Abenaki Daring

MCGILL-QUEEN'S NATIVE AND NORTHERN SERIES
(In memory of Bruce G. Trigger)
Sarah Carter and Arthur J. Ray, Editors

Abenaki Daring

The Life and Writings of Noel Annance,
1792–1869

JEAN BARMAN

McGill-Queen's University Press
Montreal & Kingston • London • Chicago

© McGill-Queen's University Press 2016

ISBN 978-0-7735-4792-6 (cloth)
ISBN 978-0-7735-9967-3 (ePDF)
ISBN 978-0-7735-9968-0 (ePUB)

Legal deposit third quarter 2016
Bibliothèque nationale du Québec

Printed in Canada on acid-free paper that is 100% ancient forest free
(100% post-consumer recycled), processed chlorine free

This book has been published with the help of a grant from the Canadian
Federation for the Humanities and Social Sciences, through the Awards
to Scholarly Publications Program, using funds provided by the Social
Sciences and Humanities Research Council of Canada.

McGill-Queen's University Press acknowledges the support of the Canada
Council for the Arts for our publishing program. We also acknowledge
the financial support of the Government of Canada through the Canada
Book Fund for our publishing activities.

Library and Archives Canada Cataloguing in Publication

Barman, Jean, 1939–, author
Abenaki daring : the life and writings of Noel Annance, 1792–1869 /
Jean Barman.

(McGill-Queen's Native and northern series ; 88)
Includes bibliographical references and index.
Issued in print and electronic formats.
ISBN 978-0-7735-4792-6 (cloth). –ISBN 978-0-7735-9967-3 (pdf).
–ISBN 978-0-7735-9968-0 (epub)

1. Annance, Noel, 1792–1869.   2. Abenaki Indians – Québec (Province) –
Biography.   3. Authors, Canadian (English) – Québec (Province) –
19th century – Biography.   I. Title.   II. Series: McGill-Queen's Native and
northern series ; 88

E99.A13B37 2016   971.4004'9734   C2016-902421-0
                                            C2016-902422-9

To Morag Maclachlan (1920–2011)
for uncovering, tending, and sharing
Noel Annance's story

Contents

Annance's Writings Reproduced in the Text

Illustrations, Maps, and Table

ILLUSTRATIONS

MAPS

TABLE

Preface

The story of Noel Annance belongs to many people – to his descendants, to the Abenaki people, and to everyone, past and present, who has been highly educated and Indigenous. In interrogating Noel Annance's life and writings, I do not pretend to adopt an Abenaki or Indigenous perspective, nor can I do so as a non-Indigenous person.[1] Neither do I pretend to have a full understanding of a time and life that survive in snatches.[2] I share what I know in the hopes that it will be useful to others and that it will spur interest in finding out more from different perspectives.

I did not plan to write this book. Noel Annance came to me, as opposed to my searching him out. The instigator was fellow historian Morag Maclachlan, who in 2011 on realizing she did not have enough time left in her life to tell the whole story of Noel's engagement with the fur trade, which had consumed her for two decades, secured my promise that it would be done. Except for Morag's initiative, Noel Annance's life and writings would linger in the shadows of the past.

Morag's wish was that two primary sources she had discovered from the years that Noel Annance spent in the Pacific Northwest fur trade would be used to expand upon her seminal article "The Case for Francis Noel Annance," published in *The Beaver* in 1993, and upon mentions of him in her fine edited book *Fort Langley Journals, 1827–30*, published in 1998. The first of these newly located sources was a manuscript journal Noel had written in 1824, and the second was what Morag termed "love notes" he had penned a decade later. Both are included here in their entirety. Our mutual friend, fur trade historian Bruce McIntyre Watson, was indispensable in sorting through Morag's files, transcribing primary documents, and giving support and assistance along the way.

I soon realized that, to do justice to Morag's request, it would be necessary to go backward and forward in time from Noel Annance's years in the fur trade so as to interrogate his whole life, 1792–1869. Others have made it possible to do so. Dartmouth College Library responded generously to my queries concerning Noel's education at Moor's Charity School and Dartmouth College. Sarah Hartwell and her associates at Rauner Special Collections located and made available relevant materials, including correspondence of numerous members of Noel's extended family. Morgan Swan followed up respecting images. *Dartmouth Alumni Magazine* found back articles. I am especially grateful to Colin Calloway for writing *The Indian History of an American Institution: Native Americans and Dartmouth* (2010), which enormously assisted me in sorting out students across the generations, and for his many other fine publications giving guidance along the way.

The door to Noel Annance's life after the fur trade was inadvertently opened by the Canadian Senate's Standing Committee on Aboriginal Affairs. Its urgent request for me to testify in Ottawa on another topic turned my mind, at the instigation of my husband, fellow historian Roderick J. Barman, to what might be hidden away in Library and Archives Canada (LAC). My interest had been piqued by Stéphanie Boutevin's fine doctoral dissertation, "La place et les usages de l'écriture chez les Hurons et la Abénakis, 1780–1880" (2011), which references some beginning points in LAC's microfilm holdings. Then accessible only onsite, some of the materials I sought can now be read at LAC's invaluable Héritage website, which digitizes Canada's documentary history. Briefly in Ottawa, I returned several times, benefiting from generous assistance.

Many others have helped along the way. Morag Maclachlan corresponded early on with Louis Annance, David Benedict, Jean Murray Cole, Gordon M. Day, Yvonne Klan, Jean-Louis R. Obomsawin, Christopher A. Roy, Bob Walters, and I expect others. Nichole Vonk, as archivist of the General Council, United Church of Canada, made available the microfilmed correspondence of Noel Annance's Abenaki counterpart Peter Paul Osunkhirhine with the American Board of Commissioners for Foreign Missions. Emily Walhout of Houghton Library, Harvard University, which holds the original copies, located a critical letter written by Noel to the American Board, whose member the Reverend Dr James A. Moos generously gave me permission to use in its entirety. Holly McElrea of the Hudson's Bay Company Archives at Archives of Manitoba checked through its holdings for relevant materials. Paul Carnahan, librarian of the Vermont Historical Society, provided back articles in *Vermont History*, and the Fogler Library, University of Maine, uncovered materials concerning Noel's older brother, Louis. The Kansas City Genealogical Society, Missouri Historical Society, and New York State Archives located items related to Noel's younger brother, Joseph. The interlibrary loan division of the University of Washington Library generously searched out and reproduced an image of Noel Annance's older brother. Nicole St-Onge gave access to the Voyageurs Database, now online. The National Archives of the United Kingdom, British Columbia Archives, and University of British Columbia Library's Special Collections Division made relevant materials available for consultation. Jan Hare, Malcolm and Alexandra King, Jack Little, and Jeannie Morgan encouraged me at critical moments, as did Bruce Watson at every step along the way. Roderick J. Barman's ongoing support was invaluable. Emily Barman generously shared her expertise as a sociologist.

At McGill-Queen's University Press, executive director Philip Cercone, acquisition editor Mark Abley, managing editor Ryan Van Huijstee, and copy editor Robert Lewis were encouraging and astute. I could not have had a more supportive team. The manuscript's readers were observant, knowledgeable, and helpful. Bill Nelson drew two excellent maps.

Most importantly, I thank the thirty plus Indigenous doctoral students and many more master's students I have worked with and come to know over the years at the University of British Columbia and elsewhere. Your commitment and persistence in the face of obstacles, some not unlike those faced so long ago by Noel Annance, have inspired me time and again. You have taught me that to be well educated and Indigenous is still no easy matter. The search for belonging goes on.

Chronology

1683 The Jesuit mission of St Francis is established on the south side of the St Lawrence River in the French colony of New France

Late 1600s Abenakis begin migrating from New England to St Francis

1697 Nine-year-old Samuel Gill is taken captive to St Francis from his Massachusetts home

1700 The St Francis mission acquires a land concession of 12,000 acres

c. 1703 Young Rosalie James is taken captive to St Francis from her Maine home

Early 1700s Samuel Gill and Rosalie James marry in St Francis, to have seven children

c. 1750 Eldest Gill son Joseph-Louis becomes Abenaki sachem, or grand chief

c. 1750 Gill daughter Marie-Appoline weds Gabriel Annance, almost certainly Abenaki

1755 Britain establishes within the Department of Indian Affairs an Indian Department with oversight of Indigenous peoples

1759 A British militia unit of Rogers' Rangers unsuccessfully seeks to destroy St Francis

1760 Britain conquers New France, causing France to depart from North America and to put its Indigenous peoples under the Indian Department within the Department of Indian Affairs

c. 1760 Following his Abenaki wife's death, Joseph-Louis Gill marries a French Canadian woman, as do his younger brothers, Francis Louis and Robert

1825 Noel is the Okanogan post's sometimes head

1826 Noel is transferred to second-in-command at the larger Thompson River post

1827 Noel is dispatched to help construct Fort Langley, being kept on as a clerk

1828 Darling Report commissioned by the governor general of British North America opposes the Colonial Office's goal of encouraging Indigenous peoples to intermingle with whites

1829 Duncan Campbell Napier is appointed to oversee Quebec's Indigenous peoples within the Department of Indian Affairs

1829 Noel's second cousin Peter Paul Osunkhirhine, who also studied at Moor's Indian Charity School, returns to St Francis to preach and teach

1829 White farmers petition for possession of Durham lands

1830 Noel is transferred between various Pacific Northwest posts in succession

1832 Noel writes the Canadian governor general requesting a Pacific Northwest land grant

1833 Noel is transferred to Fort Simpson on the Mackenzie River

1833–34 Noel has an affair with Mary Taylor, who lives with Fort Simpson's head

1834 Noel returns home to St Francis

1836 Noel marries fifteen-year-old Marie Josephte Nagajoa, whose mother is a Gill, to have ten or more children

1836 Noel briefly opens a grocery store in St Francis

1837 Former students of Moor's Indian Charity School, including Noel, unsuccessfully petition for a voice in St Francis governance

1838–39 Noel serves as an officer during the Quebec Rebellion

1840 Noel requests a land grant pursuant on his War of 1812 service, which is rejected in 1849

1842 Noel translates the New Testament's Book of Mark into Abenaki for Peter Paul Osunkhirhine, who appears to pass it off as his work

1844   Noel secures employment on a Canada-US boundary
       survey

1844   Blaming the Indian Department within the Department
       of Indian Affairs for inaction, the Bagot Report, commis-
       sioned by the governor general, argues for Indigenous
       peoples to intermingle with newcomers

1846   Opposed by the local priest, Noel fails to secure a teach-
       ing job in St Francis and thereafter teaches intermittently
       at nearby white schools

1857   The Province of Canada passes the Gradual Civilization
       Act, enabling individual Indigenous men to be "civilized"

1858   The Pennefather Report, commissioned by the Legislative
       Assembly of the Province of Canada, argues for Indige-
       nous peoples to be excluded by means of separation onto
       reserves, for á single economy tied to farming, for the
       exclusion of women who marry out, and for children
       to be forced into residential schools

1858   Duncan Campbell Napier retires as head of Indian
       Affairs in Quebec

1859   Noel requests to be "civilized," only to have nothing
       ensue for years on end

1863   Noel testifies in a pivotal Montreal court case for
       legitimacy of fur trade unions outside of legal marriage

1867   A date is hurriedly set for Noel's examination as to his
       suitability to be "civilized," which he does not attend for
       unknown reasons

1867   The British North America Act creates the Dominion of
       Canada, comprising Quebec and Ontario, along with
       Nova Scotia and New Brunswick

1869   Noel dies on 4 September

1876   The Indian Act is passed, premised on the Pennefather
       Report's recommendations, an act still in force today
       with amendments

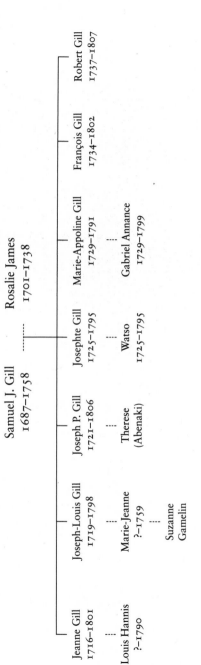

ILLUSTRATION 1

Gill family tree through two generations

ILLUSTRATION 2

Annance family tree through three generations selectively

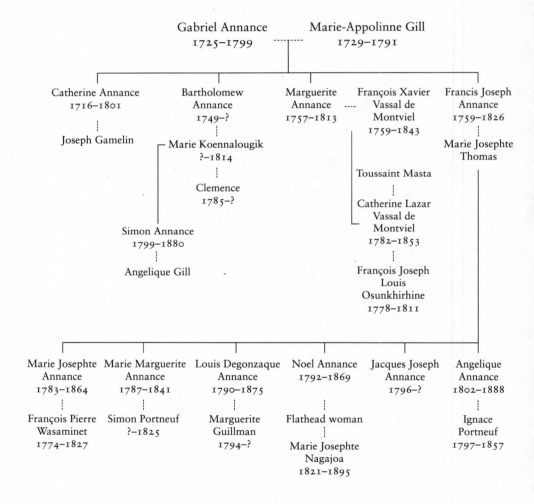

Abenaki Daring

Introduction

Abenaki daring and its counterpart of Indigenous daring have taken many forms. Noel Annance dared in a major battle of the War of 1812 and in seeking to make a career for himself in the far west fur trade, but much more importantly he dared with his pen. Made aware in midlife that to be, as he was, highly educated and Indigenous was a wholly different proposition than to be highly educated and white, he returned home. From the Abenaki stronghold of St Francis, Quebec, he wrote to those in charge of a Canada in the making respecting both Indigenous peoples' and his own search for belonging. Noel dared them to read what they did not want to hear. He dared them to consider that there might be a different way ahead.

Noel Annance's life, 1792–1869, cut across a time of fundamental change for Indigenous peoples throughout North America. At his birth, they were still perceived as having utility; by the time of his death, they had been cast aside. Considering as a young man that Indigenous inclusion was still possible, Noel sought to realize literacy's promise. Deterred, he redirected the Abenaki daring fundamental to his sense of self toward contesting Indigenous exclusion. Noel Annance's life and writings speak to what might have been.

For a brief moment, everything had seemed possible. The observation made about Noel Annance as a youth in 1808, when he was a student and boarder at Moor's Indian Charity School in New Hampshire – that he "was so studious and so 'dignified'" that he refused "to play 'tag'" – was soon borne out.[1] Arriving at Dartmouth College two years later, he like the other students gave two-thirds of his time to Latin and Greek. The other third went to a combination of advanced mathematics, logic, natural and moral philosophy, geography, surveying, astronomy, and English grammar. Each weekday began with chapel at 5:00 AM or as soon as it became light, followed by an early morning class, breakfast, individual study, an 11:00 AM class, dinner, more study, an afternoon class at 3:00 or 4:00, and evening prayers at 6:00. Students were regularly called upon to speak in chapel, and from the second year onward, they each gave a public oration three times a year.[2]

Dartmouth College was not only about scholarship. Noel also proved his popularity with fellow students, equally important on the way to becoming the gentleman that was Dartmouth's goal for its students. He was among those invited at the end of their first year into one, or possibly both, of the two campus debating and literary societies.[3] Noel joined United Fraternity and Social Friends, limited to students displaying "respectability of talents and acquirements, and a fair moral character."[4] Included among its past members was lawyer Daniel Webster, a decade Noel's senior, who had been recently elected to the US House of Representatives and would have a distinguished career. Students at Dartmouth, one of North America's most prestigious post-secondary institutions of the day, were expected to become the professionals and politicians of their generation, and for the most part they did so.

The future that Noel Annance had every reason to anticipate was not to be. Once he entered the real world, not governed by classics and the relatively closed sphere of college sociability, he was set apart. He might have acquired the attributes of a gentleman of the day, as indeed he did do, but for all of his determination and tenacity, he lacked one critical aspect of belonging that the others possessed. They were by descent "white," the general term of the day, which is for that reason used here, whereas Noel was Indigenous. More precisely, he was three-quarters Abenaki and one-quarter white.[5] His great-grandparents had been white child captives who married each other and made their lives among the Abenaki people in his home village of St Francis 120 kilometres, or 75 miles, northeast of Montreal. It was their captivity narratives that gave Noel Annance the opportunity to become one of North America's most highly educated persons, Indigenous or not, of his generation.

All his life Noel Annance bore the consequences in a North America that was increasingly unaccepting of persons perceived as Indigenous. The tiny minority educated in English or French were tolerated only as long as they put their learning to use as missionaries or possibly teachers to their own people. Their task was to conciliate their fellow Indigenous peoples to the tremendous changes being imposed upon them by outsiders.

Noel Annance did not retreat but persisted. He dared literacy's promise, just as Abenakis had dared across the generations to be their own persons in the face of the changing times around them. Noel's higher education was a consequence of his great-uncle, grandfather, and father having dared to accept the invitation proffered their families given their status as captivity descendants to partake of newcomer schooling. They had taken chances, just as, drawing on Abenaki daring, Noel would do all his life.

Noel Annance acted, as occasion warranted, as the gentleman of his higher education. Travelling in midlife with an Arctic expedition, Noel was evoked by the Englishman in charge, Richard King, in his private journal as "my esteemed friend and companion, Mr. Annance."[6] In a key court case tried in Montreal three decades later, Noel was one of the principal witnesses, his testimony among the most cited in the favourable decision.[7] Whenever Noel put pen to paper, he did so with the sure hand and eloquent style of a gentleman of the day. It is Noel Annance's surviving letters and other pieces of writing that reveal the complexities of being highly educated and Indigenous.

Noel did not, importantly, play the gentleman at the cost of his Abenaki descent. He might from time to time have paraded his scholarship, but he never, as far as can be determined, affected to be wholly white. As tents were being pitched for their nightly stop, Noel and his northern travelling companion sometimes took a "stroll through the woods," and it could have been after one of these walks that Richard King wrote almost in admiration as to how Noel was "a 'métif,' or, as the Canadians would term him, a 'brois brulé.'"[8] Noel did not hide his combination of Abenaki and white descent. During the years he spent as a young man in the fur trade, he was repeatedly described by others, including those in charge, as Abenaki.

Noel sought to be the gentleman of his higher education, even as he was Abenaki, and for a time considered that he could be both based on his capacity. The bar of race – the assumption that skin tones irrevocably trumped ability – need not operate, or so he thought. During his childhood and that of his parents, grandparents, and great-grandparents, newcomers and Indigenous peoples warily engaged with each other as sometimes allies. His family played prominent roles in the Abenaki daring that became for a time the stuff of legend. Not only had his white great-grandparents been child captives of the Abenakis, but their eldest son was the Abenaki grand chief, or sachem, who negotiated alongside his brother-in-law, Noel's Abenaki grandfather, a middle ground during the American War of Independence with the goal of protecting St Francis from incursions into their territory.

As conflict subsided following the War of 1812 between the young United States and Britain, Indigenous peoples lost whatever utility they had possessed. Conciliation gave way to competition, grounded in newcomers' sense of entitlement premised on their paler skin tones and the asserted superiority of their ways of life. The more attitudes hardened, as they did both in the United States, where Noel was educated, and in Canada, whence he came and to which he returned, the more he was made aware he did not belong. Indigenous exclusion became the order of the day. Conversely, the more Indigenous peoples were dispossessed of their ways and denied access to the emerging dominant society, the more wary they became of persons sharing a common inheritance who did not behave quite like themselves.

Noel Annance returned home from a decade and a half in the fur trade to the captivity narratives that had formed him. Setting himself down not that differently from other Abenakis, he again dared. Drawing on his higher education, Noel wrote regularly for the next third of a century to officials in Canada's Department of Indian Affairs, which was responsible for Indigenous peoples, and to public persons in high places whom he considered needed to know what was happening. Whether or not Noel's persistence effected change, his carefully crafted, suitably deferential letters were read, as attested by the notations jotted on them.

All his life Noel Annance dared to be both highly educated and Indigenous. He was caught out by virtue of others seeing him so very differently from how he saw himself. Inferring from a surviving image of his older brother, none having been located of Noel, he may have been visibly Indigenous, as well as being so in his sense of self.

Noel's search for belonging as a highly educated Abenaki encompassed a lifetime, so he explained at age seventy: "I feel my self ashamed to be among gentleman – tho I have been called a gentleman – an officer – a teacher of languages – but, alas! To have scanned Homer, Virgil, and Horace, to have traced Euclid through abstruse regions of mathematics has not expiated the crime of being called an 'Indian.'"[9]

Two years later, Noel again reflected on his circumstances: "If my ancestors were savages, I am not – if they were uncivilized, wild and barbarous I am not: consequently I ought to be treated in a different way; res mutantur et nos mutamur in illis [the times are changed, are perpetually changing, and we ourselves change with them]. A man who has been employed in various situations no matter of what origin, as a gentleman, should not be denied the access to the same privileges as enjoyed by his fellow citizens."[10] Noel's higher education, combined with his daring, could take him only so far in the face of the rapid changes engulfing Indigenous peoples.

Noel Annance did possess a critical asset in his exercise of the Abenaki daring on which he drew across his long life. Whereas his great-uncle, grandfather, and father dared by their actions, he also did so with his pen. Noel's higher education gave him a fluency with the written alongside the spoken word. Face to face, his words may have been Indigenously inflected from the perspective of others, but on paper this was not so. Rather than his writing running the danger of being dismissed out of hand, his words were more likely, if not assuredly so, read on their own terms as written. Only from the late 1850s, by which time the Department of Indian Affairs had more than ever set itself apart from the Indigenous peoples it was intended to serve, was "Indian" routinely scrawled across the covering note to his letters, likely to alert whoever would be reading them.

Noel Annance was one of a tiny number of Indigenous peoples across North America with the means to speak back to the dominant society on its own terms. Like a small handful of others who were similarly well educated before him or were his contemporaries, he witnessed fundamental change, to whose essence he gave voice. His life puts the lie to the easy assumption, common at the time and to an extent into the present day, that Indigenous peoples are somehow lesser than their non-Indigenous counterparts.

SOURCES

Noel Annance's life is visible only in parts that may or may not reflect its entirety or even its principal direction. Much about him as a person has not come into view. It is the life of the mind emanating from his taking a chance on literacy's promise that can be most fully glimpsed.

Noel Annance wrote as a matter of course, and although part of what he put on paper has been lost, other parts made it into sets of records that have in whole or part survived. They include those of Moor's Indian Charity School and Dartmouth College, which he attended from 1808 to 1810 and from 1810 to 1813 respectively, held at Dartmouth College; those of the British-based Hudson's Bay Company, by whom he was employed from 1821 to 1834, held in the Archives of Manitoba; and those of the Department of Indian Affairs, especially its Indian Department, with which he corresponded from 1834 to 1869. The name by which others knew Noel possesses a certain fluidity between sources. As will be evident, he sometimes signed himself "Noel Francis" or "Francis Noel" and was so addressed in response.

The Indian Department's records, which are partial, are held in Library and Archives Canada, as well as now being accessible at the Héritage website. In 1856 a government commission discovered to its consternation that the Indian Department's archive "has been in part mislaid, and was only placed before us in an incomplete form."[11] When surviving files were much later microfilmed for public use, they were kept in their original erratic state, with no subsequent indexing, making it an adventure to find relevant items, if in fact they do exist.

Together with twenty some letters unearthed in other locations, a hundred letters written and signed by Noel Annance were located in the records of the Department of Indian Affairs and transcribed, along with another twenty-five on which he was one of several signatories and possibly the writer. Some of these letters were written to persons of influence whom Noel considered might be responsive to him, being forwarded to the Department of Indian Affairs in order to be followed up. Fifteen of Noel's letters in Indian Affairs records and twenty located elsewhere are reproduced in the text, along with two other pieces of writing originating with him. A much longer piece is included as an appendix. Another fifty some letters are referenced in the text, many by quotations taken from them. Other letters from Noel are undoubtedly still hidden away in the files of the Department of Indian Affairs, with yet others residing elsewhere in other sets of correspondence. As well as incoming letters often containing annotations as to their likely response, twenty-five drafts of letters to Noel were located in the letter books of the Indian Department official in charge of Quebec's Indigenous peoples from 1830 to 1857. Numerous of these are quoted or cited.

The disorganized and unindexed state of Indian Affairs records implies that many other accounts echoing that of Noel Annance are likely also hidden away. Numerous letters were written in an Indigenous language, to be variously translated or not on being received. For this reason and generally, the larger story of Canada's Indigenous peoples, of which Noel was one small part, is woefully incomplete.

More generally available are printed and manuscript primary sources originating with the British Colonial Office, which had overall charge until 1860. Its correspondence with North American counterparts has been published in whole or part for 1825 to 1839.[12] Two reports on Indian affairs in Canada, dated 1844 and 1858, were sufficiently significant to have been printed in their entirety.[13] Four internal Colonial Office reports, dated 1835, 1837, 1843, and 1844, survive in the National Archives of the United Kingdom in London.[14] Taken together with other materials, these sources document Indigenous peoples' betrayal over Noel Annance's lifetime by those supposedly responsible for their wellbeing.

PARTS AND CHAPTERS

Abenaki Daring engages with Noel Annance's life and writing in three chronological parts, each introduced by a historical overview of the period.

"Part One: An Inheritance of Wary Engagement" attends to Noel Annance's background and early years. The introduction describes how for more than a century Indigenous peoples warily engaged with the growing numbers of newcomers in their midst.

Chapter 1, "Of Abenaki Daring and Captivity Narratives," begins Noel Annance's story, as it must, with his white great-grandparents. Captured as children from their New England homes at the turn of the eighteenth century, they made their lives together among Abenakis who had themselves recently resettled from New England to St Francis. Doing so under French Catholic tutelage, Abenakis repeatedly fought on the French side against the British in charge to the south.

Chapter 2, "Taking a Chance on Literacy's Promise," describes how Moor's Indian Charity School, the leading American boarding school of the day enrolling Indigenous students, came calling at St Francis because it considered captives' descendants more likely to perform well, due to their "white blood," than their wholly Indigenous counterparts. Literacy's promise caught up young Noel, along with numerous others of his extended family, including his father, who had earlier attended Moor's and Dartmouth College.

"Part Two: Pursuing Indigenous Inclusion" interrogates Noel Annance's two decades subsequent to leaving Dartmouth College in 1813. The introduction sets out the changes in the relationship between newcomers and Indigenous peoples once the latter lost their utility in times of war.

Chapter 3, "In Search of Belonging," tracks Noel Annance's pursuit of an occupation attuned with the genteel status inculcated by his higher education. The chapter first takes a step back in time to set the scene by introducing some of his similarly educated Indigenous predecessors.

Chapter 4, "Hopes for the Fur Trade," transitions to the occupation on which Noel Annance fixed as both genteel and accessible. For all of his Abenaki daring, his hopes would be dashed. Although I am unable to demonstrate cause and effect, it seems very likely Noel's inability to rise in the ranks was more than chance.

Chapter 5, "Letting Go," engages with Noel Annance's final posting in the fur trade. By now well aware that he was marked out by virtue of his indigeneity, he let go. He dared with aplomb. The chapter reproduces his intimate notes to the woman living with the officer in charge of the remote northern post to which he had been dispatched.

"Part Three: Contesting Indigenous Exclusion," follows Noel Annance's life from his return to St Francis in 1834 to his death in 1869. During these years, Noel contested Indigenous exclusion on paper to a generation of officials in the Department of Indian Affairs. He dared time and again despite their having virtually no apparent interest, for reasons explained in the introduction, in the Indigenous peoples who were their mandate.

Chapter 6, "Returning Home to Captivity Narratives' Legacies," explores the ways that the captivity inheritance Noel shared with so many others in St Francis affected how he could and could not belong as an Indigenous person. His goal of teaching the next generation in his home community on the model of his father before him came to naught.

Chapter 7, "Land No More," centres on the principal issue then agitating Canada's Indigenous peoples, as it has done into the present day. Noel fought with words literally to his death for land that he and other Abenakis had every reason to believe was theirs.

Chapter 8, "To Belong or Not to Belong," tracks the choice accorded an elderly Noel Annance of whether or not to seek enfranchisement and thereby, so he considered, to be a gentleman consistent with his higher education. Government's seeming inability to act implies that the relevant legislation was a sham.

Together with summing up Noel Annance's life, a postscript points up the betrayal of Canada's Indigenous peoples effected during his lifetime, which continues in part to the present day.

LARGER IMPORT

The history of Indigenous peoples in today's Canada has most often been considered only from the time of Canada's becoming a Confederation in 1867 or from the time of the Indian Act's passage in 1876. Rather, as Noel Annance's life attests, policies premised on dispossession and exclusion that are still in effect today were already well in place.

Noel Annance's life and writings give the lie to the recurrent inference that during the century prior to Canada becoming a Confederation, Indigenous peoples were unwilling or unable to participate in the overwhelming changes going on around them. They were not inert but variously versatile. Just as did Abenakis, Indigenous peoples dared. For a moment, if only those in charge had dared to listen, a Canada very different from the one that emerged was at hand.

PART ONE

An Inheritance of Wary Engagement

Noel Annance was born in 1792 into the Abenaki family described in chapters 1 and 2 and into the larger setting introduced here. His access to higher education had its origins in the wary engagement that had long marked the relationship between his home community of St Francis in present-day Quebec and outsiders. It was a combination of Abenaki daring and captivity narratives, considered in chapter 1, that made it possible, as explained in chapter 2, for Noel to take a chance on literacy's promise.

Wary engagement went back to the first newcomers who had reached North America from Europe in the sixteenth century. France and Britain soon became the two principal colonial powers commercially and militarily. France had loose oversight of a broad swath of North America not unexpectedly called New France, to the east of which were tucked Britain's thirteen colonies. Both countries' keen eye for the profits to be had from animal pelts made Indigenous people valuable adjuncts to do the trapping. Most highly valued were those of the beaver, whose matted underfur became the felt that went into the hats worn by everyone with the least pretension to gentility.

Indigenous peoples were also sought as allies during the ongoing conflicts in which France and Britain engaged in North America during the late seventeenth and eighteenth centuries as accompaniments to wars in Europe. The two countries brokered alliances with "chiefs and warriors," to use the term of the day, who fought either on their behalves or jointly with their soldiers. A typical exchange ran, "I sincerely console you for the loss of so many Chiefs and Warriors," to which came the response, "We, the Chiefs and Warriors here assembled ..."[1] Among the two countries' strategies, and the one responsible for Noel Annance's inheritance, was that of each side capturing soldiers and civilians living in the other's territory to be exchanged for needed cash. Noel's great-grandparents were among a very small number of captives who not only remained with Indigenous peoples but also married each other.

Wary engagement also had a spiritual component that similarly emerged out of a larger context. France's and Britain's colonial adventures acquired their legitimacy, such as it was, in the unquestioned belief in the superiority of Christianity in its respective Catholic and Protestant iterations. Where priests and missionaries did not accompany arrivals hoping to profit economically and perhaps to settle down, they were not far behind. It did not take long, if any time at all, for Indigenous peoples, who had their own spiritual ways, to become objects of conversion.

Partly for this reason but also more generally, neither France nor Britain was able to conceive of Indigenous peoples even in the best of circumstances as on a par with its white subjects. France employed the language of family life to evoke the distinction. As with children, Indigenous peoples needed to be protected by a benevolent father who was, as the intendant of New France put it in 1681, predisposed to "flattering them, giving them presents," even as he watched over them to ensure they behaved to the mother country's advantage.[2] If Indigenous peoples were necessarily allies, they were subordinately so. Be it negotiating to fight on France's behalf or brokering territory through treaties, the consequence was, to borrow Gilles Havard's apt phrase, "an unequal alliance."[3]

Unequal the alliance might have been, but it was an alliance nonetheless and so acknowledged in the terms of capitulation brokered on Britain's military defeat of France in 1759, ending the latter's North American adventure.[4] By the Articles of Capitulation of the next year, "The Savages or Indian allies of his most Christian Majesty, shall be maintained in the Lands they inhabit; if they chuse to remain there; they shall not be molested on any pretence whatsoever, for having carried arms, and served his most Christian Majesty; they shall have, as well as the French, liberty of religion, and shall keep their missionaries."[5] In this spirit of reconciliation, the peace treaty signed in 1763 between Britain and France granted all inhabitants of the former New France, Indigenous peoples or not, "the liberty of the Catholick religion."[6]

In the short term, the strategic aspect of wary engagement took priority. In its Royal Proclamation of 1763, the British government affirmed that "the several Nations or Tribes of Indians with whom We are connected, and who live under our Protection, should not be molested or disturbed in the Possession of such Parts of Our Dominions and Territories as, not having been ceded to or purchased by Us, are reserved to them, or any of them, as their Hunting Grounds." As for acquiring additional land for newcomer settlement, "no private Person" was permitted "to make any Purchase from the said Indians of any Lands reserved to the said Indians." Rather, "if at any Time any of the Said Indians should be inclined to dispose of the said Lands, the same shall be Purchased only for Us, in our Name, at some public Meeting or Assembly of the said Indians, to be held for that Purpose by the Governor or Commander in Chief of our Colony respectively within which they shall lie."[7] The Royal Proclamation did not take into account the distinctive circumstances in the former New France, where land grants for Indigenous peoples had been routinely lodged with the Catholic Church as the agent charged with their oversight.[8]

On paper the Royal Proclamation ensured Indigenous peoples' wellbeing. Those living in the former New France would henceforth be overseen by the Department of Indian Affairs that Britain had established in 1755 to service its North American colonies, within which an Indian Department had charge on the ground. Successful businessman Sir William Johnson, whose credentials were burnished by his partnering with Mohawk Molly Brant, had been appointed superintendent general of Indian Affairs, to be succeeded in 1768 by his nephew Guy Johnson and from 1782 to 1828 by his son Sir John Johnson, born of an earlier union with a white woman. The consequence was, Douglas Leighton explains, that "a 'Johnson tradition' of firm but fair decision-making and a respect for Indian customs and institutions became an important, if unwritten, part of the policies practised by the Indian Department's employees, especially those who had begun their careers under the Johnson aegis."[9]

Britain also continued two established French protocols. "Our Father" would long be used to refer to those in charge, with "Our Great Father" and later "Our Great Mother" being reserved for the British monarch. The complementary use of "our Children," "our

Red Children," and "red skins" denoted Indigenous peoples as being, by inference, if not explicitly so, lesser than their "white" counterparts.[10] Also in line with French practice, Britain annually gave every Indigenous man, woman, and child residing in territory over which it now had oversight a substantial annual present affirming the reciprocal nature of the wary engagement marking these years.[11]

Another shift in political power occurred not long afterward. Beginning in 1776, thirteen of Britain's North American colonies militarily defeated the mother country to become in 1783 the United States of America. During the hostilities, each side continued the longstanding practice of recruiting Indigenous peoples to its side or at the least inducing them to be neutral. One of the first actions taken by the new nation was, echoing British policy, to consolidate authority to deal with Indigenous peoples, including treaty making, in what would become the Bureau of Indian Affairs. As fear of Indigenous peoples' military capacity lessened, wary engagement gave way in the new nation to a wholly one-sided perspective.

At war's end, Britain retreated northward into today's Canada, as did the Department of Indian Affairs along with it. So did thousands of Indigenous peoples and others who during the hostilities had remained loyal and who, particularly if white but not necessarily so, had been promised grants of land to restart their lives. The consequence was the division of remaining British territory in 1791. To the east was Lower Canada, also called Quebec, with a French legal system and freedom of religion for Catholicism. To the west lay Upper Canada, the future Ontario, with a British legal system and intended for Loyalists, as adherents to the British side during the recent American War of Independence were known. To acquire the promised land grants, between 1783 and 1836 the British government negotiated under the terms of the Royal Proclamation eighteen agreements by which Indigenous peoples now living in Upper Canada surrendered, supposedly on their own volition, 16,137,836 acres of their land, per an official count, in exchange for £8,000 in cash or goods and £6,435 in annuities promising a small sum annually.[12]

Due to Indigenous lands in Lower Canada being lodged with the Catholic Church, the land grab did not reach into Quebec, which the Department of Indian Affairs, with its firmly Protestant ethos, largely ignored. More so than in Upper Canada, Indigenous lives in St Francis, as elsewhere in Quebec, went on much as before. Wary engagement held, at least for the interim.

I

Of Abenaki Daring and Captivity Narratives

Noel Annance's life has value both in itself and for what it reveals about the times out of which he came and in which he made his way. The Abenaki daring and captivity narratives into which he was born, and which formed him, went back in time more than a century before his birth in 1792 in the Abenaki village of St Francis. Since the late 1600s, Abenakis had dared in the face of outsiders' determination to have their lands and overturn their ways of life. Integral to the times was the taking of white captives, whose later accounts reveal much about Abenaki everyday life. Except for Abenaki daring and captivity narratives, Noel would not have been the person he was.

OF ABENAKI DARING

Once we move beyond the traditional tendency to envisage the history of North America from the perspective of newcomers interpreting the past in their own self-interest, we uncover a story equally or more powerful in its impetus and telling. We come to realize just how persistent and ingenious were the tactics of Abenakis and their Indigenous neighbours in defence of their rightful interests.

The Indigenous peoples coming down through time as Abenaki knew who they were and saw no reason to accommodate themselves to others' agendas. Spread across northern New England from Maine to Vermont and based around patrilineal extended families (see map 1), Abenakis spoke related yet distinctive languages and followed similar seasonal rounds. Summer villages might be located near fertile land used for growing mainly corn, which was supplemented for food by hunting, fishing, and gathering at different times of the year.

If self-sufficient, Abenakis were not isolationist. They welcomed the first outsiders to New England in 1620 and took advantage of their arrival to trade pelts for newcomer goods.[1] Despite the Abenakis' numbers being sharply reduced by imported diseases, they did manage for a time to retain their independence from the two major European powers of Britain and France, which were increasingly in conflict with each other at home, with spillover into North America. As the numbers of outsiders grew, Abenakis repeatedly dared in their own best interests as they perceived them. As to the reason, in David Ghere's words, "the Abenakis considered themselves independent equals of the French and English and subject to neither."[2]

Over time, as Abenaki lands were usurped by stealth or force and as military hostilities intensified, Abenakis became more closely allied to New France, centred in today's Quebec, than to the English in what became the United States. Doing so was mutually advantageous: Abenakis sought to maintain their ways of life, and the French sought to have a buffer that could turn back British expansion. As summed up by Olive Dickason, "for the Abenaki, the French connection meant making the best of a bad predicament."[3]

The ease with which Abenakis moved about during the yearly round undoubtedly influenced some of them to migrate in the late 1600s roughly 160 to 240 kilometres, or 100 to 150 miles, north via Lake Champlain and the Richelieu River to the south side of the St Lawrence River. Located upriver from the capital of France's North American empire at Quebec City and downriver from the future economic centre of Montreal, their new home lay on the east side of the St Francis River not far from where it empties into the St Lawrence. The site became known as "St Francis" or "Saint-François" after both the river and a Jesuit mission established there in 1683 and as "Odanak," which it would officially become in 1916, for the fortified village that the Abenaki constructed in 1704 for protection.[4] The St Francis mission acquired its land base with the concession on 22 August 1700 of 12,000 acres on the two sides of the St Francis River.[5] The largesse was firmly grounded in Catholicism, the seigneurs who made the grant reserving the right "of dispossessing the Abenaquois as soon as the Religious Mission should cease to reside upon the conceded land."[6] Abenakis could come and go almost at will, and they long did so in and out of both St Francis and the Abenaki community of Bécancour, also known as Wôlinak, located sixty kilometres, or forty miles, downriver along

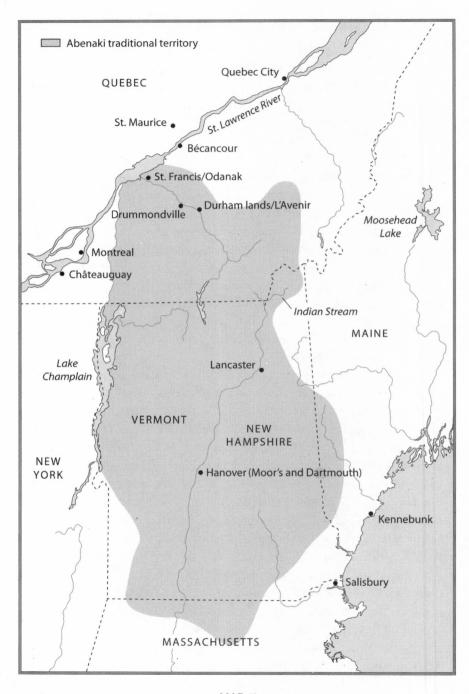

MAP 1

Early North American Northeast, showing Abenaki
traditional territory

the St Lawrence.[7] According to Gordon Day, "more than one tribe contributed to St. Francis' population," but precisely which ones, whence, and when is in good part historical conjecture.[8] Nonetheless, the numbers there for a shorter or longer time held consistent despite the hostilities marking French-English relations.[9]

From France's perspective, alliances not only with Abenakis but also with Iroquois, Mohawks, Hurons, and others were strategic given that New France's non-Indigenous population was much smaller than that of Britain's colonies. New France's white population surpassed 15,000 only in the last decade of the seventeenth century, by which time New England's was approaching 100,000. According to Gordon Day, by the mid-1700s, when St Francis was home to "186 warriors" out of a population of 1,000, "an almost continual stream of war parties, small and large, [flowed] from Canada to New England."[10] Jack Little terms Abenakis "the shock troops of the French war effort."[11]

THE FORCE OF CAPTIVITY NARRATIVES

The most contentious aspect of Abenaki conduct related to the taking of captives by the French and their Indigenous allies, also practised to a lesser extent by the British. Significant in its own right, this activity paled both before the 21,000 slaves who had been brought from Africa to North America by 1700, a number that had grown tenfold by 1760, and before the unknown thousands of Indigenous peoples snatched, in the words of June Namias, "for profit, for novelty, and for sexual misuse."[12] Unlike their French counterparts, it was almost universally accepted in the British colonies and later in the United States that whereas blacks and browns, being Africans and Indigenous peoples, could by virtue of their skin tones be denied the most basic human rights, it was unacceptable for "whites," as newcomers styled themselves, to be captured, even if it occurred in far fewer numbers and resulted mostly in servitude only until ransoms were paid.[13] In the words of Colin Calloway, "the prospect of being taken captive by Indians was one of the greatest terrors for pioneers of the American frontier."[14]

The moral indignation generated by this phenomenon found its expression in what have become known as captivity narratives, being the enormously popular accounts written from the 1680s onward by or on behalf of former captives who had been "redeemed," as their return to the societies whence they came was sometimes termed.[15] Captivity narratives were premised on a tripartite set of circumstances: the first was an enclosed setting that made escape impossible or highly unlikely, the second was individuals being subjected to the will of others, and the third was a retrospective rendering from the perspective of the returned person. These narratives' appeal lay in their fusing of autobiography and adventure with the religious and social prescriptions of the age, all with the goal of enlisting sympathy against supposedly perfidious Indigenous peoples, who could thereby be dispossessed without any sense of guilt or sin in this deeply religious age. As Calloway usefully reminds us, "writing was an instrument of dispossession that also exercised 'conceptual violence' on Indian peoples, their world, and their ways of knowing"; it "dehumanized and demonized [them] as 'savages' while their conquerors were ennobled as 'civilized.'"[16]

Although Indigenous peoples most often acted at the encouragement of the French or possibly the British, sometimes alongside volunteers or regular soldiers, and took their prisoners in several directions, "merciless captivity" has been almost wholly attributed to "Indian savages" taking New Englanders north to New France.[17] Two generations of primary research by C. Alice Baker and Emma Coleman enumerating 1,641 captives taken to New France from New England between 1677 and 1760 show that the phenomenon was far less about Indigenous peoples than about British and French colonialism, given that all but 237 of them were taken during spillovers from European conflicts.[18] King William's War of 1688–97, Queen Anne's War of 1702–13, and King George's War of 1744–48 accounted for around 300 captives each, and the French and Indian War of 1754–63, culminating in France's loss of its North American empire, accounted for somewhat over 500.[19] In other words, 85 per cent of the recorded abductions, as opposed to being random acts of terror, occurred in the course of these four English-French conflicts intended to weaken the other side by whatever means possible. At the same time, Alden Vaughan and Daniel Richter point out, "Indian allies, on whom both the English and the French relied heavily, entered the Europeans' struggles primarily for their own reasons and waged war mainly by their own rules."[20]

Unsurprising given the nature of war, three-quarters of those captured were males.[21] Of the 1,280 enumerated by Baker and Coleman whose certain or possible fate is known, 770 (60 per cent) eventually returned home, very possibly on being ransomed, with the remainder roughly dividing between those who died and those who opted not to go back.[22] It was from returnees that the captivity narrative genre emerged, with its emphasis on the harsh conditions experienced. According to Vaughan and Richter, of the 228 who stayed, and likely also the 48 who might have done so, almost all "remained among the French rather than among the Indians."[23] Almost a third of those who stayed were females taken mostly between the ages of seven and fifteen who had learned the French language, had converted to Catholicism, had become attuned to the way of life, and saw no reason to leave.[24]

Contrary to the impression left by James Axtell, the total number remaining with Indigenous peoples was minute.[25] As Vaughn and Richter explain, "There is conclusive evidence of only 24 prisoners who became 'white Indians' – just 1.5 percent of the total number of cases and 6.2 percent of those known to have spent the last part of their captivities with Indians – while there are indications that an additional 28 prisoners (1.7 percent) perhaps stayed with their Indian hosts. At most, therefore, 52 of the recorded New England captives, or 3.2 percent, underwent completely the cultural transition from British American to American Indian." Age at captivity mattered, with thirty-eight, or three-quarters, of the fifty-two who remained or perhaps remained with Indigenous peoples being under the age of sixteen when they were taken.[26] Among these thirty-eight were Noel Annance's progenitors.

DOUBLE CAPTIVITY NARRATIVES

Alongside many others, Abenakis participated in the captivity phenomenon. Among "the many, very many captives" taken were Noel Annance's great-grandparents Samuel Gill and Rosalie James.[27] Their stories argue that the phenomenon was more complex in its character and outcomes than sometimes considered.

On 10 June 1697, at the age of nine and three-quarter years, Samuel Gill was "carried away" from the small northeast Massachusetts village of Salisbury (see map 1). By this time, his hometown was sixty years old but still subject to periodic attacks from Abenakis and others whose land was being usurped.[28] The boy's family had been among the earliest arrivals. His grandparents John Gill and Phoebe Buswell farmed there from the mid-1600s, as did his parents, Samuel Gill and Sarah Worth, from the 1680s.[29]

The sequence of events that followed young Samuel's capture, which had by now been ritualized, saw British officials negotiating directly with their French counterparts, to whose territory captives had been taken, in order to secure their release. Among "Captives yet in the Indians hands" on a list compiled on 24 January 1698, seven months after his capture, was "Sam Gill of Salsbery Caried to Cannada."[30] Two years later, on 29 May 1700, his father, a sergeant in the militia, petitioned colonial officials on his and his wife's behalf for an explanation of why their son, along with several "English captives," was being "deprived of the means of being instructed in the true Protestant Religion."[31] For that reason, if for no other, funds should have been granted for their release. The senior Gill followed up a year later, again urging that money be allocated to secure the release from "the french and Indins of Canida" of "Samuel gill taken from Salsbery jun 10th 1697 agged nine yeres," along with the release of four others.[32] No further reliable information has been located.[33]

Noel Annance's maternal great-grandmother arrived at St Francis sometime after Samuel Gill and at a younger age. According to family recollections of a century and two-thirds later, the little girl dubbed Rosalie was "the daughter of a Protestant minister named James" and too young to know her first name when taken along with her parents, who were almost immediately killed, from near a mill at long-settled Kennebunk, Maine (see map 1).[34] No one had been left alive in her family to attempt to rescue her. The location suggests that the capture occurred during an attack by French forces, with whom the Abenaki and others had formed an alliance in order to counter attempts by the English to expand north from Maine into Acadia, in today's Nova Scotia, over which Britain did get control in 1710. Rosalie James's abduction might have happened during a major and widespread French and Abenaki raid of 10 August 1703, not all of whose victims were, by one account, "anywhere recorded."[35]

Neither Samuel Gill nor Rosalie James was returned home, perhaps not to their disliking. According to parish priest Joseph-Pierre-Anselme Maurault, who arrived at St Francis in 1841, learned the language, and remained there to his death in 1870, the Abenakis "adopted them as their own children and treated them tenderly," which included overseeing their conversion to Catholicism.[36] A glimmer of the pair's young lives may survive in the captivity narratives of Puritan minister John Williams and his ten-year-old son, Steven, who were taken not long afterward, along with family members and a hundred others, in a French-led attack on Deerfield in western Massachusetts.[37]

Published just three years later in 1707 and eight times reprinted by the end of the century to widespread acclaim, John Williams's narrative includes a brief account of his short stay in St Francis in the spring of 1704: "We found several poor children who had been taken from the Eastward [Maine] the summer before, a sight very affecting, they being in habit very much like Indians and in manners very much symbolizing with them."[38] Although Williams's son Steven penned his separate account not long after returning home, it remained unpublished for over a century, perhaps not to upstage his father. Steven Williams had a parallel but more intimate experience given his young age: "While I lived here I observed that some English children would scoff at me when before the Indians worse than the Indian children. But when alone they would talk familiarly with me in English about their own country and etc., whereas before the Indians they would pretend they could not speak English."[39] Whether or not Rosalie James and Samuel Gill were among their number must be left to the imagination.

In the account passed down through descendants, on Rosalie and Samuel reaching the age for marriage, the Abenaki leadership held a council as to how best to proceed. "Some wanted them to marry each other so as to have some white people in the tribe, but as many were of the opinion it was better to marry the young man to an indigenous woman and the young girl to an indigenous man so as to mingle their blood with indigenous blood, to tie them more closely to the Abenaki, and to protect their descendants."[40] In this version of events, the local priest, aware of the pair's feelings for each other, got the meeting adjourned and that evening married them to each other.

By the various stories that have come down through time, the couple both adapted to their circumstances and remained their own persons. Samuel Gill is remembered for having "lived like indigenous people of his time, that is to say on the products of hunting fur-bearing animals as well as they themselves, on deer, caribou and others." At the same time, "Samuel Gill never forgot English and all his life interpreted for the Abenaki of St. Francis."[41] Because St Francis church records were destroyed in a British raid in 1759, it is impossible to know precisely when the couple died, save that the last of seven known children was born in 1737. A family history considers that Rosalie James died around 1738 and Samuel Gill about 1758.[42]

The Gills had four sons and three daughters reaching adulthood, all of whom made their lives in St Francis (see illustration 1). Born in about 1719, eldest son Joseph-Louis Gill ran a dry goods store.[43] His first wife, with whom he had two or possibly three children, was the daughter of the Abenaki sachem, or grand chief. Joseph-Louis would himself become chief, by one account being so elected on returning from a French military expedition in 1747 and by another account doing so on his father-in-law's death.[44] Following his wife's death in 1759, Joseph-Louis married a French militia captain's daughter, Suzanne Gamelin-dit-Châteauvieux, from whose father he inherited considerable property and by whom he had a second family of six sons and two daughters – who, unlike his first family, were by descent wholly white.[45]

The senior Gills' second son, Joseph-Piche, wed two Abenaki women in succession, and his younger brothers, Francis Louis and Robert, wed French Canadian women, as had their eldest brother the second time around. Joseph-Piche and Robert also became, according to a descendant, "chiefs of the Abenaki tribe." All three are thought to have been literate in French, as attested by their signing a document in 1768; if so, they were likely taught by the local priest.[46]

Of the three Gill daughters, the eldest, Jeanne-Magdeleine, married a man remembered as Louis Hannis, said to be of mixed German and Indigenous descent, whose father was a onetime captive.[47] Josephte wed an Abenaki called Watso. Marie-Appoline wed Gabriel Annance, who was, according to a family memoir, an Abenaki of "pure blood," although an oral account describes him as an Iroquois from Caughnawaga outside of Montreal.[48] Marie-Appoline and Gabriel Annance were Noel's paternal grandparents.

UTILITY OF CAPTIVITY NARRATIVES

For all that Abenakis played a prominent role in the ongoing hostilities between the French and the British, only a handful of narratives, as with those of John and Steven Williams, speak to captives' experiences in St Francis and, by inference or directly, to the Gill clan.[49] One of those doing so comes from Mary Fowler, taken in 1746 at the age of sixteen along with her family from their eastern Massachusetts farm. In her nineties, she recalled being carried "through the wilderness to St. Francis in Canada," where she was "detained for the term of three years." Fowler told of being sold "to a squaw," who released her on her feigning illness following "three years' hard labor in planting and hoeing corn, chopping and carrying wood, pounding *samp* [corn meal], gathering cranberries and other wild fruit for the market."[50] The account of twenty-six-year-old Titus King, taken in June 1755 during an attack on a regiment of militia in which he was serving, describes how on arriving at St Francis he was expected to run a gauntlet, the traditional means by which captives exchanged one identity for another. King may have been referring to one of the Gills in describing how "the Indian goveners Son Step^t in bteen me & the young Indians y^t [who had] ye sticks [and] told [them to be] gone home."[51]

The narrative of Jemima Howe, captured the same year as King in her early thirties along with numerous of her children, may or may not refer to the Gills. By the published version of her oral account, soon after reaching "St. Francois, the metropolis, if I may so call it, to which the Indians, who led us captive, belonged ... a council, consisting of the chief Sachem and some principal warriors of the St. Francois tribe, was convened; and after the ceremonies usual on such occasions, were over, I was conducted and delivered to an old squaw, whom the Indians told me, I must call my mother."[52] A French army engineer visiting on his own accord three years earlier, in 1752, described St Francis as "a considerable and wholly Abenaki village consisting of 51 long huts covered with boards and bark, and 12 others constructed in French style."[53] Much like Mary Fowler, Jemima Howe at least in her memory used her wiles to protect her small child and to prevent her daughter from "being shortly married to a young Indian of the tribe of Saint Francois, with which tribe she had continued from the beginning of her captivity."[54]

The only published account assuredly referencing the Gills is that of Susanna Johnson, who was captured in 1754 together with her husband and children but who only crafted her narrative four decades later, by which time it was "impossible to give the reader a minute detail of events that occurred while there."[55] Abducted from southwest New Hampshire in the late summer of 1754, the twenty-five-year-old was taken along with some others to St Francis, where together with her infant daughter Elizabeth and six-year-old son Sylvanus, she spent about six weeks prior to beginning the next phase of what would be a four-year captivity. Despite the time lag, the narrative respecting the Gills' eldest son, Joseph-Louis, is immediate and persuasive.

Susanna Johnson and the others who were with her experienced a ritualized Abenaki welcome, as had Titus King at about the same time. As she explained with the knowledge and understanding that came with the years, "whenever the warriors return from an excursion against an enemy, their return to the tribe or village must be designated by warlike ceremonial; the captives or spoil, which may happen to crown their valor, must be conducted in a triumphant form, and decorated to every possible advantage." Cheeks, chin, and forehead having been painted with vermilion mixed with bear's grease, Johnson along with the others had to run the gauntlet. The horrific accounts in earlier narratives meant that they "expected a severe beating, before we got through, but were agreeably disappointed, when we found that each Indian only gave us a tap on the shoulder." Her ritualized welcome into a new self culminated with the ceremonial placement over her shoulders of "a large belt of wampum," being beads or shells having symbolic meaning, which crossed in back and front.[56]

Initially, Susanna Johnson was assigned to another "master" but within a day found herself "allied to the first family: my master, whose name was Gill, was son-in-law to the grand sachem, was accounted rich, had a store of goods, and lived in a style far above the majority of his tribe." By her recollection, "he often told me that he had an English heart, but his wife was true Indian blood." Through an interpreter, who according to a descendant was Joseph-Louis's father, the now elderly Samuel Gill, Johnson was introduced to the family and told to call them "brothers and sisters," in response to which she expressed her "gratitude, for being introduced to a house of high rank."[57] Joseph-Louis Gill and Marie-Jeanne were the parents of Antoine and Xavier, aged ten and seven. By this time Joseph-Louis's older sister Jeanne-Magdeleine was married, his younger brother Joseph-Piche had four years earlier wed an Abenaki woman and now had a two-year-old, and the other siblings were not yet wed.[58]

Although Susanna Johnson's circumstances were likely far easier than if she and the Gills had not shared common descent, it still took accommodation on her part. Her initial living arrangements, prior to being taken in by the family, had consisted of "a large wigwam without a floor, with a fire in the centre, and only a few water vessels and dishes, to eat from, made of birch bark, and tools for cookery, made clumsily of wood." Her first evening meal of *samp* she identified as "hasty pudding," being a common newcomer dish of the day made by stirring corn meal, boiled water or milk, and possibly molasses for sweetening into a batter-like consistency. As to eating, "a spacious bowl of wood, well filled, was placed in a central spot, and each one drew near with a wooden spoon." It was not so much the hasty pudding as the lack of seats that perturbed her. "The squaws first fall upon their knees, and then sit back upon their heels," a position she could not physically achieve. She was similarly disconcerted by her sleeping arrangement, being the first evening "pointed to a platform raised half a yard, where upon a board covered with a blanket, I was to pass the night," whereas "the Indians threw themselves down, in various parts of the building in a manner that more resembled cows, in a shed, than human beings in a house."[59]

Despite being welcomed into the Gill family, Johnson very understandably felt herself alone with her two young children in "an unnatural situation." As she explained, "I was a novice at making canoes, bunks, and tumplines [leather slings worn over the head or shoulders for carrying things], which was the only occupation of the squaws." And "another time, I went with a party to fish, accompanied by a number of squaws." Johnson accommodated, "washing some apparel at a little brook," milking the cows morning and night, and visiting the other captives, but it was the boredom likely occasioned by her preferential treatment that most grated: "The rest of the time I strolled gloomily about, looking sometimes into an unsociable wigwam, at others sauntering into the bushes, and walking on the banks of brooks."[60]

Susanna Johnson evoked St Francis remarkably sympathetically given her reason for being there, so much so that some of her recollections, or alternatively how they were put into print, verge on romanticism. She described "a church, in which mass was held every night and morning, and every Sunday the hearers were summoned by a bell; and attendance was pretty general ... [The priest] appeared to be in that place, what the legislative branch is to civil government, and the grand sachem the executive. The inhabitants live in perfect harmony, holding most of their property in common. They were prone to indolence, when at home, and not remarkable for neatness. They were extremely modest, and apparently averse to airs of courtship." As to the basis of the economy, Johnson noted hunting and corn growing, which explains samp cum hasty pudding. Her time there caused her to reflect on the link between the St Francis she observed and the Abenakis' reputation for taking captives: "Perhaps I am wrong to call necessity the only motive; revenge, which prompts them to war, has great power."[61] The Abenakis had reason from past events to act as they did.

Despite having with her "my son and infant, in this strange land, without a prospect of relief," Johnson along with six-year-old Sylvanus and baby Elizabeth benefited from the Gill relationships into which she had been thrust. Aware of a century of captivity narratives by the time she wrote, Johnson realized "few have fallen into the hands of savages disposed to more lenity and patience." During her six weeks at St Francis, "my new sisters and brothers treated me with the same attention that they did their natural kindred," showing "no other resentment, than calling me 'no good squaw,' which was the only reproach my sister ever gave, when I displeased her." As a consequence, "I had a numerous retinue of relations, whom I visited daily; but my brother's house, being one of the most decent in the village, I fared full as well at home. Among my connexions was a little brother Sabatis, who brought the cows for me, and took particular notice of my child. He was a sprightly little fellow, and often amused me with feats performed with his bow and arrow." Johnson reciprocated by accepting "the privilege of making shirts for my brother." When in early November 1754 her husband wrote from Montreal, where the rest of the family had been purchased by respectable families, requesting that she persuade her cap-tors to take her there to be sold, which he had arranged, "my brother and sister" agreed, and "we set sail in a little bark canoe" for the four-day trip.[62]

ST FRANCIS'S ALMOST DESTRUCTION

Susanna Johnson's ties to St Francis did not end with her departure for Montreal. The impetus to the renewed contact was a British raid on St Francis in October 1759, not long after she returned home. During the same years that the Johnsons were negotiating their freedom, hostilities between Britain and France intensified, with the Abenaki stronghold of St Francis becoming a target. Up to then, its remote location in French territory had shielded it, but no more.

A British militia group known as Rogers' Rangers, after the name of its leader, was ordered to attack St Francis "in such a manner as you shall judge most effectual to disgrace the enemy, and for the success and honour of his Majesty's arms." Reflective of the state of mind that by this point had been memorialized in a host of published captivity narratives, the raid's head was commanded to "remember the barbari-ties that have been committed by the enemy's Indians on every occasion ... without mercy" and to "take your revenge."[63]

Approaching by water and having reconnoitered "the Indians in a high frolic or dance" celebrating a marriage, Rogers' Rangers attacked the next morning "at half an hour before sunrise ... when they were all fast asleep," setting "fire to all their houses, except three, in which there was corn" that the militia wanted for food.[64] Indicative of the religious tensions between Protestants and Catholics that were so prominent during these years, the church was gutted of its treasures, in-cluding baptismal, marriage, and death records.

The head of the militia estimated they "had killed at least two hun-dred Indians," including those burned to death by virtue of concealing themselves "in the cellars and lofts of their houses." As well, "twenty of their women and children" were taken prisoner, of whom Rogers claimed to have released fifteen, the remaining "two Indian boys, and three Indian girls" being taken away.[65] Among the dead was Chief

Joseph-Louis Gill's Abenaki wife, Marie-Jeanne, captured along with fourteen-year-old Antoine, who survived, and eleven-year-old Xavier, who appears to have died.[66] As Abenakis dispersed in the face of the disaster, St Francis's population fell to around 400, down from earlier estimates approaching 1,000, and then decreased over time to a steady 350 or so.[67]

Again, captivity narratives elucidate the course of events. The ferocity of the attack on St Francis was very likely heightened by the Rangers' second-in-command having been seven years earlier, in 1752 at age twenty-four, captured in southern New Hampshire. After he was ransomed, despite being by his own account "well treated by the tribe" during his five weeks at St Francis and, as with Johnson, "adopted by the sachem," John Stark returned home ambivalent.[68] Even though he acknowledged that "he had received more genuine kindness from the savages of St. Francis, than he ever knew prisoners of war to receive from any civilized nation," his gender had not been respected.[69] Whereas he took pride in running the gauntlet "without much injury" by swinging a pole at those attempting to make contact, he had refused to tend the corn patch, "declaring that 'it was the business of squaws, and not warriors.'"[70] Such work was clearly expected of captives, with Titus King describing how, when there in 1755, "my business now was to hoe corn."[71]

In Stark's retrospective view, "this tribe of Indians was notoriously attached to the French, and had for a century past, harassed the frontiers of New England, murdering people of all ages and sexes, in the most barbarous manner, and in times of peace, when they had no reason to suspect their hostile intentions." Indicative of Stark's greater concern to lambaste than to describe Abenakis as he found them was his copying into his memoir, virtually word for word and without credit, Susanna Johnson's long paragraph in her narrative respecting the character of the village of St Francis, by then several times printed, to which he appended a final denigrating sentence of his own: "In fact, the passions of avarice and revenge exciting them to war and plunder appear to be the most powerful stimulants which operate upon the savage mind."[72]

Susanna Johnson was drawn full circle into the raid's aftermath by virtue of one of the captives taken by Rogers and his men at St Francis soliciting her protection. She recounted in her narrative what occurred shortly after she returned home:

> Soon after my arrival, Major Rogers returned from an expedition against the village of St. Francis, which he had destroyed and killed most of the inhabitants. He brought with him a young Indian prisoner, who stopped at my house, the moment he saw me he cried, my God, my God, here is my sister; it was my little brother Sabatis, who formerly used to bring the cows to me, when I lived at my Indian masters. He was transported to see me, and declared that he was still my brother, and I must be his sister. Poor fellow! The fortune of war had left him without a single relation, but with his country's enemies, he could find one who too sensibly felt his miseries; I felt the purest pleasure in administering to his comfort.

Subsequently, Johnson continued, Sabatis "met my son Sylvanus, who was in the army ...; he recognized him, and clasping him in his arms, 'My God,' says he, 'the fortune of war!' – I shall ever remember this Indian with affection; he had a high sense of honor and good behaviour, he was affable, good natured and polite."[73]

The said Sabatis's identity is confused. A history of the Abenakis published a century later in 1866 named him as Joseph-Louis and Marie-Jeanne Gill's son Antoine, who had been captured in the Johnson raid, but a family historian writing two decades later in 1887 was not so convinced that he was the same person.[74] Whether or not he was Sabatis, Antoine returned home to have a family of his own with an Abenaki woman.[75] This incident points out, as do captivity narratives read between the lines, that everyday relations between Abenakis and the outsiders in their midst were more complex and sometimes more intimate than stereotypes would make them out to be.

ABENAKI DARING AGAIN TO THE FORE

Rogers's raid coincided with Britain's military defeat of the French a month earlier in 1759, culminating four years later with France's withdrawal from North America. Despite the Articles of Capitulation's assurance that "the savages or Indian allies of his most Christian Majesty, shall be maintained in the Lands they inhabit; if they chuse to remain there," it behooved Abenakis and others to cooperate with the very British against whom they had dared for almost a century.

The stationing of a contingent of British troops in St Francis likely encouraged Sachem Joseph-Louis Gill's strategic profession of loyalty to the new order of things. By 1768 St Francis had rebounded from its almost destruction nine years earlier. Having rebuilt their church, Abenakis took pride in explaining to government officials how "we complied with your desire" following the British takeover and Rogers's raid "to collect our selves, and to light our fire again at our Village."[76] Responding to a complaint the same year by Joseph-Louis Gill and three others, a British government proclamation of 1769 forbade whites to settle on St Francis land.[77]

As though the raid and the British takeover were not dislocation enough, a little over half a dozen years later, the British colonies to the south of St Francis, from which numerous of its inhabitants had come, rebelled. The consequence was another war, this time pitting Britain, to whom St Francis now belonged, in a losing struggle against the self-styled United States, whose territory included New England, whence the Gill parents had been forcibly taken to St Francis and where numerous Abenakis made their homes.

Colin Calloway's close interrogation of events points up Joseph-Louis Gill's strategic role during the American War of Independence in protecting St Francis from another devastating raid in the pattern of 1759, when his wife had been killed and two children captured. "Like many Indian peoples, most Abenakis desired neutrality in a struggle that was not of their making and not in their interests."[78] Since such was in practice impossible and as long as it remained unclear in whose territory St Francis would end up, Gill played the Americans and British off against each other.[79] As sachem, he travelled extensively to find out as much as he could about what was happening. A Vermont shop located about 250 kilometres, or 160 miles, south of St Francis at which Indigenous people traded pelts became "a place of randevews, for scouts, Indins and Desarters." The owner recalled how in the fall of 1776 "Gill the Cheff of the St Frances tribe came to our house and stayed nearly a week." Although "he could speak but few words of English," Gill's host "understood many words of the Indian dialect, and between us we could make each other under stand, so that he appeared to be Quite happy."[80] Given that Gill had to have grown up speaking English and two decades earlier had conversed freely in English with Susanna Johnson, his apparent inability now to do so appears to have been a ruse intended to garner as much information as possible.

Joseph-Louis Gill's brother-in-law Gabriel Annance, who was Noel Annance's grandfather, similarly crossed boundaries in what he considered to be his people's best interests. The story is told of how, the morning after Gabriel Annance returned to St Francis in February 1778, British authorities stationed there discovered an American secreted in a cabin about five kilometres, or three miles, away from the village. A search of Annance's house uncovered four letters, two of them intended for Joseph-Louis Gill. Gabriel Annance and the American were summarily dispatched to Montreal, where they were set free in exchange for information about a likely imaginary imminent American invasion.[81]

Joseph-Louis Gill so successfully manoeuvred between the two sides on behalf of the Abenakis that in November 1779 Commander-in-Chief George Washington requested that the Continental Congress appoint "Capt. Joseph Louis Gill Chief of the Abeneeke or St. Francois Tribe of Indians" a major in the American Continental Army, of which Washington had charge. The future United States president had two reasons for doing so: first, Washington explained, Gill could take charge of a never-formed Abenaki contingent consisting of "a number of his Tribe as are willing to take part with him"; second, and perhaps more importantly, Washington intended to "ensure the neutrality of those of his Allies who remain in Canada." Gill had a hand in the initiative, having "heard that Continental Commissions have been granted to some Chiefs of the Northern Indians, and therefore expects something of the same." It was not, however, just any commission that Gill sought but, Washington noted, "the rank of Major, to which he thinks himself intitled as having been a long time a Captain," a likely consequence of earlier French military service.[82]

Washington's request was referred to the Board of War, which resolved the next April "that a commission of major, to be dated the first of May, 1779, be granted to Joseph Louis Gill, an Indian chief of the St. François tribe, and that all Indians of that tribe who are willing to enter into the service of the United States, to be collected and formed into a company or companies under the command of the said Joseph Louis Gill and receive while in service the like pay; subsistence, and rations, with the officers and soldiers of the continental army."[83] Congress followed up by "granting a Commission of Major to Joseph Louis Gill, an Indian Chief," with additional "Commissions for a certain Number of Officers who may be recommended to command under Joseph Gill" from among "those of his Tribe who are willing to enter the Service of the States."[84] The Abenaki sachem's feat was considerable.

Not just the emerging United States but also the British considered Joseph-Louis Gill to be central to the course of events. In February 1779 the British dispatched Gill's son Antoine and a Gamelin brother-in-law to track him down so as to reconcile opposing groups in St Francis, as also did a scouting party, which three months later offered him amnesty in exchange for his agreeing to return.[85]

As it became unlikely St Francis would fall to the Americans, the elusive sachem astutely changed his allegiance. According to a British report, he was soon "full of Contrition for his past Conduct and [made] Professions of Loyalty for the time to Come."[86] On 9 October 1780, just six months after the American Continental Congress had commissioned him a major, the sachem formally swore an oath of allegiance to Britain: "I Joseph Louis Gill promise sincerely and affirm by oath that I will be faithful, and that I will bear true loyalty fidelity to his majesty King George ... renouncing all indulgences and exemptions of former powers and persons whatsoever."[87] Gill was thereupon permitted to return home to St Francis, only to behave much as he had done before in negotiating between the two sides until the war's end in 1783.

As assessed by Calloway, Gill's actions assume

> greater clarity and consistency if that role is viewed as one phase in a continuing Abenaki struggle to maintain their lands and independence against all comers, if necessary by dealing with them all ... Joseph Louis Gill assured first the Americans and then the British that Abenaki support was certain, Abenaki action a possibility. To British and Americans, such behaviour appeared duplicitous, but the central objective of Abenaki strategy remained

unchanged … The Abenakis fought no major actions, and their ambiguous stance frustrated Britons and Americans alike. But by successfully keeping the Revolution at arm's length, they avoided devastating losses.[88]

The Abenakis had once again dared.

ABENAKI DARING REWARDED

More than a century of Abenaki daring, culminating in Sachem Joseph-Louis Gill's astute manoeuvring during the War of Independence, sometimes with Noel's grandfather Gabriel Annance at his side, was rewarded. The Abenakis had got themselves on the winning side. As Calloway explains, "having done so, they were able to request a grant of lands in subsequent years in recognition of their services."[89] As early as 1781, Abenaki chiefs reminded British authorities how "during the last war they had promised to extend their lands if the services they rendered were worthy, which they had tried to do."[90]

The promise of land acquired new urgency with the migration north into still British territory of thousands of supporters of the losing cause, who had been promised land grants on coming north. Although it did not include St Francis, the region where they settled, known as the Eastern Townships, came within seventy-five kilometres, or forty-five miles, of the Abenakis' stronghold and included their principal hunting grounds.

By 1797, a year before the death of Joseph-Louis Gill and two years before that of Gabriel Annance, the latter's son, who was Noel Annance's father, was made a chief and in that capacity pursued the promise of land. In his petition of 1803, Francis Joseph Annance reminded the governor general of the Canadas, Sir Robert Shore Milnes, of the promise, in exchange for which the grantees would "be restricted from the power of selling & alienating the said land."[91] Francis Joseph's proviso echoed the British home secretary's earlier stipulation to the lieutenant governor of Lower Canada that "the Land so granted shall on no account be capable of being alienated or disposed of."[92] On 26 June 1805, 8,900 acres located in Durham Township thirty to forty kilometres, or twenty to twenty-five miles, southeast of St Francis were granted to seventeen

Aebenaki male family heads, each of whom received a designated portion (see map 1).[93]

Indicative of the consequences of St Francis's captivity narratives, two-thirds of the seventeen families acquiring Durham land descended in whole or part from Samuel Gill and Rosalie James. Among these descendants were their now almost seventy-year-old youngest son, Robert, who had a family with a French Canadian woman, and their grandsons Francis Joseph Annance and Antoine Gill, the latter being Joseph-Louis Gill's son, who had at age fourteen been captured by Rogers' Rangers. Four of the other recipients had Gill wives, and five had Annance wives.[94] The captivity narratives' legacies were powerful and ongoing.

TO SUM UP

It was in the aftermath of a century of Abenaki daring and double captivity narratives that Noel Annance was born in 1792. Not only his chiefly great-uncle Joseph-Louis Gill but also his grandfather Gabriel Annance had repeatedly dared in the recently concluded War of Independence, manoeuvring between Britain and the young United States in St Francis's best interests. Noel's father, Francis Joseph Annance, had played a leading role in the subsequent acquisition of additional land. Abenaki daring was alive and well.

Taking a Chance on Literacy's Promise

Noel Annance was heir not only to Abenaki daring and to double captivity narratives but also to literacy's promise in respect to reading and writing. The three inheritances had become intertwined by the time of his birth in 1792. His captive great-grandparents' third and youngest daughter, Marie-Appoline, had wed Gabriel Annance, almost certainly an Abenaki. According to family tradition, their youngest son, Francis Joseph, was born on the same day that Quebec City fell to the English in September 1759. Francis Joseph took a chance on literacy's promise, as did in due course his three sons, including Noel, by an Abenaki woman.[1] The two generations doing so was to come full circle, for inherent within the acquisition of literacy's promise was a variant of the captivity narratives that had long defined the Gill family.

THE COMPLEXITIES OF LITERACY'S PROMISE

Acquisition of newcomer literacy by children of Indigenous descent, such as were many of the Gills of the second, third, and subsequent generations, was fraught with contradictions and inconsistencies. The few schools giving Indigenous youth an entryway to literacy in English, French, or possibly their own language were premised on a form of captivity comparable to that experienced by Samuel Gill, Rosalie James, Susanna Johnson, and a host of others similarly taken from their families and homes into wholly other ways of life. Indigenous children and youth had to undergo rituals not unlike those experienced by captives on entering Indigenous territory. They were expected to forgo their whole selves in favour of another way of being. The goal of transformation into other selves underlay both iterations of captivity.

The captive nature of the schools enrolling Indigenous students was due to their origins. Almost all of them were run by religious denominations. Their goal was not so much literacy as it was religious conversion, be it to the Catholicism of the former New France or to a variant of the Protestantism girding Britain and the young United States. Literacy was a means toward that end, as opposed to being an end in itself.[2]

In reality, very few schools admitting Indigenous children and youth existed during the mid and later 1700s, when the third-generation Gills were growing up, or by the early 1800s, when the fourth generation did so. The principal purpose of the handful of church-run day schools and mostly short-lived boarding ventures was to train their almost wholly male students as missionaries or possibly teachers to their own people, as opposed to welcoming them into the dominant society coming into being.[3] Their function as adults was to conciliate Indigenous peoples to changes not of their making.

MOOR'S INDIAN CHARITY SCHOOL

The educational institution that would alter some St Francis lives was Moor's Indian Charity School. Founded in 1754 in central Connecticut with the financial assistance of, among other donors, the Boston commissioners of the London-based Society for the Propagation of the Gospel in Foreign Parts, it had been relocated in 1768 to Hanover in north-central New Hampshire. As meticulously compiled by Colin Calloway, up to its closure in 1856 the broadly Protestant Moor's admitted 150 Indigenous students, all but 18 of them male.[4]

Moor's was, as explained by Hilary Wyss, "unquestionably the longest lasting and most well funded, publicized, and ambitious institution for educating Native Americans in the eighteenth century."[5] James Axtell describes its founding head, Congregational minister Eleazar Wheelock, as "the leading exponent of Indian education in the eighteenth century."[6] No other early school for Indigenous children and youth more systematically intertwined literacy acquisition and the captivity narrative than did Moor's.

Although Moor's was intended primarily, yet never solely, for Indigenous youth, its curriculum followed that in place generally at this time, which added to its captive character. Students were taught to read and write English, alongside Bible study and instruction in Latin and Greek. Their regimented days began and ended with prayers. Moor's did everything it could to prevent contact with relatives for fear of undoing its supposed good work. Wheelock considered it essential that students were "taken out of the reach of their Parents, and out of the way of *Indian* Examples, and kept to School under good Government and constant Instruction."[7] As concluded by Calloway, "English soldiers rarely took Indian prisoners, but the Indian children at Wheelock's school … surely felt themselves captives in the process of cultural conversion."[8]

Students' captivity was not intended to end on their leaving Moor's but was to extend through their lifetimes. As well as continuing in the ways inculcated in them, former students were expected to write regularly in deferential fashion testifying to their doing so. Wheelock's heart must have been gladdened by lines in their letters such as "educated people are so well-bred" and "the Carnal effections, rising in my Heart were so strong, they almost overcome me, had it not been the Divine Assistance."[9] The numerous literary scholars and historians who have analyzed the letters of former students point up how they remained ensnared whether or not they adhered to the school's desired life course for them.[10] In Wyss's determination, "central to Wheelock's concept of Native education is that the English must control and supervise Indians at all times, even the Indian missionaries and teachers his school produced."[11]

If Wheelock had not been so blinkered, he would have realized, Sylvia Gale helps us to understand through her close reading of the letters of former students, why they at one and the same time acquiesced to and resisted their ongoing captivity. Carrying "the weight of both the education they received and the social history of the communities they served," students sought "an 'advanced' education even when that education is apparently unnecessary or incidental" to their intended future occupation.[12] Indigenous peoples viewed literacy as an entryway to newcomers' worlds while at the same time not forgoing their own, whereas newcomers conceived it as part of a wholly transformational narrative. It was not that students rejected what they had been taught but rather that they resisted being stripped of their selves, much as several generations of writers of captivity narratives describe.

MOOR'S COMES A CALLING

The intertwining of Moor's with Gill descendants on the eve of the American War of Independence had two impetuses. The first was the family's self-acknowledgment that, however tied they might be to the Abenaki, they were also non-Indigenous – if not entirely, then partially so. The second was the dilemma in which Moor's increasingly found itself.

For all that Samuel Gill and Rosalie James's eldest son, Joseph-Louis, had been the long-time sachem at St Francis and so bound the family to the community, offspring were very aware of their inheritance's complexities. The second generation lived in an Abenaki context and was Abenaki in spirit and outlook, if not necessarily or wholly genetically so. With the passage of time, particularly on their parents' deaths, which likely freed them to do so, offspring sought to know their whole selves. Whether or not Rogers's raid with its intent of obliterating St Francis played a role, nine years later, in 1768, all seven Gill offspring, then aged between thirty-one and fifty-one years, joined together to find out who they were.

In their request for information, the Gill offspring foregrounded what they knew about the captivity narratives out of which they originated. We "seek the relatives of our father, a native of New England ... brought 80 years ago by the Abenaki Indians to the village of St. Francis at about seven or eight years of age." By their understanding, "our grandfather Sergeant Gill made two attempts to search" for his son, but "having been taken so young he became attached to the Abenaki and never wanted to leave." It was not only their father's family whom offspring sought to contact: "Our mother was taken at Kennebec, sometime after the capture of our father, near to a mill where the whole family was taken and led away to Canada with the exception of the father and of the mother who were taken out to the field."[13] The request for information went on to explain how their parents had been married in the local church when they were very young, but the records of their being so had been lost in the British action of 1759 against the village.

Deputized by the siblings to lead the search for relatives, thirty-year-old youngest son Robert took with him a letter of support from no less than Quebec governor Guy Carleton. Family historian Charles Gill, who told the story a century later, was unable to determine whether

Robert actually made it to Boston with the letters, as was the plan. In any case, nothing was turned up until Charles Gill began his own search, which would in 1892 uncover the senior Gill's unsuccessful 1700 and 1701 petitions for the return of his captured son.[14]

The captivity narratives that distinguished the Gill clan also came to the fore in the matter of schooling, where options had up to then been limited to the long-time Catholic presence in St Francis. It was due to the practical difficulties of Moor's acquiring and retaining Indigenous students who met its head Eleazar Wheelock's expectations that another option came into view, rebounding on the Gills.

Early Moor's students had been mostly Narragansett or Mohawk, the latter including eighteen-year-old Joseph Brant, dispatched in 1761 at the behest of Indian Affairs head Sir William Johnson, who had partnered with his sister Molly.[15] For all that the majority of Indigenous students had in Wheelock's view "generally behaved well while they were with me," a minority sank down into as "low, savage and brutish a manner of living as they were in before."[16] In response to this perception and to growing tension with Johnson, Wheelock did not wholly close Moor's, as some writers erroneously indicate,[17] but rather adapted it to changing circumstances.

The first of Wheelock's two new initiatives was to redirect the £12,000 – well over $1.5 million today and more "than any educator up that time had at his disposal for missionary work" – that his early Mohegan protégé Samson Occom had collected during two years of fundraising in England and Scotland for the purpose of furthering Moor's as a school for Indigenous students.[18] Wheelock instead used the funds to found Dartmouth College in 1769 in Hanover as a higher-level, almost wholly non-Indigenous extension of Moor's, to which he subsequently committed his principal attention.[19]

Dartmouth College would be just the tenth postsecondary institution to be founded in English- and French-speaking North America after Harvard, Laval, William and Mary, Yale, Princeton, Columbia, Pennsylvania, Brown, and Rutgers, all intended in the thinking of the day to train "gentleman," being the language then used, to take their places at the forefront of the emerging dominant society. Wheelock's shifting attitude toward the potential of Indigenous peoples caused him to believe that whites such as those to be educated at Dartmouth must be the crit-

ILLUSTRATION 3

Head of Moor's Charity School Eleazar Wheelock with students
at the founding of Dartmouth College, 1769

ical agents of change, whether as missionaries and teachers or as businessmen and politicians. Wheelock named himself Dartmouth College's inaugural president, to be succeeded on his death in 1779 also as head of Moor's by his eldest son, John, who had been a member of Dartmouth's first graduating class. Needless to say, this breaking of literacy's promise to Indigenous people did not go down well with Occom.

The elder Wheelock's second initiative was for Moor's to refocus student recruitment. Wheelock increasingly looked to Britain's recently acquired New France, whose Catholic character made its Indigenous population, he considered, in particular need of remediation at this time, when Protestants deemed Catholics to be damned and vice versa. Wheelock also sought, alongside wholly Indigenous students, descendants of captives who by choice or circumstance had made their lives with Indigenous people. This turn would, Wheelock considered, moderate "the Difficulty of Educating an Indian" due to their "Sloth," "Sordid Manner of Dress," "no Care for Futurity," and so on. He was hopeful that white descent, even if partial, would win out. In 1772 Moor's snared, among ten new recruits, two captives' sons with Iroquois mothers, which whetted Wheelock's appetite for more.[20]

It was two years later, in the summer of 1774, that Moor's came a calling at St Francis in pursuit of descendants of Samuel Gill and Rosalie James. The interpreter with the group had made a reconnaissance trip six weeks earlier, which means that by the time of the return visit, minds were likely made up. Although we cannot know what occurred in the interval, it seems possible the Gill siblings consulted with each other, much as they had done six years earlier in deciding to search out their whole selves. Demonstrating the Abenaki daring long guiding the community, they decided to take a chance on literacy's promise. As explained by Wyss, "such engagement was a choice made by Native Americans as a means of forwarding their own goals."[21]

The visitors' close account gives their version of events:

In the evening *Joseph Lewis Gill*, the Chief Sachem of the Town, came to visit us, he is an *Englishman* by Blood, tho' an *Indian* by Education, being descended from two English Captives, who about 70 or 80 Years ago, were in their Childhoods brought Prisoners to this Town, grew and became naturaliz'd among the *Indians*, married and had Six or Seven children, who were inter-married among the *Savages*, and have a Number of Children by them, Three of which are to go with us to the School; *Joseph*, the aforementioned Sachem, also sends a Son, which he has by a *French* wife; an *Indian* Woman, whom he had before, having been killed by Major Rogers when he destroyed this Town. – *Joseph's* Wife and her *French* Relations are much against his sending his Son, they tell him that the Boy will turn Heretic, and be ruined forever; but he encourages himself and his Brethren and Sisters against these Insinuations, by telling them, that GOD will preserve their Children, and lead them in the right Way, and when they are instructed in both the Papist and Protestant Religions, they will be capable of choosing that which is best.[22]

Whether or not Joseph-Louis Gill was so aware, the distinction was considerable between the Catholicism of the Jesuits ensconced in St Francis and the school's fierce Protestantism.

No time lost, the visitors met their four charges the next day, a Sunday, to set out Monday morning for the month-long trip to the school:

The little Boys who are to accompany us came to see us … They seem very fond of the Journey; and look like fine sprightly lads; the oldest is not above Fifteen years old; and they all have a good share of *English* Blood in their Veins. [The next morning] Set out for *Montreal* in a Canoe, with our Four little Boys, who were very joyful at our Departure. – Their Mothers bid them farewell with great Tenderness and Affection, but without any appearance of Sorrow or Regret, at parting with them … *Joseph Lewis*, and an *Indian*, his Brother-in-Law, with some others, went down with us in a Canoe to the Mouth of the River, took leave of their Sons with an affectionate Satisfaction, committed them to our Care with a great Appearance of Confidence in our Fidelity and Friendship.[23]

Noel Annance's father, the now fifteen-year-old Francis Joseph, was one of the four leaving home. Francis Joseph's father, Gabriel Annance, was almost certainly the unnamed brother-in-law accompanying Joseph-Louis Gill by canoe to bid their sons a final farewell. Joseph-

Louis's son was eleven-year-old Antoine, the eldest by French Canadian Suzanne Gamelin, his second wife. The other two were named Benedict Gill and possibly Montuit Gill.[24] Their parentage is unclear from surviving family records, and they may have been offspring of Samuel and Rosalie Gill's daughters, being, like Francis Joseph Annance while at the school, bequeathed the Gill surname in recognition of the captivity inheritance responsible for their being there.

It is not hard to intuit why Joseph-Louis Gill along with the others engaged literacy's promise, with all of the complexities that thereby ensued. His and his siblings' search for their origins half a dozen years earlier speaks to their understanding of their double inheritance. There were also strategic considerations. Knowledge of the Abenaki and French languages no longer sufficed. The British had by now been in charge for a decade, giving priority not only to proficiency in the English language but also to understanding British ways of thinking. For all that Joseph-Louis was a sachem, he well understood, as did his brothers and sisters, as indicated by their interest in their parental descent, that a much larger world was out there. Whatever the family might have known previously about faraway Moor's, its link with one of North America's very few postsecondary institutions in Dartmouth College may have enhanced its appeal. Finances were not a consideration. As well as providing transportation, Moor's as a charity school picked up all the costs, which for "Provisions, Cloathing, &c," including "mending, and other incidental Charges," added up to a tidy £1 to £2 per student per month.[25]

LITERACY'S PROMISE FOR GILL GRANDSONS

If literacy acquisition made sense to the Gill clan in St Francis, the family's presence was even more critical to Moor's. Wheelock gloried at how the visit had "brought to this School, Four Boys whose Grand Parents were captured from *New-England*, by that Tribe many Years ago." Indicative of his prejudices in respect to Indigenous peoples, he enthused about the four Gill grandsons, "though they were born among the *Indians*, and have been exposed to their national Vices, such as Cohabitation, that such early Connections could inspire; yet they appear to be as sprightly, active, enterprising, benevolent towards all, and as

sensible of Kindnesses done them, as English Children commonly are."
The quartet's presence portended a better future for Moor's: "Indeed, it
appears to me, that the coming of these Boys to the School, with all
these concurring Circumstances, exhibits the most encouraging, and
animating Prospects of future Success of this great Design, that has ever
yet opened to View in this Land."[26]

At the time the four arrived, although Moor's had earlier educated
some girls intended to become suitable wives, the six Indigenous students already there and the two attending Dartmouth, mostly Iroquois
or Huron, were male like themselves.[27] Moor's used the new arrivals
not only to refurbish its reputation but also to buttress its finances. In
September 1776, just two months after declaring the American colonies
independent, the Continental Congress resolved that, "as it may be a
means of conciliating the friendship of the Canadian Indians, or, at
least, of preventing hostilities from them in some measure, to assist the
president of Dartmouth college, in New Hampshire, in maintaining
their youth who are there, under his tuition, ... five hundred dollars be
paid to the Rev. Dr. Eleazar Wheelock, president of the said college."[28]
Another such grant followed two years later.[29]

A paucity of sources makes it impossible to know precisely how literacy's promise unfolded for the four Gill grandsons, but enough correspondence and other information survives in the Dartmouth College
Archives to determine that it did so differentially.[30] Wheelock explained
in a letter of November 1777 to "Sachem Gill" that his son "Anthony"
sought to return home, with which decision he agreed, given that "he
don't love his books, but loves play & idleness much better." Antoine
was not the only Gill grandson to falter. "Benedict did not get the English tongue so easie as some do & is not so forward in reading & writing as I could wish." On the other hand, Wheelock wrote in the fall of
1777, "[Francis] Joseph entered [Dartmouth] college last August &
bids fair to make a good schollar," and the likely Montuit "will be fit
to enter college as soon as he is old enough." Wheeler was hopeful that
"their Fathers are wise enough to let them go through their learning &
not take them away."[31] Antoine, Benedict, and Montuit had all left
Dartmouth by the end of 1779, by some accounts as early as 1777,
very possibly due to the hostilities between the incipient United States

and Britain, but also due to their disinclination to be held captive to a way of life so different from what they had known previously.[32]

FRANCIS JOSEPH ANNANCE'S PATHWAY

It was Noel Annance's father, Francis Joseph, who persevered not only at Moor's but also at a higher level. Entering Dartmouth College in the fall term of 1777 as the fourth Indigenous student to do so, he remained three of the four years and so did not graduate before returning home, almost certainly due to the ongoing war between Britain and the United States. Now twenty-one, he came back wearing his schooling.[33] As explained by a contemporary, he was "non pas comme un Sauvage, mas habillé à la façon d'un petit maître [no longer a savage, but dressed in the fashion of a little master]."[34] Francis Joseph later described himself as "employed during the said American War as a Scout on His Majesty's Secret and Confidential Service, and also on Scouting parties in common with the other Indians of his tribe."[35]

Wedding Marie Josephte Thomas, likely a local Abenaki woman, Francis Joseph Annance used his higher education to serve the Abenaki people as a sachem in the pattern of his maternal uncle. His name appears time and again, sometimes alongside various Gills, on public documents, thus testifying to his status. Francis Joseph was one of eight St Francis signatories to a land deed in 1798, one of thirteen as "war captain and interpreter" to another two years later, and among the seventeen St Francis family heads granted land in 1805 as a consequence of his skill with the English language in petitioning the governor general of the colonies.[36] Later, in 1819, he would be one of seventeen signatories on a request to rebuild the Catholic parish church burned down in a recent fire.[37]

Francis Joseph also sought land on his own account. In 1803 he petitioned the governor general of the Canadas, Sir Robert Shore Milnes, as to how he was "averse to that kind of idle and indolent life to which Indians are generally attached, was desirous of cultivating lands and settling himself more in a state of civilization, ... hoping thereby to provide for his wife, three sons & three daughters, so they do not thereafter be obliged to follow the Indian mode of life." To give the request credibility, he enumerated his children, describing how "his three sons are of the age of nine, eleven, & thirteen and his daughters of the age of twenty, sixteen, and one years." His sons were Joseph, preceded by Noel and Louis, and his daughters were Marie Josephte, Marie Marguerite, and Angelique (see illustration 2). In the petition, Francis Joseph requested, in line with newcomers obtaining land, that he be granted "an Island in the River St Francis" known as Long Island, some fifty-eight acres in size, where he had already settled his family and to which he would six years later, in 1809, be given a twenty-one-year lease.[38]

Francis Joseph used his higher education to advantage as opportunities came his way. A just arrived Englishman encountering him in 1804 described "meeting with a person not unknown to Lord Dorchester [governor general of the Canadas, 1786–96] and General Prescott [governor, 1796–99], Francis Annance, chief of the Abenakee nation," who "in his plain sensible manner, informed me that he had been within a few leagues of my estate, and marked upon my map the road, ... To use his own words, 'he had had the honour of shaking hands with these Governors, and he loved them because they had favoured his nation, and had caused Government to be their friend, and they felt themselves bound to serve the friends of the Government.'" Later the newcomer passed by St Francis, where "the nephew of my friend Annance" arranged his transportation back to the place whence he had come.[39] Boundaries dividing Indigenous peoples and newcomers were not yet fully in place.

Following on legislation passed in 1801 establishing a free primary school system across Quebec, then Lower Canada, St Francis became two years later, at Francis Joseph Annance's initiative, the second Quebec Indigenous community to have a local school. Its only predecessor was the Huron community of Lorette outside of Quebec City, where Louis Vincent, recruited to Moor's two years prior to Francis Joseph and having graduated from Dartmouth in 1781, began a school in 1792.[40] Francis Joseph as teacher received a salary of £10 a year.[41] An 1820 list compiled by the "Office of the Indian Department" included him as "Interpreter and Schoolmaster" with a double salary of £20.[42] A count from this time had 65 families comprising 300 persons living in St Francis.[43] Stéphanie Boutevin and Mathieu Chaurette separately emphasize how these initiatives put St Francis and Lorette to the fore in the matter of schooling, not only among their Indigenous counterparts but also in comparison with French Canadian communities.[44]

An account two years before Francis Joseph Annance's death on 13 January 1826 described him as having charge of "a common week school" enrolling "nineteen scholars, who attend constantly," being "children of his own tribe."[45] This "aged Indian ... educated at Dartmouth College" instructed his students in "the objects of such Institutions," together with "the more important objects of civilization and refinement," at least partially "in the English language." Teaching materials included "seven dozen and a half of London school books" provided by the American Sunday School Union, a Protestant nondenominational organization promoting Bible-based Sunday schools across North America. In appreciation of the gift, Francis Joseph emphasized his commitment to literacy as informed by his own higher education: "The interest I feel for the instruction of our Indian children will always lead me to do all in my power to promote it; and I am convinced that no information can be effected without the knowledge of the Holy Scriptures."[46]

Francis Joseph Annance was not, however, a convert to Protestantism. For all of Moor's proselytizing of its students, he held to the Catholicism into which he had been born, but within a broader framework than he would likely otherwise have done. As a visiting missionary discovered in the early 1820s, "though he is a Roman Catholic by profession, he is willing his tribe should read the Bible," and he was willing to be an intermediary to their doing so: "Captain Francis Annance thinks he can distribute a number of French bibles to those who will be glad to read them."[47]

THE NEXT GENERATION AT MOOR'S

By the time Noel Annance was born in 1792, the family had become firmly established in St Francis. His and his siblings' childhoods passed within the context both of their privileged family and of Abenaki life generally. Their Dartmouth-educated father and perhaps also the local Catholic priest taught them reading, writing, and numeracy, and their

Abenaki mother, Marie Josephte, imparted practical skills.[48] Farming based in corn, hunting, fishing, and gathering remained critical components of the food economy, and they acquired these skills along with expertise in trapping. Animal pelts had value both of themselves and as local women turned them into moccasins, gloves, and other items of clothing. Abenakis continued to be self-sufficient.

The promise of Moor's was not lost on Francis Joseph, especially as his sons and their St Francis contemporaries grew older. Moor's had been closed to Indigenous students in 1785 due to its indebtedness, which had been occasioned by Dartmouth College's foundation, to reopen in 1800 after John Wheelock had for the sole purpose of funding indigenous students negotiated to secure £90 per year in interest earned on earlier Scottish donations.[49] In practice, despite its still being known officially as Moor's Indian Charity School, only a very small handful of the thirty plus students there at any one time from 1800 onward were, as at Dartmouth, Indigenous.[50] Joseph Brant Jr and Jacob Brant, sons of former student Joseph Brant, now a Mohawk sachem, had enrolled on the school's reopening, but on their departure in 1803, Moor's was "destitute of Indians."[51]

From the perspective of Moor's, captives' descendants were still to be preferred by virtue of embodying some white descent, which suited Francis Joseph Annance just fine, much as it had earlier his uncle Joseph-Louis Gill. On the dispatch of the four Gill grandsons a quarter of a century earlier, the school's founder, Eleazar Wheelock, had written enthusiastically of how "the Sachem of the Tribe at St. Francis ... sent me Word, that he had more Sons, and designed to send them all, as soon as they were big enough, to be educated at this School." Wheelock had almost gleefully anticipated "an Increase in my Number of Indian Children from the Province of *Quebec*, and particularly of Descendants from Captives among the Tribes there."[52] The promise would be fulfilled for Wheelock's son John on his becoming head of both Dartmouth and Moor's. He again turned to the Abenakis, along with "the Mohawk, the Oneida, the Caghnawaga," all of whom had also earlier sent students. By 1803, according to John Wheelock, "Capt. Annance" was "in hopes that one or two more may be received from his tribe."[53]

Francis Joseph Annance, now a sachem, strategically used the opening to secure the entry into Moor's over the next decade of ten students to be educated at the school's expense, being his two eldest sons, relatives' offspring, and others in the village whom he considered promising. Justifying the arrangement, Wheelock wrote glowingly to the Scots society overseeing the annual £90 sum: "Captain Francis Annance, since he left the School, has held his fixed abode at St Francis. A great part of the time, he has been concerned in instructing the children of that village in reading, writing, and good principles; and received some allowance from government for his support. He has been concerned in surveying the lands of his tribe; in assisting them with his advice; and in negotiating, matters of their national interest." The younger Wheelock's self-serving praise, which it was, extended outward to St Francis: "From the period when they began to send their children to the school to the present day, they appear to have made greater advances than almost any other tribe in North America."[54]

Like his uncle Joseph-Louis Gill, Francis Joseph was cognizant that the school's Protestant ethos was at odds with St Francis's Catholicism. Apart from bland generalities about students' time at Moor's, such as the claim that "god would improve them in some station in which they might be useful to their Maker and comfort to their Parents in days to come," Francis Joseph did not mention the topic of religion in his substantial correspondence with John Wheelock, considering as had his uncle that theological differences were less relevant than was literacy's promise.[55] Whether it was tacit or deliberate, neither did Wheelock in writing back.

Of Francis Joseph Annance's three sons, the eldest, Louis, was the first to attend Moor's. Louis was enrolled in March 1803 at thirteen years of age after having, by his recollection in later life, "received a Catholic tuition from the Jesuits in his neighbourhood," which may have been supplemented by lessons from his father.[56] Louis headed off with another local boy, being followed in October by a second and also by a Gill relative.[57] Indicative of the acuity of Noel's father, the arrangement was, according to Wheelock, "made pursuant to the wishes of Capt. Francis Annance, a Sachem of the tribe there, long ago communicated to me." As was his wont, Wheelock added in his letter to the oversight society a reminder of the school's past good works: "This Francis was in a savage state received and taught at the school. He sustains a good character, and is usefully exerting himself to inform his nation. The enclosed is one of his letters written in his own hand. I send it that you may see his spirit & improvement, and as one among many samples of the past utility of the School to the Indians."[58] Facility with writing mattered.

Francis Joseph Annance knew exactly how to play Wheelock to his family's and community's advantage. His postscript to a follow-up letter read,

> For I have experienced the art of reading & writing to be more than common benefit to man~~kind~~ in respect to his present occasions & the bettering of his understanding & judgement by giving him in Sight into things both of Civil & Spiritual nature which would otherways undoubtedly have escaped his knowledge but this advantage is quite unknown to my Nation. Therefore they see not the value of it but if I should be supported from this government to whom I have applied for the same so that I may be able to instruct our children here steadily for four or five years they would then begin to see the beauties of learning.[59]

It was about this time that Francis Joseph was appointed to head the new government school established in St Francis, which caused Wheelock to report the next June how "Capt. Annance devotes a large portion of his time to the instruction of the children of his village" and how Francis Joseph received for his school "£100, annually, from the king."[60] Wheelock sought to ingratiate himself with the community from which he was drawing so many of the school's students, with Francis Joseph doing the same in reverse. One such letter described how "the Chiefs are greatly obliged to your honour's kind remembrance to them & unite with me in reverence and respect to your honour and family."[61] The relationship was in every respect mutually advantageous.

Francis Joseph Annance was at the same time well aware of the school's captive nature and in 1805, much as he would have admonished Noel in the same circumstances, sought to mollify fifteen-year-old

Louis on being informed "of your attempting to leave the College without the Consent and knowledge of the President, who you ought to esteem as a parent and benefactor, and without my advice." In a letter written to "Dear Child" from "your affectionate parents," which survives in the Dartmouth College Archives, Louis was reminded, much as his counterparts of a similar age have been through the generations, that "youths do not know what is good and commendable and therefore ought to submit to the mature judgement of their parents, who are daily striving for their ~~good and~~ welfare and interest – you must remember that time lost never can be recalled and therefore if you neglect to improve your mind in your early days, you will in vain lament it when you enter into the world to act for yourself."[62]

Louis's father played the guilt card as to why his son was now in his seeming captivity: "I preferred your advantage than my pleasure and I could not give more convincing proof of my love for you, than to send you to so great a distance for your own good. I sacrificed my fondness to duty." There was also the usual encouragement: "You must be sociable," value "the art of reading & writing," and persevere "until you finish your literary career."[63] Whether or not the letter ever reached Louis, its essence must have passed from parents to son, given that he spent another four years at Moor's, during which "his conduct has been sober and regular, and his habits are virtuous and chaste."[64] Louis's departure in July 1809 was prompted by "his mother being very sick, his parents wishing his return."[65] As of early January 1810, the then twenty-year-old appears to have been back at Moor's, but how long he remained is uncertain.[66]

TURNING TO NOEL ANNANCE

Noel Annance, sometimes known at the school as Obean Noel, Noel Obean, or Noel Joseph, followed his older brother, Louis, to Moor's in July 1808, being also preceded at his father's request to Wheelock by an Annance cousin and a Gill relative.[67] St Francis had by then become the school's sole feeder of Indigenous youth, accounting for all four such students, including Louis and now Noel, among its thirty-five otherwise white, mostly local boys.[68] Set in a small farming village on a riverbank and surrounded by pine forests and foothills, Moor's was, by

a contemporary account, "now almost exclusively devoted to the instruction of the children of the neighbouring inhabitants," and it differed "in nothing from the other grammar-schools, called academies,
which are established in different parts of the country."[69]

It is therefore unsurprising that Wheelock shortly thereafter wrote
enthusiastically to the Scottish society funding Indigenous students concerning his decision "to admit Obean Noel Annance," who "is sixteen
years of age" and already literate. "By some instruction received from
his father, who was many years ago a member of the school, he begins
to read without spelling, has a fair character," and promises to do
well.[70] Wheelock reported a year later that young Annance was "steady
and attentive" and the next year wrote similarly.[71]

However much Noel had heard about Moor's, the actual experience
went beyond words. John Wheelock, who headed both the school and
Dartmouth, set the tone. By the recollection of Alexander Plumley, a
local student there at the same time, "He dressed in the old style, in
small [informal] clothes, with long, black silk stockings, large knee-
buckles, bootees, hat, and ruffled shirt, of ample dimensions. He was
very dignified and remarkably polite, bowing almost to the ground to
every man, woman, and child, as he walked across the College Green.
When lecturing to the students on politeness, he used to enforce his
precepts with the cogent argument, having proved it by his own experience, that bows cost nothing, but often brought much."[72]

Although it is not possible to know all of Noel's studies, the courses
being taken by a Gill relative are indicative: "He has read all Homer's
Iliad in the original, the most of Livy's history 4 vol., and the minor classical authors."[73] His older brother, Louis, was by the end of Noel's first
year at Moor's "well acquainted with reading, writing, & the catechism"
and proceeding "in his studies into Virgil."[74] The most immediate information concerning Noel comes from a formal public examination held
for "members of Moors Indian Charity School on Friday the 17th August
1810."[75] Of the thirty-two students to be examined, just two were
Indigenous, based on the various school lists compiled over time.[76] An
Algonquin named only as Ignatius was examined at the lowest of the six
levels, being "Reading and Spelling," and Noel was among seven otherwise local students examined at the highest level, respecting "Cicero Orations & Greek Testament."[77]

Alexander Plumley's recollection captures the Annance brothers' different approaches to literacy's promise. His mother knew the Wheelocks going back to her childhood, which contributed to the intimacy, and thereby the validity, of her son's perspective: "My playing in the beautiful field of that old school with the Indian boy, Lewis Annance ... and other boys, is one of my earliest and most pleasing recollections. But I well remember that Noah Annance, Lewis' older [*sic*] brother, was so studious and so 'dignified,' too, that we could not induce him to play 'tag' with us."[78] Noel took literacy seriously indeed.

FROM MOOR'S TO DARTMOUTH

On the model of his father before him, Noel Annance reaped the rewards of his combination of persistence and capacity. His success in the 1810 examination almost certainly propelled his admission into Dartmouth College, given that entering students were examined in Cicero's orations, the Greek Testament, Virgil, their ability to translate English into Latin, and the fundamental rules of arithmetic.[79] A year later, in October 1811, "Noel Annance" from "St. Francis, Canada," was among 40 "Sophomores," being second-year students, listed in a Dartmouth catalogue alongside 24 freshmen, 61 juniors, and 47 seniors, for a total of 172 students.[80] Among a student body mostly from nearby farms and small towns, Noel was the only one from British North America and almost certainly the only one of Indigenous descent.[81]

Dartmouth College at the time of Noel's arrival was physically prepossessing. In the centre of an enclosed green stood a three-storey hall with a cupola flanked by several other buildings, including dormitories lodging students in single or double rooms. As well as a library containing 3,000 volumes, Dartmouth sported a museum whose collection included mineral specimens and a set of red deer horns acquired west of the Allegheny Mountains.[82]

The course of studies and the daily routine were prescribed. During the first three years, two-thirds of students' time was given over to Latin and Greek, with the other third going to advanced mathematics, logic, natural and moral philosophy, geography, surveying, astronomy, and English grammar. Chapel began the day at 5:00 AM or as soon as it became light. The religious service was followed by an early-morning

ILLUSTRATION 4
Dartmouth College, 1803, by then student George Ticknor

class, breakfast, individual study, an 11:00 AM class, dinner, study, an afternoon class at 3:00 or 4:00, and evening prayers at 6:00. Students were expected to speak in chapel and from the second year onward to give a public oration three times a year.[83] The teaching staff was headed by President John Wheelock, who had charge of chapel and prayers, oversaw student speeches and orations, and taught civil and ecclesiastical history. Four faculty divided the other courses between them, assisted by two tutors, who were likely recent Dartmouth graduates.[84]

In February 1811 Wheelock described the now nineteen-year-old Noel as "pure" in his "moral conduct, attentive to religious duties," and "making good improvements" in his studies.[85] "Noel J. Annance" of "St. Francis, L.C.," was among the students invited at the end of their first year to join one, or possibly both, of Dartmouth's two debating and literary societies. He became a member of United Fraternity and Social Friends.[86] Limited to students displaying "respectability of talents and acquirements, and a fair moral character," United Fraternity included among its past members the prominent US politician Daniel Webster. Together with more informal manifestations of a sense of belonging, United Fraternity held a weekly literary event with debates and orations and maintained a library available to its members. On a list extending from the society's beginning in 1786 to 1840, Noel is alone as being from St Francis and was one of only two of the half-dozen Indigenous students enrolled at Dartmouth during the first half-century who were invited into membership.[87]

Dartmouth College's implicit and also explicit goal was to form the next generation's leaders. Students were routinely addressed as "gentlemen" or "young gentlemen" and were expected to behave accordingly both while at Dartmouth and in their subsequent lives, and they overwhelming did so.[88] Of Dartmouth students who graduated between 1811 and 1814 for whom information was located, a good one-third became professionals, mainly physicians, judges, or politicians, including two state governors, two speakers of state legislatures, a US senator, and the fervent antislavery advocate in the US House of Representatives Thaddeus Stevens. Another almost one-half served their communities in the other fashion of the day for gentlemen as teachers or ministers. The remaining one-fifth went into business.[89]

TABLE I

Direct costs to Moor's and Dartmouth for Noel Annance, 1809–12

	1809	1810	1811	1812
Individual tuition	$8.00	$8.66	$9.00	$13.35
Special textbooks	–	$0.72	$1.12	$7.25
Board	$46.45	$69.33	$69.33	$67.22
"Bed & bedding"	$5.70	$2.47	$5.20	$5.20
"Washing and mending"	$6.65	$2.70	$4.78	$8.67
Clothing	$26.05	$52.38	$24.77	$33.42
Travel	–	$5.00	$5.00	$16.44
Sundries	$1.30	$0.49	$0.58	$1.85
Totals	*$94.13*	*$141.75*	*$119.78*	*$153.40*

Whereas other Dartmouth students had to pay tuition, Noel continued to be funded as he had been while at Moor's. His and his brother's
literacy acquisition was, as his father put it in a letter to Wheelock, a
"Privilege freely given them by their benefactor."[90] Surviving accounts
remitted to the Scottish society allocating £90, or $375, a year to sup-
port Indigenous students make it possible to estimate how much was
spent on each of "the Indian charity youths," as Wheelock termed
them.[91] The direct costs for educating Noel Annance included individual tuition, textbooks, bedding, washing and mending, clothing, travel,
and sundries (see table 1). Among school texts bought on his behalf
were in 1810 a "Greek Testament" for $0.72, in 1811 "Cicero de
Orate" for $1.89, and in 1812 "Webber's Mathematics" for $3.25 and
a music text for $4.00.[92] Annual total expenses ranged between $100
and $150, which may explain why only two or three Indigenous stu-
dents were enrolled at any one time. Reminiscent of how his father returned home from Moor's wearing his clothing, items provided to
Noel, which were sometimes made to measure and other times purchased, included coats and pants, shirts, vests and pantaloons, woolen
hose, shoes, handkerchiefs, greatcoats, and in 1812 for the first time a

hat. It is unclear from the accounts whether Noel lived in the college dormitory or boarded elsewhere. Be it an economy measure or intended to provide familiar food, "Ind. corn" was specially noted as an item of his board.[93]

Noel Annance acquired a classical education of the day, similar to that of white counterparts so privileged. To whatever extent the fervent religiosity practised by John Wheelock's father still held, it was not obvious either in the books purchased for Noel or in the examinations he is recorded as taking at Moor's or at Dartmouth. As to a possible reason, a knowledgeable history of early Dartmouth evokes a "state of unbelief or indifference manifested by the students."[94] Neither would religion permeate, except as generic phrases in passing, his surviving writing.[95]

Noel Annance left Dartmouth College prior to graduation for reasons not of his making. On 18 June 1812 the United States declared war on Britain, with the goal of annexing British North America, but even before then what a Dartmouth historian terms "the rising temperature of politics prior to the War of 1812" had precipitated the enthusiastic adhesion of both past and present Dartmouth students to the American side.[96] "The war precluding an idea of the return of Noel" was how Dartmouth president John Wheelock diplomatically phrased it.[97] Noel Annance most likely left Dartmouth College in the spring of 1813.

TO SUM UP

On the pattern of select members of the previous generation, Noel Annance and his older brother, Louis, were among very few persons, whatever their backgrounds, given an opportunity to engage literacy's promise. Double captivity narratives, combined with Abenaki daring, had made it possible for his father to do so at the highest level then available in North America, to be followed in due course by his two eldest sons. Having excelled at the historically most prestigious American school enrolling students of Indigenous descent and then at the postsecondary level, Noel Annance had every reason to consider that he was poised for success.

PART TWO

Pursuing Indigenous Inclusion

By virtue of his higher education, Noel Annance should have been able, if any Indigenous person could, to find a measure of acceptance in the dominant society. Chapter 3 turns to his search for belonging in the context of others before him similarly seeking to reconcile their schooling with their indigeneity. Chapter 4 tracks Noel's pursuit of Indigenous inclusion in the fur trade beyond the political boundaries of British North America or of the United States. Chapter 5 engages with Noel's letting go on facing up to the impossibility of his belonging as the person he knew himself to be.

Noel may not initially have fully realized that the trappings of a gentleman did not, if one was perceived as Indigenous, a gentleman make. His taking literacy's promise seriously went only so far. The comparative ease with which he glided through Moor's Charity School and Dartmouth College was deceptive. A captive in the pattern of Noel's great-grandmother, taken in 1773 at the age of five and only located by her brothers half a century later, by then a chief's widow, explained with the wisdom of age how "it is very easy to make an Indian out of a white man, but you cannot make a white man out of an Indian."[1] As Noel would discover for himself, Frances Slacum's judgment had more to do with hardening attitudes in the newcomer society than it did with Indigenous peoples.

The War of 1812, which took Noel Annance away from Dartmouth, was the last North American military conflict to engage Indigenous peoples as allies. Once it ended and no further confrontations were in the offing, Indigenous peoples lost their utility. As neatly summed up by John Milloy, they "drifted into colonial backwaters."[2] In line with generally hardening attitudes toward persons whose skin tones did not accord with those now in charge numerically – be it in the United States, where Noel had studied, or in the future Canada, whence he

came – little if any consideration was given to the diverse interests and
capacities of the different tribes and bands, much less of individuals.
The dismissive category of "Indian," to use the common term of the
day, was rarely if ever disaggregated.

Policies enacting these assumptions did differ between the two
countries. The American government opted for a version of what we
today easily condemn as "ethnic cleansing." The growing conviction
that the United States belonged to white folk precipitated the 1830
federal Indian Removal Act. Over the next decade 100,000 Indigenous persons were forced west of the Mississippi River into what
was termed Indian Territory, a policy justified with more than a
touch of irony as being in their best interest in the face of, in Stephen
J. Rockwell's words, "violent and corrupting white settlers."[3] The policy advantaged Moor's and Dartmouth. So as to continue to be able
to access outside funding restricted to Indigenous students, Moor's recruited a dozen and a half from Indian Territory, who attended alongside later Gill descendants and a couple of others from St Francis.[4]

To the north in still British territory, government policy toward
Indigenous peoples stagnated, due in good part to two levels of
authority. The Colonial Office in London oversaw British North
America as one of a collection of diverse geographical entities from
which it sought to profit economically, whereas successive governor
generals of the Canadas looked to the interests of white settlers who
were their principal and to some extent sole constituency. The distance was enormous, literally and figuratively, between the two levels
of government. The one in Britain provided funding but was remote
from events on the ground and perhaps overly idealistic as to Indigenous peoples' potential to make their own way. The other in British
North America was too close in the everyday to newcomers.

This impasse was evident from at least 1827 when the British secretary of state for war and the colonies, under whose mandate Indigenous peoples came, proposed in the interest of economy to replace
goods with cash payments in the longstanding practice of giving
annual gifts, and to reduce and eventually abolish the Indian Department. Canada's Indigenous peoples would effectively be freed of
government intrusion into their everyday lives and be permitted to
intermingle on their own terms with the newcomer population.[5]

The governor general of the Canadas was having none of it, his vehement opposition being grounded in stereotypes that tended toward exclusion and dispossession. As for converting gifts to cash, "every man here knows that money to Indians is instantly spent in spirituous liquors; and the system adopted in making useful presents as payment was intended expressly to avoid temptation and take way the means furnished to that dreadful state of brutal drunkenness, to which all Indians, men, women and children give themselves." In respect to the Indian Department's dissolution, "that is impossible, so long as the Indian tribes continue to be warlike in their ideas and recollections."[6] This position, which would win out, points up the lack of trust, tinged by fear and self-interest, that would long prevail among those in charge and, to some extent, into the present day.

Determined to ward off change not to his liking, the governor general used the commonplace tactic of delay by commissioning a report. He passed off its construction to his military secretary, Henry Charles Darling, who was soon named chief superintendent of Indian affairs, succeeding the Johnson reign of the past three-quarters of a century. Not unexpectedly given its impetus, the 1828 report argued against the Colonial Office's proposals.

As opposed to Indigenous peoples and whites intermingling, the Darling Report sought separation grounded in the assumptions of the day respecting inferiority and superiority: "In Lower Canada, so in the Upper Province, an Indian is little better than a child as respects any land or other property assigned for his support ... If the interference or protection of their great father be withdrawn, the consequences to the public will become as inconvenient and embarrassing, as they would be ruinous and destructive to the Indian."[7] The report continued the use of the term "Children" by government officials when speaking or writing to Indigenous groups, with its counterpoint of "Father" to be used by Indigenous people in addressing their supposed betters:[8] "Father, we have nothing more to say ... Children, I have listened with much pleasure to your talk ... Continue to be good children, and you may depend that your great father will always love you."[9] Children needed to be differentially treated from adults for their own good as determined by others. So it was with Indigenous peoples.

The 1828 Darling Report is also noteworthy for its attitude of dismissal respecting Quebec. At a time when religion was fundamental to virtually all levels of human activity, Lower Canada and Upper Canada, as Quebec and Ontario were then termed, were as far apart as it was possible to be. Although British North America, in line with Britain itself, was officially Anglican, the terms of the peace treaty had ensured Quebec's "Roman Catholic subjects may profess the worship of their religion according to the rites of the Romish church." In accordance with this commitment, the Indian Department funded five Catholic missionary priests to minister to Quebec's principal Indigenous communities, including St Francis. This funding the appointees equated with their being in charge to the extent of vigorously and successfully opposing nondenominational, Protestant, or English-language schools as opening the door to religious pluralism.[10] From the perspective of a Protestant – in good part, Anglican – bureaucracy, Catholicism's hold justified the Indian Department's passivity in respect to half of its geographical mandate. Per the Darling Report, "while the Indians of the Lower Province remain in their present state, having attained only civilization sufficient to subject them to the impositions of their priests," nothing much could be expected of them.[11]

The Colonial Office, to its credit, persisted in searching out a way ahead that was not wholly defeatist. It was, however, one thing for officials in faraway London to ruminate on policy from time to time and another thing for their counterparts on the ground, who in any case disagreed, to carry it out. In the interim, the relationship between the two levels of governance, and thereby attention to Indigenous peoples, languished.

It was within this context that Noel Annance engaged literacy's promise unaware, as he would find out, that he was too highly educated to be Indigenous and too Indigenous to be accepted as the gentleman he considered himself to be by virtue of his higher education. All of his Abenaki daring on the model of his great-uncle, grandfather, and father would matter for naught, or so it seemed.

3

In Search of Belonging

Noel Annance was among a very small number of Indigenous persons across North America, earlier in time or in his generation, given the opportunity to access literacy's promise. Others not doing so reflected the limited attention given generally to reading and writing, magnified many times over in respect to Indigenous peoples. Noel had few predecessors or counterparts.

Noel Annance left Dartmouth College determined to be a gentleman, consistent with its mandate for its students, a direction that got a boost from the War of 1812. Following outstanding service as a military officer, Noel briefly sought to be a teacher in the pattern of his father before opting for employment in the westward-expanding fur trade.

FEW PREDECESSORS

Noel Annance's educational accomplishment was considerable. His father Francis Joseph had been only the fourth Indigenous student admitted to Dartmouth College, the fifth being a white Gill relative. Noel was the sixth, and the seventh would not be accepted for another quarter of a century. The three earliest, each of whom had attended Moor's Charity School and graduated from Dartmouth, were Narragansett Daniel Simon in 1777, Stockbridge Peter Pohquonnapeet in 1780, and Huron Lewis Vincent in 1781, who had organized the Lorette school. The next Indigenous student to graduate from Dartmouth would not do so until 1840.[1]

Dartmouth College's uniqueness was even more pronounced given that at this time only two other postsecondary institutions, Harvard and Princeton, appear to have admitted Indigenous students at the postsecondary level. Both had done so, as with Dartmouth, as funding vehicles.

Almost as soon as Harvard College was founded in Massachusetts in
1636 as the first postsecondary institution in North America, it became
cash-strapped, and the newly formed London-based Society for the
Propagation of the Gospel among the Natives in New England agreed
to assist. Its offer depended on the college supporting at an advanced
level the society's goal of training "learned and able [Indian] preachers
unto their countrymen."[2] Six years later, the society funded a two-
storey brick Indian College able to "accommodate about twenty scholars with convenient lodgings and studies."[3] Harvard's charter of 1650,
which still governs the institution, committed the college to educating
both "the English and Indian youth of this country in all manner of
good literature Artes and Sciences."[4]

Several factors limited Harvard's enrolment of Indigenous students to
five. Those in charge were at best nominally committed. Indicative of his
own attitude and possibly also of the general view at the time, eminent
Harvard historian Samuel Eliot Morison described in the 1930s how,
"from the founding of Virginia [in 1607] to the American Revolution,
the delusion persisted that there wanted but money and organization to
make scholars and ministers out of selected Indians."[5] As interrogated
by Drew Lopenzina, the practical difficulties were enormous.[6] It took
several years, if not more, of study at one of the few select preparatory
schools of the day to pass Harvard's rigorous entrance examinations:
"When any Scholler is able to read and understand Tully Virgil or any
such ordinary Classicall Authors, and can easily make and speake or
write true Latin prose and hath Skill in making verse, and is Compe-
tently grounded in the Greeke language ... hee shall be capab[le] of his
admission into the College."[7] Once students were there, both their routine and dress were closely structured, much as would be that of Noel
Annance a century and a half later.[8] Indigenous students' inability to realize, almost always through no fault of their own, the aspirations set
for them attested, in the minds of others, to their lack of capacity.

For these reasons, and also due to epidemic diseases and other causes
of premature death, just one of the five Indigenous students admitted to
Harvard at the London missionary society's expense graduated. A
Wampanoag sachem's son named Caleb Cheeschaumuck did so in
1665, only to die shortly thereafter of consumption, being tuberculo-
sis.[9] Fellow Wampanoag Joel Hiacoomes died as a consequence of a

shipwreck a few months before his projected graduation at about the same time. Nipmuc John Wampas left less than a year after being admitted, likely in 1665. A Wampanoag recorded only as Eleazar almost immediately succumbed to smallpox on entering in 1675. Nipmuc Benjamin Larnell, who arrived only in 1714, died of fever three years into his program of studies.[10]

According to knowledgeable accounts, Larnell would be "probably the last Native American student to attend Harvard before the 1970s," and "not a single Native American student would return to graduate until three centuries later."[11] All these factors caused the opinionated Morison to conclude – in justification of Harvard's retreat, as evidenced by the Indian College being as early as 1656 eyed for a "better use ... than to house Indians" – that "the Indians could not absorb higher learning to any advantage."[12]

Harvard's sole Indigenous student to survive his stint there, John Wampas, in attendance under a year in the mid-1660s, left a substantial trace. He did so, however, not as the preacher that was Harvard's goal for its Indigenous students but as an enthusiastic convert to newcomers' ways. It is unsurprising Wampas did so given he had been away from home since his Nipmuc father had handed him over as a child to a visiting missionary "to be trained up among the English."[13]

Part of the reason for Wampas's brief stay at Harvard may have been the conflicted nature of his time there. That it was so is indicated by the double inscription in a copy of Cicero's *De Officiis* published in London in 1629. One side reads, "John Wompowess His Booke 1665," and on the other side in someone else's crude scrawl is written "John Savage." Wampas got his own back soon after leaving Harvard by purchasing for himself and the Mohegan sachem's daughter he married a fine house fronting Boston Common, the most desirable location to live in the then city of 3,000 or so residents, for which he paid an impressive £78.[14]

Wampas's actions repeatedly clashed with his Nipmuc inheritance. Around 1670 a group of Nipmuc, primarily "because he spake English well & was agreeable to the English," requested that he "get sealed and recorded the Indians title & Right" to their lands.[15] A year later, Wampas deeded to an Englishman a 100-acre tract that he had inherited from his father and that was thereby his own "proper right and inheritance," or so he thought. The Nipmuc viewed the transaction differently, claiming that it was part of their tribal lands and so able to be transferred only by the grand sachem.[16] On his wife's death in 1677, Wampas did much the same with her father's land, with similar consequences, despite his father-in-law having been a sachem.

By the time of Wampas's death in 1679, he had enraged so many by his dealings that he was briefly thrown into debtor's prison, lost the Boston house, and was at the centre of various proceedings ranging from an inconclusive inquiry conducted by the superintendent of Indian affairs to an appeal to the Privy Council in London. For all that Wampas may have been a scoundrel, two approaches to land tenure, and more generally to belonging, collided. "Thinking like an Englishman, a direct result of his upbringing," put Wampas, to quote his biographer, "into direct conflict with the traditional communal values of his Nipmuck relatives," this at a time when they still had influence.[17]

The only other college apart from Harvard early on admitting Indigenous students on a par with whites, and the fifth to be founded in North America, was the College of New Jersey, later Princeton University, which opened its doors in 1746. The impetus was, as with Harvard, access to external funding, in its case from a Scottish missionary society. The first of three Delawares arrived in 1751 to die in his second year, the second was a former Moor's student who enrolled a decade or so later to be found academically incompetent, and the third was forced to leave when the American War of Independence cut off his funding.[18] The initiative was not only self-interested but also brief and inconsequential.

Another institution, the College of William and Mary, founded in Virginia in 1693 as the third postsecondary institution in North America, did an end run. Like Harvard a few decades earlier, it admitted Indigenous students in order to access external funding, but unlike Harvard, it did not admit them on a par with their non-Indigenous counterparts but at a much lower level. The impetus was the will of English philosopher, scientist, and inventor Robert Boyle to provide £90 annually, a goodly sum at the time, "for the purpose of maintaining and educating Indian scholars."[19] Once the funds had been accessed, a two-storey Indian School was constructed in the middle of the campus. There, a handful of students, some of them captives or hostages to ensure their peoples' quiescence, were housed and taught separately at a level much lower, being precollege, if not elementary, than that of their white counterparts, who were the college's principal and almost sole focus. Indicative of William and Mary's priorities, as soon as the War of Independence stemmed the flow of funds, the Indian School, through which fifty Indigenous students at most and likely fewer had passed, was turned over to white students.[20]

One of the best documented William and Mary students is John Nettles, remembered as "the first literate Catawba."[21] David Hutchison,[22] a nearby settler who knew him during the two decades prior to his death in about 1812, recounted Nettles's story as it was told to him: "A boy by the name of John Nettles was selected, being the most promising boy in the Nation. He was taken to Virginia, placed in the College of William and Mary, and was kept there five or six years. The object was to give him a liberal and finished education, and to send him back to improve his tribe."[23]

Having "behaved well and stood high as a student," Nettles was "waiting for an opportunity to return home" when "he was found lying in the street drunk." Admonished by college officials, Nettles acknowledged his fault. "But, when they were done speaking, he called their attention to a window, and pointed to a hog walking in the street, and said, 'Take that hog and wash him clean, and as the weather is warm it might be very agreeable; but let him go, and he will lie down and wallow in the first mud-hole he comes to, for he is still a hog' thus intimating that an Indian would be an Indian still."[24] Whether or not the lesson of Indigenous inferiority had been instilled at William and Mary during his time there in the 1760s, it was firmly implanted in Nettles's thinking.

Nettles did not so much search for belonging as he lived its contradictions by virtue of being well educated and Indigenous. Young Massachusetts engineer Elkanah Watson, who visited the Catawbas in 1787, made this point: "I there noticed a savage who had been educated at the college at Williamsburgh, Virginia, degraded into his native savage habits – to all intents an Indian." Worst of all, Watson realized, it was at least in part an act: "Ten days ago I was introduced to him in Albany, a polite, well informed *gentleman*. To day, I beheld him splashing through the mud, in the rain, on horseback, with a young squaw behind him, both decently drunk."[25]

By the time David Hutchison became acquainted with Nettles a few years later, he "ranked among the lowest" from the Catawbas' perspective: "His time spent at school had unfitted him for the habits of Indian life, which was to make a support by hunting, fishing, and a small portion of labor, to all of which he was a stranger." Perhaps deliberately making the point, Nettles differed in dress, "adopting the breeches of the whites instead of the breech-clothes of his tribe," which "rendered him contemptible in the eyes of the Nation." From Hutchison's outsider perspective, "all the time I knew him, his habits were peaceable, moral and temperate, and yet he ranked as above."[26]

Nettles did not, all the same, neglect his obligations to the Catawbas. As well as his signature turning up on repeated petitions, virtually from the time Nettles returned home, he interpreted at meetings with government officials and others.[27] The Catawbas now demanded that even speeches be put in writing so "that the Interpreter Might Read it to them and Explain it when they were by them Selves."[28] When Elkanah Watson was first introduced to Nettles in 1787 in a genteel urban setting as "a polite, well informed *gentleman*," Nettles was almost certainly acting in the interests of the Catawbas. His initiative is perhaps best evidenced by the Catawbas sending a petition to state officials in 1801, on which the now aging Nettles was a signatory and possibly the author, requesting "to have two or three of our young boys taught to read and right [*sic*] ... that they might be assistance to our Nation."[29] To be well educated and Indigenous was no easy matter but had its rewards.

Another well-educated Indigenous predecessor to Noel Annance who leaves a trace acquired his learning, unlike Wampas and Nettles, outside of an institution and for that reason may have been more comfortable, indeed almost joyous, in his search for belonging. French aristocrat Gilbert de Motier, Marquis de Lafayette, who fought on the American side in the War of Independence, returned for a brief visit in 1784, at which point he encountered Peter Otsiquette, then fourteen or fifteen years old. Lafayette's biographer considers Otsiquette's father to have been an unnamed Frenchman and his mother an Oneida woman.[30] The Oneida having permitted Otsiquette's departure to France, he spent three years living in the Lafayettes' household. Otsiquette was sufficiently literate in English by March 1786 that when Lafayette wanted to contact former Moor's student and Mohawk sachem Joseph Brant, then visiting London, "the epistle to Brane [*sic*] was written By My Young Indian who I requested to ask Brane what were His Views and His Hopes."[31] Indicative of Otsiquette's acceptance, Lafayette's wife felt comfortable explaining to a visiting Thomas Jefferson, then American ambassador to France and a family friend, how "Otchikeita" had to be elsewhere and therefore "could not wait for you tomorrow."[32]

Otsiquette so caught the public fancy that on his return to the United States at the end of July 1788 he merited an almost admiring, if not wholly accurate, announcement in Boston's first newspaper, the *Boston Advertiser*: "In the late vessel from France came passenger Peter Otsiquette, who we are told is a son of the King of the Six Nations, and whom the Marquis de La Fayette sometime since sent to France to be educated. He speaks the French and English language with accuracy, and is acquainted with most branches of polite education – morals, etc., and is on his way to the Indian country."[33]

On 31 July 1788 an eighteen-year-old white woman who was Otsiquette's contemporary in age boarded the early morning train in Boston to visit a friend in Providence, Rhode Island, only to find an unexpected companion among the four sharing her carriage. Suan Lear's diary describes their chatty encounter:

At first I felt very much afraid of him, but he turned out to be the most agreeable of the company ... After breakfast the Indian Chief played several tunes on his Clarinet. He played very well. In short, he is quite accomplished. 'Tis about three years since the Marquis De la Fayette sent for him over to France and he has since been at the expense of giving him a very liberal education. He appears to have improved his time well. His observations are just and his manners are very agreeable. He entertained us with a number of anecdotes he picked up in France. He also gave us a very entertaining account of the manners and customs of his own Nation. At every place we stopped, he serenaded us which made our journey quite agreeable.[34]

Susan Lear was so taken that she persuaded her host to invite Otsiquette to dine with them:

He came dressed in a scarlet coat trimmed with gold lace. He really made a very good figure. After dinner ... I danced a cotillion with him. He dances by far the best of any person I ever saw attempt it. He also danced the War dance for us which was very terrible ... In the course of the evening he came and sat by me and paid me a number of compliments, among the rest he said I resembled the Marchioness de la F.[ayette] very much. He requested me to give him my name on a paper which I did. He assured me he would not part with it while he lived.[35]

Otsiquette acquitted himself so well that he was invited to a follow-up party the next day, at whose end "he regrets very much that he is obliged to leave us so soon" and "says he never spent his time so happily." Susan Lear mused, "I don't wonder but the ladies of this place are all in love with him and striving who shall pay him the most attention."[36] Unlike Nettles, Otsiquette saw no reason why gentility and indigeneity could not coexist in the same person.

Otsiquette's attendance a month later on behalf of the Oneida at treaty negotiations extinguishing Indigenous titles in the state of New York, during which he kept a watching brief and signed the resultant treaty, had a contrary effect on two white men also present.[37] Whereas Susan Lear accepted Otsiquette for whom he was, including his determination not to surrender one identity for the other, Elkanah Watson and Thomas Morris could not countenance his refusal to do so.

Elkanah Watson, a contemporary in age who had earlier scorned Nettles, began his account on a positive note: "A young Indian, of the Oneida nation, was also at this treaty; who has just returned from France, where he has been for several years, under the patronage of a distinguished public character, who took him when a boy. He is probably the most polished savage in existence. He speaks French and English perfectly; is master of music, and many branches of polite literature, and in his manners a well bred Frenchman." As for what Otsiquette signified, Watson was scathing: "He is a remarkable instance of the folly of attempting to civilize an Indian: Generally speaking, we may as well attempt to civilize a bear."[38]

During the treaty negotiations, government interpreter Thomas Morris affected an intimacy that would have a duplicitous edge: "Having received the early Part of my own Education in France and being well acquainted with the French Language, I would frequently retire with Peter into the Woods, and hear him recite some of the finest Pieces of French Poetry, from the Tragedies of Corneille and Racine." The edge was not long in coming: "He had not been many Months restored to his Nation, and yet he would Drink raw Rum out of a brass Kettle, take as much Delight in Yelling and Whooping as any Indian; and, in Fact, became as vile a Drunkard as the Worst of them."[39]

Visiting the reservation laid out for the Oneida three years later, in September 1791, recent Dutch immigrant John Lincklaen was less judgmental. He described "a certain French Peter, son of an Indian woman & a French man, the Marquis de la fayette took him with him to Paris where he received an education for 3 years, he speaks French & English very well & a little German, on coming home he married an Indian woman, has 2 children & is 22 years old."[40]

Six months later, in March 1792, Peter Otsiquette again comes into full view, this time as a member of the Oneida delegation to a large gathering of chiefs called together by the US superintendent of Indian affairs. On the way to Philadelphia, then the US capital, the group stopped off at a mission school where the centre of attention was, for one of the young girls studying there, "the adopted son of the Marquis de la Fayette, Peter Otsiquette, who lived for 3 years in Paris, & speaks besides his own, the French and English Languages very fluently." Mary Magdelene Flagg was impressed: "He appears to be a very accomplished young Indian, and it appears plainly, that he has ... lived for a good while among White and Civilized People."[41]

Just ten days later, twenty-two-year-old Peter Otsiquette was dead of an inflammation of the lungs. The Philadelphia setting made the funeral of "M. Peter Jaquette, one of the principal sachems of the Oneida Nation of Indians," so significant as to be covered in a popular local magazine: "The corpse was proceeded by detachments of the light infantry of the city, with arms reversed – drums muffled – music playing a solemn dirge. The corpse was followed by six of the chiefs as mourners, succeeded by all the warriors now in this city – the reverend clergy of all denominations – the secretary of war, and the gentlemen of the war department – Officers of the federal army, and of the militia – and a number of citizens. The concourse assembled on this occasion is supposed to

have amounted to more than 10,000 persons."[42] Among those in attendance was then US secretary of state Thomas Jefferson, who had known
Otsiquette in France. The next day, he described the event in a letter to
his daughter Martha, who had in 1784 as a twelve-year-old accompanied her widowed father there: "I believe you knew Otchakitz, the Indian who lived with the Marquis de Lafayette. He came here lately with
some deputies from his nation, and died here of pleurisy. I was at his funeral yesterday. He was buried standing up, according to their manner."[43] Otsiquette managed the rare feat of belonging in death as he had,
at least for the most part, in life.

Wampas, Nettles, and Otsiquette took literacy's promise seriously,
each in his own distinctive fashion. Their actions ran the danger, as
would those of Noel Annance, of putting them at odds with whites'
growing determination to have it all. Up to the time Noel entered Dartmouth in 1810, just thirteen Indigenous students appear to have studied across North America at the postsecondary level, of whom one at
Harvard and three at Dartmouth had graduated. Even these few entryways were too many from the perspective of whites. Noel would be the
last enrolled at Dartmouth for a decade and a half, with only a handful
studying there or elsewhere over the next century.[44] The small numbers
who were well educated, as described by Donald Smith and others,
were intended to preach or teach like their predecessors with the goal
of moderating Indigenous peoples' wariness of the enormous changes
being foisted on them in newcomers' self-interest.[45] They were intended
to be tools of dispossession.

Looking ahead in time, as late as the 1930s Harvard historian
Samuel Eliot Morison would justify Indigenous peoples' exclusion from
higher education by explaining, in reference to the early College of
William and Mary, how "the experiment there was not such a complete
failure as at Harvard and Dartmouth, since no attempt was made to
take Indians beyond grammar-school learning." Indigenous youth were
in his view inherently unable, or alternatively not to be permitted, to
compete with their white counterparts. Literacy's promise was not for
them. As for Moor's, which continued to enrol Indigenous students
into the mid-1850s, almost half of them from St Francis, it had been in
Morison's view a "failure equally conclusive."[46] To be well educated
and Indigenous was, from his perspective and almost certainly that of

most others in similar positions of authority well into the twentieth century, irreconcilable.

THE RELIGIOUS IMPERATIVE

The actions of Wampas, Nettles, and Otsiquette were fundamentally flawed from most whites' perspectives for one very important reason. By virtue of taking literacy's promise seriously to the extent of daring to compete with their supposed betters, they flaunted the religious imperative intended to constrain their actions.

The linkage between the religious imperative and schooling went back in time to the first newcomers to North America. One of the earlist Indigenous youths to be caught up was Louis Amantacha, among a tiny number in New France sent to France with the goal of his entering a religious order. Huron born in about 1610, Amantacha was dispatched at age sixteen with his father's permission. Baptized as Louis de Sainte-Foi, Amantacha spent two years learning to read and write before being returned to New France, where he sought both to ingratiate himself with the Jesuits and to prove himself as a Huron warrior. The consequence was his being killed, likely by the Iroquois, in 1636 while still in his mid-twenties.[47]

If not for the religious imperative in its Protestant iteration, Harvard, Princeton, William and Mary, and Dartmouth would not have admitted Indigenous students. Be it through one of these institutions or some other means of formal education at least up to the secondary level, the almost singular goal of those financing the undertakings was not to turn Indigenous students outward as participants on their own terms in white society but to turn them inward as missionaries, or possibly teachers, who could conciliate Indigenous peoples to the changes that newcomers were imposing on them.

No school was more committed than Moor's in intensity and over time to the Protestant iteration of the religious imperative. The two early students who became Dartmouth graduates, Daniel Simon and Lewis Vincent, preached. So did founding head Eleazar Wheelock's protégé Samson Occom, who became embittered when the funds he had raised as a preacher in England and Scotland to further Indigenous education at Moor's were redirected to found Dartmouth College almost

wholly for white students. Occom was also frustrated, in David Silverman's words, by "colonial New Englanders' discrimination against
even Christian Indians," which rebounded in little support for his
labour, never mind respect.[48] "Now you See the difference they made
between me and other missionaries; they gave me 180 Pounds for 12
years Service, which they gave for one years Services in another Mission ... I *must* Say, 'I believe it is because I am a poor Indian.' I Can't
help that God had made me So: I did not make my self so."[49]

To be constrained by the religious imperative was not necessarily to
acquiesce. In the astute characterization of Bernd Peyer, even Occom
"finally came to the realization it was practically impossible for Indians
to live in 'civilized' society according to the principles he had been taught
to believe in by Protestant missionaries."[50] The consequence was for him
and a cohort of former Moor's students to rebel, although not against
the religious imperative but against the unequal treatment accorded them
by virtue of their indigeneity. In 1785 Occom, along with a dozen and a
half others who were similarly disenchanted, including early Dartmouth
graduate Peter Pohquonnappeet and two of Daniel Simon's four siblings,
founded in east-central New York their own Protestant religious self-
governing Indigenous community of Brothertown.[51] Just as would later
occur with Stockbridge in western Massachusetts, one of whose founders
was Occom admirer Hendrick Aupaumut, a Mahichan who had been
taught in a bilingual mission school run by a Yale graduate, Brothertown's originators sought to live according to the religious imperative
independent of whites' influence on them.

Laura J. Murray contends more generally that "every one of Wheelock's Indian students who lived long enough or studied long enough to
take up a post in the field did break with Wheelock," if not necessarily
rejecting the school's Protestant religious imperative.[52] Some former
students acted more subtly than others, as with Noel Annance's father,
who drew on the school's and related resources to benefit both his family and St Francis generally. Margaret Szasz observes somewhat optimistically about a broader swath of Indigenous youth who were early
on made literate in English or French that theirs was "a balancing act
some accomplished more successfully than others," but almost all of
them "achieved a degree of dignity and a sense of their own self worth,
which was an uncommon feat in a period of staggering change."[53]

IN THE MATTER OF WRITING

A critical advantage of Indigenous people becoming literate that over-shadowed the religious imperative was their learning to write, as well as to read, in English or French and possibly in their own language.[54] This assessment encouraged the Gill family's decision of 1774 to accept the invitation to send their sons to Moor's. The matter of writing went beyond whether individuals held to, modified, or rejected the religious imperative.

As Stéphanie Boutevin has demonstrated in respect to the Hurons and Abenakis over the critical century of outsider intrusion into Indigenous lives, 1780–1880, the force of the written word cannot be overestimated.[55] It was, and remains, the means of everyday communication across time and distance. In an age before common schooling, before everyone in the emerging dominant society becoming literate in childhood, as occurred over the nineteenth century, the minority who could read and write stood out. They had a powerful advantage both in the everyday and in specific circumstances.

Writing, very importantly, gave Indigenous peoples a disembodied means to contest power. A name signalled authorship but not in the same way as did individuals in their person. Words on paper took on meaning in and of themselves apart from the physical appearance and dress of their author.

It may be in part for this reason that the handful of Indigenous persons who early on learned to write in ways that survive through time has very justifiably garnered so much recent attention among Indigenous and also non-Indigenous literary scholars. The impetus may have been Robert Warrior's insight in his *Tribal Secrets*, published in 1995, that a "Native written intellectual tradition reaches back at least to Samson Occom's (Mohegan) missionary writings in the 1700s."[56] As well as the observation being several times reprinted, it almost certainly encouraged the subsequent sustained attention to Occom's words.[57] Also interrogated have been the writings of Occom's son-in-law Joseph Johnson, educated at Moor's and a preacher; Hendrick Aupaumut, who sustained Stockbridge on the pattern of Brothertown; and William Apess, a self-educated Pequot and preacher half a generation younger, who published an autobiographical narrative in 1829.[58]

The early Indigenous writers receiving attention share two important attributes. First, their words are, not unexpectedly so given the time in which they wrote, religiously inflected. Second, they each wrote at least in part for public consumption. Their words might have been printed, delivered as sermons, or retold as stories. Whichever the means, the solitary activity that is writing took on a life of its own apart from its originator.

The interest in Indigenous writing is expanding. A welcome consequence of the growing interrogation of the past has been the work of Indigenous scholars, including Lisa Brooks, Daniel Heath Justice, Niigaanwewidam James Sinclair, Robert Warrior, Jace Weaver, and Craig Womack, to link early writing to the present day.[59] What came before is increasingly being valued.

The challenge for the present and the future is to interpret words sympathetically within the periods they were written as emblematic of what educated Indigenous persons could become, as opposed to critiquing them as showing that such writers behaved as those in charge would have them do. Just as with Abenaki daring, its larger manifestation of Indigenous daring has many manifestations.

Early Indigenous writers' diverse pathways to belonging have much to offer in the present day. It has for too long been perceived that Indigenous peoples, conveniently for others, lacked the capacity to dare. They have been narrowly perceived as not becoming their own persons, except possibly to rebel within the religious parameters inculcated by their schooling.

Re-examining texts, as well as searching for new ones, has the potential to be rewarding. From Eric Gary Anderson's perspective, "while it seems reasonable to assume that some lost, neglected, or long unpublished Native authors and texts have yet to be recovered, the larger project of early-twenty-first-century Native studies seems less about recovery than about learning how best to teach, think, write, connect, and just attend more closely to what is already available."[60] Whichever way the balance swings between locating new writings and rethinking those already in view, the possibilities, as recent scholars have made visible, are real and dynamic.

RETURNING TO NOEL ANNANCE

The young Noel Annance had to have been aware, at least to some extent, of predecessors' and contemporaries' pathways. Stories were likely passed down at Moor's and Dartmouth, and also during visits back home in St Francis, respecting relatives and other Indigenous persons who had studied at one or both of them.

Perhaps because Noel was at Moor's just that much later in time, perhaps because he overlaid his teachings there with those at Dartmouth, or perhaps because it was in his character, he was not, as far as can be determined, influenced in his writing by the Protestant religious imperative. It was the case that, not unlike with Samson Occom and others, the writing and actions of several of Noel's contemporaries at Moor's were religiously inflected, notably those of his second cousin Peter Paul Osunkhirhine, with whom he later in life interacted at length.[61]

Noel Annance's writing also differs from his predecessors in having a private, rather than a public, purpose. He wrote clearly and precisely respecting the subject at hand with the intent of persuading on an individual level, as opposed to his writing being disseminated. Although not denying his indigeneity, Noel sought to showcase himself as the gentleman of his higher education. He sometimes used his ease with the classics and knowledge of the law to make his points. Noel's letters were overall virtually identical to those of similarly well-educated gentlemen of his time, as evidenced by comparing them with their counterparts written by others.[62]

Perhaps more than at any other time in his life, when Noel wrote, he belonged. He belonged to the generations of predecessors whose writings he had studied at Moor's and Dartmouth and whom he likely continued to read, he belonged to all those to whom he wrote in the hope that they would understand what it was he sought to convey, and he belonged to his self as he imagined it to be. Words on paper had the potential to be transformational, just as they had been for his Indigenous predecessors and would be for his contemporaries and successors.

SERVICE IN THE WAR OF 1812

Noel Annance's first foray on leaving Dartmouth College, and his almost certain reason for doing so, related to his geographical origins. His
departure in the spring of 1813, at a time of fellow students' strident
American patriotism respecting the War of 1812, was so prompted. His
brother Louis later explained about himself how he had been "summoned to his home in Canada, to serve with his tribe under the British
government," and Noel was likely also requested to do so.[63] Noel followed in the footsteps of their father, who had also left Dartmouth prior
to graduation – in his case, consequent on the War of Independence.

Louis and Noel Annance were not alone among those from St Francis
who joined up. The small Abenaki community contributed two companies to the British side. Attesting to how "all the able bodied men
served in the War of 1812," Gordon Day counts sixty-four volunteers
who over a century and a half later still had family in St Francis. The
list includes the Annance brothers and five Gill relatives.[64]

Noel Annance's contribution to the War of 1812 on the British side
was outstanding. First and very importantly, unlike his immediate family or any of the Gills, he served as an officer. Reflecting his facility
with French, English, and Abenaki, he acted as an interpreter. On 25
August 1813 Noel was made a lieutenant and interpreter at 6 shillings
and 6 pence a day. An official account recorded him as interpreter in
the military's Indian Department among the "Indian Warriors–Corps
des Sauvages."[65]

Second, the twenty-one-year-old distinguished himself in the Battle of
Châteauguay, where American forces were repulsed in their campaign
to invade Canada and ultimately attack Montreal (see map 1). The confrontation on 26 October 1813, according to an account at the time, was
"the first in which any considerable number of natives of this Province
[of Quebec] have been engaged with the Americans." Warned of approaching Americans, the British forces, composed mainly of French
Canadian militia units, created a series of strong defensive positions on
the Châteauguay River. The frontline consisted of three companies of infantry. Stationed to the right was a company of the Canadian Fencibles
Regiment, augmented by a force of Indigenous men. Despite the "in-

ILLUSTRATION 5
Battle of Châteauguay, 1813, by Henri Julien

vading American Army" being much larger in size, by one account "the enemy lost about 100 men killed in that affair, while we lost only 5."[66]

In the dispatch recounting the engagement, Noel Annance and two others also in the military's Indian Department were singled out for praise: "Their conduct throughout was highly meritorious."[67] Much later in life, Noel recalled how "he served during the late American war as a Lieutenant in Indian Department and was honored with a medal from General [Duncan] Daroch of the Meuron's Regiment, then stationed at Kingston, for successfully interpreting and taking deserters from our side at a certain island opposite to the town and again he received a medal from the Great and Illustrious Mother across the Great Waters for his services at the decisive battle of Chateauguay in the fall of 1813."[68] The second medal was engraved with "Chateauguay" and "Annance, Lieut."[69]

Noel was promoted the next year from lieutenant to captain. On 8 August 1814 the Indian Warriors were reorganized, and he was one of four captains given charge of the "Comp^y of St François Bacancour & Three Rivers."[70] The Indian Warriors were to be "brought forward as circumstances may Require," and Noel and the other officers "must at all times, hold themselves in readiness to move at the Shortest Notice."[71] Noel's brother Louis was likely engaging in a bit of retrospective bragging when he told in old age how, to quote his interviewer, his brother "had command of all the Indian forces during that war, and both [he and Noel] were noted for their bravery and daring in battle."[72] The treaty ending the war was signed on 24 December 1814. The Abernaki daring exhibited by Noel's great-uncle, grandfather, and father had passed down to the next generation.

WAR'S AFTERMATH

Noel Annance returned home from the War of 1812 buoyed by his newfound status as an officer and a gentleman, as indicated by the letter he penned to Moor's and Dartmouth president John Wheelock in the spring of 1815. For all that the style was suitably deferential, employing the language and tone that the school expected former students to use, it hinted at a certain independence of spirit.

The now twenty-three-year-old Noel was speaking back in sending the letter directly to Wheelock in the interests of two prospective students seeking to be accepted by Moor's. The letter's bearer was Noel's cousin Simon Annance, half a dozen years his junior. The second hopeful student was Noel's much younger brother, Joseph, born in about 1800. By virtue of including a nondenominational reference to religion and a throwaway line echoing what must have been Wheelock's attitude to Indigenous people, Noel was skilfully doing what was necessary, and no more, to secure his relatives' access to literacy's promise. The letter attests that the young Noel had a fine hand and a good mind.

Louis and Noel Annance's younger brother, Joseph, followed his older siblings to Moor's in 1816, a year after Simon Annance did so. Times had, however, changed. Unlike his two brothers, Joseph would not be wholly supported by the school. His father paid at least part of

Letter to Moor's and Dartmouth president John Wheelock
requesting relatives' admission to Moor's, 10 May 1815

St Francis May 10th 1815

Hon^d Head, Sir,

The want of a good opportunity to communicate has, for a
long time, deprived me of expressing my humble acknowledge-
ments for the kindness and humanity I experienced during my
residence at Hanover. Perhaps my not writing sooner might have
induced you to think that I am indifferent of the favors conferred
upon me and unmindful of the persevering watchfulness you
shewed for me, while under the care of your fostering and protecting arms. I would be guilty of the highest and most shameful in-
gratitude should I be insensible of so many favors bestowed upon
me for which I shall never be able to give satisfaction to my Bene-
factors. While Education will be the highest honor of man while
gratitude is an armament to humanity, this memory of your
exertions for my education will ever be grateful to my heart,
as I daily feel their happy and beneficial effects.

The Bearer hereof is a young man of our village wishing to be
admitted a member of Moor's Charity School; there are two men,
of whom one is my brother, who greatly desires to go as soon as
an answer can be had, what time there can be a way provided
for them.

May the everlasting God prolong your dear and useful life, and
may He crown your labors with abundant success in your endeav-
ors to civilize poor and ignorant Barbarians who sit in darkness.

    is the Prayer of
    your most humble
    and obedient
    servant
    N. Annance

Hon. J. Wheelock Esq. &c

Source: Noel Annance to John Wheelock, 10 May 1815, Dartmouth College,
Correspondence and Papers, 815310.

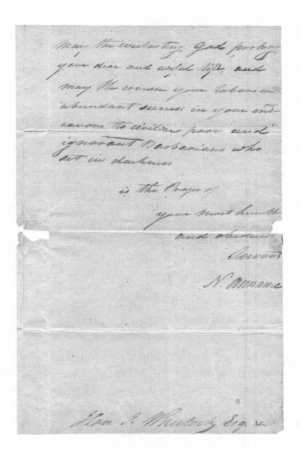

the costs, including "thirty dollars on account of his son" in January 1818.[73] Moor's would subsequently be intermittently closed to Indigenous students for financial reasons.

LOOKING TO TEACHING

As for Noel, he sought to get on with his life in a fashion befitting his higher education and meritorious service in the War of 1812. In doing so, he had before him the obligation Moor's put on its Indigenous students of becoming, if not a preacher, at the least a teacher. To pursue the latter was in the pattern of his father, Francis Joseph, who had been St Francis's schoolmaster since 1803 and would continue to be so until his death in 1826.[74] Given that St Francis contained, by Francis Joseph's count, sixty-five families comprising 360 Abenakis, and since the government provided for only a single school, teaching locally was not an option.[75]

Perhaps for this reason, not long after recommending his younger brother to Moor's, Noel sought to carve out a teaching career for himself in Lower Canada's capital of Quebec City, located 180 kilometres, or just over 100 miles, down the St Lawrence River from St Francis. Then Lower Canada's largest city, it had a population approaching 15,000, with a majority, but just, of French over English speakers.[76]

Since 1763 Quebec City's literate minority had had access to the weekly bilingual *Quebec Gazette/La Gazette de Québec*, with its combination of official government notices, advertisements, and news. The newspaper's 400 local subscribers, among its total reach of approximately 1,350 persons, comprised a literate core group potentially looking to their children's formal education.[77] It was there that private schools of various kinds made their pitch for students, among them Collier's Academy, with which the highly educated Noel Annance appears to have made contact and where he possibly taught.

Opened in the fall of 1814, Collier's Academy was, according to Bruce Curtis, one of the top two private schools in Quebec City due to the stature of E.C. Collier, the man in charge. Intended to "prepare young gentlemen for a *College* or *Compting-room*" by combining "*scientific instruction, with polite and elegant literature*," Collier's seemed ready made for Noel's range of attributes. Collier was, however, soon being lambasted for the school's Protestant ethos, resulting in its temporary closure, to be reopened in April 1816 teaching both the Catholic faith and female students. Various attempts followed to keep the school viable prior to Collier departing in the spring of 1818 to try his luck in a growing Montreal.[78]

The consequence of these shifts was that Noel Annance had to step out on his own. The notice he placed in the *Quebec Gazette/La Gazette de Québec* on 9 May 1816 echoed those of others seeking similar appointments. There was no hint of his indigeneity respecting what may have been intended by Noel as the beginning of a private school of his own, or at least an entryway to private tutoring.

No information has been located respecting how long or how successful, if at all, was Noel Annance's stint in Quebec City as a teacher of "young Gentlemen." What is clear is that within a year, or two at most, he was again looking to reset his life congruent with his higher education. For all of Noel's Abenaki daring, the venture had not worked out.

Notice placed in *Gazette de Québec*, 9 May 1816

CLASSICAL EDUCATION

MR. N. ANNANCE who has been regularly educated, respectfully informs the inhabitants of this City, that he is desirous to receive a select and limited number of Young Gentlemen on the first of June, to instruct in any of the following branches, viz. Mathematics, Algebra, Geography, Arithmetic, Greek, Latin and French Languages, Syntactically, to whose improvement he will devote his most sedulous attention. Mr. ANNANCE begs leave to refer to Mr. COLLIER, who will bear testimony to his moral character and professional capacity. The terms may be known on application to Mr. ANNANCE at Mr. COLLIER'S ACADEMY ON Mount Carmel.

Quebec, May 9th, 1816

Source: Noel Annance placed only one notice, as indicated by the single reference in the typescript *Gazette de Québec: Index from 1764–1824*, online.

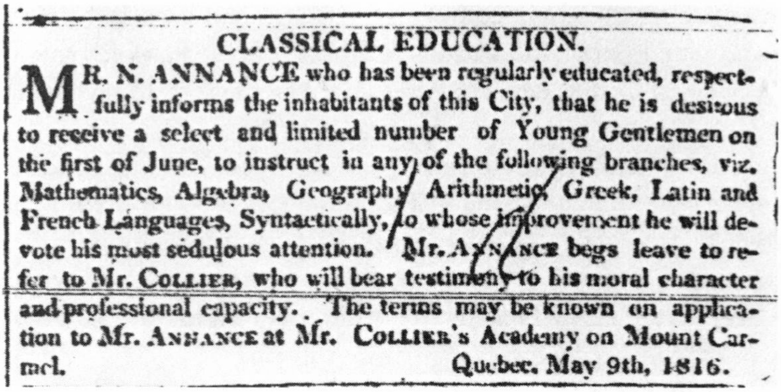

CLASSICAL EDUCATION.

MR. N. ANNANCE who has been regularly educated, respectfully informs the inhabitants of this City, that he is desirous to receive a select and limited number of Young Gentlemen on the first of June, to instruct in any of the following branches, viz. Mathematics, Algebra, Geography, Arithmetic, Greek, Latin and French Languages, Syntactically, to whose improvement he will devote his most sedulous attention. Mr. ANNANCE begs leave to refer to Mr. COLLIER, who will bear testimony to his moral character and professional capacity. The terms may be known on application to Mr. ANNANCE at Mr. COLLIER's Academy on Mount Carmel.

Quebec, May 9th, 1816.

ILLUSTRATION 7

Notice that Noel Annance placed in *Quebec Gazette/La Gazette de Québec*, 9 May 1816

OPTING FOR THE FUR TRADE

As his older brother, Louis, was doing at about the same time, Noel now turned in another direction. They each sought to make it on their own. Whatever role, if any, Francis Joseph's aspiration that his children would not "be obliged to follow the Indian mode of life," as he put it in 1803, played in their stepping out is impossible to know but intriguing to contemplate.[79]

Louis Annance shared in old age, as retold in the third person by an interviewer, his reasons for structuring his life as he did. Louis's years at Moor's, with its fervently Protestant ethos, had made him dissatisfied with Catholic St Francis: "At this time his people were all Catholics, but Louis, after devoting considerable thought to the subject, became convinced that the priesthood and Church were serious impediments in the way of any intellectual or moral advancement of his race, and about the year 1817, he publicly renounced Catholicism, severed his connection with that body, and joined the Congregationalists." The eldest Annance son's disaffection had consequences at home in St Francis: "At about this time, he became by the laws or rules of his tribe successor to his father as chief and ruler; but having become an avowed Protestant, and his religious convictions subjecting him to some persecution and annoyance, he removed in 1818 to New Hampshire," which he knew from his schooling there.[80]

Like Louis, Noel sought to escape St Francis's shadow but did so in a wholly other direction. He opted for the fur trade, which was at one and the same time familiar and distant. Demand in Europe and elsewhere had long been seemingly insatiable for beaver pelts in particular, upon which New France's economy had been in good part based. Following the British takeover in 1763, the fur economy gradually consolidated under the North West Company, formed in Montreal in the early 1780s as a loose association of mainly Scots merchants with employees principally recruited from Quebec. Montreal-based merchants and their principal competitor, the London-based Hudson's Bay Company in the far north, controlled the British North America fur trade.

Noel Annance appears to have tested his affinity for the fur trade on a local level. As well as Abenekis trapping with their own resources

north of the St Lawrence River, several companies hiring Abenakis operated out of St Maurice, some seventy kilometres, or forty-five miles,
northeast of St Francis (see map 1).[81] Following two short-term contracts, tracked by François Antaya, Noel looked farther afield.[82]

On 8 August 1818 "Noel Francis Annance" signed on with agents of
the North West Company at a wage of £50 a year "for three consecutive years in the Columbia River area in the North West."[83] Given that
the Columbia River emptied into the Pacific Ocean, Noel was heading
as far away from home as it was possible to go (see map 2).

Noel may have been propelled to act as he did by virtue of securing
a status consistent with his higher education and his service in the War
of 1812. By the contract's terms, "During the summer he will assist in
the rank of clerk as much as he can in his power. In the winter he will
be employed all the time as a hunter."[84] The agreement acknowledged
both Noel's skills as a hunter, a skill learned at home, and his superior
schooling, transforming him from just another employee to a gentleman, as clerks and others having charge of the fur trade were considered to be.

Noel was not alone in opting for the fur trade but among a swath of
St Francis men signing up between 1815 and 1819 whose contracts survive.[85] Three were his Gill great-uncles' sons or grandsons who became
voyageurs, being the all-purpose *milieu*, or middlemen, in the canoes
taking goods from Montreal into fur country and returning with pelts.[86]
Eight others were Obomsawins, Plamondons, or Portneufs, into all of
whose families relatives had married. Noel had served in the War of
1812 with the literate Ignace Portneuf, both seeing action at Châteu-
guay. Ignace and his brother Joseph had contracted a year and a half earlier in January 1817 as all-purpose middlemen and hunters. Both were,
like Noel, dispatched west of the Rocky Mountains.[87] Another St Francis recruit was Pierre Charles, a literate Abenaki who signed up in June
1818, two months before Noel, as a *bout*, or prestigious canoe steers-
man, and hunter, also in the Columbia River area.[88]

Yet another addition a few years later was Noel's younger brother,
Joseph, whom he had successfully recommended in 1815 for admission
to Moor's. Joseph enrolled in 1816 and remained a couple of years, but
what he did next is uncertain until 1822, when he followed in his
brother's footsteps west of the Rockies – in his case, as a hunter. He

would be among fifty plus men dispatched in February 1824 on a nine-month trapping expedition, during which he garnered nary a mention in its journal, except for being issued at the onset, as were the other men, "1 gun, 3 traps, 2 horses."[89] The trip was marked by ongoing contention over harsh conditions, making it unsurprising that a dozen men, including Joseph, deserted the Hudson's Bay Company on the subsequent expedition and in May 1825 approached a nearby American competitor offering higher prices for pelts. To whatever extent the brothers made contact in the Pacific Northwest, the interlude was over.

John Milloy explains the fur trade's appeal for Noel and the others in his apt observation that, "with the single exception of the fur trade," the British "colonies had no natural place for the Indian, no inclination to mix the blood of races, no need for Indian labour and no undeniable compulsion to civilize him."[90] Noel may have been already "civilized," but the logic still held. He could in the fur trade, by the terms of the agreement he signed, be a gentleman who just happened to be Indigenous, as opposed to the two attributes being in opposition to each other.

Whether or not it was a consideration, and it may have been, the Pacific Northwest to which Noel and the others headed lacked external governance. No country cared enough about this far corner of North America lying west of the Rocky Mountains, north of Spanish California, and south of Russian America, the future Alaska, to declare unilateral sovereignty. In the wake of the War of 1812, Britain and the United States had agreed on joint oversight, but that was all. Abenakis, as well as others, could at least in principle be their own persons.

BASIS FOR OPTIMISM

Noel Annance's contract signed in 1818 obliged him to "winter for three consecutive years" in the Pacific Northwest.[91] By the time of its completion, his employer had changed. The North West Company (NWC) was in 1821 amalgamated into the Hudson's Bay Company (HBC), which had up to then not had a presence west of the Rocky Mountains.

The HBC was not obliged to keep on the entirety of NWC employees and did not do so. Its headquarters in London put a priority on "reducing the Establishment of Clerks" with "discretion and discrimination" to the minimum "necessary to carry on the trade in an efficient

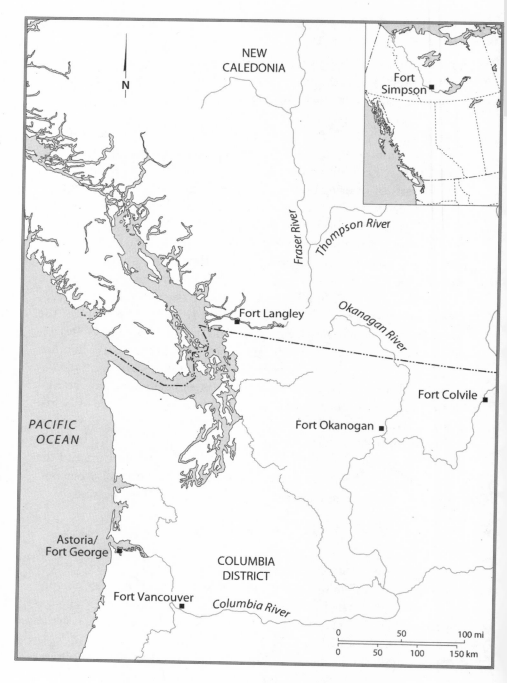

MAP 2

Pacific Northwest during Noel Annance's years there, 1818–33

and economical manner."[92] The HBC continued Noel as a clerk, as signified by "Mr." being routinely inserted before his name to signify his status as an officer rather than a regular employee. Several other St Francis men, including Pierre Charles, were continued as regular employees. Among those now posted west of the Rockies was Simon Plamondon, Noel's second cousin by a non-Indigenous branch of the Gill family.[93] Noel, Pierre Charles, and Simon Plamondon would briefly be stationed together in the late 1820s.

To be a clerk was the first step in the HBC hierarchy to being named a chief trader and then possibly a chief factor, each of which were accompanied by higher salaries and a financial share in the company.[94] Not only was Noel now assuredly a gentleman, but he was so in a setting where his higher education mattered. Although it is impossible to know with certainty, he may have been the best educated of his HBC cohort. Among those he surpassed by a length was HBC head George Simpson, brought up by his aunt and grandparents, who had sent him to the local Scots parish school to be taught basic grammar, copybook writing, arithmetic, and bookkeeping.[95]

Simpson's fullest assessment of the HBC's officer corps over which he had charge, penned in 1832 at a time Noel was still employed, makes clear the very great extent to which "Education," always capitalized, mattered. Simpson variously appraised the 138 clerks, chief traders, and chief factors then at work across North America as "illiterate,"[96] "deficient in point of Education,"[97] "can read and write which is about the extent of his literary acquirements,"[98] "had not had the advantage of a good Education,"[99] "not well Educated,"[100] "very limited Education,"[101] "tolerably well Educated,"[102] and "plain good education."[103]

It was not only the level of schooling but also its use that mattered. The great distances between trading posts meant facility at writing mattered. In reference to diverse individuals, Simpson recorded how he "writes a good hand, but his Education has been very limited,"[104] "writes a good hand expresses himself tolerably well altho' not correctly on paper,"[105] "has had the benefit of a good plain Education, both writes and speaks tolerably well,"[106] and "tolerably well Educated but assumes a high lofty style of Writing which is quite ridiculous and his misapplications of long words in which he deals unsparingly is quite laughable."[107]

Simpson described only Noel and six others in the HBC's North American officer corps totalling 138 persons as "well Educated," one of them being further distinguished as "the most finished man in the business."[108] An individual who had been "in a Lawyers Office in Scotland for 3 Years" had an "excellent education," another was "a good classical scholar," and a third was "one of the most finished Scholars in Aberdeen College" in Scotland.[109] Noel's higher education, of a level matched only by a few others, all of them Scots, caused him to stand out. His employment of literacy's promise was, it would seem, reaping its reward.

TO SUM UP

Noel Annance was among a tiny minority of Indigenous North Americans who, consequent on their higher education, had an opportunity to engage literacy's promise. His predecessors had found it difficult to reconcile their schooling with their indigeneity, excepting when their search for belonging was cloaked with the religious imperative intended to reconcile Indigenous peoples to the wrongs being done them. Not so Noel, who had, after a couple of short-term ventures, opted for the fur trade. The direction he took appeared to be a wise one.

4

Hopes for the Fur Trade

Noel Annance's status as a clerk in the fur trade gave every appearance of being propitious. An opportunity to consolidate his status came almost immediately, resulting in the longest single piece of writing surviving in Noel's hand. Noel was buoyed, convinced a successful career was assured, and for a time it seemed to be so. Abenaki daring would have its reward. The long-term reality would be quite different, as Noel's Indigenous descent, almost inevitably so it seems, pushed him to the edge of belonging.

DISTINGUISHING HIMSELF

Not only did the Hudson's Bay Company (HBC) continue to employ Noel Annance, but he also soon distinguished himself among its Pacific Northwest workforce of around 250, one in ten being fellow officers and the others regular employees.[1] Subsequent to the HBC taking charge, he was posted as an interpreter at the outlying post of Okanogan, an adjunct to Thompson River, the future Kamloops, which functioned as a storage depot and staging post (see map 2).

A year later, in the summer of 1822, Noel was dispatched to prospect trapping at the unknown headwaters of the Thompson River in today's southern British Columbia.[2] He accomplished his task so well that George Simpson enthused the next July, "With Mr. [William] Connolly [in charge of New Caledonia, being present-day central British Columbia] I have had much conversation in regard to the tracts of country explored last summer by Mr. Annance; it lays between the head waters of the Smoky and those of Canoe and Frasers River, and by his account abounds with beaver ... does not appear to have been frequented by hunters of any description and little doubt remains it may produce some valuable furs."[3] Noel had dared to good effect.

The opportunity for Noel even further to distinguish himself soon followed. The 1821 amalgamation had taken the London-based company across the Rocky Mountains, whereupon the British government granted it a twenty-one-year monopoly on British trade across the Pacific Northwest. The goal became the region's exploration and exploitation.

Simpson headed west in late summer 1824 from the HBC's North American base of operations at York Factory on Hudson Bay to take charge of what were two quite separate Pacific Northwest nodes (see map 2). The New Caledonia District originated with North West Company (NWC) partner Simon Fraser's establishment between 1805 and 1807 of the first trading posts to be located west of the Rocky Mountains. Situated 1,100 kilometres, or 700 miles, to the south near the mouth of the Columbia River dividing the present-day states of Washington and Oregon, the New York–based Pacific Fur Company had in 1811 established Astoria. The NWC acquired Astoria and its environs in the course of the War of 1812, meaning that it also went to the HBC in 1821, as the main trading post of a separate, distinct entity known as the Columbia District.

From the onset, Simpson looked to the two districts' integration in the interests of expediency and economy, but there were complexities. The intervening territory, which included the mighty Fraser River down which Simon Fraser had descended, was unknown apart from Noel's 1822 foray commended the next year by Simpson. The first step toward integrating the two Pacific Northwest districts, so distant from each other, was to more fully discover the space in between them, briefly explored by Noel.

Simpson personally organized a large expedition to gain "a knowledge of the Frazers River and the adjacent country," looking to the establishment of a new post lying between the two nodes to facilitate cheaper transport of goods and pelts.[4] The expedition's head was to be forty-year-old Scot James McMillan, a chief trader already familiar with the Pacific Northwest who had accompanied Simpson west. On the way there, Simpson introduced his "dangerous and unpleasant mission" to his travelling companion. "I imparted to M^r McMillan my views in regard to extending the trade" and "the importance of having an Establishment at the mouth of Frazer's River ... with a view that he should volunteer his services."[5]

McMillan may have recommended to Simpson the three younger men he considered best suited to accompany him on this potentially hazardous venture, being clerks Noel Annance, John Work, and Thomas McKay. All three prospects met with Simpson's approval. The HBC head privately characterized Noel as "a cool determined fellow, can act in the capacity of a Clerk trader or stronger & just cut out for a new country, can head a War Party & be the Indian if necessary."[6] Irishman John Work, Noel's equal in age at thirty-two years, was a "very steady correct man good clerk & trader, looks to promotion thro' merit."[7] As for Thomas McKay, four years younger than Noel and also part Indigenous, he was from Simpson's perspective a "first rate man under the Direction of another, never happy except on dangerous service, can live by his Gun like an Indian, very useful on the West side of the Mountains."[8] Aware of Noel's and McKay's Indigenous descent, Simpson was not put off. It rather appears to have been perceived as an asset.

McKay, the stepson of recently appointed Columbia District head John McLoughlin, was already part of Simpson's entourage. Simpson met with Work a week later and a couple of days after that with Noel at Fort Okanogan. As recorded by Simpson, "Here we likewise found Mr Annance Clerk who had come from the Post of Thompson River with some necessary supplies."[9] Noel so impressed Simpson on personal acquaintanceship that the same day, 1 November 1824, Simpson requested Noel's release from his current employment so that he could take part: "Mr. Annance is particularly required to accompany Mr. McMillan on a very hazardous expedition to the mouth of Frazers River in the course of the winter."[10]

Just two weeks later, the expedition headed out from Fort George, the former Astoria, at the mouth of the Columbia River toward the Fraser River. Among the three dozen men taking part was Noel's St Francis compatriot Joseph Portneuf and a couple of other Abenakis, along with a mix of French Canadians, Iroquois, an Englishman or two, and some Indigenous Hawaiians, employed in the Pacific Northwest fur trade since the time of Astoria.[11]

Each of the three clerks had designated duties. Work's main task was to record occurrences along the way, whereas the other two were to keep daily journals supplementary to their principal obligations. McKay "was in charge of hunting and expected to keep the party supplied with fresh meat," and Noel was to help search out a location for the new post, to trade and otherwise interact with Indigenous peoples encountered along the way, and to assist with hunting as needed.[12]

A TALE OF TWO JOURNALS

Although all three clerks on the projected expedition up the Fraser River were deputized to keep journals of the six-week expedition, only those of Work and Annance have survived.[13] Work's was kept in a white-covered notebook of five by nine inches and Noel's in an HBC standard-issue journal with a marble cover, perhaps indicating that it was the copy sent to company headquarters.

Noel Annance's journal, reproduced in full in the appendix, illustrates a very different approach to writing, the use of language, and the expedition's function than does Work's more copious and detailed counterpart. Noel perceived himself in relationship to the principal task allocated to the expedition, which was the determination of the best site for the proposed new trading post, whereas Work discounted Noel as being a hunter, a task most often associated with persons of Indigenous or part-Indigenous descent. Work's perspective may have been coincidental, but it could have been intentional.

Overall, Work was wordy and Noel pithy. In line with journaling being his principal task, Work detailed geographical terrain crossed by what means, daily weather and mileage, animals and trees, Indigenous peoples, and most everything else encountered along the way. His doing so was strategic given that the HBC wanted to extend itself through this still unknown territory. Work's was a fine-grained travelogue that made it possible for others to follow in the expedition's wake.

In respect to Indigenous peoples, Work wrote somewhat like an early ethnographer, to the extent of noting individuals' clothing or lack of it. Noel was similarly attentive to differences but more so to understand those encountered along the way and in the course of doing so to give credit, thus writing on 9 December, "Fine Indians!" He was more aware of domestic life, as with his observation on 17 December that "in the lodges we saw a sort of loom, with which they manufacture blankets with the hair of dogs and the down of ducks and geese," which Work described as "an instrument resembling in shape a salmon spear, but for what purpose it is used for, its size leaves me at a loss to determine."[14]

Consistent with his higher education, Noel approached journaling more conceptually and imaginatively than did Work. A day out, he was already appraising locations through which they passed as to their potential for a new post congruent with the expedition's mandate, in contrast to which Work measured the distance travelled to the nearest yards and paces. Noel may have been in closer ongoing contact with McMillan, only he describing the latter's decision of 19 December respecting a location for the post, made apparently in conjunction with local Indigenous people and affirmed by carving "HBC" on the trees. Noel was still thinking on the subject the next day, writing that a second possible location lay near the mouth of the Fraser River at Point Roberts. Work's journal says nothing about potential locations.

Noel was at the same time more practical than Work. When the expedition found itself in need of food, he sought out fellow St Francis resident Pierre Charles. Charles, who on the HBC taking charge from the NWC had gone to live with the local Chehalis people to which the woman with whom he had partnered belonged, was persuaded to join the expedition as a hunter.[15]

Noel's writing style is overall distinguished, in comparison with Work's flat prose, by literary echoes of his classical education. Work described what he saw, whereas Noel emphasized the larger meaning he associated with what he perceived. Work's "weighty rain" contrasts with Annance's reflection as to how "in some countries we pray for rain; but in this we receive it in abundance without the intercession of prayers, and enjoy it without gratitude."[16] Of unhelpful local people, he wrote, "here you will find no Egyptian to detail you to the history of this country, or converse with you by signs," and five days later he described "a large Chinook hat ornamented with white shells quite in the style of a Grandee," referring to a Portuguese or Spanish nobleman of the highest rank. Of a breathtaking natural setting, he noted, "it would require the fire and genius of a Homer to do justice to the scene." Returning to Fort George on the last day of December, Noel concluded his journal, "I may say in the language of Caesar, Veni, vidi, vici: We came, we saw every thing, and overcame every thing."

Noel was more able, or willing, to put circumstances within larger contexts. More so than those around him, he lived in the world of ideas, of mental agility, and of interpretation. Passing "Possession Bay"

on 9 December, he noted how British sea captain George Vancouver
had a third of a century earlier named the location. A day later, relative
to indigenous trading practices, he mused about how "we find Customs
house officers in this country as well as on the way from Montreal to
Canton; but we were up to their tricks, they did not get many blankets,
as they expected." Noel was, unlike Work, unafraid to express his emotions, despairing on 10 December over "Rain, rain and storm!" and
eight days later over "Rain without mercy." The almost graduate of
Dartmouth College engaged literacy's promise as a matter of course
and may also have employed it for effect. Whether or not such a perspective served the purposes of the fur trade, particularly Simpson with
his much plainer background, remained to be seen.

ON TRACK

As Noel Annance completed the last lines of his journal on the last day
of 1824, he must have considered that he had proven himself in the fur
trade. As the journal illustrates time and again, he had not denied his
classical training at Moor's Charity School and Dartmouth. He had
dared to follow up on literacy's promise fully and imaginatively. He
had not been afraid to take initiative to the benefit of the larger group.
After just over half a dozen years in the fur trade, Noel was ready to
move forward and upward.

The six-week expedition had been a success and, indeed, had lain the
foundation for the HBC's way ahead. Simpson reported enthusiastically
in its aftermath on how "the Channel which divided Vancouvers Island
from the Main land they found studded with Islands which afford a
safe and well sheltered navigation for any Craft," how "the Shores of
the Main land they found densely peopled the Natives being collected
in Villages," and how "from the Natives they learnt that the Country
abounded with Deer and that Beaver were numerous in all the Small
Streams."[17] In detailing each aspect of the trip, Simpson drew on its
members' respective mandates: "Messrs McMillan & Work have prepared a Journal of the Voyage and Chart or rough sketch of their route
and Messrs Annance and McKay have furnished similar documents
which were handed to me by Mr McMillan accompanied by a Letter or
general report of the Expedition."[18]

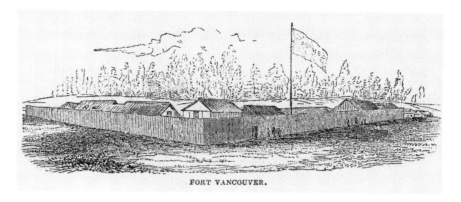

FORT VANCOUVER.

ILLUSTRATION 8
Fort Vancouver, 1841, headquarters of the fur trade in the
Pacific Northwest, by Joseph Drayton

Within this framework Noel Annance had every reason to consider
his career was on track. His journaling and activity during the 1824 expedition were one dimension of the HBC's consolidation and expansion
overseen by Simpson under the immediate command of John McLoughlin, who had charge in the Pacific Northwest from its newly constructed
headquarters of Fort Vancouver (see map 2). Perhaps for this reason, or
due to some other consideration that did not make it into the public
record, Noel did at some time thereafter come under scrutiny. Just as
McMillan had done when Simpson travelled westward, Noel accompanied Simpson part way on his return east in March 1825.

Likely based on their topics of conversation along the way, Simpson
noted in his daily journal, "Put Mr Annance in charge of Okanogan for
the Summer with Two Men."[19] The assignment was both an informal
promotion and a test on Simpson's part, as he explained to McLoughlin: "If he does not give satisfaction it will not be for want of threats
and promises as I spoke to him in terms that could not be misunder-
stood. Present appearances are in his favor and I am much mistaken if
he does not turn out to be better than you expect."[20] McLoughlin's
concerns did not make it into the public record. In contrast to whatever
they might have been, in August 1825 when Noel was at Okanogan,
McLoughlin reported from Fort Vancouver that he was having "Mr.
Annance sent down here, who would Assist us from his knowledge of

the Country hereabouts more than any other that could be sent."[21] Such responsibility was a necessary step to assuming authority consistent with promotion.

Still with his eye on Noel, Simpson recommended to McLoughlin that he continue to be in charge of Okanogan over the next winter. Noel carried out his duties with a certain aplomb, as indicated by the favourable impression he made on visiting Scots botanist David Douglas when they met in April 1826: "Arrived at the establishments on the Okanagan River, one of the northern branches of the Columbia at eight in the evening, where we were very cordially received by Mr. Annance, the person in charge."[22]

Thompson River, including the Okanogan post of which Noel had charge, was in 1826 put under the command of the promising Archibald McDonald, a Scot two years Noel's senior, who had come west as an accountant to sort through the Columbia District's finances.[23] On his second visit west the same year, Simpson raised Thompson River's status by designating it the connecting link between the principal HBC post of Fort Vancouver and remote New Caledonia.

Likely because Noel had been stationed at Okanogan, he became McDonald's right-hand man at Thompson River, which included keeping the post journal while McDonald was away.[24] Noel's entries followed in form and substance those of McDonald, except for concluding, "signed, Francis Noel Annance," as he was principally known in the fur trade. As was expected in post journals, nothing distinguishes the two men's entries from each other.

Among Noel's tasks was to negotiate sufficient salmon from local peoples along the Fraser River to feed the men over the winter.[25] On 17 October 1826 "Mr Annance and three men [were] making another trip for the salmon at the usual place," and on 3 December "Mr Annance ... made another trip to Fraser River, but not quite so successful as we had reason to expect."[26] As to the reason, "the Indians all along the upper part of that river were in a complete state of warfare & it would seem the flame in great measure has caught those we visit in this lower part."[27]

Noel's personal life, which up to then existed in the shadows, now comes into view. McDonald's wife of mixed Indigenous descent, Jane Klyne, and their two young children arrived at Thompson River in September 1826, along with the unnamed Flathead woman with whom

Noel had partnered and their young son. The McDonalds and Annances shared the officers' quarters, where an employee was soon "preparing Wood to fix up a small Apartment off the Hall for the Accommodation of Mr. Annance and family."[28] A second son was born on 26 December 1826.[29] The two men's personal lives reflected the partnering options available at this time in this far corner of North America.

Noel now rose in the all-important measure of Simpson's favour. His 1827 private assessment was crisp and buoyant: "Active determined fellow well adapted for a new country being a good hunter, Clerk & trader."[30]

IN FAVOUR

In June 1827 Noel Annance reaped the rewards of his hard work. McMillan had kept his eye on him, so when Simpson put McMillan in charge of constructing the new trading post of Fort Langley, resulting from the earlier expedition, Noel was among the twenty-five men dispatched there on 27 June 1827, along with his St Francis contemporaries Pierre Charles, who had been cajoled into HBC employ as a middleman and hunter, and Simon Plamondon, also as a middleman.[31] The two other clerks assigned to Fort Langley along with Noel were Donald Manson and George Barnston, Scots eight years Noel's junior who had been transferred west across the mountains to Fort Vancouver a year or two previous.

As Fort Langley's journal kept by McMillan testifies, Noel proved himself handy. A day after setting out, "Mr. Annance was immediately dispatched to find Horses and returned in the evening with two: he says we will get more from the Indians on the morrow."[32] The animals were needed in order to cross over land along the way, despite which "the men had each about 80 lbs. weight of Luggage & Provisions still to carry."[33] Having done so, the entourage needed water transportation, and Noel and a fellow clerk "contrived to purchase" canoes in the local Indigenous village so as "to depart in the morning."[34] As well as a negotiator, Noel was a proficient hunter and three days later "killed a Red Deer, the meat of which was brought to the Camp."[35] Noel was also knowledgeable on the water. On reaching the entrance to the Fraser River on the vessel being used, the captain "& Mr. Annance were off twice in the Boat during the day to sound for a Channel."[36]

The trip up the Fraser River echoed the earlier expedition. Along the way McMillan honoured Noel by naming after him a large island in the Fraser River, which they had passed on the earlier expedition, Annance's Island slurring over time to become today's Annacis Island, located southwest of New Westminster not far from Vancouver.[37] Physical evidence of the earlier expedition was noted: "Tuesday 24th [July] ... At noon we passed a small village on the south side where there are two trees marked HBC, which was done by the Party under Mr. McMillan in 1824–25."[38] Perhaps because neither of the other two clerks who had been part of the earlier expedition were along, as John Work was now based at Fort Colvile and Thomas McKay was on a trapping expedition, Noel was at the centre of events. Three days later, "Mr. MacMillan accompanied by Messrs. [Chief Trader Alexander Roderick] MacLeod [who had just joined the expedition] and Annance and [Cowichan chief] Shashia went off up the River to look for a more eligible site for an Establishment," which they found.[39]

All hands were thereupon put to work on post construction under the charge of Noel and the other two clerks, who also had responsibility for keeping watch and, more generally, overseeing relations with curious local people. Plamondon and Charles – in whom Noel may have taken a special interest given that his St Francis counterparts were, respectively, a decade and seven years his junior – were among those "squaring Logs for the Bastion," intended for protection against potentially hostile Indigenous peoples.[40] By mid-August "the Bastion has only to be covered," and Charles and others were "busy raising Cedar Bark for that purpose."[41] The next steps were to erect pickets around the new post, again for protection, and to construct the necessary buildings.

In the interim, men had to be fed, and as soon as feasible the acquisition of beaver pelts, which was at the heart of the fur trade, had to be begun. Trapping was a seasonal activity, one in which Pierre Charles and one or two others engaged from early October through the winter even as, more importantly, local people were cajoled to trade pelts for goods. Come winter, the versatile "Pierre Charles the Hunter" constructed "Snow Shoes, which are required by the People to bring to the Fort the meat which was left out."[42]

Indicative of the favour in which Noel now stood, in September 1827 McMillan wrote to John McLoughlin that either Noel, who was "as usual very useful," or Scots clerk Donald Manson was capable of taking charge of Fort Langley during his upcoming absence.[43] Not unexpectedly, then, on 26 November Noel oversaw Fort Langley's official opening, so the post journal fulsomely recorded: "This morning a Flag Staff was cut in the woods, and prepared, and in the afternoon erected in South east corner of the Fort. The usual forms were gone through – Mr. Annance officiated in baptizing the Establishment, and the men were regaled [with liquor] in celebration of the event. The Firing which took place on the occasion was heard by our hunters who were not far distant and they came home very much alarmed."[44]

Numerous of Noel's responsibilities concerned Indigenous peoples. On 24 December 1827 he was dispatched along with another clerk to rescue a Fort Vancouver counterpart, Alexander McKenzie, who on his way there with dispatches had found himself "disagreeably situated" by some Musqueam.[45] Its having been a false alarm resulting only in minor pilfering, two days later Noel was off again: "Mr. Annance with Six men was dispatched to fetch Mr. McKenzie's Canoe on the Ice to the Fort, and to recover what had been stolen from that Gentleman in the Misquiam Camp. In the Latter Business they succeeded nobly, but the Canoe they found impracticable to bring up, as the Ice was too weak to bear them, and at the same time too strong for them to break their way through it for any distance with the canoe."[46] McMillan took Noel with him on accompanying McKenzie back to Fort Vancouver on 3 January. A month later, the journal recorded, "Annance went to a small Village above to inquire about a Canoe for sending the Party with the Spring Express to Fort Vancouver," returning "with an Indian who is to accompany him tomorrow to a Village Below, where it is expected a suitable one will be easily procured," which proved to be the case.[47] A French Canadian stationed at Fort Langley a few years after Noel's departure recalled how "it required patience, tact and a sharp wit to be an Indian trader, and Annance possessed all these qualifications," so much so "the Indians named [him] 'The War Chief.'"[48]

Noel Annance also acted as an enforcer as needed to dispense the rough justice integral to the fur trade: "A Quitland [Kwantlen] was rather insolent on the wharf, for which he got a few Sound Kicks from Mr. Annance."[49] As indicated by a journal entry a day later, Noel did so within judicious limits: "Towards Evening, Indians were heard Speaking in the woods below – Mr. Annance embarked in a Small Canoe and paddled toward the quarter from whence the noise was heard, and in turning the point he heard them very distinctly but being alone he did not think it advisable to go too near – We Cannot Imagine who they are unless Some more war parties from Vancouver's Island going up the river."[50] Another day later, "Mr. Annance with some men went down to see who these Skulkers were ... Saw plenty of fresh marks in the woods, and tracks along the beech [sic]. I suppose being perceived they thought proper to turn back – Or at least gone down the river for a few days."[51] A few months later, respecting some visiting Musqueam, the journal recorded, "One of them asked for some of the deer to eat in a very rough way – No notice was taken for Some time, until he became troublesome. At last Mr. Annance asked him what he had to give for a piece. 'Nothing,' says he, 'but I have a Cock,' putting his hand on it. 'Perhaps you want it.' No Sooner Said than he got Such a kick on the very Spot, which settled his talk – and a Couple more Sent him down the hill. They went all in a very short time."[52]

IN A HOLDING PATTERN

With the passage of time, Noel would have been justified to have considered that he was in a holding pattern. James McMillan, under whose oversight Fort Langley was founded and constructed, was in the fall of 1828 permitted to go on leave, furloughs being allowed some officers after so many years of employment. His replacement was neither Noel nor Donald Manson, both of whom McMillan had a year earlier recommended to HBC's head in the Pacific Northwest, John McLoughlin, as able to take charge, but rather Archibald McDonald, with whom Noel had served at Thompson River and who had just been elevated to a chief trader. In another change, anglophone Montrealer James Murray Yale, who had until recently served in remote New Caledonia, replaced a departing Donald Manson at Fort Langley. Characterized by Simpson as "deficient in Education," Yale was Noel's junior in age by four years.[53]

Unlike McMillan's practice, McDonald distinguished between the two clerks in his first report to his superiors. Noel he described as attending "to the Trade & Indians" and Yale "to the People & Stores."[54] Despite his earlier acquaintance with Noel, or perhaps because of it, McDonald played no favourites, as indicated by his first running entry, which read simply, "Mr. Annance Continues Indian Trader."[55] The title McDonald accorded Noel, even if informally so, is telling, as Morag Maclachlan and John Foster separately explain, given that the positions of Indian trader and postmaster were typically the highest to which persons of Indigenous descent could aspire in the fur trade and were for that reason linked to such an inheritance.[56] To be an Indian trader or a postmaster was not to be a gentleman, as were clerks and those above them in rank.

In line with McDonald's greater emphasis than his predecessor on profitability, Noel now from time to time hunted and trapped, tasks previously relegated to Charles, Plamondon, and other regular employees. At the beginning of December 1828, "Mr. Annance with Six men is dispatched up the river – they have 12 Beaver Traps – provisions for 7 days and otherwise well-equipped – they cannot be expected to go far."[57] A few days after returning, "Mr. Annance and 6 men with our large wooden Canoe descended the main river and are to strick [*sic*] back to the Southward behind Point Roberts in Search of Elk – they leave their Craft at a place called 'HBC' tree."[58] At least once, Noel and Yale foraged together: "Messrs. Annance & Yale did a turn into one of the little Creeks and Shot a Couple Geese (& 1/2 doz. Ducks)."[59]

The tasks assigned to Noel varied. While returning in March 1829 from a ten-day exploratory trip with Yale, "on entering this river yesterday morning, they had to encounter a most daring attack from those of the Gulf of Georgia."[60] According to McDonald, it was "Mr. Annance and his Rifle" that saved the day.[61] Perhaps for that reason, McDonald was "accompanied by Mr. Annance" a month later when, for the "first time since I Came here," as McDonald explained, "I went with a Canoe and Eight men ... to examine the nature of the Country in the neighbourhood, and the practicality of Cultivating a good Spot with but little labour."[62] That fall, he wrote, "to day with Mr. Annance I visited another Small Stream in this neighbourhood for the Site of a mill, but is not the thing."[63] In October 1829 when McDonald "resolved on a visit to the Columbia" to enquire about the shortage of

trade goods dispatched to Fort Langley, he took with him Noel and
eight men on what was "a profound Secret to this moment when the
party was advertised & even now the trip is given out merely to the
Sound."[64] The month-long trip, during which Yale was left in charge,
included twelve days at Fort Vancouver determining Fort Langley's position in the larger scheme of things as set forth in a plan made up by
Simpson in consultation with McLoughlin during a recent visit. The
plan's intention was to reduce Fort Langley's personnel to a single clerk
and a dozen men.

To the extent Noel had his own life, as opposed to responding to the
wishes of those in command over him, it was in respect to his family.
Separate houses were constructed at Fort Langley for clerks and senior
officers with families, and just a week before the post's inauguration, its
journal recorded four men "putting up a chimney in Mr. Annance's
House, the one which was first built having fallen down."[65] Officers,
unlike regular employees, received rations not only for themselves but
also for their families. Over the course of 1829 Annance's and Yale's
families, according to McDonald's account, together consumed 60
pounds of flour and three gallons of molasses, compared to the fourteen men stationed at the post being allotted between them 155 pounds
of flour and just one and three-quarter gallons of molasses.[66] Noel's
family grew. On 24 June 1829 "Mrs. Annance brought another Boy
into the world last night," who added to the two sons the couple already had.[67] Of the two sons whose names survive, Archie was named
after Archibald McDonald and Johnnie after John Work or possibly
John McLoughlin.

THE HBC'S ORGANIZATIONAL MODEL

As the 1820s ran their course, it must have looked to Noel Annance as
though his hopes for the future were in jeopardy. As a clerk and
thereby a gentleman, he should have been able to anticipate that continued hard work would have its reward in the form of promotion in
the ranks. He likely considered that he had exerted all his efforts to
make it so, but nothing had ensued.

Understanding at least part of what may have occurred requires
turning our attention to Noel's employer. The Hudson's Bay Company

was distinctive as an organizational model. Its success depended on workers' isolation from alternative ways of life. Men in such circumstances needed to internalize their employer's singular goal of profit so completely that all other considerations fell by the way, being in this sense another iteration of the captivity narratives lived by Noel's great-grandparents and by him and others as students. As summed up by Bruce McIntyre Watson, the HBC was premised on, "structurally, an inherently paternalistic master-servant relationship demanding complete loyalty by employees."[68]

The HBC was organizationally a single squat pyramid extending across North America with the apex both very small and all-controlling downward. Regular employees were overseen by clerks, who were in turn under the charge of chief traders and above them chief factors, with George Simpson at the apex. Simpson was accountable to company headquarters in London, whose singular purpose was to maximize profit for the company's shareholders. It was in the HBC's interest for the organizational structure to be as conducive as possible to doing so, which meant creating the illusion, if not the reality, of cohesion. The consequence was at the officer level a small inbred cohort. A bias toward Scots along with some Irishmen and Englishmen was common knowledge, as indicated by a contemporary's advice to a long-time HBC clerk desirous of promotion that "your name will have to be changed" by putting a "Mc- before it."[69] Jennifer Brown astutely links the likelihood of promotion to "the cultivation of patronage, kinship, and friendship ties."[70]

George Simpson moved men across North America rather like pawns on a chessboard, be they regular employees or officers. The absence in the Pacific Northwest of external governance or other means of employment meant the HBC was especially able to act with impunity. Noel would over a dozen years, from 1821 1833, have at least half a dozen postings, being in sequence Fort Okanogan in northern Washington, Thompson River and then Fort Langley in southern British Columbia, Fort Vancouver on the border between Washington and Oregon, New Caledonia in central British Columbia, and Fort Colvile in northeast Washington (see map 2). However much men might have resented their circumstances, they consented on the assumption hard work would be acknowledged and rewarded.

TOWARD THE EDGE OF BELONGING

For all that Archibald McDonald repeatedly acknowledged Noel in reporting to his superiors, the latter's ties with Fort Langley may have been fraying as the decade moved toward a close. Indigenous descent, possibly combined with Noel's fraternization with ordinary employees, notably Plamandon and Charles, also from St Francis, may have accounted for McDonald's linking the men in his observation of September 1829 to McLoughlin: "I think that Mr. Annance also is getting indifferent to Fort Langley and Plamondon and Pierre Charles will be following his example."[71]

McDonald did not for his part want to lose Noel. A few months earlier, in June 1829, McLoughlin had requested that he "send here Mr Annance" along with six others in order to reduce the number of men stationed at Fort Langley given the completion of post construction. McDonald resisted, and Noel stayed. A little over a year later, in September 1830, McDonald enthused to McLoughlin how he had persuaded Noel to renew his contract: "Mr Annance is arranged with for three years." And in respect to a request to reduce Fort Langley's complement to a single clerk, he replied, "if you insist on it I shall return you Mr. Yale," who was the other clerk.[72]

Shortly thereafter Noel along with his family departed Fort Langley as passengers on a schooner for Fort Vancouver.[73] As to the reason, McLoughlin had immediate need of his expertise with horses, this at a time when numerous men stationed there who might have assisted him were ill with intermittent fever, being malaria. Noel had in 1826 been part of a large group, including Archibald McDonald and John Work, that successfully secured seventy horses from Indigenous peoples.[74] Now his designated task was to head to Fort Colvile some 300 kilometres, or 185 miles, to the northeast and return to Fort Vancouver with as many horses as he could acquire from local people. It was no easy operation, and McLoughlin flattered Noel in his letter of instructions as being "so experienced a hand" as to be up to it.[75] The return trip of almost a month with eighty horses was over "very bad Roads," during which, according to McLoughlin, "14 were lost by Mr Annance on his way here."[76] The inference left was that the loss came about because Noel did not adequately "take care of them."[77] Although McDonald had earlier demanded that Noel "be sent back immediately" once the task was completed, at least for the interim he remained at Fort Vancouver.[78]

INTO DISFAVOUR

Whether or not the implied criticism by McLoughlin respecting the loss of horses rebounded to Noel's discredit is impossible to know. What is certain is that George Simpson turned against Noel. Exactly when and why is impossible to determine, given the consistently favourable descriptions in the Fort Langley journal, a copy of which would have made its way up the pyramid of command. Simpson's 1830 private assessment was damning: "Has been a Schoolmaster an excellent Classical Scholar but flighty & unsteady, talks & writes nonsense and cannot be believed on oath, an excellent Walker, good shot, firm & savage & a good Trader."[79]

Based on her study of ninety-five sons employed by the NWC or the HBC who had similarly employed Scots or English fathers and Indigenous of part-Indigenous mothers, Denise Fuchs argues by inference that Noel Annance's fall into disfavour was structural. Fuchs describes how the "race consciousness which began in the 1820s" grew so that by the end of the decade "being a 'halfbreed' was detrimental in and of itself." The reason, according to Fuchs, was that Simpson both practised and "sanctioned the practice of judging and often discrediting a person's abilities and the nature of his character on the basis of mixed parentage alone."[80]

Noel's expectations emanating from his higher education may have played a role in his falling into disfavour. As explained by Morag Maclachlan, "An employee such as Francis Annance, however, found that a white man's education did not bring him the privileges he desired. That Native strain in his mixed blood prevented him from rising."[81] Maclachlan's assessment echoes Simpson's complaint earlier in the decade to his London superiors, in reference to mission schools not that different from the one Noel had attended, "I have always remarked that an enlightened Indian is good for nothing ... even the half Breeds of the Country who have been educated in Canada are blackguards of the very worst description, they not only pick up the vices of the Whites upon which they improve but retain those of the Indians in their utmost extent."[82] Noel's higher education, rather than the advantage he must have considered it to be, worked against him.

Events elsewhere may have contributed. Simpson had a couple of years earlier been made aware of St Francis's Abenakis to his displeasure. The HBC had been among those establishing a Quebec operation at St Maurice on the north side of the St Lawrence River, where Noel had earlier honed his skills. The HBC's profits were being eroded by the region's being, in Simpson's words, "principally hunted by a Tribe of Indians or rather Half breeds called 'Abinakees' who inhabit the village of St. Francois on the St. Laurence."[83]

Simpson's outrage caused him, deliberately or not, to misconstrue the Abenakis as farmers or to contend that, if not, they ought to be so: "These hunters are as much civilized as is the generality of Canadian Voyageurs and make the chase more a matter of pastime or amusement than the main source of their living. Their families are left at home during the hunting season, so that their Outfit or equipment can be a mere trifle, and this they purchase for cash or with produce of their farms, or get a credit from the surrounding Shopkeepers, and their furs they hawk to the towns & villages, getting higher prices from the Canadian public they would realize in the London or New York Markets."[84] By Simpson's lights, Abenakis did not play fair. They had no right to impinge on his fiefdom, which the HBC soon sought to circumvent by compelling Abenakis and others to sell it their pelts.[85]

It is plausible, given that Simpson characterized Abenakis as "Half breeds," he was linking the unwanted competition directly to Noel. One of the men the HBC employed at St Maurice was his cousin Simon, with the same last name of Annance, whom he had successfully recommended to Moor's in 1815. Following a three-year HBC contract, from 1822 to 1825, based at St Maurice, Simon had signed on for a year with the HBC's principal competitor in the region, to return to the HBC on short-term contracts in 1827, 1828, and 1831.[86] It may have been that Simon Annance's behaviour, or misbehaviour by Simpson's lights, contributed to his antipathy toward Noel.

SOCIABILITY'S BOUNDARIES

Another factor was also at play. Noel would have been more attune to the HBC's undercurrents if he had been part of its gossipy inner circle of junior officers sustaining each other by a mutually supportive sociability. Although the upwardly mobile Archibald McDonald appears to have accepted Noel as a useful employee, he and the others formed circles of acquaintance that, deliberately or not, excluded Noel. In their lengthy "private letters," composed in part out of loneliness, men requested news of each other but never about Noel.[87]

Noel was not disparaged in the sources that survive, but neither was he among "our friends," "a dear friend," or "a private friend," as his fellow clerks routinely referred to each other.[88] For reasons very possibly related to Noel's combination of non-Scots sensibilities, Indigenous descent, and higher education, he was tolerated but not embraced and may not have been liked on a personal level. Archibald McDonald's observation a few years later in reference to his own growing sons that "all the wealth of Ruperts Land will not make a half breed either a good Parson, a Shining Lawyer, or an able physician" is telling.[89] Whatever the mix of reasons, Noel was an outsider who did not belong.

Whether or not others' views reached Noel, he must have been dismayed by his lack of advancement within the HBC, of which the sons in Fuchs's study had virtually no possibility.[90] Noel was by now in his late thirties and had to have been consternated by numerous of his contemporaries being made chief traders, which meant a higher salary and a share in HBC profits. Archibald McDonald was made a chief trader at the time he took charge of Fort Langley in 1828, and Noel's fellow clerk on the 1824 expedition, John Work, was likewise promoted in 1830, whereas Noel and the third clerk along, Thomas McKay, who was also part Indigenous, were not.

That more Pacific Northwest clerks did not overall rise in rank was linked to the HBC's organizational structure as a single squat pyramid across North America. It was not a matter only of men who had proven themselves in the Pacific Northwest being considered for advancement. Rather, they competed with a whole slew of Scots, Irish, and Englishmen stationed east of the Rockies, some with highly placed fathers, who during these years Simpson repeatedly parachuted into the Pacific Northwest as chief traders.[91]

The disparity respecting Noel went beyond lack of promotion. What he may not have realized as a consequence of his outsider status was that his remuneration was not keeping pace with that of his peers. As a fellow clerk explained in a letter of 1826, when both he and Noel were being paid £60 a year, to "remain under 100 Per. An." is "a breach of which I shall not easily excuse."[92] When Noel's contract expired in 1830, he agreed to a three-year renewal at £75 a year, even as fellow clerk John Murray Yale, with whom he had served at Fort Langley, received £100, as did Thomas McKay of the 1824 expedition.[93] Noel would have been even more dispirited if he had known that official HBC policy remunerated clerks "according to their Education and Abilities," with the lowest level of £50 to £75 annually limited to clerks who "as from want of Education are not qualified for the higher situations."[94]

TAKING DIRECT ACTION

For these reasons or possibly in ignorance of them, Noel Annance opted for direct action to make his case for greater consideration of his service. Having earlier been in Simpson's favour, he had no reason not to believe that, if he could speak directly to him, he would be heard. Abenaki daring came to the fore.

To do so, Noel requested permission shortly after arriving at Fort Vancouver in the fall of 1830 to travel to York Factory with the annual spring brigade heading east. Simpson was said to spend time there, although he increasingly preferred the HBC's main depot of Lachine outside of Montreal and also the burgeoning HBC settlement at Red River near present-day Winnipeg.[95] The Pacific Northwest's seasonal isolation meant McLoughlin was able to pass Noel's request onto Simpson only in March 1831: "Mr. Annance came here last fall with the intention of going to York Factory this Spring, but on my representing to him, that such a proceeding would be equivalent to a resignation of his situation in the service, he consented to remain and requests to be permitted to pay a visit to York."[96] When an answer finally came, it was the opposite of what Noel wanted to hear. Simpson responded in a letter of July

1831 that if Noel persisted in heading east, "he will be considered as on the retiring list and provided with a passage to Canada accordingly."[97]

In the interim, Noel was bounced around, which likely fed whatever dissatisfaction he already felt. In June 1831 John McLoughlin dispatched him to assist Fort Colvile's head over the summer.[98] In November 1831 the post journal of Fort St James in New Caledonia had Noel in charge of the very remote Chilcotin post.[99]

INSIDE SIMPSON'S PRIVATE CHARACTER BOOK

By now the all-controlling George Simpson had even more turned against Noel. As part of a private "character book" written over the winter of 1831–32, a vituperative Simpson assessed all twenty-five factors, twenty-five chief traders, eighty-eight clerks, and nineteen postmasters then employed by the HBC across North America based on his experience with them over his decade in charge.[100] Every one of the clerks, Noel among them, was described first of all by racial descent, with the resulting appraisal of job performance giving the appearance of being derivative of it. For all of his quibbles on mostly small matters, Simpson was favourable overall to two-thirds of the almost eight in ten white clerks, including the almost three-quarters of them who were Scots.

In sharp contrast, all nineteen clerks and the one chief trader whom he described as a "half breed" fared badly. Perceived failings that might have been glossed over in the others were almost always so attributed. Where Simpson did not yet know an individual well enough to make a personal judgment, he simply noted that, if he should turn out well, "I shall be agreeable surprised as it is a lamentable fact that very few of his breed have hitherto conducted themselves with propriety."[101] About another, Simpson observed, "Country & Color disqualify him for his situation as neither Gentlemen nor Natives will have confidence in or respect for him."[102] The most that individuals embodying Indigenous descent could hope for was the backhanded compliment about one of them that he was "tolerably steady considering his breed."[103]

Simpson's critique of Noel was personal and vituperative in respect to his Indigenous descent, against which he now appears to have been principally measured. It read in full, "Annance, F.N. About 40 Years of Age. 13 Years in the Service. A half breed of the Abiniki Tribe near Quebec; well Educated & has been a Schoolmaster. Is firm with Indians, speaks several of their Languages, walks well, is a good Shot and qualified to lead the life of an Indian whose disposition he possesses to a great degree. Is not worthy of belief even upon Oath and altogether a bad character altho' a useful Man. Can have no prospects of advancement. Attached to the Columbia Deptmt."[104]

Simpson's sketches were intended to be private to him alone. He identified individuals only with a number, kept the codes separate, and put both under lock and key, where they remained for the rest of his life. By some accounts, their essence, if not also their substance, leaked out.[105] Simpson himself later referred to "the information, which was intended to be strictly confidential, finding its way back to the interior, leading, as may be readily imagined, to personal difficulties and other inconvenient results."[106] Whether or not it did so, the reality was that the character book assessments reflected and legitimized Simpson's assumptions, attitudes, and actions in the everyday, with others taking their cues from him.

PROSPECTING ANOTHER WAY AHEAD

Noel sought another way ahead. However long he had been so contemplating, the direction he took may have crystallized during his stint in New Caledonia. There, he likely came into contact with disgruntled fellow clerk John Tod, a Scot two years his junior who had been posted there since 1824. In a lengthy letter written in 1830 partly out of loneliness, Tod described his frustration over his lack of advancement, a sentiment he and Noel shared: "I was once a great builder of castles in the air but, for the most part, I have now given it up as unprofitable speculation."[107] By the spring of 1831, Tod had "determined on quitting" the HBC and, like Noel, was looking to the future.[108] Given Tod's "flagging spirits," to quote his biographer, it is unsurprising he was receptive to Noel's similar exasperation.[109]

The consequence was a letter in its essence intelligent, resourceful, and imaginative, in which Noel, referencing John Tod in the content, looked in a wholly different direction drawing on his almost decade and a half in the Pacific Northwest. Over the past few years, a handful of HBC employees, almost wholly from today's Quebec, as was Noel, had set themselves down south of Fort Vancouver in the fertile valley fed by the Willamette River running north to the Columbia River where the post was sited. They sought the independence that came with a farm of their own and, together with the Indigenous women in their lives and their families, had withstood the HBC's opposition to their doing so.[110]

Noel sought to form another such enclave north of the Columbia River, which was mooted during these years as a likely boundary between the United States and Britain once it was determined. Echoing Noel's classical education, the "Tyne" in his letter referred to the strategic port that the Romans had established in the second century on the River Tyne near present-day Newcastle in England.

Noel had shared with others his hopes for the proposed settlement and its location on the northwest coast of the future Washington State. Two months after HBC physician William Fraser Tolmie arrived in the Pacific Northwest in May 1833, Montrealer Jean Baptiste Ouvré, who had been employed west of the Rockies since 1810, took him to see the spot "frequently talked about as a spot favorable" for soon-to-be retirees like himself. Tolmie noted in his journal how "the prairion so much admired by Mr. Annance & Ouvre" was located "about 20 miles [or 35 kilometres] N. of [Fort] Nisqually on the same side of the [Puget] Sound."[111]

Noel's daring echoed his father's achievements of early in the century. Not only had Francis Joseph and the others been granted land not far from St Francis in recognition of their services during the War of Independence, but Noel's father had also petitioned the governor-in-chief of British North America for the island where the family lived. There were also other precedents of which Noel was almost certainly aware. By the time he attended Moor's, the story was likely well known of how his predecessors there half a century previous, in 1780, had founded their own self-sustaining community of Brothertown. Noel's initiative may also have harked back to earlier Moor's student Joseph Brant, who had assumed a leadership role among the Mohawks and, in the wake of their service on the British side in the War of Independence, had negotiated a large land grant in present-day Ontario.[112]

Both the Abenaki and Mohawk grants came through authorities in charge of Britain's remaining North American territory. Brant had worked through Quebec's governor general, Sir Frederick Haldimand, and Noel's father through the governor general of the Canadas, Sir Robert Shaw Milnes.[113] In line with these two precedents, Noel sent his letter of request to the then sitting governor of the Canadas, Lord Aylmer.[114] Noel also built on the earlier precedents by linking his request to his military service in the War of 1812, in whose aftermath numerous soldiers had been rewarded for their allegiance to the British side with land grants. Noel's letter attests both to his widespread knowledge of the politics of governance and to his understanding of land's centrality to the course of events.

The letter's envelope was boldly addressed in Noel's sure hand to "His Excellency Lord Aylmer[,] Governor General of the Canadas[,] &c – &c – &c –[,] Quebec," to whom it in due course arrived.[115] Whether or not the letter would have reached its destination passing through the hands of the Hudson's Bay Company, it is feasible that it left with John Tod on his heading east from New Caledonia to York Factory in May 1832 on the expiry of his contract.[116]

The letter, which resides among the "Land Petitions of Lower Canada" files at Library and Archives Canada, was on its November 1832 arrival taken seriously. Given that the British parliament's grant to the HBC in 1821 of a twenty-year British trading monopoly west of the Rockies contained a proviso that there be no colonization, it is intriguing whether or not the governor general could have granted this request by a third party. What is clear is that Lord Aylmer considered the proposition important enough for him or an aide to pencil on the envelope that the letter was to be passed on to the "Civil Secrty" on "Tuesday even^g Nov. 13," as "I should like to communicate personally wth Mr. Burroughs on the subject of this letter tomorrow at one o'clock." Across the letter's coverpage sideways in another hand is written, "[illeg.] requests [illeg.] Answer may be sent to him."[117]

If the governor general's response, whatever it was, reached Noel, it has not been recorded. In the interim, likely awaiting a reply, he was once again sent to Fort Colvile, whose head relegated him to the outlying post of Flathead House, used for collecting beaver pelts.[118]

Letter to Governor General Lord Aylmer requesting Pacific
Northwest land grant, 20 March 1832

Columbia River North Pacific Ocean
20th March 1832

To His Excellency Lord Aylmer
Governor General of the Canadas
&c – &c – &c –
Quebec

My Lord
   The subject is my only apology for troubling your Lordship by
the present address. Impressed with the highest sense and venera-
tion of that noble generosity and spirit of enterprise which pre-
dominate in the breast of a British Nobleman, I take the liberty of
applying to your Lordship for advice and assistance on the subject
which I consider to be of greatest importance. Colonization is an
object always worthy of attention. Emigration, relieving old countries of their over growing population, has of late much occupied
the attention of our modern statesmen. In all my travels from the
Atlantic to the Pacific I have not seen a country so well adapted
for a settlement than the spot I have in mind near the mouth of
the Columbia. Therefore I humbly beg that your Lordship would
condescend to inform me and my colleague Mr. John Tod of York
Factory, whether we can get a grant from Government to colonize
that part of the country. There are [a] great many [French] canadi-
ens, who having retired from the service of the H. Bay and other
fur companies, are dispersed about that country, doing very little
good to themselves or the Natives with whom they are often at
variance. These men have often applied to me to assist and head
them in settling themselves on the beautiful and luxurious plains
between the Columbia and Fraser's rivers. By beginning with these
men accustomed to the country, in the course of three or four
years several thousands can be admitted yearly. Vast number of
whalers and coasting vessels that now in vain apply to the Sand-
wich Islands for fresh supplies in provisions and timber would
soon crowd into our harbours and the place would be a second

Tyne in a very short time. As soon [as] I can ascertain the possibility of obtaining a grant I shall send out a regular chart of the country and detail the vast advantages that would result from the colony – I humbly pray that your Lordship would communicate the sentiments of the government on the subject and oblige, my Lord,

> Your Lordship's most humble and devoted Servant
> Francis N. Annance.

To his Excellency
Lord Aylmer Governor Genl.
of the Canadas &c &c &c

P.S. Your Lordship's humble Servant was a Lieutenant in the Ind Dept and took an active part in the last war [War of 1812].

Source: Francis N. Annance to Lord Aylmer, 20 March 1832, Library and Archives Canada, Land Petitions of Lower Canada, RG1-L3L, vol. 32, pp. 16698–700, reel 2505.

REVEALING HIS SELF

About this time, personal tragedy struck. Responding in October 1832 to a letter from fellow Fort Langley clerk James Murray Yale, still stationed there, Noel laid open his grief at the death of "my beloved, poor little Johnny!"[119] The letter is, almost certainly for this reason, the only one of some 120 of Noel's located letters that was religiously inflected on a personal level. In writing a decade and a half earlier to the head of Moor's on behalf of his younger brother and cousin, Noel had used religious language for effect but not now.

Tucked away among James Murray Yale's papers in the British Columbia Archives, Noel's letter is also distinctive in other ways. In lamenting his son's death and also in writing on other topics, Noel revealed his self more fully than in any other piece of correspondence unearthed. Still at Fort Colvile, Noel had by now cut his ties emotionally

Letter of farewell to James Murray Yale, 17 October 1832

Colvile, Oct. 17, 1832
Mr. J. M. Yale,
My dear sir: –
I had the pleasing satisfaction to receive your much esteemed
favour on my arrival at Okanogan, and I now most affectionately return you my warmest thanks for your kind remembrance of me. My
memory shall ever dwell with tender emotions on the many happy
hours we have spent together. The recollection of Joys that are past,
of scenes of pleasure, anxiety and danger passed through with
friends in whom there is no guile, are always dear to the heart, even
when many years have rolled away. I am now on the eve of my departure: and however grieved I may be to leave some of my friends,
I feel no regret to leave a service which I am beginning to detest.
There is a species of tyranny in the country that would do honor to
the spirit of a hero. There are some who as soon as they rise a little
above their former insignificance, fancy themselves setting on the
throne of the Caesars, and glory in the acts that would grace the
abominations of a Commodus or a Caligula [Roman emperors].
Unprincipled and unfeeling, hardy and ferocious, they stifle every
sentiment of humanity and trample on every principle of honor.
I dare say you heard of the distressing calamity that has befallen
me in the untimely end of my beloved, poor little Johnny! I was the
most miserable being in existence all the winter. But, my dear Sir,
these things cannot be escaped, and we must bear in silent grief to
the awful Providence of God. I am glad to hear that your little girl is
doing well: and sincerely hope that it may not be your lot to feel that
anguish which so keenly preys on my heart for the loss of my boy:
but let me say in the language of inspiration, "the Lord giveth and
the Lord taketh away; blessed be the name of the Lord."
Give my compliments to Mr. [Archibald] McDonald and tell him
I have no time to write him. Remember me to Pierre Charles and all
your men, not forgetting our Quotland [Kwantlen] and Hoomis
[Sqamish?] friends — tell them if I come back I shall go to see them.

I am, Dear Sir
Your affectionate friend
F. N. Annance

Source: Francis Noel Annance to James Murray Yale, 17 October 1832, British
Columbia Archives, MS-0182, box 1, file 2, item 17.

and practically with the fur trade: "I am now on the eve of my departure: and however grieved I may be to leave some of my friends, I feel no regret to leave a service which I am beginning to detest."[120] An unspecified "tyranny" against which he railed contrasted sharply with his warm feelings toward his long-time colleague Archibald McDonald and St Francis compatriot Pierre Charles, who would make his life in the Pacific Northwest. Noel's request to Yale that he "tell them if I come back I shall go to see them" likely stems from his springtime letter to the governor general requesting land, to which he had not yet had a response, if indeed he ever received one.

The death of Noel's son presaged the end of his apparently stable relationship with the unidentified Flathead woman with whom he had made his life. Posted to Fort Colvile in 1832, Noel requested she also be transported there, as was the usual HBC practice, but McLoughlin alerted a clerk stationed there of more pressing needs than to do so.[121] Whatever transpired, a chapter in Noel's life was over. However he managed and whatever happened to his third son, Noel would then or later take charge of eight-year-old son Archie with the goal of having him schooled.

The unravelling of Noel's personal life corresponded with his transfer out of the Pacific Northwest. From Flathead House in March 1833, "Mr. Annance ... requested that his engagement might be cancelled."[122] The consequence was his being dispatched to work out the remainder of his contract at remote Fort Simpson, located on the Mackenzie River in today's Northwest Territories, to which he headed alone with the 1833 spring brigade (see map 2).

TO SUM UP

To make a successful career as an officer in the fur trade was to anticipate promotion, with its increase in pay and status, as reward for enterprise, loyalty, and hard work. To whatever extent Noel's lack of recognition lay with his capacities, and there is no way to know, attitudes toward him were compounded by assumptions respecting Indigenous peoples that he could not overcome. His higher education and his daring had gotten him to the entry rank as a clerk but could not take him further.

By 1833 Noel Annance had been at the service of the Hudson's Bay Company for a dozen years. Among a small minority of gentlemen with the privilege of having "Mr." in front of his name, he had worked at the behest of others with the ups and downs that thereby ensued. Now entering his forties, the time had come for him to take account of what had ensued and what was possible.

5

Letting Go

For a decade and a half, Noel Annance performed in the Pacific Northwest fur trade at the behest of others in a form of captivity not unlike his years at Moor's Charity School and Dartmouth College or, much earlier, reminiscent of his great-grandparents' experiences. The Abenaki daring Noel exercised had come to naught. Although Noel's decision to depart the Pacific Northwest was not wholly his, it did give a certain freedom of action.

Perhaps for the first time in Noel's life and the only time whose record survives, after arriving at the remote northern post of Fort Simpson to finish out his final contract following a satisfying experience along the way, Noel let go. His six months there were emotionally charged, due in the first instance to a woman but also to a clash of personalities. His "love notes," to use Morag Maclachlan's term for them, are reproduced here in their entity. The consequence of his daring was that Noel departed the fur trade not with a whimper but rather with a bang.

ON THE WAY

Founded in 1822 and named for George Simpson, Fort Simpson was about as far away as it was possible to get from the Pacific Northwest. Noel headed "across the mountains" with the Hudson's Bay Company's (HBC) spring 1833 brigade taking out pelts.[1] Making it by mid-June to the post of Norway House northeast of Lake Winnipeg on the established route between the Pacific Northwest and York Factory, he was by arrangement given a passage on an Arctic expedition being supported by the HBC.

Having been subject to the ups and downs resulting at least in part from George Simpson's perspective on persons like himself, Noel must have been buoyed by the relationship that quickly grew up between him and the expedition's naturalist and medical doctor, twenty-three-year-old Englishman Richard King, who had charge of the supply boats carrying provisions to an anticipated Arctic post. Noel found himself treated from their first encounter as the gentleman he had hoped to be in the fur trade.

King narrated events in his journal. On the expedition's next stop at Cumberland House about 500 kilometres, or 300 miles, west of Norway House in today's western Saskatchewan, "while the men were occupied in pitching our tents and preparing the supper, Mr. Annance and myself took a stroll through the woods in pursuit of some pigeons that had been seen to alight." King was admiring of his companion's prowess and also, possibly, his storytelling: "Mr. Annance, who ranks in the country as a first-rate shot, had made himself so great an adept, that, at a distance not exceeding twenty yards, he even preferred the hatchet to the rifle; and on several occasions he had handled it with great success against marauding parties of Stone Indians, who inhabit the extensive plains of the Saskatchewan."[2]

Perhaps as a consequence, Noel had no compunction about revealing his self not long after leaving Cumberland House. He was, as King put it in his journal, "a 'métif,' or, as the Canadians would term him, a 'brois brulé,'" both words referring to persons of mixed Indigenous and non-Indigenous descent.[3] It is impossible to know whether Noel used the terminology in so describing his inheritance or only King did so.

Come the end of July, the two boats, with their crews of eight carrying King and "my companion, Mr. Annance," departed Île-à-la-Crosse about 500 kilometres northwest of Cumberland House on their way to Fort Chipewyan, another 500 kilometres distant. Along the way a bond grew between the pair, separated by two decades in age but clearly attune to each other. On a very hot day as goods were being carried across a difficult portage, "we found the men in a high state of fever; and rather dead than alive, from excessive thirst; yet not a murmur escaped them. Mr. Annance and myself seized each a kettle, and started, as if impelled by wings, for the creek where the boats were left, and soon obtained a supply of water to quench the thirst." A wolverine having marauded the camp at night, "Mr. Annance thought it so favourable an opportunity for using his rifle," but finding it too far away, "we contented ourselves therefore with hallooing as loudly as possible."[4]

In due course, King headed out to join the main part of the expedition, Noel thereupon making his own way in stages to Fort Simpson: "I gave Mr. Annance a few pounds of pemmican, and he hoped to kill a few ducks, to enable him to reach his [initial] place of destination on the banks of the M'Kenzie River, distant about five days' march" from Port Resolution, located about 500 kilometres north of Cumberland House, where they parted company.[5] On the morning of 7 September, King took leave of "my esteemed friend and companion, Mr. Annance," whose first stop was the outlying fishing grounds attached to his new posting as a clerk.[6]

The two men's amiable encounter became the stuff of HBC gossip. A fellow clerk explained admiringly to another officer as a matter of course how "with such aids as ... Annance, tis hoped" all would go well with the expedition.[7]

IN GEORGE SIMPSON'S SHADOW

Five weeks after separating from the Arctic expedition and a good half-year after leaving the Pacific Northwest, Noel arrived at Fort Simpson. Its head, John Stuart, recorded in the post journal on 16 October 1833 how "Mr François Noel Annance a Clerk sent to this Dist." brought with him "a copy of the Minutes of Council and further instructions for the Guidance of the District."[8]

Tension between the two men was visible from the outset. They each walked in George Simpson's shadow at a fur trade post named in his honour. Just as did Noel, Stuart had reason to blame Simpson for his present situation – in his case, following on a distinguished career. The now fifty-five-year-old Scot, whose time in the fur trade went back over a third of a century, had travelled down the Fraser River in 1808 with Simon Fraser, a year later taking charge of the newly established fur trade region of New Caledonia. Named a chief trader on the HBC taking control of the Pacific Northwest in 1821, Stuart had known such success that on Simpson's second trip west in 1828, he commended Stuart's "great exertions and unwearied perseverance" and praised him as "the Father, or founder of New Caledonia."[9] Some viewed Stuart's unexpected appointment to remote Fort Simpson in 1832 as untoward given his seniority, but Stuart represented himself on his way there as being "in high spirits."[10]

Stuart's appointment was linked, as was Noel's being dispatched there, to the total control George Simpson exercised over employees' careers. According to Stuart's entry in the *Dictionary of Canadian Biography*, his appointment "to the Mackenzie River district, an unusual posting for an officer of his service and inclination, may have been a punitive act."[11] If so, the impetus lay in Simpson's treatment of the women in his life. Being in the words of his biographer "an active philanderer," Simpson fathered at least ten children by half a dozen women.[12] Among their number was Peggy Taylor, whom Simpson had encountered in 1826 as a consequence of her younger brother Tom being his personal servant.[13] Their father was an English sloop master earlier in the service of the HBC, and their mother was a Cree woman, an inheritance giving daughters little manoeuvring power on being propositioned by fur trade officers, as was common in a place and time without white women. Consistent with that frame of behaviour, Peggy's sister Mary had been fancied and then abandoned by Scots HBC clerk James Hargrave about the time Stuart either left or lost through death the woman with whom he was living. If much older than Mary, Stuart had the advantage of being a chief factor, and in 1827 she accepted his invitation.[14]

Stuart's relationship with Simpson had soured over the HBC head's abandonment of Mary's sister Peggy in 1829 preparatory to his wedding a white woman.[15] Stuart turned on Simpson, who in response turned on Stuart.[16] Much as Simpson had been toward Noel, he was vituperative respecting Stuart in his 1832 character book: "Exceedingly vain, a great Egotist, Swallows the grossest flattery, is easily cajoled, rarely speaks the truth ... Has of late become disgustingly indecent in regard to women."[17]

By any measure, it would have been difficult for Noel to come to terms with Fort Simpson. It seems virtually impossible that he was not privy to the gossip respecting the Taylor sisters and now found himself under the authority of a disgruntled Stuart, with Mary an everyday presence at the remote post. Stuart for his part flexed his muscles, describing Fort Simpson to a fellow officer shortly before Noel's arrival as "the only place I know where a person can act The Chief Factor."[18]

Perhaps for that reason, but more likely due to a perspective shared by fellow fur trade officers in their gossipy letters, Stuart baited Noel. He was from Stuart's perspective "an Abenequi Indian of more than common education that came up from Canada as a Trapper in 1819, was employed since in various capacities and unfortunately sent here as a Post Master," a position of lesser status than that of a clerk with no pretensions to being suited to a gentleman.[19] The fabricated characterization speaks to Stuart's everyday attitude toward Noel.

A TINDER BOX

Not long after his arrival at Fort Simpson, Noel Annance encountered the impetus for letting go. Now in her mid-thirties, Mary Taylor had for the past six years lived with Stuart, almost two decades her senior. In perspective and appearance, he seemed even older, as Simpson had observed a couple of years earlier: "About 57 Years of Age, calls himself 47 – 70 winters at least, however, are marked on his countenance."[20]

Mary Taylor was attractive. Even as James Hargrave disposed of her half a dozen years earlier, he was plaintive: "Had I an eye toward picking up a play-mate, between ourselves, I have scarcely seen a young woman of her Caste [skin tones] I would have preferred before her."[21] In 1830, when Stuart and Simpson were still in contact, Stuart bragged to him as to how "she is uncommonly attentive to me – apparently as caressing and anxious to please as if I was a young man."[22]

Fort Simpson became a tinder box with Mary Taylor its flame, to be ignited by Noel a little over a month after his arrival on 16 October. For almost three months, Stuart remained ignorant of their intimate relationship for reasons that are not wholly clear. He might have been unable to conceive of Noel, whom he persistently diminished as Indigenous, as a competitor for her affection. It was also the case, Stuart later acknowledged, that he and Mary had grown apart.[23]

Only on 7 February 1834 did Stuart find the couple out, whereupon Mary turned against Noel. A few days later, she handed over to Stuart fifteen notes he had written her, which Stuart dated as best he could and copied alongside editorial comment into a private version of the Fort Simpson post journal that he kept for himself, as opposed to its official counterpart yearly sent to HBC headquarters.[24] It is these notes, along with the information accompanying them, that make it possible to track the relationship.

The surviving notes are not the only ones Noel and Mary exchanged. She later explained to Stuart how "there were many more notes some of which she had burnt & others she had lost."[25] On the couple being found out, Noel handed over to Stuart "some notes which he said was the handwriting of Mary."[26] These were not copied into Stuart's private version of the post journal, very possibly due to their compromising content respecting Stuart.

BEGINNINGS

By Mary's recollection of events, as retold by Stuart in her self-defence, Noel was immediately attracted to her: "She states that no more than three days after his arrival here in the fort he began to ingratiate himself into her favour." Just over a month later, according to Mary, Noel had forced himself on her: "Going out by the back gate of the Fort as her custom was before going to bed she found him wrapped in his cloak standing by the Bastion that he caught hold of her arm and forcibly dragged her to the branches by the Garden fence and then violated her person against her will in having carnal communication with her."[27]

A day later and many times subsequently, Noel accosted Mary intending in Stuart's words to salvage her reputation in his self-interest: "While I was occupied in the Interpreter's house he called her into his room … dragged her in, and then a second time against her will and consent and by force had carnal knowledge of her, that from that time she … became subservient to his will in every thing and from fear pretended great love and attachment to him."[28]

Stuart's account narrates growing tension between the two men, Noel coming to perceive him as a romantic rival, and Stuart playing "The Chief Factor." Stuart outwardly scorned, but may have secretly envied, Noel's learning. According to Simpson in his private assessment of 1832, Stuart "had not the advantage of a good Education but being studious improved himself very much and having a very retentive memory is superficially conversant with many subjects."[29]

Differing levels of literacy may have been the impetus to a mid-December flare-up that Stuart described at the time in the public version of the Fort Simpson journal, this prior to his knowledge of the relationship between Noel and Mary. The confrontation began with Stuart refusing to read a letter Noel had handed him, as "he could communicate any thing he had to say to me verbally." Thereupon, in Stuart's words, Noel "commenced a insolent rhapsody too deep for my learning."[30]

The journal entry reveals Stuart's knowledge of Noel prior to his arrival: "Mr. Annance is a classical scholar but I could not say whether what he uttered was Greek, Latin, or Abonakee & before I could have time to ask him, even if I had been so disposed to do which it is likely I would not he left the room and did not come to either dinner or supper. Poor Mr Annance has been in difficulties wherever he had been."[31]

The gossipy private letters that flowed back and forth between HBC officers were the almost certain source of Stuart's assessment. What is revealing is that Stuart considered their contents sufficiently valid for their implications to make their way into a post journal intended to be read by others. In the entry Stuart explicitly referred, in respect to the intended purpose of journals in the fur trade, to "the gentlemen for whom I write."[32] Noel subsequently apologized, as also recorded in the post journal.

Note of apology to John Stuart, 17 December 1833

Mr Stuart. Upon consideration I find that I have been wrong and inconsiderate both as regards the duty and respect I owe both to the company and to yourself which I now regret, and you will forgive and forget what passed and allow me to return to my duty as formerly most respectfully &c &c &c.

Source: HBC, Fort Simpson (NWT) Post Journal, 1834-35, as copied by John Stuart, Hudson's Bay Company Archives, Archives of Manitoba, John Stuart papers, E.24/5.

FIFTEEN NOTES

In the tinder box that was Fort Simpson over the winter of 1833–34, it was two weeks after the December flare-up when Noel wrote the earliest of the fifteen surviving notes to Mary Taylor, which are perforce reproduced here in the form Stuart copied them into his private journal, as opposed to how Noel might have written them.[33] Now six weeks into their relationship, Noel considered it sufficiently solid to anticipate their having a child together.

First note to Mary Taylor, 1 January 1834

> New Year's day verses
> May bliss and Joy crown our eternal love
> And Heaven grant our union happy proof
> Rain a lively offspring in our tender care
> You and I the pleasing task will share.

Stuart explained that Noel's second note was written in anticipation that Stuart was about to accompany Chief Trader Murdoch McPherson, who had just arrived to take charge of the district, on an extended visit to Fort Liard, located 275 kilometres, or 170 miles, to the south. Noel feared Mary would be expected to join Stuart at Fort Liard prior to his own anticipated departure for York Factory on his way home. Noel hoped his relationship with Mary would be ongoing and expected her to accompany him on his departure. The note is the earliest to refer to Mary's sharing with Noel her alleged mistreatment by Stuart.

Second note to Mary Taylor, 15 or 16 January 1834

My Love.
He [Stuart] takes all his Papers and he will work then with Mr.
McPherson till next March then he will bring you down with the
Express, then he will want to send me up but I will not go. I shall
leave this for York [Factory]. Now can you believe him. My dear
is it possible that you can leave me for ever. Why need you do
such a thing. Think my love. He will abuse you again.

A third note written at about the same time expressed concern over
Stuart having told McPherson that he had put laudanum, a form of
opium commonly used at the time to reduce pain and induce sleep, into
Mary's evening chocolate drink. Stuart acknowledged in his accompanying notes having done so on the night of 15 or 16 January or there-
abouts.

Third note to Mary Taylor, 15 or 16 January 1834

My Dear Love.
I am anxious to hear from you. Take care my dear, he told
McPherson that he put Laudanum into your chocolate and you
slept so hard that he could not waken you.

Another note written about the same time was longer and more emotionally charged. Noel urged Mary to share with the visiting Murdoch
McPherson, who was Stuart's superior, the concerns she had expressed
to him over Stuart's treatment of her. Noel feared for her wellbeing and
used, as a reason for her to do so, her fading physical appearance.
Again, he declared his love for her. Nangua and Lizette, who have not
been identified, were likely servants.
    According to Mary's later confession to Stuart, the "Paper" men-
tioned in the note was a four-sheet document written by Noel detailing

the charges she had made to him against Stuart. Mary would later
claim to Stuart she had no knowledge of the document's contents.

Fourth note to Mary Taylor, likely 16 January 1834

Be easy my dear Love.
   I will not tear my heart to refuse any thing you request. You
have only one thing to do never consent that he should call you
his wife. No never, or all is lost. If Mr. McPherson speaks to you
for him, tell him so at once that his treatment of you has been
such that it is impossible for you [to] live with him and if he com-
pels you in this manner you have not long to live and, believe me,
I am astonished and pained to death to see you so much changed
in your looks. Believe me, my dearest love, do not trifle away your
own life, if you do you destroy two. If you do not, keep away
from his bed and speak to me and see me, as you wish. Your dearest heart, my Love will Break and I will follow you to your grave
to lay my bones with yours. Sign and send me the Paper. Nangua
tells me that Lizette told her if she carries any papers from me to
you she would get a thrashing.

Stuart described in his accompanying narrative how at about this
time he and McPherson had spotted "A. going out of my room by the
back door," but having "not the least suspicion that there was any intrigue of a criminal nature between them," he had not followed up.
Stuart did not do so even though he was convinced, he wrote in retrospect, that Noel had "stolen Books and Sugar both the Companys
Property out of the Store."
   On 18 January, Stuart informed Noel that "I desired him to hold
himself in readiness to accompany Mr. McPherson to Fort de Liard,"
or alternatively to give assistance at a nearby post. Noel refused, responding that "he was told by Governor Simpson he would not be
asked to perform any winter voyage, that he was determined to go to
York Factory either by the March conveyance or by the Boats as would
best suit him, and that no one could prevent him." Stuart attributed
Noel's response to his "being like all other Indians."

It was in this context that Noel again wrote to Mary in what would be the fifth note between them to survive. He recounted to her the sequence of events much as Stuart later retold them, but he did so from a very different perspective. Noel's motivation in acting as he did was to facilitate his and Mary's being able to leave together in the spring. According to Noel in the note, the sugar pilfering charge against him had been withdrawn. Tandella has not been identified.

Fifth note to Mary Taylor, 18 January 1834

I thank you my love for your affectionate and kind expression and I shall certainly obey you. I am happy to hear that Mr McPherson spoke to you in the manner you tell me. I am much obliged to him. Tell the old scamp that you care very little whether he drives himself to despair or not. You have your own soul to save and your happiness to think of and let him do the same and not tempt you to sin against God and bring ruin upon you. Mr McPherson tells me he has been telling lies about him and very likely they will Quarrel before he leaves this. The old Jebusite says now that he will remain here another year that he may punish us. He tells me to go and find Mr. McLeod [at a branch post], I told him I will not shall not go there. I shall remain here till the Boats go, then I shall embark for Norway House. No one will stop me. So my Dear Love, stand firm, separate yourself from him that we may go both next spring and leave him behind with his friend Tandella. You shall go with your friend, my Love, and let him go with his. I made him humble as a boy to day and he is trying every thing to please me. He told Mr. McPherson that he was sorry that he told me to day that I stole Sugar from the Store and carry it to Lizett's house and wanted to excuse himself but I will not forgive the villain. He said again today that we both stole Books from the store before Mr. Mcpherson. Good bye my Love. Tell him you will neither kill him nor have any thing to do with him. Now take care he may play some dirty trick upon you when you sleep.

Written two days later, the sixth note centred on what Stuart described as "a Diamond Souvenir ring belonging to me value about thirty Guineas," which he had "never given but lent to Mary 19th Jany." According to Stuart, Mary wore it that evening and the next day. Noel's note described his strong emotions on seeing it on her finger. He also once again attempted to persuade her to sign the "paper" he had written respecting Stuart's maltreatment of her.

Sixth note to Mary Taylor, 20 January 1834

My Love.

    I was very much hurt when the old villain was pointing to the Ring he had given you, I thought we were lost. I began a terrible letter, but before I got half through tears burst out of my eyes and my face fell on the table. When I recovered, I looked at what I had written and threw it into the fire. Then you were saved. My heart bled when I turned away from you at the window, because I thought you had deceived me. That infernal Ring stabbed one through the heart. Let me never see it again if you have not ruined yourself. Send the Paper. I will not make use of it without your consent.

According to Stuart respecting the ring lent to Mary, on "the 21st it disappeared and is not now to be found." In this version of events, Mary later told Stuart that Noel had forced it from her finger and that "some times when she was reluctant to continue the connexion he would threaten to show the ring and disclose the whole to me."

Perrish, referred to in this seventh note, has not been identified, nor has the nature of the events so disconcerting to Noel. On the surface, it appears as though Mary was going from man to man.

Seventh note to Mary Taylor, likely 24 January 1834

Please take time to read this and think upon it seriously. You have
broken a most awful promise – a decent woman should rather die
than do such a thing – you swore that you loved me – now this
love is gone – an abominable falsehood which no man can forgive
– you prefer to please an old villain detested by every one well
known to be the most dirty profligate, who will run after any
dirty Bitch in his way. If he thinks he can succeed, to despise you
and make other women laugh at you – a villain who has done
everything a Dog can do upon your body – to insult you – where
is your heart? Have you any feelings, must we be forced to believe
what he says, that you are a strumpet, a Liar, &c, &c. Will you
expose yourself to every one that you are really so – will you
allow every one to know all you have done, and every dirty trick
he has played with and on your body, for depend upon it I will
hide nothing, if I am offended. You know if I say a thing I will do
it not like you, nor like that I considered you are so anxious to
embrace every night. For him you need not be afraid. He is too
mean, too much a coward, that he will do anything. But be afraid
of exposing your character which will be damned forever. My
heart is getting better and I am not so much pained because I am
sure you do not love me as you are too much in a hurry to lay
aside that dirty caress to receive his filthiness on your body. You
know well that I can do little about that villain. You know what I
have told him & what I will tell him, and perhaps I may tell him.
It is in my power to get him kicked out of the country. Perrish
says they will tell the Governor that they would not remain here
because they have a Bourgeois who is a fool. He does nothing but
hang after his wife continually. He neglects the Company's work
for the sake of his wife.

Mary told Stuart that she likely received the eighth note to have survived on the morning of Noel leaving the post for work responsibilities.
He had "previous to his departure showed himself at her window &
left the note which she herself went for having seen him leave it there."
His goal in doing so was, as with the previous note, to give Mary the

courage to be true to herself as he envisaged her. He was hopeful she would end her relationship with Stuart, but if not, so be it. From Noel's perspective, "a woman may remain with a man as long as she finds herself happy, but the moment she finds herself unhappy she can go away."

Eighth note to Mary Taylor, on or after 26 January 1834

My Love.

I now tell you what you must do. If you are afraid that you will not succeed, I tell you try. You must try, then if it will not do, it is very easy for you to go back. You have been trying so long, and nothing is done. Now this is my advice, follow it as you say you would, then leave the rest to me. Do you think, that if I did not know what I was about, that he would be so humble now, doing every thing to please me? If I did not know what is due to me, he would not have told me. He would have done every thing to please himself, but I have too much regard for myself to allow others to do as they please with me and if you have any regard for yourself, for your own happiness, do as I do. You have the same right as I have. Go to your room and sleep there. You must tell him first that you are unhappy & miserable with him, and it is your duty and your right which no one dares dispute to do what you think proper to make yourself happy. Do my love, do follow this advice. This is the last I shall give you. [Do] not be afraid. He will not, he dares not, do any thing to distress you. Do not believe what he may tell you. You know no one believes what he says. If he threatens you, do not mind him. If he says he will not allow you, tell him you do not want his permission. A woman may remain with a man as long as she finds herself happy, but the moment she finds herself unhappy she can go away. If she is not a slave, no Law can make her remain with a man against her own will. Do. my Love, know your own right. Speak to him as I did, then he will hang down his head with shame. If you do not stand up for your right I shall do. My love, try. I say, only try, and if I do not make every thing smooth you can go back to him, and not think of me more. Follow my advice and, dear, if you do not, you know there will be something very disagreeable to me and you.

I kiss you my Love. Good bye.

On 5 February the men from the post who had gone with Chief
Trader Murdoch McPherson to Fort Liard on 22 January returned to
Fort Simpson, which led to speculation as to who might accompany
them on their return to Fort Liard. From Noel's perspective, if Mary
went to Fort Liard, he and she could later leave together from there. He
was making plans for their life together, even as he acknowledged that
he might love her more than she did him. Yet he pressed his case in this
ninth note to have survived.

Ninth note to Mary Taylor, 5 February 1834

My dear Love.
  If he tells you to go to Fort de Liard, tell him at once, yes, that
you would go and let him get every thing ready. If he does let you
go, Mr. McPherson will be sure of seeing me there next March.
But if he afterwards tells you no you will not go, then tell him that
you will no longer remain with a man who is doing every thing to
harass you and worry you to death. Now, my love, for whom
have you done all that you have been doing, for whom have you
suffered and been so ill treated? Is it not for me? Is it not because
you have loved me & thought you would be more happy? These
are very strong reasons, the only reason for which a woman ought
to remain with a man, and do I not love you perhaps more than
you do me? Can I not support you as well as he? You know that
you would not be pitiful then, dear Love. Why not trust every
thing to me? You know that I would rather die than see you miserable. Since you obeyed me in one thing, you should obey me in
all because if you are happy I am also happy. Why do you suspect
that you would be badly off? No one can think so. The old villain
may so, but he knows well that it is not in his power to destroy
me or to prevent me from doing what I please. You know that I
have my foot on his neck and he dares not show his teeth. Perrish
told his wife last night that in Montreal, even if a woman was regularly married to a man, she would not be allowed to remain with
him if she was so unhappy as you are with the old Villain. My
dear, do not allow all that you have suffered pass for nothing. If
you will give way to him and allow him get the better of you, it

will appear foolish and he will be more cruel to you after. Allow me, my dear, to tell him today that you appear to be very unhappy and, if he asks you if you told me so, tell him, yes, that you did so, my love. I will not say anything to hurt your feelings. Me, I will give you my dear heart. Trust me. Fear not. What ever you do, every one will praise you.

P. S. Now, my love, tell him since he wants to send you away that you will and must go and let him get every thing ready immediately.

On the evening of 5 February, Stuart told Mary of his intention to send her to Fort Liard, but he said nothing about going with her. The next day, it seemed as though he would do so. Noel's tenth surviving note urged Mary not to consent to go to Fort Liard since Stuart was being conciliatory about his remaining at Fort Simpson as the storekeeper. Noel might as a consequence not leave for York Factory in the spring, as he had planned to do.

Tenth note to Mary Taylor, 6 February 1834

Be easy my dear Love. I completely gained my point with the old scamp. He came to me just now and begged like a Beggar, and begged again that I would forgive and be good friends with him and not leave this place to go to York this Winter. Then he put every thing in the first place. He told me I was Master to do what I liked with anything in the store, that he would not meddle with any thing, that I shall do as I think proper. I told him that I will do so, but it will depend upon his conduct to me till next Spring whether I shall go to York or not. O! my dear love, if you can gain your point as I have done, we will soon be happy. [Do] not be afraid, my dear, do what you like, speak to me and he does not get angry according to his promise. He tells you that he will never say any thing disagreeable to me, so that he may see us sleeping together. Keep him always at a distance. My Love. Secure my heart, my Angel. If he tells you to go to Fort Liard with him, do not consent to go. My Love, you are not too well yet.

Noel reiterated his point about Mary not leaving in a very brief note, the eleventh to have survived, written shortly after its predecessor.

Eleventh note to Mary Taylor, 6 or 7 February 1834

My Love
    Do not with him on any account go, not for the world. What will Mr. McPherson think when he sees you? No, my love, do not go (on any account) on no condition.

The twelfth surviving note followed not long afterward. Here, Noel referenced having put Mary's notes to him in his pocket.

Twelfth note to Mary Taylor, about 7 February 1834

My Love.
    You must tell me immediately whether you go with him to Fort Liard. All I require is yes or no – lose no time. I am now ready with all your notes in my pocket. Perrish could not tell him last night what was the matter with you. I will soon explain the whole to him. Is it possible, my dear, that whenever the old villain wants to impose upon you he has only to speak to another man then you consent at once.

In yet another note, the thirteenth to have survived, written on the same day, Noel expressed consternation at having had no answer from Mary. He reminded her that the notes from her to him were in his pocket preparatory to showing them to Stuart at dinner, when "I shall tell him all." The letter appears to have been a kind of ultimatum to Mary, whereby he would stay at Fort Simpson if she did but would otherwise leave in March for York Factory. The note acknowledged he had Stuart's ring in his possession and would hand it over if Mary left. Dandella has not been identified.

Thirteenth note to Mary Taylor, 7 February 1834

For Heaven sake answer me before supper because at supper I shall tell him all – show him your notes, ring and tomorrow, if you go, I will give the ring to Dandella. I write Mr McPherson I leave this in March for York, but if you remain I will not go. Tell him at supper that you will not go with him.

Noel wrote again to Mary at 9:00 on the same evening in what comes across as a final appeal to her. In this fourteenth note to have survived, he viewed the "paper" with Mary's list of charges against Stuart, now in her possession, as a means for them to secure the future he envisaged could be theirs together.

Fourteenth note to Mary Taylor, 7 February 1834, 9:00 PM

My Dear love, do for the sake of our mutual promise and mutual love, do obey me once more then we are happy. You have nothing to do but to come into my room. Come into my room this evening and ask my protection, then you are as safe as if you were in Montreal [intelligible]. Mary Love, believe me for heaven's sake, only once more, then every thing is safely over. If he comes for you, tell him no, I will go to you. Then I shall turn him out. You must bring the Paper. In case he wishes to make a noise, we will show him that Paper to let him know the danger that is before him.

In Stuart's words accompanying the notes in his private version of the post journal, "Mary did retire into his room but the result was different from what it is probably either expected." The couple were found out, but by whom and how are left unclear.

Stuart described how on the evening of 7 February, in anticipation of leaving for Fort Liard, he had just finished writing in the post's daily journal and had made arrangements to put the post while he was away in charge of "Francois Noel Annance an Abenaqui Indian of more than common education." It was then that events cascaded: "It was found that the said Francois N. Annance had inveigled Mary Taylor, her whom I tenderly loved and since the 15th August 1827 both considered and treated as my lawful wife and sincerely intended before God and man to make her such, into his room with intent to make her leave my bed and board and kept there against my will."

It appears Stuart had physically feared Noel all along, as indicated by his calling together seven employees for self-protection. Stuart "told them I must go for my wife, and at the same time requiring their assistance in case resistance was made and violence offered me, and to be careful that no injury was done to my person in case my life was attempted which from the character of the man I had reason to expect, at the same time cautioning them against using violence if none was offered me."

In what must have been a letdown to Stuart, "on opening the door I found the Gentleman and the Lady both standing by the fire ... talking openly together." Asked what they were doing, Noel responded, in Stuart's paraphrasing of his words, "there was no secret at all, that a woman who was no slave might go where she pleased, that such was the law and that no one had a right to prevent her." To this, Stuart "stated in French that said Mary Taylor Stuart was my wife" and that "while I retained life no one would either take or keep her from me."

According to Stuart, "Francois N. Annance then said in a blustering manner common with most Indians that such was the law ... and that no one had a right or would take her out of his room, on which of a sudden and before he could make use of his Pistols I seized him by both arms & called to the men to secure him." First, however, Stuart "aimed a blow at him and as a justice due both to myself and the unfortunate woman he has so grossly abused." The last was a bit of literary licence given that Stuart did not, by his own account, yet know what had occurred between Noel and Mary, whom Stuart now ordered to her room. Once Stuart did find out, it was, in his view, "but justice to say that ... she is now become perverse and a disgrace to her sex." Noel used the opportunity to hand over both Stuart's ring and Mary's notes to Stuart, as he had already told Mary he was going to do that evening if she refused him.

Noel's final surviving note to Mary, written two days later and the fifteenth and last in the series, made clear that she, not he, had broken off their relationship.

Fifteenth and final note to Mary Taylor, 9 February 1834

My dearest love.

Now the fatal die is cast and we part for ever. I suppose you heard me when I told him that I was determined to go away next March. If my heart bleeds I only blame myself for having loved an object which is not for me. I shall always remember with sorrow and tears those places which saw us once happy. Farewell, may you enjoy that happiness which you have refused me.

The fifteen notes narrate a sequence of actual and anticipated events. By the time of the earliest one that survives, celebrating the New Year, Noel and Mary were comfortably intimate. At least from his perspective, the relationship was meant to endure past his intended departure as soon as the breakup of the ice made it possible for boats to run, and he had reason to believe that Mary was receptive to their leaving together. Noel wrote and acted as he did out of his own self-interest but also, it is possible, out a genuine concern for Mary's wellbeing. The closing warning in the 15 January note that "he will abuse you again" indicates that, from Noel's perspective, desire was tinged with empathy for her physical self as he perceived it from her descriptions to him. Over the course of the notes, Noel became increasingly exasperated with Mary's response to his overtures and calls to action, but he did not give up on her.

Nobody was without culpability. By her own admission Mary Taylor was in a physical relationship with Noel from sometime in November, which she could easily have escaped by alerting Stuart. Her later claim that Noel had forced himself upon her was what Stuart wanted to hear, but given the relationship's duration of over two months, something more was occurring. It was not a case of Noel beseeching Mary in words alongside deeds but rather a written correspondence of which unfortunately only one side survives. James Hargrave, who eight years earlier had fancied and then abandoned Mary Taylor, was not unsympathetic to her acting as she did, "poor Mary having found herself unable to resist the manly attractions of Annance."[34]

Noel's motives are not readily intuited. Mary Taylor was obviously an appealing woman, and he fell for her. He let go. He dared. Even as he did so, he could have been looking to get his own back with Stuart, who clearly resented having been asked to treat him as a gentleman rather than as the lowly Indigenous person he perceived him to be.

The couple's discovery dropped whatever pretenses to gentility Stuart had previously displayed toward someone from his perspective unworthy of such treatment by virtue of his indigeneity. According to his addendums respecting the notes, he had back in December forbidden Mary to talk to Noel on the grounds he was "a thief and nothing more," a charge he later sought to demonstrate by having HBC supplies meticulously counted out in the hope of finding disparities. Without much success, Stuart also claimed that Noel, whom he repeatedly characterized as an "Abinekie Indian," had been out to kill him, as evidenced by his practice of wearing pistols. Both men walked in George Simpson's shadow, which likely exacerbated the tension between them.

AFTERMATH

The relationship having been found out, Noel apologized for his actions to Stuart, who was having none of it, writing two weeks later how "I will now unless something very particular discontinue in future to soil the journal with the name of Annance or anything that regards him."[35] Three weeks hence, on 18 March, the annual spring express went off to York Factory and "with it the Blackguard Annance."[36]

Despite Noel Annance again prior to his departure, as he had done earlier, apologizing to John Stuart in line with his gentility, the deed was done. Stuart dispatched his version of events to a fellow Scots chief trader on the same outgoing express as took Noel away with the undoubted intention that it would become the stuff of gossip. Stuart was more candid than earlier in acknowledging not only that Mary had previously grown apart from him but also that she "fell over head and ears in love" with Noel: "The poor infatuated victim of delusion retired publicly into the bed chamber of that vile Abenaki, the abominable Annance, under a written promise he would both protect her and turn me out of the House." To ensure nothing more happened, Stuart had in the aftermath deposited Mary at Fort Liard "until open water," being the time of Noel's departure.[37]

In his retrospective account, Stuart at one and the same time bragged about his physical prowess before Noel, whom he deemed inherently inferior to himself by virtue of his indigeneity, and was anxious as to Simpson's perspective:

> Like most Indians he is blustering in words, like all Indians also, he shrank into himself when he saw the danger was evident and before him and he is now leaving the District – not because he seduced my wife – but because he either neglected or refused to perform every duty I assigned him, threatened my own life – and is both a thief and a villain, altogether unfit for this part of the country. I do not know what their mightiness will think of the matter – but if they side with the Abenaki I am certain that in the eyes of the public it will do no great credit either to them or to the company.[38]

From his own perspective, Stuart was more determinedly racist than he feared Simpson and the others might be.

Stuart had good reason to fret over the outcome, for HBC head George Simpson essentially washed his hands of events, as he informed the two men on 4 July 1834. No question exists but that Simpson was biased against both of them but more so it seems against Stuart. Writing to Stuart, Simpson was almost brutal:

> I have to acknowledge your letter of 15th of March, which has been laid before the Council, and it is with much concern I have to say I have not heard one solitary opinion favourable to your management of the affairs of McKenzie's river. With regard to the differences which have existed between you and F.N. Annance Clerk, we must decline taking any cognizance of them, from the various documents we have perused, the details of which are most disgusting and disgraceful, it would appear these differences have arisen out of private or family broils, totally unconnected with public business under our management. You bring several grave charges against that person, and he, in turn, brings many serious charges against you; both are unsupported by evidence.[39]

Stuart was nonetheless granted the furlough due him.

Simpson's letter to Noel attests to his longstanding enmity toward him: "You have for some years past been a most troublesome useless servant to the Hon'ble Company." On a gentler note, the letter informed Noel that a bill was being returned unpaid that he had on 10 March drawn under pressure from Stuart "in favour of Mary Taylor Stuart, per £250" but had later protested against "on the ground that it was exhorted from you 'under most awful threats.'"[40] Not to be undone, Stuart would pursue the debt while on leave in London on the grounds the HBC had reneged on paying up.

The little drama did not take long to become the talk of HBC officers, just as the actions of George Simpson and others had done over the past decade. James Hargrave, being a recently promoted chief factor at the HBC's North American headquarters of York Factory, was centrally involved, as he described:

> A discovery & war in miniature was the result, attended by all the
> usual accompaniments of arms, personal violence, imprisonment,
> & guards. Both parties filed Bills of accusation before [the HBC
> annual] Council; – both most voluminous, minute in detail &
> broadly expressed. It fell my lot to entertain & by reading them in
> Council, & I speak seriously when I say that I believe in conse-
> quence I never spoke so much *Parody* in all my life together, –
> composed of all topics from simple fornication up to the unheard
> of charge of a husband committing a rape on his own wife. But to
> avoid this dirt, – let me hasten to the end.[41]

Despite the good time had by all, no action was taken by the HBC officers present: "The Council declined interfering in what they justly considered a private charge."[42] It is tempting to speculate that the HBC governing council's decision to consider the Fort Simpson happenings a private matter had as much to do with some others' similar behaviour as it did with the determination that a larger policy had not been breeched.

John Stuart and Noel Annance were left to their own devices. The consequence was a litany of claims that were ongoing when Hargrave wrote in August 1834:

Both parties are hastening out, & both breathing threats of fire & revenge, the one for seducing of what the owner says he considered "his legal wife before God & man," the other spouting about arranging imprisonment, personal violence including an assault for the purpose of castration, and bolstered up with charges of robbery (obtaining signatures of Bills in favour of the seduced) for the full amount of Annance's means by threats & violence. The details would fill a volume – but the upshot is at present that both have full permission to leave the country & the result may be that our unfortunate character for Morals will yet receive a deeper dye by this exposure of the acts of two worthless & degraded fools.[43]

Hargrave considered Stuart was not about to abandon Mary Taylor, at least not immediately: "I ever yet would not wonder to see A[e]sop & his Sposa come out lovingly as ever in the lap of the Portage Boats, if I may so judge from his language regarding her throughout ... where she is described as 'contaminated in body but not in mind.'"[44] Four months later, Hargrave reported how "Old Stuart ... came out to the portage, as I suspected, with Mary more loving than ever."[45] According to Sylvia Van Kirk, Stuart decided to sever the relationship when in the next year, 1835, he travelled to Scotland on what would become an extended leave due to illness, whereupon he made financial provisions for her and freed her to find another attachment as long as it was a white man. Several years later, Stuart changed his mind, persuading Mary to join him in Scotland with the promise of a church marriage, on which he then reneged despite her adopting European dress and manners. She refused to accommodate to his half-measure, and he arranged for her to be returned home in the spring of 1838.[46] Hearing the news, her still single, onetime suitor James Hargrave approved of her pluck: "I cannot help admiring the spirit of my old friend Mary in her resolution of separating from Old Aesop when she found he boggled at the Noose Matrimonial. In that he was a fool – for with all her slips aside in this land – she was every way worthy of having this justice done her by him."[47] Mary eventually moved in with her brother Tom and his family by one of George Simpson's discards.[48]

Noel's departure from Fort Simpson on the March 1834 express took him away from the far part of the continent that had been his home for a decade and a half.[49] Simpson had given him a choice of working out the final year of his contract, which would have been at Oxford House in today's northeastern Manitoba, or returning "to Canada, by the last canoe of the season."[50] He opted for the latter, it taking another two years for him to settle accounts with the HBC.[51]

TO SUM UP

George Simpson shadowed that northern winter in which Noel Annance let go. The HBC head's earlier actions respecting Noel, Fort Simpson's head John Stuart, and the Taylor sisters hung over a sequence of events echoing Simpson's own behaviour. Whereas with Simpson it was tolerated because he was the man in charge, with Noel it gave the excuse for naming him the Indigenous person he already was in some others' minds, certainly in that of Simpson and Stuart. As for Noel's motivation, the notes do not tell us with certainty whether he acted with his heart, out of frustration, for revenge, or just out of physical need and desire. What the notes do is bring us just a little closer to his versatility as a writer and uniquely so to his humanity.

In the aftermath of that winter's drama at remote Fort Simpson, Noel Annance acted the gentleman John Stuart would not have him be. He twice apologized for the wrong he had done Stuart in attempting to entice away Mary Taylor. Noel behaved badly, and he knew it. His higher education as a gentleman entailed the obligation to apologize, be it at Moor's and Dartmouth or in the far north.

The two apologies brought to an end a major chapter in the life of Noel Annance. Ever since leaving Dartmouth College over two decades earlier, he had sought acceptance as a gentleman consistent with his higher education who, by the way, happened to be Indigenous. He had repeatedly dared in the effort to make it so. The façade he had erected around himself, he must have now realized, was just that. He did not belong.

PART THREE

Contesting Indigenous Exclusion

Back home by the end of 1834, Noel Annance thereafter lived outwardly as an Abenaki person.[1] Just as he had earlier sought to pursue
Indigenous inclusion as the gentleman he had been educated to become, he now contested Indigenous exclusion, with writing the instrument of his renewed vigour. Abenaki daring again came to the fore.
Aspects of Noel's life over the next third of a century, to his death
in 1869, are tracked in chapters 6, 7, and 8, with their larger setting
introduced here.

Noel Annance had been away a decade and a half, but as far as
Canada's Indigenous peoples were concerned, he might never have
left. The Colonial Office in faraway London still anticipated Indigenous peoples intermingling on their own terms with newcomers, its
counterparts in Canada giving priority to white interests and thereby
to exclusion and dispossession. Neither took into consideration what
Indigenous peoples might have wanted for themselves.

Owing to what Michel Lavoie and Denis Vaugeois aptly term
"l'impasse amérindienne," Indigenous peoples were in a holding pattern even as white society charged ahead.[2] Between the end of the War
of 1812 and Canadian Confederation in 1867, the white population
grew by roughly three times in Quebec to over 1 million and by
fifteen times in Ontario to 1.5 million. Indigenous numbers, in sharp
contrast, were in decline, by one measure from 15,000 in Lower
Canada and 28,000 in Upper Canada to 3,301 and 8,862 respectively
by 1844.[3] Indigenous peoples could for that reason alone be treated
with impunity as inconsequential objects to be acted upon to others'
advantage rather than as the fellow human beings they were and are.

To the extent that those in positions of authority agreed about
Indigenous peoples, it was in relation to Quebec, of which everyone

essentially washed their hands, both generally and during the administrative division of 1830–45 between Lower and Upper Canada. By the time of Noel's return home, the Colonial Office in London had disengaged: "It will however be vain to expect that the Canadian Priests, themselves an ignorant body, will encourage, or even not oppose, education among these people: and it is at the same time almost impossible for the Government to take any active steps in the matter without an appearance of interfering with religious liberty."[4]

The inability of the primarily Anglican officers of the Indian Department to come to terms with Quebec rebounded in few personnel. Put in charge of its Indigenous peoples in 1829 and serving almost singlehandedly to his retirement in 1857 was Duncan Campbell Napier, a former British army officer addressed as "Lieutenant Colonel" or "Colonel" and by title as the "Secretary of Indian Affairs for Quebec."[5] As of 1829 the number of personnel was roughly equal between Ontario and Quebec, but by 1844 that of the former had been expanded by three and that of the latter been reduced by four, with those remaining being a combination of Catholic priests, who received an annual stipend to manage individual communities, and local agents, who worked on commission. The dearth of officials would be justified by how "in Lower Canada no surrenders of Land have been made to the Crown, by the Indians, and consequently the Government is no further concerned in their affairs than to appoint or sanction the appointment of Agents, to receive the rents and seigneurial payments on account of their lands, and the tenants upon them, and also to receive and examine the accounts rendered by the agents, and to control their proceedings."[6] In this sense, as was the case earlier, the Royal Proclamation of 1763 did not apply.[7] Together with priests, local agents managed relations with the Indian Department, writing petitions and letters on behalf of Indigenous peoples and generally keeping a watching brief.[8] In lieu of salaries, agents kept 10 per cent of whatever they collected, which could be substantial. In the case of St Francis, with a population of around 350, the agent's annual commission in 1841 amounted to £263/8, being considerably higher than Napier's annual salary of £185.[9]

In like manner, whereas the annual Colonial Office grant between 1836 and 1843 held steady for Upper Canada at £13,380, it was cut for Lower Canada by a third from £6,000 to £4,000.[10] To this was added for Upper Canada annuities from earlier land sales of £4,000 to £5,000 per annum, which went into schooling and other projects deemed worthy by those in charge, whereas with Quebec there was nothing to be siphoned off.[11]

For the British government, which paid the bills but saw little happening in its preferred direction of Indigenous peoples intermingling with the newcomer population, economy increasingly came to the fore. It did so in respect both to the ongoing annual presents, which accounted for most of the monies allocated, and to the Indian Department, whose time seemed to be so taken up.[12] By Noel Annance's return, it was generally agreed the presents would gradually be restricted and discontinued, which meant in the Colonial Office's view that "the Indian Department may be greatly reduced, if not entirely abolished."[13]

Much as happened earlier with the 1828 Darling Report, in 1842 Governor General Sir Charles Bagot appointed a commission in the hopes of warding off unilaterally imposed change. The difference was that this time, unlike its predecessor, the Bagot Report of 1844 looked to Canada's populations intermingling, much as did the Colonial Office: "The true and only practicable policy of the Government, with reference to their interests, both of the Indians and the community at large, is to endeavor, gradually, to raise the said Tribes within the British Territory to the level of their white neighbours; to prepare them to undertake the offices and duties of citizens; and, by degrees, to abolish the necessity of its farther interference in their affairs."[14]

The Bagot Report was striking in its common sense: "To this there appears to be no insurmountable impediment. It is the universal testimony, that there is nothing in the character of the Indian race which is opposed to such a result. They possess all the higher attributes of the mind ... neither are they wanting in a desire to improve their condition."[15] In what was a tacit bow to the tiny, formally educated minority whose numbers included Noel Annance, "Many are acting as Missionaries and Interpreters among their brethren in Canada and the Territories of the Hudson's Bay Company, with credit to themselves, and infinite advantages to those under their charge. Most, if not all of those who have received a good education, are equal, in every respect to their white associates."[16]

As to why the preferred British policy respecting Canada's Indigenous peoples had for so long lain fallow, the Bagot Report affixed
blame squarely on the Indian Department, much as the Darling Report, with its different conclusion, had done. Since the War of 1812,
according to the earlier 1828 report, "the officers of the department
have done little more than superintend the issue of presents, while the
more important object of keeping alive the affections of the Indians
to the Government, by a vigilant protection of their interests, and by
encouraging their disposition to settle into useful subjects, has been
altogether overlooked."[17]

The 1844 Bagot Report was scathing. Mandated by the Colonial
Office to "conciliate the good will of the several Indian Tribes, and
possess their confidence; attend to their endless representations, remedy their grievances or report them ... &c &c.," the Indian Department had long since become a holding operation. Rather than being
"somewhat in advance of the pressing necessities of the day" in respect to "the extensive and varied duties which it ought to preform,"
it displayed an "entire inadequacy to the present state of the Indians
and their property."[18]

Scholars attest to this damning assessment. According to Douglas
Leighton, Indian Department officials saw themselves first and fore-
most as jobholders. Very possibly "related to one another by blood,"
they were at best "narrow rather than bigoted, and discriminatory
rather than racist," and at worst "corrupt sycophants ... who
regarded their positions as little more than sinecures." Their "frustra-
tions and disappointment at the lack of rapid promotion to more
glamorous postings" rebounded on Indigenous peoples.[19] Due to
"massive corruption and incompetence in the Indian Department,"
Sidney Harring writes, "Indian policy was in shambles."[20] As to how
this situation was allowed to continue as it had and would, according
to Robert Surtees, the Indian Department's "looseness and confusion"
was masked by "the arrogance of the British officer," which most
officials had formerly been.[21]

The Bagot commissioners' scathing indictment did nothing to benefit Indigenous peoples but rather the reverse. For all that the Colonial
Office, as Harring stated, "was increasingly concerned that colonial
governments were potentially the instruments of local forces that had

an interest opposed to indigenous rights," it had by now lost interest in Canada as compared with other parts of the empire.[22] The consequence was reduced Colonial Office funding, curtailed presents, cuts to the Indian Department, and an announcement in 1856 that all funding would be withdrawn within four years. Canada would be on its own.

In what appears in retrospect to have been a remarkable response, the Legislative Assembly of the Province of Canada turned for advice to the very Indian Department that had been so vehemently denounced. Superintendent General of Indian Affairs Richard Pennefather, who had overall charge of the Indian Department, was appointed to chair a committee comprising a long-time Indian Department employee and a government administrator, both based in Ontario, then known as Canada West.[23] The future of Canada's Indigenous peoples was turned over to the very same entity responsible for their predicament.

The result was predictable. The three commissioners disagreed with the majority of the responses they had solicited from missionaries, who were the nearest outsiders to be involved on a day-to-day basis with Indigenous peoples. Well over half of the two dozen who were queried, Protestant and Catholic, hoped for the intermingling of populations.[24] A Church of England missionary recalled "having during the first years of my connection with the Indians, been strongly in favour of their isolation from white settlements," but "the experience of many years has convinced me that such isolation is not the best mode of securing the desired results."[25] A Methodist preacher did not equivocate: "Give them an English education in religious principles, encourage them to adopt English customs and habits, and give them all the privileges of 'bona fide' British subjects."[26] A pair of Church of England missionaries considered that "the best mode of promoting the moral, intellectual and social improvement of the Indians" was "to treat them as we do the white people, and to let them see that we do not look [on] them as degraded or inferior."[27]

Catholic missionaries responded similarly, one of them describing "manners and customs, which differ but little from those of their neighbours."[28] Joseph Maurault, the priest based in Noel Annance's home village of St Francis, was fervent: "Let them no more be considered as minors, &c. in the eye of the Law, enable them to hold property, and they will then be respected. Soon they will have sympathies and interests in common with the whites, and make equal strides in advancement with them." More specifically, "the Abenakis are, as a rule, more intelligent than the Canadians."[29] The commissioners were having none of it: "We confess we are unable to agree with the recommendations of several of these Gentlemen, that the Indians generally should be at once placed on the footing of their white neighbours."

Determined to protect what were referred to as "white" interests and to justify the Indian Department in its attitudes and actions, the 1858 Pennefather Report was premised on isolation and separation aimed at exclusion and dispossession. It is hard not to perceive the report's recommendations, which two decades later would become the basis for a century of Canadian government policy, as retribution for the scorn earlier heaped on the Indian Department. Three aspects of the report were uppermost.

First, in respect to land, which had been an explicit component of its mandate, the Pennefather Report was all about dispossession. It turned on its head the Royal Proclamation of 1763. Lands not expressly given up were now described as "Indian Reserves," being in size "disproportionate to the numbers and means of the bands residing in them." More land needed to be removed, and with white interests uppermost and in apparent disregard of the Royal Proclamation, the commissioners did "not see that it would be absolutely necessary in most cases to obtain the consent of the Indians to a surrender, where such surrender appeared to be clearly for their benefit." In their view, "the Aborigines have been hitherto treated to a certain extent as Sovereign Princes, as Lords of a soil which yet they were not possessors of."

This state of affairs would no longer obtain: "In cases where the Indians obstinately refuse to accede to any terms of surrender, we are of opinion that gentle means of coercion might be applied without prejudice to their real interests." To act otherwise was unthinkable: "A country situated as Canada is ... not adapted for locking up large tracks of fertile land for the sake of a few individuals, who are too idle to reap the benefit of them." This direction would be encouraged, when the Province of Canada took over from the Colonial Office in

1860, by the absorption of the Department of Indian Affairs into the Crown Lands Department, charged with the sale of "surplus" Indigenous lands.

Second, to put the first recommendation into practice, the Pennefather Report stipulated for Indigenous peoples the single occupation of very small-scale farming, a measure serving to keep them out of the way. It was even then limited, conditional, and to be surveilled:

> Each head of a family shall be allotted a farm not exceeding 25 acres in extent, including an allowance of woodland where they can obtain fuel; and that for such farm he shall receive a license giving exclusive occupation of the same to him and his heirs for ever, on condition of clearing a certain number of acres in a given time. These documents should be so drawn as to prevent the Indians from disposing of their interest in the land, except with the consent of the government; and might be revocable for proof of habitual intemperance, or for a continual neglect of the same.

Third, the Pennefather Report broke up family life both within and between generations. Indigenous women were to be treated differently from Indigenous men in respect to marriage: "An Indian woman marrying a white man loses her rights as a member of the tribe, and her children have no claim on the lands or moneys belonging to their mother's nation." Offspring were to be separated from their parents and vice versa. The report parroted the view of an influential Indian Department stalwart who, on being asked by the commission whether it was possible for Indigenous peoples to change their ways, had responded, "I do not, except in cases where the child is from its infancy separated from the natives and educated; and even until the third or fourth remove, the character of the individual is often marked by indecision, and the impatience of restraint that predominates in the blood of the aborigines."[30] These recommendations would two decades later become the basis for the Indian Act, in operation with amendments into the present day.

The attitude underlying the Pennefather report explains why Indigenous peoples had for so long been left to languish. It was within this setting that Noel Annance now sought to counter Indigenous exclusion as he perceived it. The role played by his captivity inheritance in doing so is interrogated in chapter 6, the critical importance given to land is described in chapter 7, and Noel's search for belonging as the person he still considered himself to be is treated in chapter 8. To know how the story turns out in respect to Canada's Indigenous peoples is not to deny agency to Noel Annance.

6

Returning Home to Captivity Narratives' Legacies

Back home by late 1834, Noel Annance reset his life. Since leaving Dartmouth College two decades earlier, the erudite scholar and some-time romantic, as revealed in his 1824 Hudson's Bay Company journal and love notes a decade later, had lived outwardly as a highly educated person who happened to be Indigenous. Now it would be as an Indigenous person who happened to be highly educated.

Pursuing Indigenous inclusion as the gentleman he had been educated to become, Noel had been caught out by others' attitudes toward persons perceived as inferior to themselves. They were appraised not by virtue of who they were but by their indigeneity. Returning to captivity narratives' legacies, Noel was set apart by his higher education, which made him, from some perspectives, suspect. Writing became his tool of choice to contest Indigenous exclusion to the advantage of both himself and others around him. With his pen, he dared time and again.

WRITING FOR CHANGE

In one very important sense, Noel Annance might never have been away. As he must have soon realized on returning home, whereas Quebec – particularly Montreal, through which he likely passed on his way back – was changing, St Francis and the Abenaki people were seemingly stuck in place.

For this reason and generally, from his return home in late 1834 to his death in 1869, Noel Annance corresponded with officials in the Department of Indian Affairs and others who had little apparent interest in effecting change. He all the same persisted in attempting to nudge them into seeing the errors of their ways by his lights. In doing so, he remained the officer and gentleman he was, treating others with respect and meriting, if rarely a resolution, usually a response. To the extent

Catholic Church, Montreal.

ILLUSTRATION 9
Montreal, 1834, at the time of Noel Annance's return home,
by Robert Auchmuty Sproule

that Noel belonged, he did so whenever he put pen to paper, knowing his recipients would, if not necessarily agreeing with the content, understand his words as he wrote them down. Literacy's promise held.

Responses to Noel's letters were generally speedy. Noel was able to act as he did, sometimes effectively or almost so, due in part to a postal system that made it possible to get a response within a month from the Department of Indian Affairs in Montreal. A letter posted from "Indian village of St. Francis 20th March 1838" was noted as "Received 26th March" and answered "28 March 1838."[1] Whatever was his means of access to the newspapers and other printed materials of the day, Noel's everyday knowledge of current events, which grounded his correspondence, was considerable.

Noel was not alone among his Indigenous contemporaries in his facility with writing and reading. He shared St Francis's captivity inheritance with numerous others similarly educated who returned home from school comfortable in English and almost certainly also in French and Abenaki. The parallel consequence of this cohort's schooling in a Protestant setting at Moor's Charity School and possibly also Dartmouth College was their being perceived as outsiders both in St Francis, premised as it was on the French language and Catholicism, and in the future Canada, which was determined to pursue Indigenous exclusion.

ILLUSTRATION 10
Abenaki scene, 1848, the other aspect of Noel Annance's return home, by Cornelius Krieghoff

ILLUSTRATION 11
Quebec Royal Mail, 1848, which made it possible for Noel
to correspond rapidly with government officials and others,
by Amelia Frederica Dyneley

Whether or not this cohort realized that their writing for change was doomed to fail, they made the attempt. None did so more determinedly than Noel Annance, along with his second cousin Peter Paul Osunk-hirhine, who while at Moor's had been snared by its Protestant religious imperative and had returned home a half-decade before Noel to ply his craft as a preacher and teacher.

SETTLING DOWN

Noel Annance did and did not return to his immediate family. Whereas his parents had died, his mother in 1808 and his father in 1826, and his two brothers, Louis and Joseph, had gone their separate ways, three sisters lived nearby. Noel's eldest sister, Marie Josephte, had married

Pierre Wasaminet, a War of 1812 veteran and among those receiving land in the 1805 grant.[2] The two others were married into the Portneuf clan, Noel's older sister Marie Marguerite to Simon, who had also been among those granted land in 1805, and his younger sister, Angelique, to Ignace, who had been Noel's comrade in the War of 1812 and in the fur trade. Having departed the Pacific Northwest at the time the Hudson's Bay Company took charge in 1821, possibly due to a lingering war wound, Ignace Portneuf had wed Angelique a year later, to have a large family together.[3] By the time of Noel's return, Ignace Portneuf was grand chief of the St Francis Abenakis and would long remain so. Among other relatives were Simon Annance, whom Noel had recommended to Moor's, and Charles Annance, who had fought at Châteauguay as a regular soldier, or "warrior," and had settled down in St Francis a decade or more prior to Noel's return.[4]

As indicated by the return addresses on his letters, Noel itinerated over time between several locales: St Francis; Durham, where his father had been among those receiving a land grant in 1805; Long Island in the St Francis River, which had been in the family since his childhood; and other nearby locations where he may have had employment. He preferred Long Island. Noel lexplained how "in the year 1799 my late father made a small clearing and planted some potatoes on Long Island, and in 1802 moved his family unto it, built a house, barn &c and we lived there till my late father was appointed schoolmaster for the village of St. Francis but the farm was always occupied by some of the family."[5] In 1809 the governor-in-chief of British North America had granted Noel's father a twenty-one-year lease, to expire on 8 February 1830, which he had in 1814 transferred to Noel.[6]

It is unclear whether Noel's far west son, Archibald, born in 1825, returned with him to St Francis or arrived separately, but he was integral to Noel's settling down. Likely for that reason, almost immediately on arriving, Noel raised the issue of the Long Island lease verbally with Governor General Lord Aylmer, to whom he had earlier sent the petition for Pacific Northwest land. Noel was introduced to him by the governor's aide-de-camp, Frederick George Heriot, under whom he had served in the War of 1812.[7] Whether or not they also discussed the earlier request, in respect to Long Island, "I was promised by Lord Aylmer when governor of this province that I should get a grant of it."[8] Noel acted on that assurance: "In 1835 I built a new house on it, and it has always been cultivated either by myself or by some one for me. It contains 40 acres clear."[9]

Noel completed the settling-down process by finding himself a wife. The elusive Mary Taylor perforce a memory, on 10 September 1836 in St Francis, the now forty-five-year-old "Noël François Annance Sauvage Abenquis," according to the Catholic record, wed fifteen-year-old Marie Josephte Nagajoa, whose mother was a Gill and thereby comfortably related.[10] As to how they might have gotten together, Marie's older sister Marie Marguerite had a year earlier married Noel's cousin Simon Annance, whom he had earlier recommended for admission to Moor's. Noel and Marie Josephte's family came to include, according to baptismal and other records, Pierre (b. 1841), Marie Victoire (b. 1846), Julie (b. 1847), who died at age thirteen, Lucinda (b. 1850), Charles Emery (b. 1854), Noel (b. 1855), Marie (b. 1856), who died young, Anne Marie (b. 1860), Marie Anne (b. 1861), who died in infancy, and Absalom (b. 1864). Unmentioned in Noel's letters, his wife and children are not followed here.

AN ENDURING CAPTIVITY INHERITANCE

Noel Annance returned not only to a family but also to a community. St Francis had never been that large, earlier 1,000 at most and now roughly 350 in population.[11] From Indian Department and white outsiders' perspectives, the community had little to recommend it. The 1828 Darling Report dismissed St Francis out of hand as "a small village of the rudest construction, their habitations consisting chiefly of square huts built of thick bark, which, though certainly better than the ordinary wigwams, have little resemblance to the habitations of civilized life."[12] A much cited topographical dictionary of Lower Canada published in 1832 was cutting: "The village consists of about 40 cabins or houses of wood indifferently built. These converted Indians subsist upon their own lands in the seigniory by raising, in their peculiarly careless manner, some Indian corn and potatoes, and by rearing poultry and pigs; they sometimes increase their means by fishing and sometimes by hunting parties." That it was such did not much matter, given that Indigenous peoples, according to this account, had been "nearly exterminated."[13]

The Indian Department's expectation of deference toward its actions or inactions held almost as a matter of course. Indicative was a governing council held in St Francis in 1836 at which a government official addressed the chiefs as "Brothers," as opposed to the more usual "Children," to which they nonetheless responded, "we have heard our Father's Words" and have a message for you to take back to "our Father at Quebec."[14] Less often, as in an exchange between two officials in the Indian Department concerning an upcoming visit to St Francis, those in charge were still referred to as "Chiefs and Warriors."[15] The written word in the form of petitions and letters was the preferred means of communication, which made it very tempting for the missionaries or local agents who did the crafting to massage the contents in their own interest. As Mathieu Chaurette astutely concludes about one such Quebec instance, "despite the false accusations and the petition being falsified by the missionary, the government closed its eyes to events."[16]

St Francis's captivity inheritance contrasted sharply with outsiders' perceptions. Its consequence was that a large proportion of its residents were related not in the crisscross way that characterized many Indigenous and also non-Indigenous communities of the day but by virtue of, as did both Noel Annance and his wife, sharing common progenitors in Samuel Gill and Rosalie James. As of 1866 long-time local priest Joseph Maurault counted 952 living descendants from the onetime captives, not all of them resident in St Francis.[17]

Among the 952 descendants, 213 had the Gill surname, sometimes written as "Guille" or "Guile," and were white or mostly white by descent. According to Maurault, of the other 739 descendants, perforce part or mostly Indigenous, 318 lived among the Abenakis and 421 among French Canadians.[18] Two decades later, in 1887, according to great-great-grandson and family historian Charles Gill, "there is hardly anyone among the Abenakis of St. Francis not descended from Samuel Gill."[19] Having interrogated Abenaki family history, Christopher Roy described in 2012 how "almost every Abenaki person I know descends from Samuel Gill, a white child taken captive," being thereby, as had Charles Gill, sadly neglectful of Rosalie James's causative role.[20]

The consequence was, as an Indian Department official explained in 1836, that St Francis Abenakis were "rather more civilized (at least the greater part of them) than the other Tribes of the District."[21] One of the ways that St Francis was distinctive related to language, an official visiting there three decades later explaining, "I opened the proceedings by reading the charges in French and English. Some Indians understand English better than French, others understand French better than English, but they all prefer being addressed in their own Abenakis tongue."[22]

It was also the case that by the time of Noel Annance's return, St Francis's formative captivity inheritance was no longer, to the extent it had ever been, a cohesive force. Two contingents among descendants were by their actions tearing the community apart.

THE GILL CONTINGENT

One group of descendants was centred on those carrying the Gill surname, who enjoyed the social and economic benefits of being Catholic and French-speaking in line with Quebec's character and of being wholly or mostly white at a time when Indigenous peoples were being set apart and excluded.[23] The group's composition went back to second-generation Gills, all perforce white by descent. Eldest son Joseph-Louis's offspring by his second marriage continued to be so, as did those of his two brothers, Francis and Robert, and then some of their children by virtue of their unions with whites, and so on through the generations.[24] Such families increasingly engaged in farming and other economic activities that drew on their own resources. The most prominent of the white Gills, in a line of succession from Joseph-Louis Gill's second marriage, descended from his son Thomas, whose children, Catholic and educated in French as a first language, were said to have no longer spoken Abenaki.[25] In 1830 Thomas's eldest son, Ignace, opened a store whose presence sharpened local Abenakis' sense of their being used economically by the Gills. In the fashion of the day, he permitted at least some customers to run up bills, thus putting them under obligation to him.[26]

As Thomas Charland describes in his close history of St Francis, a consequence was that in 1832, prior to Noel's return, "the savages, tired of the authority of the Gill family over the tribe, petitioned the

Government to have it removed from the [Indian] Departmental census," used to determine eligibility to receive the traditional annual gifts.[27] The process of delisting white Gills as Abenakis would take some time, given how integrated they were into the community. The Gill surname accounted in the 1822 St Francis Indian census for 14 of 91 family heads, in 1831 for 14 of 76, and in 1841 for 13 of 85, but owing to their delisting, it was absent among the 90 family heads in the subsequent census of 1844 and among the 112 in the census of 1850.[28] The surname disappeared from the lists even though in 1844, as he had done earlier, Thomas Gill's brother Augustin certified the census, their brother Louis was for twenty-two years the Indian Department's local agent, and one of them or some other Gill acted as postmaster.[29]

That the Gills no longer belonged may have no longer mattered to most of them from their perspectives. Even as Ignace Gill continued to operate his store, he acquired hunks of the Durham land that had been granted the seventeen Abenaki families in 1805 on the way to his constructing the village of L'Avenir on part of it.[30] He built on his accomplishments to enter politics and in 1854 won election to the Parliament of the Province of Canada, only to be defeated seven years later amid charges, possibly emanating from his still remembered captivity inheritance, that Abenaki women had been dressed in greatcoats and made to vote for their "cousin."[31] Ignace Gill's son Charles would become the family historian.

Other Gills found it economically expedient to continue to act as though they were Abenakis, to the extent of serving as chiefs in the pattern of their forefather, confident no one had the authority to challenge their doing so.[32] The 1840s and 1850s saw repeated complaints respecting timber cutting on St Francis lands and cattle grazing in "the Indian common" by Gills "not considered as Indians." Long-time sachem Joseph-Louis Gill's grandsons by his second white wife were said to be the principal culprits.[33]

In typical fashion, one of the St Francis chiefs' numerous complaints "against the Guille family," this at the beginning of the 1840s, was passed on to Augustin Gill for him to request that "all the children of the elder Guilles, will desist from committing any species of degradation whatsoever on the Domain of the Abenaquois Indians of St. Francis."[34] Following Abenakis' stymied attempt to go through the courts to get action, one of those in opposition lamented, "They do with us just as they please and have no fear, they say what can the Indians do. They cannot go to law, for they have no means and the government will not spend money for them."[35] The disputes ended only because, by the late 1860s, "there is not now much wood."[36]

Other descendants carrying the Gill surname argued that "they are part Indians and therefore have right" to act as they wanted, in response to which seven of the principal St Francis chiefs turned in 1845 to the Indian Department official responsible for Quebec, Duncan Campbell Napier, for advice respecting Indigenous men with white wives:[37] "The Chiefs apprehend a danger of losing a part of the property belonging to the tribe if the same rights and privileges be extended to the children of Canadian women married to Indians as those whose parents are both Indians. Can such half Indians be considered as Indians if they should in future follow the example of their father in taking Canadian wives."[38]

The passage in 1850 of land legislation defining "Indians" as being "all persons intermarried with any such Indians and residing amongst them, and the descendants" precipitated a follow-up letter of the same year protesting how it would permit "whites to be considered Indians on account of their having some Indian blood, or married with the Indians, or adopted," as the Gills considered themselves to be.[39] The dispute, along with similar complaints from Quebec Iroquois communities, presaged, and was likely responsible for, the Pennefather recommendations removing rights as "Indians" from Indigenous women married to non-Indigenous men, which would in due course be incorporated into the Indian Act, in force with amendments into the present day.

The 1850 letter protesting the land legislation is unique for being explicitly grounded in St Francis's captivity narratives as common knowledge, so much so that they did not need to be elucidated. The chiefs' letter, whose principal author was Noel's brother-in-law Ignace Portneuf, baldly narrated the community's captivity narratives as a principal factor in the course of events, albeit not wholly accurately as to chronology:

We hope our Father, the Governor, will consider the matter for our main difficulty is from such persons and will always be, if there be no remedy. Now as soon as the Gills heard of the Bill, they immediately cry out that they are confirmed to have right in the Tribe, because, as they say, their great grand father and great grand mother were adopted by the Tribe; but it is not certain that they were adopted, for they were taken prisoners by the Indians in the revolutionary war between the English and the Yankees, so they were Yankees made captive by the Indians. Whether prisoners or captives can have the same right as adopted persons, if adopted persons must be considered as Indians by adoption, we are not able to judge.[40]

THE MOOR'S CONTINGENT

The second activist contingent among captivity descendants consisted of Abenakis who together with a couple of white Gills had been educated at Moor's, with its English-language Protestant ethos. Of the fifty-three Indigenous students who attended the school from 1774, when the first of those from St Francis arrived, including Noel's father, to its closure in 1856, twenty-eight, or over half, were from St Francis. Not only did all but one or two of them descend from the long-ago child captives, but, indicative of the limited options for educated young men perceived as Indigenous, most of them also returned to St Francis. Fully half of the twenty-eight Moor's students were roughly of Noel's generation, if mostly a bit younger, by virtue of studying there between 1800 and 1832.[41]

The Protestant ethos of Moor's did not initially challenge St Francis's Catholicism. The village's land base of 12,000 acres had been ceded in 1700 with the proviso that it contain a Catholic mission, and by inference its residents were Catholic. Although Noel's chiefly father had dared to utilize Protestant teaching materials, he had remained a Catholic, as did the community. The priest in charge at the time of Noel's return, despite his employment of the pejorative assumptions of the time, took pride in Catholicism's prominence among St Francis's residents:

They attend their religious duties very regularly, and from religious motives. The Christian Religion has alone reformed the manners of the Indians, who, before their conversion, were full of faults of every nature. The character of the Indians being light and haughty, it can only be kept in check by religion, which alone renders them docile. I see no improvement in the Indians as far as regards temporal things, since I have been with them; but as regards their spiritual concerns, their condition appears to me to leave nothing to be desired. I know of no heathens among the Abenaquois.[42]

By the time Noel returned in late 1834, the Protestant religious fervour that some earlier Moor's students as well as others educated elsewhere had brought back to their home communities was lapping at St Francis. Whereas Noel does not appear to have defined himself in religious terms, making up for lost time were three of his relatives who had returned during his absence in the fur trade.

Following a year at Moor's in 1815–16, Simon Annance, who from 1836 was Noel's brother-in-law as well as his cousin, had been ensnared by the Foreign Mission School established in Connecticut to educate Indigenous youth, initially mostly from the Hawaiian Islands and India, "for missionary labours among the heathens" – in other words, their own people.[43] On the death of Noel's father in 1826, Simon had sought to succeed his uncle as schoolmaster in St Francis, to be rejected by the local Catholic missionary due to an unspecified "character disorder," and had subsequently worked intermittently for the Hudson's Bay Company in Quebec.[44]

At Moor's from 1829 to 1831, James Joseph Annance then spent a year at Kimball Union Academy, a long-established boarding school, where he was the only "Indian" recorded through 1876.[45] James Joseph, whose precise relationship to Noel is unclear, subsequently attended Dartmouth for three years without graduating, to return home about the time Noel did.

The zealot of the trio was Peter Paul Osunkhirhine, whose career Stéphanie Boutevin has perceptively tracked and assessed.[46] While at Moor's in the mid-1820s, already a young adult, Osunkhirhine became determined to teach "my own people the religion of the Bible."[47] On returning home, he got himself appointed Francis Joseph Annance's successor at the local school at an annual salary of £20, whereupon he confided to the American Board of Commissioners for Foreign Missions in Boston, which also sustained him, how he started each day with "a lesson in the Bible."[48] In 1831 Osunkhirhine did a kind of end run by marrying the daughter of prominent St Francis chief Simon Obomsawin in a Catholic ceremony, to which faith he is said to have returned only long enough to snare her, all of which contributed to the opposition growing against him in St Francis.[49] Shortly thereafter, the local priest initiated a petition signed by thirty prominent Abenakis, all but two with their marks, demanding Osunkhirhine's dismissal as teacher.[50] Napier concurred with the proviso that he be employed as "interpreter to the Abenaquois Tribe (being I believe the only Indian of St. Francis, who is conversant with the English language)."[51]

Osunkhirhine was not to be mollified, and persuaded his Boston sponsors to fund an independent English-language Protestant school in St Francis under his charge even as he also got himself ordained and financially supported as a Congregational minister. Thereupon he proceeded, despite widespread community opposition, to erect a missionary-funded chapel on Abenaki land. Whereas Noel would be ever the outsider, Osunkhirhine by virtue of his religiosity stood in his own mind on solid ground. In one important sense, he was justified in doing so, being at the time one of only five "native preachers" supported worldwide by the American Board of Commissioners for Foreign Missions, two of the others preaching to the Cherokees in the southeastern United States and the other two in Ceylon.[52]

LOOKING TO MAKE A LIVING

The captivity narratives' legacies soon caught up the returning Noel Annance. Looking to make a living, he ran afoul of the plenitude of prohibitions regulating all aspects of Indigenous life that whites across the future Quebec and Ontario were turning to their advantage. According to an Indian Department account, "Mr. Noel Annance did in the year 1836 keep a sort of a grocery shop in the village of St Francis." To compete with Ignace Gill, who was not only the local storekeeper but also a recently appointed justice of the peace, was to invite retribution. Noel had been, in his words, "threatened with persecution and banishment if we dared set up a shop for trade in the village," yet his complaint went nowhere on the grounds he had violated a ban on "the sale of liquor to Indians."[53] Gill's store would continue to operate to 1850.

Noel was similarly stymied in respect to teaching on the pattern of his father. The two religious constituencies now active in St Francis gave priority to outdoing each other at the cost of the schooling of the next generation. The Indian Department funded a Catholic missionary priest in each of Quebec's principal Indigenous communities, including St Francis, at the rate of, as of 1837–38, £46/8/6 a year, being over twice the salary of its teacher, which was £20/16/o.[54] The local priest, who took his responsibilities seriously, was not about to consider as a teacher anyone tainted by Protestantism, given the recent experience with Osunkhirhine and especially as long as he remained religiously active in the community. Noel had been wed in the Catholic church and, as far as can be determined, would not until late in life embrace Protestantism, but that mattered for naught.

In August 1836 Noel attempted to rewind the situation to his advantage, and also to that of St Francis from his perspective, by having Osunkhirhine removed elsewhere. Noel used his knowledge of the fur trade to make the argument for greater need among remote Indigenous peoples for a Protestant missionary than in long-established St Francis. To make his case as persuasive as possible, he underestimated distances between locations. Whatever the mix of motives, the letter Noel penned to the missionary group that sustained his second cousin exuded a self-confidence consistent with his gentility.

Letter to American Board of Commissioners for Foreign Missions, 2 August 1836

                                                    Sherbrooke, 2 Aug 1836
To
        the Rev. D. Greene
            Dear Sir
                    In conversing the other day with my relative Peter P. Osunkhirhine, he made me understand that he had been ordained minister for foreign missions, and that St Francis village was to be the scene of his labor and I suggested to him what a grand thing it would be for him to be sent to the North West where I had been, and proclaim the Gospel and establish Christianity there! There can be no difficulty in establishing missionary

stations between Fort de Prairie [the future Edmonton] and Cumberland House [northern Saskatchewan] – an extent of country of about four hundred miles, inhabited by numerous tribes of Indians, much given to superstition and ready to receive any kind of information on the subject of religion. I have been fourteen years in the fur trade of the Northwest, over ran the Columbia River country, north and south; came across the Rocky Mountains several times, of course I know the state of the Natives on those countries. If the Board for foreign missions were disposed to favor an enterprise so vast, so grand and so important, I would communicate with them, and lay the plans and explain the whole country to them. The distance is not great: not more than perhaps one hundred miles from Red River colony which is much known. My friend Peter is industrious and active and it is pity that he should be kept where he is, teaching two or three children and as many old women – The fact is that the Indians of St. Francis have been in a civilized state hundreds and odd years and have been reared up in the Roman Catholic Religion, and are so deeply rooted in that faith it is of no use to try to convert them. Not only the Priest, but the chiefs are opposed to the establishment of Protestantism among them. The Priests have too much influence over the minds of the Indians – no set of Christians are more successful in making themselves respected, feared, and revered than the Roman Catholic clergy. For those reasons I am of opinion that Peter would do more good by going among the poor unenlightened savages of the north than to be contending against the combinations and intrigues of the bigoted priests and incur the displeasure and hatred of his own countrymen. There is more certainty to be stationary there, but there is more glory to venture into the regions of the wilderness and announce the glad tidings of the Gospel – I now will act independent – but I told Peter that I would go with him, and only return when I see his church planted among the lost tribes of Indians.

I am, Rev Sir,

with profound respect

your most hum^{ble}

obdt Servant

N.F. Annance

P.S. The country abounds in provisions – thousands of deer and millions of buffalos – and the H.B.Company who carry on the fur trade with the Indians have beautiful farms thro' out the country – I and Peter both live in the Indian village of St. Francis.

On the envelope:
The Rev. David Greene
Secretary of Foreign Missions
Boston
By the postmistress
of Mrs. Fisher

Note that received August 23 and answered Sept 22

Source: Noel Annance to David Greene, 2 August 1836, in Noel (N.F.) Annance, Correspondence, Houghton Library, Harvard University, American Board of Commissioners for Foreign Missions papers, 18.6.3, vol. 1, 183.

The American Board's response to Noel aligned with Osunkhirhine's optimistic reports to the missionary body: "It seems to us that as Osunkhirhine has made so good a beginning among his own people and is becoming so much interested in his work there, that it would be scarcely advisable for him to change his sphere of action at present. He has not expressed any desire himself, on the subject."[55] The Boston official appreciated hearing about the circumstances Noel described and hoped it would be possible to do something at some future date.

Learning from his Boston sponsors of Noel's letter, as indicated by his awareness of the secretary's misreading of the initials of Noel's first names in his response to him, Osunkhirhine was outraged. His strategy in replying to his sponsors was to discredit the messenger: "I learn that Mr. N. Annance who wrote to you for my removal, intends to write again, I will therefore let you know that he is in a pitiful condition, for he is unfortunately a man of no religion, who means to be more cunning than the priest, and all the rest of those who have attempted to remove me from the place."[56]

Noel kept a watching brief on Osunkhirhine. He and James Joseph Annance witnessed a petition of December 1836 from five prominent St Francis chiefs, including Osunkhirhine's Catholic father-in-law Simon Obomsawin, composed in French by the local priest, to be dispatched to the governor general of the Canadas. Not only did Osunkhirhine seek, in the petition's words, "to detach the children from the religion of their fathers and from the obedience and the subordination due to the Chiefs of the Nation," but he also openly scorned them, considering that "there is neither Chief nor Government which can command him." Respecting Osunkhirhine's school, "financed by a Society in the United States," the petitioners asked provocatively, "Is it intended to alienate the hearts of the savages from their God and their King?" The petition asserted with some historical justification, but an overstatement, that Osunkhirhine's erection of his chapel "would be to deprive the said Tribe of the property and the fiefs that it occupied in St. Francis since it was conceded and given to them on the express purpose that they had among them a Catholic Missionary to keep them in the exercise and profession of the said Religion, as it appears by the contract executed at Montreal before Maitre Adhemar in the year 1700."[57] The response to the petition was not located.

COALITION FOR CHANGE

Whatever may have been individuals' misgivings with each other, Osunkhirhine and his Moor's counterparts, including Noel Annance, soon came to consider that they had more to unite than to divide them and in early 1837 joined forces in what they deemed to be St Francis's betterment. Doing so pitted them against the local priest, almost all the chiefs, and Catholic French-speaking Gill descendants. Describing themselves as "not of the canadian part of the tribe, but the majority of the Indians," and including Noel's brother-in-law Grand Chief Ignace Portneuf, this coalition for change petitioned for a voice in local governance. Four of the St Francis chiefs were linked to the Gills, and the coalition requested that the "most unfit" among them be replaced by former Moor's, Kimball Union, and Dartmouth student "James Joseph Annance as Chief."[58]

The coalition for change would have been buoyed if its members had realized the Colonial Office was at about the same time lamenting similar circumstances to those troubling the St Francis cohort. According to an internal Colonial Office document of 1837,

> In Lower Canada many of the young men are employed in conducting Bateau, Rafts &c; & the women manufacture various ornamental articles for sale to the colonists. Their social state appears to be most deplorable. They enjoy but little opportunity of acquiring a knowledge of the Christian Religion, or the arts of civilized life. The instances are very rare, in which they have missionaries or schoolmasters resident amongst them – receiving only casual visits from those who are settled in their neighbourhood. The persons too who are devoted to their instruction appear to be little qualified for the task. Some schools were established in Lower Canada by the Gov[t] & by benevolent individuals which promised to effect much good. They were well attended at first by the Indian children but, owing to the opposition of the Catholic Priests occasioned partly by the pupils being taught in English, the schools were soon abandoned.[59]

It was, of course, a far cry from the Colonial Office's high-minded enunciations to action on the ground.

In retrospect, it was inevitable Indian Department officials would come down on the side of a principally illiterate status quo able to be managed in its own self-interest as opposed to change premised on higher levels of knowledge and understanding with the potential to rock its very comfortable boat. The petitioners were understandably distraught on learning that the official dispatched a few months later to examine the situation they had described "for the purpose of making some kind of report" did not alert them to his coming but met only with "the accused party" in the house of the Gill family member at the centre of their complaints before hastily departing.[60] The local priest may have played a role in ensuring that nothing ensued, apart from the complainants being set apart in the community with the acquiescence of the Indian Department.[61]

The petitioners sputtered along on their way to giving up. Their principal vehicle, they initially considered, was their literacy: "if the subject is not attended to, we shall be obliged to make it known abroad by publishing it in some of the public papers."[62] They truly believed that words on paper mattered.

In a follow-up petition to the governor general of the Canadas, wherein they referred to themselves in line with the expectations of the time as "dutiful children," they deplored what "we look upon as the most daring and nefarious attempt on civil liberty."[63] It was met wih an imperious response: "The Governor General is unable to discover that the Abenaquois Indians have any grounds for the complaint preferred in their petition."[64] James Joseph Annance and Osunkhirhine in particular were chastized for "having for these several years given trouble to the chiefs," and perhaps for that reason a possibly embittered James Joseph was reputed to say that Darmouth "spoiled a great many good Indians and made very poor white men."[65]

Official British government policy toward Indigenous peoples might have anticipated, in the words of the secretary of state for the colonies a couple of years earlier, their "Instruction in the Arts of the civilized Life, as the principal Object to be kept in view in our Intercourse with these Tribes," but its practice was a very different matter.[66] The petitioners were well aware of how Indian Department officials had targeted them. In response, James Joseph and Osunkhirhine, supported by Noel, petitioned defensively in March 1839 that "no future complaint against us will be believed by the Supt. [of Indian Affairs] before it is investigated and proved; because great injustice has been done us by the particularity of our Supt., not willing to investigate whether we have any grounds to support our complaints."[67]

DISSENSION FROM WITHIN

To the extent the coalition for change collapsed, as it did do, another factor at play was Osunkhirhine's ambivalence toward the others. He assumed, on the one hand, that they were "better able to help on account of their education" and, on the other, that they were thereby mocking him. Whereas he had a fairly plain schooling, having entered

Moor's by his own count at the age of "two and twenty," others had studied what he sometimes ridiculed as "the dead languages."[68] Osunkhirhine suspected that they "treat me as a foolish fellow ... saying that there is no harm to drink a little of the ardent spirits, as well as to be indulgent in harmless amusements, such as playing cards, or some other plays & peaceable dances." As to the reason, "they say that all those are not forbidden in the Bible, to any one who understands in original Greek."[69] They claimed, in Osunkhirhine's words, that he knew "nothing about Greek, therefore he cannot understand the Bible correctly," and that "his instruction is only to trouble & distract the minds of peaceable people, says the one who had studied the original tongues."[70] Given Osunkhirhine's zealotry and his inclination to "cut off from the church" that he headed anyone not measuring up to his exceedingly high expectations, he could, despite his deeply held religious convictions, be his own worst enemy.[71]

Osunkhirhine's ministry was from the perspective of outsiders sufficiently worthy that in 1840 Dartmouth College's president afforded it a visit. While there, he encountered Noel's son, the now fifteen-year-old Archie, who as a consequence a year later followed in his father's and grandfather's footsteps to Moor's, along with Osunkhirhine's younger half-brother, Jean Baptiste Masta. Unsurprising given how little Moor's had changed from Noel's time in its Protestant religious fervour and strict routine, it did not appeal either to Archie or to the other St Francis students then enrolled there. Changing times now made it impossible for Moor's to prevent communication with the outside world, with the result that Archie and the others, according to Dartmouth's president, were "tempted to return to their people & former habits of life by the influence of several of their tribe, who set up their wigwams & visited for a few weeks" during the summer. One of the students was removed by his parents, whereas Archie, according to the school head, "went clandestinely, taken away by some of his people in the night & without my knowledge."[72] Indicative of how literacy's promise engaged Indigenous persons in different ways, Jean Baptiste Masta continued on from Moor's to Dartmouth Medical School and became a respected New England physician in the pattern of his older brother Joseph Alex, who had also attended Moor's.

Osunkhirhine's orthodoxy proved an enduring cause of friction. James Joseph Annance and their relative John Stanislas, who returned home in 1835 from three years at Moor's, sustained Osunkhirhine's tiny congregation for a time, as did his half-brother, Ignace Masta, much more determinedly.[73] Noel's brother-in-law and cousin, Simon Annance, was in 1841 persuaded to teach in Osunkhirhine's tiny school, for which he received the missionary stipend designated for that purpose.

A FRAUGHT RELATIONSHIP

In the early 1840s the relationship between second cousins Peter Paul Osunkhirhine and Noel Annance, which was never intimate, became fraught as a consequence of their differing language skills. As well as earlier translating some religious tracts into the Abenaki language, Osunkhirhine had published in Boston in 1830 an Abenaki language primer, *Kimzowi Awighigann*, under his sometimes surname of Wzokhilain. Indicative of important linkages now being made between past and present, in writing the influential *The Common Pot* almost two centuries later, Abenaki scholar Lisa Brooks used the primer to interpret Abenaki concepts of belonging.[74]

Osunkhirhine had limited language skills when it came to doing more. In May 1840 the Canadian agent for the British and Foreign Bible Society, James Diego Thomson, visited St Francis, where he formed a Bible Society under the aegis of Osunkhirhine with James Joseph Annance as secretary. Thomson was so impressed by how "several of these Indians have received a good education at Dartmouth" that he secured a Greek Lexicon to make it possible for James Joseph, with his "pretty extensive knowledge of Latin and Greek," to translate "a portion of the New Testament into the Abenaki language."[75]

The project languished. James Joseph may have been ill or too busy, given that in 1843 he died a farmer, not an easy occupation. Osunkhirhine appears to have turned to Noel, who began with the Book of Mark. Possibily indicative of the enmity between them, Osunkhirhine did not then acknowledge Noel by name in reporting to his Boston superiors in November 1841: "We have now the Gospel of St. Mark translated by another Indian of our tribe and we are now correcting it for the press, which will be printed at Montreal by the Bible Society."[76]

A few months later, an annoyed Noel detailed his involvement in the translation project to Duncan Campbell Napier, the Indian Affairs official in charge of Quebec, in a fashion that did no credit to Osunk-hirhine. Writing from Durham, Noel described the translation project, and his involvement with it, as predating Thomson's visit. The letter, as with the others he sent to Napier, did not employ the language of deference but rather that of gentility, consistent with its use in the dominant society.

Letter on New Testament translation to Department of Indian Affairs, 26 March 1842

Durham 26th March 1842

To Col. D.C. Napier
Secry Indian Affairs

Dear Sir,

As we advance in civilization, our wants multiply, our views enlarge, and new objects present themselves which at once engage our attention and become to us a source of care and anxiety. Some three or four years ago, the religious part of our tribe desired me to translate the new testament into our language, and as I could not afford to undertake the work without some assistance, it was agreed that a contribution should be raised to enable me to go on with the translation. But unfortunately our plan was opposed by Peter the methodist preacher of our village, who threw cold water upon it. However we succeeded in drawing the attention of some members of a certain religious association to our object, who immediately undertook to have it done at their own expence, and Peter received orders from his superiors to begin the work without delay. At the end of fifteen months, after much shifting, shuffling and equivocating he gave it up, on the score of too much occupation on pastoral duties. Subsequently application was made to me to undertake the work, to which I agreed, and Peter was named Agent. He told me to write two or three chapters first for his inspection to see whether my alphabet corresponded with the one in use among the tribe. I made out the specimen and after waiting three months for his inspection I wrote to him in order to know whether he intended to comply with the order of the association and follow up the agreement he had made. He made me a very dry and surly reply, saying since I was so anxious about it, I might begin when I pleased never mentioning a word about the specimens. Not the least offended I set to work immediately and in two weeks translated one Gospel according to orders ready to be laid before the Commissioner for inspection. The minister before whom the translation was to be read, wrote a note to me previously to bring my brother [Louis, who was then visiting] with me to assist in examining the work. But the little apostle got to the place of meeting before me and had daubed my brother with his slime before the minister, that he was excluded from having any thing to say with regard to the translation. But as Peter could not english my Indian manuscript, we were brought to a sad predicament; and the minister would not allow me to do it, else it would be no examination. Then it was resolved, that Peter should go back to the village and study the translation and get James [Joseph] Annance to help him, then come up again in a few days and have the work finished off for the press. He came up the other day to the minister and excused himself that he had been sick and had done nothing towards it – at the end of seven months!!! a work that may be settled in a week because if I can translate it in two weeks, surely two persons, such as Peter and James Annance can examine it in one. As he did not think proper to come and see me on the subject when he came up to Durham the other day, I have demanded the translation, as we intend to make application elsewhere for assistance. The present communication therefore is made for the purpose of ascertaining whether we can get assistance from government, by making a proper application through you that we may accomplish so desirable an object as the translation of the new testament into the Abenequi language.

      I am

           Dear Sir

               With profound respect

                 Your ob^{dt} &

                       hon^{ble} servant

                 N.F. Annance

Source: Noel Annance to Napier, 26 March 1842, Library and Archives Canada, RG10, vol. 597, pp. 46159-62, reel 13379.

Napier, to his credit, acted on Noel's letter. He informed Noel a month later how "the agent of the British and Foreign Bible Society to whom he had written expressed his intention to communicate with you upon the subject of the assistance required for the completion of so deserved an object as the translation of the New Testament into the Abenaque language."[77] Having heard nothing subsequently, Noel wrote back to Napier in August respecting a project that clearly engaged him.

Follow-up letter on New Testament translation to Department of Indian Affairs, 6 August 1842

                                               Durham, Aug 6, 1842
To Col. D.C. Napier
Secry Indian Affairs
Dear Sir,
... [The following paragraph was circled by Napier:] I am extremely anxious to hear from the Agent of the British and Foreign Bible Society. I would feel grateful for your opinion on this subject, whether there can be any prospect of getting assistance either from Government or the Bible Society for translating the Scriptures into the Abenequi language. The subject is of vast importance in a religious point of view from New Brunswick to the foot of the Rocky Mountains, the same Indian tongue is spoken with very little variation.
                    I am
                             Sir
                         With profound respect
                             Your h^ble subject
                                 N.F. Annance

Col. Napier
Montreal

P.S. ... [The next part was circled by Napier:] I translated the Gospel of St. Mark into the Abenaqui language last year for the Congregation Union and Peter^x ran away with the manuscript and I am not paid yet. I since finished the Gospel of St Matthew and the Epistle of St Paul to the Romans.
N.F.A.

[The following was also circled by Napier:]
ˣ Peter Paul Osunkhirhine a Congregational Minister and one of the Abenaquois Tribe of Indians –

Note: The other parts of the letter are on other topics.
Source: Noel Annance to Napier, 6 August 1842, Library and Archives Canada, RG10, vol. 597, pp. 46375-78, reel 13379.

Napier responded in November 1842 that he had written again to the Bible Society, only to discover that the individual who had made the commitment to assist the project "has sailed on a mission to South America." James Diego Thomson had returned to Mexico, where he had earlier been in charge. Napier needed to know from Noel "to whom you forwarded the translation of St. Matthew's Gospel and the Epistle to the Romans."[78]

Although it is unclear what happened with Matthew and with Paul's epistle, it seems likely Osunkhirhine had held on to Noel's translation of Mark, which he published and lauded as his own work. In May 1845 Osunkhirhine reported to his Boston sponsors how "I have the Gospel of Mark in the hands of a printer in Montreal to print," for which he had, he explained, "raised money enough among my friends in Montreal."[79] He enclosed the printed chapter of twelve pages, for which he took sole credit, in a letter of October 1846 to his funders.[80]

LOUIS ANNANCE'S RETURN

The tension between Noel Annance and Peter Paul Osunkhirhine was moderated, and then exacerbated, by a returning Louis Annance. Preceding Noel to Moor's, Louis had in 1817 wed a local Abenaki woman named Marguerite Guillman. Leaving home about the same time as Noel did, he subsequently moved back and forth between the New England of his schooling and St Francis, where their children were baptized in the late 1820s. In 1827 Louis made a tentative enquiry about entering the fur trade, which was passed on to Hudson's Bay Company head George Simpson, but nothing came of it.[81]

Setting down in Lancaster, New Hampshire, about 120 kilometres, or 75 miles, north of Moor's (see map 1), Louis joined the Congregational Church, consistent with his schooling. There, he became so well established that in 1834 the North Star Lodge made him a Master Freemason.[82] Given that it was the highest possible rank to obtain, with the right to participate in all activities, Louis must have been a member for some time. This form of male sociability was unusual for having Indigenous members, including onetime Moor's student and Mohawk chief Joseph Brant.[83]

Louis may have been encouraged back to St Francis by Osunkhirhine's presence, given that his wife's family, were among his handful of supporters. In June 1841 Osunkhirhine recorded Louis's arrival and entry into his church:

There is one Louis Annance who was educated at Hanover seven years time, is been absent from the tribe twelve years, he is now here with us since few weeks, and appears well and does well. He is praying man, going about in the village to do good, and as he is related to many he has great deal of influence among the people. He appeared himself to be examined and received into the church at our next communion season in August. We examined him and are well satisfied with his experience of change, still we made him to understand that we will ask him some few questions before he shall be propounded.[84]

The relationship became, as indicated by Noel's description in his first 1842 letter respecting Noel's New Testament translation, increasingly frosty. In 1847 Osunkhirhine reported to his Boston sponsors,

The opposition is not from the chiefs of the tribe, nor so much from the priest. It is from one of my own people, Louis Annance, who was once a member of the church, but is not now, since he has fallen back to his natural state. He tries all he can to hurt my character – by misrepresentation of every thing I do and say, both in my preaching and in what I do to help the tribe, the chiefs, in their difficulties with those French people and others who are encroaching upon the Indian lands. He goes about among my people to misrepresent me in many things, trying to make them believe that I say and hold so and so, which I do not own nor hold. My people told him, Osunkhirhine does not hold such things as you say of him, still he insisted upon it.[85]

Osunkhirhine linked his enmity toward Louis with Noel's behaviour now a full decade earlier, which he suspected might repeat itself: "He is brother to the one who wrote so cunningly to the Board about me in August 2nd in 1836, who called himself S.B. Annance as it appears by your answer to him, while that was not his name for his name is Noel F. Annance. I make all this report of him because my people tell me that he has prepared a letter of complaint against me to the Board to which letter he will make some to sign with him. The intention is to break me up and send me away from this place if possible."[86]

Osunkhirhine was, in other words, persisting on the path Noel Annance had prognosticated in his letter of 1836 to his Boston sponsors. Osunkhirhine's school survived only because it was, despite periodic complaints from St Francis's Catholic missionary, irrelevant in the view of the Indian Department, educating only "a few children (chiefly his relations)."[87] The school was repeatedly closed for lack of pupils, as of 1850 enrolling twelve, compared with twenty-seven in the local Catholic school, out of a village population of ninety-four aged between five and fourteen years. Many children were receiving no schooling at all. Osunkhirhine's congregation was so minute that his church's register of Abenaki baptisms, marriages, and deaths averaged seven a year, half of them being those of former Moor's students and their families, compared with ten times as many officiated by his Catholic counterpart.[88] For all that Osunkhirhine's fervour garnered few adherents, his conviction that the people of St Francis were "altogether drunken with the Roman Catholic spirit" in what was "altogether a very wicked place" continued to strain community cohesion up to his departure in 1858 to another posting.[89] Captivity narratives' legacies had the potential to be divisive indeed.

STILL LOOKING TO MAKE A LIVING

Captivity narratives' legacies also continued to constrain Noel Annance's making a living. Osunkhirhine's presence, and thereby the stigma associated with attendance at Moor's, hindered Noel's utilizing his higher

education, as he sought to do to the benefit of others and, very importantly, of his family. His consternation over the translation points up a
critical economic difference between the two men. They both had families to support, but whereas his second cousin, for all of his perennial
plaints to his sponsors over his finances, had guaranteed annual stipends
as a minister and for his school, Noel was cast on his own resources.
Whether or not he was audacious in opening his store, it had proven to
be a short-lived venture.

Noel grabbed at opportunities as they came along. As did numerous
others from St Francis, he responded to the challenge of the Quebec
Rebellion of 1837 and 1838, which was marked by dissatisfaction
over political reform. Echoing the War of 1812, his higher education
mattered. Noel was commissioned a first lieutenant of a company of
Eastern Township Loyal Volunteers, in which he served at least from
November 1838 through March 1839 and perhaps longer. His monthly
wage of £12/2/10 contrasted sharply with the £1/5/10 accorded privates. A considerable portion of the fifty or so "Indian" privates came
from St Francis, among their number James Joseph Annance.[90] Noel
later described how he had "served as first lieutenant in the E.T. Volunteers in the late Canadian would-be-rebellion with a party of Indian
warriors as a guard stationed at Drummondville."[91] The captain in
charge of the company, along with the second lieutenant, sergeants, cor-
porals, and bugler, were all white. Although the circumstances of Noel's
service may have boosted his sense of self, it did not have longer-term
consequences.

Noel kept a watch for other possibilities, even as he farmed and
likely did a bit of everything. Consequent on the Webster-Ashburton
Treaty of 1842 between British North America and the United States,
he helped to survey the Lower Canada and New Brunswick borders. In
April 1844 Napier offered, perhaps at Noel's request or possibly on his
own initiative, to give "the officer in charge of the Boundary Survey expedition" a recommendation.[92]

In the fall of 1844 Noel was still "employed in the Boundary Commission" and expected to be so again the next spring, and as a consequence he requested that Napier arrange in advance for him to receive
"a light chiefs gun" in the annual gift giving.[93] The irony was that by
virtue of Noel being ambitious in terms of securing paid employment,

he was summarily informed "that in consequence of your continued absence no presents were issued for you."[94] In 1850 Noel again sought practical gifts for himself and Archie: "I beg leave to apply early for a gun and a large kettle for myself and son; should any such articles accompany the presents this year ... I want the gun very much."[95] No account of what ensued, if anything, has been located.

IN THE MATTER OF TEACHING

In the ongoing tension with his missionizing second cousin, Peter Paul Osunkhirhine, no issue more engaged Noel Annance than did the matter of teaching. To the extent Noel was justified in being optimistic about a position, it lay in repeated government pronouncements. The 1844 report of the Bagot Commission reiterated "that steps should be taken to establish Schools among the Indians of Lower Canada, and to avert that opposition, on the part of the Missionaries, which has hitherto prevented their successful operation."[96] As with earlier statements to that effect, the recommendation was mischievous when set against the very public position of the Catholic priest whom the Indian Department had funded since 1834 to maintain control over St Francis. It was his perspective that mattered, and he was having no truck with anyone associated with Moor's and more particularly with Osunkhirhine: "The Indians were then ... corrupted in their religious faith by an individual of the Tribe, who, by preaching a doctrine favourable to insubordination, had rendered them almost unmanageable. It was only by dint of vigilance and instruction that I succeeded in bringing them back to their good principles ... so that it may be said that the village of St. Francis contains a population of Christians, fervent Catholics, with the exception of a very few."[97]

The priest was in any case only mildly, if that, committed to Indigenous children's schooling, as indicated by his 1843 report: "There is an Elementary School for the instruction of boys and girls in the French language. The children have little taste for school, and they would not be very punctual in their attendance, if the master did not take the trouble of going to get them himself sometimes. About 30 boys and girls attend the school. They show enough aptitude for learning, but their light character hardly allows them to profit by what they learn."[98] The consequence was, when put together with Osunkhir-hine's antics, a juggernaut.

The situation gave promise of turning around under 1846 legislation that provided for the establishment "in each Municipality, Town or Village in Lower Canada" of government schools employing teachers "duly qualified to teach" children, including Indigenous children, aged between five and sixteen.[99] Indicative of the relationship that had by now developed between the two men, Napier gave Noel what appears to have been an inside track on a job: "I am desirous of ascertaining through you whether any member of the tribe is qualified and disposed to undertake the duty of teacher of the English language, writing & arithmetic to the Indian children of St. Francis – The salary will be £50 currency."[100] Noel responded the very same day enthusiastically and succinctly, in line with his full awareness of his own capacity and his conviction that he himself was the most qualified.

Letter on schooling to Department of Indian Affairs, 11 September 1846

Durham 11th Sept. '46
Lt. Col. Napier
Secy In affs Dear Sir,
    I had the honor to receive your favor of the 1st instant; and in compliance with your request in the last part of your letter, I am happy to inform you, that no one is better qualified and more disposed to be a teacher to my tribe than myself – and if agreeable to you, you have nothing to do but send me instructions then we will take the preparatory steps immediately ... I have just recovered from the country cholera.
                                    I am with profound respect
                                        Your hble servant
                                            N. Annance

Note: The omitted section of the letter is on another topic.
Source: Noel Annance to Napier, 11 September 1846, Library and Archives Canada, RG10, vol. 603, pp. 49175-78, reel 13381.

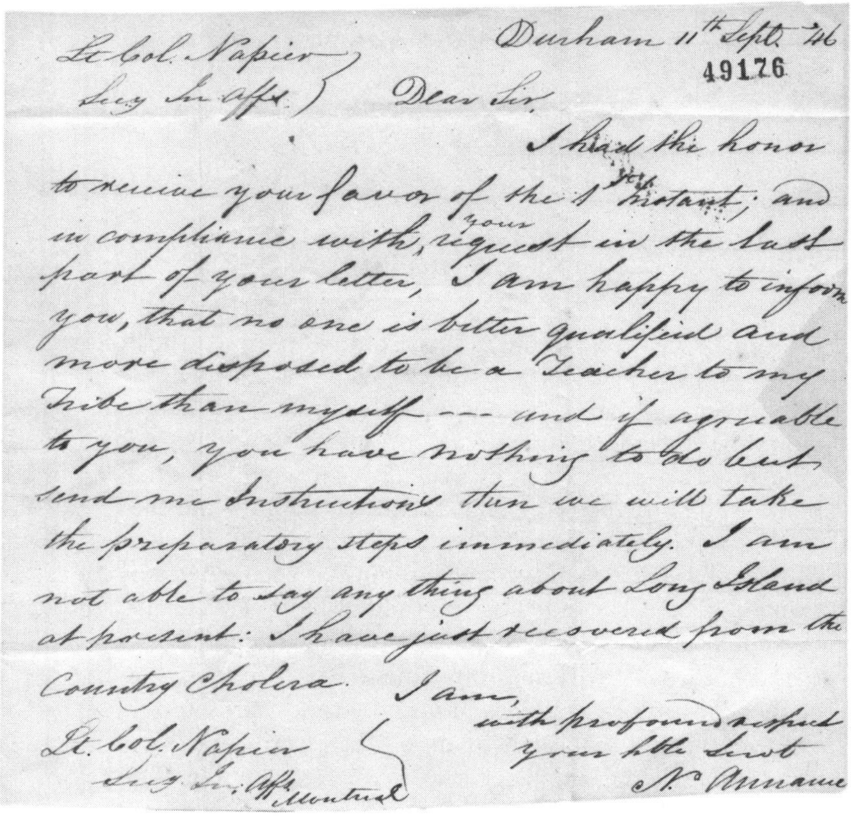

ILLUSTRATION 12
Noel Annance's letter to Secretary of Indian Affairs
Duncan Campbell Napier, 11 September 1846

In a follow-up letter to Napier, Noel reviewed the village's fraught circumstances of schooling occasioned by Osunkhirhine's now decade and
a half of proselytization and its challenge to St Francis's Catholic ethos.
Positioning himself as an outsider, which to a considerable extent he
was, Noel sought to reconcile the changing times for Indigenous peoples
with St Francis's distinctive character, an aim that he propounded not
without a couple of flourishes showcasing his higher education.

Follow-up letter on schooling to Department of Indian Affairs, 9
November 1846

Bury Nov 9, 1846

To Lt. Col. Napier
Secy In. Affairs

Dear Sir

As I answered your commu-
nication of the 1ˢᵗ Sept. only in part I now do myself the honor of
addressing you again on the subject. As it has reference to the establishment of a school in our village, I am deeply interested. I
would be extremely happy to see a respectable and permanent establishment of the kind in our village, as it would eventually anni-
hilate those little pettyfogging schools set up now and then, by the
two reverend religious rivals contending heads of the village. Peter
Masta, alias P.P. Osunkhirhine, got himself engaged at Boston
sometimes since to preach to the Indians for a certain sum; and if
he kept a school, he was to get so much more, and he has contrived to do this, by hiring some one to keep the school in his
chapel consisting sometimes of four, five and very seldom of ten
very young children. As the main object was to get the pay, it mattered little whether the teacher was competent or not. The priest,
on the other hand, not to be out done by his sectarian brethren in
their mighty zeal for the Indians, has always supported and pa-
tronized some ignoramous to teach the Indian children to read
and spell a few words, and repeat some prayers and dialogues to
be rehearsed before his Lordship, the Bishop on his circular visits.
Neither of these schools for these ten years has taught any child
arithmetic half way to the Rule of three, nor to dictate a letter!!
for all their tremendous anxieties to promote the welfare and everlasting happiness of the Indians, for all their huge professions and
promises to reconstruct and rebuild up the fallen wigwams of the
Abenaquis ...

Our tribe does not require a school shackled with pious restriction, circumscribed by holy prescriptions, or tied down to categor-
ical dogmas, to rules of bigotry or sectarian nonsense. We want a
school on the basis of freedom, of utility and humanity, teaching

the simple rudiments of English education, teaching the young
Inds how to shoot, inculcating the principles of industry; and by
infusing into the young mind, a taste and love for the comforts of
civilized life, leading the rising generation imperceptibly from the
most simple to the higher branches of science, which make man
an honor to himself and a useful member of society. And let those
favored associations or individuals who have the happiness of
being subservient in eleemosynary [charitable] benefactions, do it
from the noble suggestions of universal philanthropy, displaying
disinterested charity, a christian love, generous and dignified in its
principles and expansive in its feeling. So much for the school ...
                    N Annance

Note: The omitted sections of the letter are on unrelated topics.
Source: Noel Annance to Napier, 9 November 1846, Library and Archives
Canada, RG10, vol. 603, pp. 49186–90, reel 13381.

Nothing ensued until the beginning of 1848, or at least nothing as
described in letters that have been located. Then Noel enthusiastically
wrote Napier that his brother-in-law, long-time grand chief Ignace Portneuf, "requests me to go down to the village and begin the school," to
which he had astutely responded, "I am ready always the moment I receive orders from headquarters."[101]

Just a week later, Noel explained to Napier in a short follow-up letter that he was in a quandary, for "application was made to me to take
the Drummondville School with good encouragement; but, as I would
still prefer going down to the village with less salary, I wish you would
be kind enough to let me [know] whether there is any prospect of a
Government School being established in the village: if not I shall accept
the offer from Drummondville and begin the school immediately, as
these people seem to be very pressing and urgent." Located about
thirty-five kilometres, or twenty miles, southeast of St Francis, Drummondville had been founded following the War of Independence to
house former British soldiers and had a population of several hundred.
Their approach to Noel Annance testifies to his combination of teaching capacity and gentility from some white outsiders' perspectives. Noel

preferred the St Francis school but was pessimistic, given that "Peter, the Preacher, has created much wrangling, animosity and disturbance among the Indians."[102]

Unsurprising in the circumstances, Noel was not hired for St Francis. Despite the School Act limiting priests' role to "selecting the books having reference to religion or morals," such was not the case in practice.[103] Napier broke the news to Noel by return post in late January 1848 as to how the local priest had made a "strong recommendation" of another candidate, to which Noel responded with more than a touch of asperity as to how that individual's earlier service as the priest's cook was now being rewarded:[104] "To recommend a man to office for which he is totally unfit in every respect, is an infringement upon talent and a trespass on the rising generation. [Basilide] Desfossés is a simple good natured fellow: quite religious, punctual in his prayers; but ignorant, hardly compos mentis ... he knows nothing of English, the first and most essential qualification in a man of his qua non."[105]

As Noel's letter indicates, he and Basilide Desfossés could not have been more different in background, capacity, and outlook. Within a decade of completing his studies in 1826 at age fourteen at the parish school in Nicolet, twenty-five kilometres, or fifteen miles, distant, Desfossés had migrated to St Francis.[106] His having assisted the local priest in preparing a catechism in Abenaki published in 1832 caused the priest to propose Desfossés as Osunkhirhine's replacement as the local schoolmaster on Osunkhirhine's dismissal shortly before Noel returned home. Osunkhirhine's appointment had not worked out, and prior to being appointed in 1848, Desfossés appears to have taught off and on as well as engaging in other activities as they came to hand.[107] His middling capacity is attested by the local priest explaining to Napier how Desfossés is "a good man, but he is not educated," or as put in the original French, "Mr Desfossés est un brave homme, mais il n'est pas instruit."[108]

As for Noel, he looked to the future in a quick follow-up letter to Napier subsequent to the 1848 decision against him: "Should there be any vacancy and that a Schoolmaster is required I hope I will be remembered. I think no one has a better claim to it."[109]

UNRELENTING DETERMINATION

Noel's hopes for teaching in his home community were once again raised when in 1851 Desfossés was dismissed for incompetence:[110] "It has been rumoured down there that the man was not fit; that many withdraw their children from the school in consequence." Noel was consequently "requested by our Indians of the village below to go down and take charge of the school there as the present teacher is to leave the place the 1st of May next." He queried Napier in a short note as to "what steps to be taken that they may obtain this wish and mine."[111]

Again, hopes were dashed.[112] The possibility that Noel might this time actually get the job was such that the local priest took pen to paper to denounce what he characterized as nepotism. Ignace Portneuf "was seeking to put in his place his brother-in-law," being Noel, whom he characterized as "without faith, possibly without morals, and with whom the children will be very exposed." The priest then judiciously pulled back just a little to protect himself: "I'm not sure that will be the case, but it could happen."[113]

More than two years later, to no apparent effect, St Francis Abenakis petitioned that the "school may be placed in the hands of the educated member of the tribe," by whom they almost certainly meant Noel.[114] As Osunkhirhine put it bluntly at about that time, "the Government school ... is in the hands of the priest."[115]

The next year, 1854, an Indian Department employee wrote sympathetically that Noel Annance "tenders his services as a Teacher for his own Tribe," which he would do again in 1856.[116] Noel's capacity was in the interim attested by his various teaching positions, including one in what he described as "a large school under my charge on the main road to Durham near the village."[117] He viewed his jobs in white settler communities, including Wickham, about fifteen kilomestres, or nine miles, northwest of Durham, as stopgaps since his principal interest lay, as it had done since his return, in serving his own people. By population, the areas where he taught were two-thirds French by surname, the others being mostly Irish.[118]

Despite the loss of two allies on Napier's retirement and his brother-in-law Ignace Portneuf's death, both in 1857, Noel did not give up. He persevered despite nothing changing over time in respect to the absolute control the local priest exercised over village affairs with the concurrence of the Indian Department. He functioned as the conduit both to Catholicism, to which most Abenakis adhered, and to the Indian Department, whose longstanding subsidy to priests in the principal Quebec Indigenous communities gave them authority over schooling and most everything else.[119]

In May 1862, at the age of seventy, likely in order to increase his chances of being hired in St Francis, Noel renewed his elementary school diploma on passing the examination set forth in the School Act.[120] Perhaps for that reason, two months later he reminded the commissioner of Crown lands, now in charge of Indian affairs, of the village's distinctive educational circumstances. In doing so, Noel demonstrated his full and clear understanding of the relevant legislation.

Letter on schooling to superintendent general of Indian affairs, 28 July 1862

Indian Village
St Francis 28th [July] 1862
Hon. William McDougall
Honored Sir,
We did ourselves the honor of writing a few lines to you not long since [in a letter not located], in the shape of a complaint praying for assistance in effecting certain charges in the mode of conducting our domestic concerns among other matters in that address, the instruction of our children was of the highest importance. We have a school in our village of some fourteen years standing, but it is yet a nominal one, instead of a high school as it is falsely called. It consists, on an average the year round from four to ten children. The school room is something more than ten feet square – rather deficient in appearance for the money that was given to the priest (£90) to build the school house. From its beginning to this day, not one child has been taught to write a decent letter, or to be able to read the Bible with ease. The priest arrogates to himself the sole management of it,

but it is doubtful whether he goes into it once in twelve months.
He draws the money and pays the teacher. In all other schools in
Canada certain school laws are made, and strictly and rigidly en-
forced such as qualification in teachers: without diploma, no
teacher can be received: even in the elementary petty schools, each
must contain twenty children to be entitled to receive the school
money. There must be an examination of the scholars, at least
once in six months, and many other little ceremonies deemed conducive to the progress of education. But all these things are not in
the program of our school, nor in the dictionary of its chancellor.
The present teacher is a young Canadien not fit to teach in English
– he is clerk both of the small commissioners court and of the
magistrates court of the parish, and he also sometimes does his
carpenter work in the school house, and steps now and then into
the school room to make the children read, or sends in his wife
when he is in a hurry to finish a job. Now Sir, let common sense
judge (although sense is not common) if such complicated calling
be any way consistent or compatible with the duties of a school
teacher ...

    I am Dear Sir,
        With a profound respect
        Your most obed[t]
  & humble sert
          Noel Annance
          Late Lieut & Interpreter Indian Dept

Note: The parts of the letter not included are on other topics.
Source: Noel Annance to William McDougall, 28 July 1862, Library and
Archives Canada, RG10, vol. 273, pp. 184403-10, reel 12657.

A memo pencilled at the bottom of the 1863 letter speaks to the impediment, given Napier's retirement, that Noel now faced in securing
his much sought teaching position in St Francis: "Mr. Dorion (J.B.) tells
me the writer is not much to be relied on & a busybody but there may
be truth in his version."[121] Despite the attempt by Durham landowner
and political rabble-rouser Jean-Baptiste Éric Dorion to discredit Noel,
two actions ensued from his letter.[122]

First, an Indian Department official was sent to investigate "the complaints made by Noel Annance and other Indians of the Abenakis tribe of the Village of St. Francis against their school master." Enquiring why "seven or eight only attended," whereas "the number of children which ought to attend that school is 34," Edward N. DeLorimier was informed "the school-master was not teaching them, but was occupying them at turning a wheel." Visiting "the school house which is a few acres (arpents) from the village," he was met with "a great wooden wheel, which is used for turning wood ... for making legs of chest of drawers and other similar objects." DeLorimier was not best pleased: "Full of shavings and chips and ... in the most dirty state, we see in that house nothing which indicates it to be a school, but a regular joiners work shop. If it is allowed, I would say that the government's intention has been frustrated in appointing such an individual ... the sooner he shall be disposed of the better. From the information that I have collected nobody is interested in that school, so that the master does as he pleases."[123]

Second, Noel was asked by the deputy superintendent of Indian affairs, William Spragge, for specifics concerning the situation and responded in September 1862 shortly after the visit with more biting detail than he had shared two months earlier.[124] Even as he showcased his higher education, Noel was circumspect as to his role in events.

Letter on schooling to Department of Indian Affairs,
15 September 1862

Indian Village St. Francis
15th September 1862

C.T. Walcot Esq
       Dear Sir
              Not knowing Mr. Spragge's address in full, I address this communication to you for his information. As far as I can ascertain, the population of the Abenaki village consists of eighty men, seventy seven women and one hundred and sixteen children from the age of fourteen downwards. Between thirty and forty of

the children are able to attend the school and fit to receive instruction if we had a competent teacher, but to our sad misfortune it is not the case since the school was established by a grant of government [in 1846], as we were made to understand; the priest always had the sole management of it. He drew the school money and paid the master as he thought proper; he never put in a master who was fit to teach English. As the Indians found the children learned nothing, they prefer to keep their children at home, so that the number of scholars never exceeded ten: at times only four or five for several months. In every school in Canada, however low and small, there are some rules and regulations to be observed in their school: on the observance of these rules depends the existence of the school and the pay to the teacher. But our school is independent, nondescript, it needs none of these things. The priest is the sole trustee and dictator. The only test for fitness to teach in our school is to be a rigid Roman Catholic and no other qualification is required. Before the school began, Col. Napier wrote to me on the school affair thus: "I request you will name a native Indian who is fit and willing to be teacher to the Indian children of St. Francis: in English reading, writing and arithmetic." But the Indian I named was rejected, because he did not confess to the priest as a good Catholic. We have had five teachers, since the school began, not one of these taught English, and the present teacher is not able to obtain a diploma to teach the English language; he may be a good french scholar, but he has not been examined for a french diploma to be admitted into a french school. He is at present clerk for both the commissioners' court and the magistrates' court; and besides he is a carpenter and works in the school house part of his time. He keeps no regular journal – his school was never examined as the school act requires. In the presence of such reckless neglect and flagrant contempt of the established rules, so essential to the progress of education, has the money been drawn, allowed for the school? If it has, it must be under fool's pretexts. When Commsr Delormier came to investigate into the ... condition of our school under the sole care of our missionary, his reverence refused to go with us, he was probably aware what was to be seen. Mr Delormier did not find a school house but a carpenter shop! The building inside was full of carpenters wood, tools, unfinished boxes or bureaus &c &c: in one room was a huge wheel for turning wood for bedposts. When the teacher kept school, he made some of the boys turn this wheel for him when he was at work. Such gross imposition would be an insult to a horde of Hottentots or wild Patagonians. Therefore we humbly beg that the gentlemen of the Indian Department would interfere, so far as to sanction the appointment of the persons we recommend to be trustees to our school as to put the priest completely out of the way and those trustees will find a man to teach english and french. We have no time to lose: the priest has put the carpenter again in the school; our children are losing their precious time. We are much disappointed not having heard any thing of Mons. Delormier's report yet.

I am Dear Sir,
with profound respect
your most obdt
Servant
Noel Annance

Source: Noel Annance to C.T. Walcot, 15 September 1862, Library and Archives Canada, RG10, vol. 273, pp. 184443-47, reel 12657.

At the time Noel wrote in the fall of 1862, he had been teaching "for a few months" at Durham, but by the end of the year, he was once again optimistic about St Francis: "I will go down to take the management of that school, if the Indians succeed to put the parish priest out of it. Great and just complaints sent down against the management of it and we hope those complaints have been taken into consideration at the proper place."[125]

Noel was still teaching in Durham when, the next spring, following "several complaints ... on the subject of mismanagement" of the St Francis school, Noel once again "went down at the repeated request of the Indians to take the school there, but the priest would not allow it." In what must have been from Noel's perspective the consummate rebuff, "the priest put in Mons. Desfossés again who had been dismissed from the school" a decade and a half previous and was still "totally ignorant of the English."[126] Attracting an enrolment in the mid-thirties, another twenty-five favouring its Protestant counterpart, Defossés would occupy the position to Noel's death in 1869, putting an end to his long-held dream to teach in his home village.[127] His seeking to pass literacy's promise on to the next generation in his home community so they might dare literacy's promise in their lives, as he had done, came to naught.

TO SUM UP

The consequences of the captivity narratives from which Noel Annance descended cast a shadow over his life from the time he returned home to St Francis. The long ago captivity narratives divided the community not only between descendants and others but also among descendants. The different directions they headed were nowhere more evident than among former Moor's students. Second cousins Noel Annance and Peter Paul Osunkhirhine had the potential to be allies in effecting change. That they did not do so, except briefly and inconsequentially, reflects both on their limitations and, very importantly, on the Indian Department and the government more generally.

For the Department of Indian Affairs to deny a basic education to more than a generation of St Francis's children was far easier than to give credence to an educated minority or to an individual such as Noel Annance. For all of his persistence, Noel never became the teacher in St Francis that he had sought for a third of a century to become on the model of his father but instead scrambled to make a living for his family.

7

Land No More

On his return to St Francis in late 1834, Noel Annance was caught up not only in the consequences of the captivity narratives that had formed him but also in a broader shift respecting Quebec's Indigenous peoples. At the time he left, they were still valued for their contribution to the War of 1812 and earlier the War of Independence, and they were otherwise largely left to their own devices. By the time Noel came back, Indigenous peoples were being variously dispossessed of their land in others' self-interest.[1] Noel was quick to enter the fray.

LAND'S COMPLEXITIES

By virtue of his higher education, Noel Annance became involved in the complexities of land both on his own behalf and on that of fellow Abenakis. His facility with the written word caused him to develop a respectful relationship on the topic with Duncan Campbell Napier of the Indian Department, responsible from 1829 to 1857 for Indigenous matters in Quebec.[2] Based on skimming incoming correspondence from 1834 to 1869 to the Department of Indian Affairs on microfilm in Library and Archives Canada, it is virtually certain no other person, Indigenous or no, had Noel's sense of style, power of organization, and capacity to intuit what was wanted in a letter intended to cajole, explain, and persuade, at least a little.[3] Following Napier's retirement in 1857, rather than Noel's letters being taken on their own terms, "Indian" would routinely be scrawled across a covering note, possibly to alert their recipient prior to reading them.

As with his letters concerning a teaching position, Noel put on paper about land what otherwise might be lost from view except as oral tradition. His correspondence and related materials go some way, but only that, to sorting out Abenaki landholding. To quote Philippe Charland respecting his intensive interrogation of the related topic of Abenaki place names, "what remains of such names is only what has been retained by the colonial administrators."[4]

Indigenous landholding was not straightforward anywhere in the future Canada. Reflecting larger sets of attitudes, the convention held that Indigenous peoples might hold land but considered that, unlike all others, they had no right to dispose of it. The 1844 report of the Bagot Commission stated, "owing to the peculiar Title under which the Indians hold their Lands, and their incapacity to alienate them, they continue, as in their uncivilized state, to hold them in common."[5]

Abenakis held land both in common in respect to the large concession made in 1700 and individually in relationship to a grant made a century later.[6] The concession comprised 12,000 acres centred on St Francis, with the seigneurs who granted the land in common reserving the right "of dispossessing the Abenaquois as soon as the Religious Mission [established by the Jesuits in 1683] should cease to reside upon the conceded land."[7] Only as long as Abenakis professed Catholicism were they assured of a homeland. The other piece of land consisted of the 8,900 acres, located in Durham Township southeast of St Francis, granted in 1805 to seventeen male family heads, and then their heirs, consequent on their service on the British side during the War of Independence.

The large St Francis concession had over the years been whittled away. As acknowledged in the 1828 Darling Report, "Of the greatest part of their possessions they have of late been most cruelly deprived, by intrigue and oppression of various designing individuals who, under a variety of pleas, have got hold of nearly the whole of their properties."[8] According to an Indian Department official writing at about the time Noel returned home, all that remained for Abenakis' use was "446 acres for Indian cultivation in patches round the village," the rest being leased for small annual sums.[9] Overseen not by government officials but by local agents, Quebec Indigenous communities were reimbursed only 10 per cent of what the agents collected annually in rents or otherwise, further diminishing that "sole revenue of the Abenakis Tribe."[10] Income differentials were as a consequence enormous, with priests and some of the captivity narratives' descendants, as with Ignace Gill, on the very high side.

Remaining St Francis land had little economic utility, being likely for that reason unrented. As officials acknowledged shortly after Noel's return home, it was "of a very inferior Quality, being for the most Part a dry sandy soil without any admixture of Clay."[11] According to a report three decades later, "a good deal of the Reserve [as Indigenous lands were now being called] is bad land and scarcely fit for cultivation," with "the most valuable" portion being "altogether in the possession of the whites."[12] Some Gill descendants' sense of entitlement to use the lands as they would contributed to the worsening situation.

Even the ambitious Peter Paul Osunkhirhine was caught out. As did other missionaries and officials in the Department of Indian Affairs, he sought Abenakis' containment, whatever the resultant loss of personal freedom, self-will, and economic wellbeing: "I have tried all I can to make the Indians remain more at home and to pay attention to farming rather than their hunting and wandering life, but as they [have] been accustomed in that way, it is not easy to succeed just yet."[13] Osunkhirhine determined to lead by example, only to discover that agriculture on St Francis land was not the solution he would have it be: "The summer or fall before last I have lost so many potatoes that rotted in the field and in my cellar after they were put in; and so much buckwheat and oats that were destroyed by frost, my labor and expence was all lost ... I have almost been obliged to give up the farming business, but I thought it would be a bad example to my people if I let my own land lay waste."[14] Osunkhirhine acknowledged shortly before he washed his hands of the Abenakis in the mid-1850s how "the tribe is growing poorer and poorer every year as hunting is very much diminished everywhere, and the land here is not good enough ... Most of the Indians are in debt."[15]

The consequence was that, despite much correspondence with the Department of Indian Affairs, most Abenakis had no choice but to live much as they had long done, with some pragmatic concessions to the changing times around them.[16] According to a government official writing in 1837, "between Forty and Fifty of these Indians are actively engaged as Hunters during the Winter Season, and are supported principally from the Profits of the Chase."[17] For Abenakis to do so, including north of the St Lawrence River, was to encounter growing numbers of newcomer settlers perceiving them as intruders into "their" territory.[18] Abenaki women, by this 1837 account, "are employed making baskets, snow shoes, moccasins, and bead work, which they trade with the whites for clothing and Provisions," the result being that "they very

seldom reside at the village more than a week at a time."[19] With necessary adaptations, this yearly round would long continue.

IN THE MATTER OF THE DURHAM LANDS

Never more than an observer in respect to the St Francis lands due to his
outsider status in the community, Noel Annance was early on caught
up in the parallel and even more contentious controversy over the 8,900
acres of Durham land granted three decades prior to his return home.
Noel's father, who had charge of the transaction, had understood, in
line with the terminology he and the British colonial secretary had used
at the time, that recipients were "restricted from the power of selling &
alienating the said land," being thereby free to lease parcels, which he
did from 1820 onward on his and others' behalves.[20] The Indian Affairs
official in charge of Quebec from 1829, Duncan Campbell Napier, similarly understood that, "should they sell any of them, the Lots sold became forfeited to the Crown."[21]

Then came an end run. Three years after Francis Joseph Annance's
death in 1826, thirty-four whites, some lessees, and others wanting to
get their hands on Durham lands, the majority likely of humble background given they signed with an "X," petitioned the governor general
of British North America. What they sought was "peaceable possession" of the Durham lands, or alternatively "their taking forcible possession," on the grounds they were "forwarding the settlement of the
Country," as opposed to "the Indians never having cleared, and scarcely
made any improvements."[22]

The 1829 petition initiated what would be a lengthy government in-
vestigation into the Durham lands. The understanding at the time had
been that the parcels, which had in 1805 been granted individually to
seventeen Abenaki family heads, could not be "alienated or disposed
of."[23] On closer examination, it turned out the letters patent transferring
the parcels stated that they could not be "leased, transferred, conveyed,
or otherwise disposed of," this despite the transaction being explicitly
based on the colonial secretary's earlier letter stipulating only that they
not be sold.[24] The proviso in the letters patent invalidated the leases that
had been negotiated from 1820 onward to the detriment not only of the
Abenaki leasers but also of white lessees. Napier for his part considered

from early on that "the Abenequais Indians are so remarkably quiet and inoffensive in their manners, it appears extremely improbable that they would commit the outrage described in the petition."[25]

The Durham lands issue unresolved by the time of Noel Annance's return, he was immediately drawn in as an heir and sometimes protagonist, writing for clarification on 22 December 1834. Napier responded with the wording of the letters patent: "In case any of the Grantees or their Representatives should lease, sell or alienate in any manner the lands in question, the lot or lots so disposed of become forefeited to His Majesty."[26] Leasing out a portion of the Durham lands was to lose it.

Undeterred, Noel thereupon aimed his efforts at those higher up in the line of authority. His letter of 25 May 1835 to the civil secretary of the governor of Lower Canada evidenced much research on the Durham lands issue. Noel explained not only that some of the land had been leased but also that other portions had been "taken without any permission or authority." Pointing out how "we can no longer live by the chase," Noel framed the issue to align with government aspirations that Indigenous peoples would set themselves down in one place. The letter's genteel style and proprietorial prose ensured that it would not be dismissed out of hand. As indicated by the notations on the letter, it was referred to the attorney general, who transferred it to the commissioner of Crown lands and in due course to Napier for a cursory, inconsequential response.[27]

Letter on Durham lands to the secretary of Lower Canada's governor, 25 May 1835

St Francis 25th May 1835

To
        Lieut Col. Craig
            Dear Sir,
                    I am sorry that I am compelled to give so much trouble on a subject which should, long since, have been put at rest. It is a misfortune to the Indians that the officers in

the Indian Department should have so much business on hand of superior importance as to prevent their listening to our repeated requests, and examining into the grievances we complain of, respecting some of our lands in the Township of Durham. I have repeatedly explained to those gentlemen that some of the lands have been leased out to the Irish, or Scotch complainants, but very few; others have been taken without any permission or authority, and the intruders have often abused, beat and bullied the poor Indians whenever they attempted to recover their own! how the Indians wished the government to evict them to get their lands back, but the officers of the Indian Department do not think it their province to give themselves any trouble on the subject. So we are at a loss what to do – I am much apprehensive that quarrels will soon arise between the Indians and the whites about these lands, as the Indians have threatened to take forcible possession of their lands and drive away the Intruders – These lands are now of great importance to us: we can no longer live by the chase – those spots once rich in game, when trod by our ancestors, lands of the soil, can no longer afford us subsistence. Therefore we most humbly beg that Government would extend its protection to us by appointing some one to see this business settled as soon as possible. If his Excellency would be pleased to refer it to the Attorney General, he may name some law officer at Sherbrook to transact the business for the Indians.

I am

With profound respect
Your most humble servt
F.N. Annance

Lieut Col Craig
  Civ. Secrey

Source: Noel Annance to H. Craig, 25 May 1835, Library and Archives Canada, RG10, vol. 272, pp. 83867-71, reel 2557.

Noel kept up the pressure. At some point thereafter, Napier had passed on to him, he explained to Noel, from "His Excellency the Governor a Paper purporting to be a Petition from you, but without either a signature or date."[28] The petition, which has not been located and may not have survived, appears to have been remarkably successful. Whether or not it was coincidental, in the summer of 1837 the government conceded in respect to the Durham leases that "it does not appear, however, that the original Grantees or their Heirs were made acquainted with the terms" and thereby acted in good faith.[29]

Indicative of the trust that had by now grown up between them, in February 1838 Napier requested that Noel pass this information onto Durham landholders: "I have to desire you to inform the Grantees of the Indian Lands in Durham or their Heirs that a Communication has been made to the Persons now occupying certain portions of the said Lands, with a view to remove any misconception they may entertain in regard to the Payment of the Rent of the Lots so occupied."[30] If lessees wanted to hold on to their leases, now declared valid, they had to pay the agreed rent. Noel responded from the "Indian village of St. Francis" a month later: "In compliance with your request, I communicated the intelligence to my friends and relations of this place and Durham. We therefore in expressing our warmest thanks and sincerest gratitude for what government has done for us, beg that you would have the goodness to tell Mr. Aug. Gill the chief to go up to Durham and see the business settled."[31] Noel astutely signalled the limits of his authority.

Two related circumstances now came to the fore respecting the Durham lands. Noel used his March 1838 letter to explain one of them, namely that some heirs could not agree as to who could collect the rents now owed: "Some of the lots are claimed by two or three heirs: whichever of these heirs came forward first and gained a lease has the advantage over the others."[32] The second circumstance followed on the claim in the 1829 petition as to "the Indians never having cleared, and scarcely made any improvements."[33] An Indian Department official writing in 1837 confirmed that only "a few of the Indians are settled in the lands," and "the greater parts are laying waste."[34] An 1843 count put at Durham eleven Abenaki family heads, likely including Noel, and also thirty-six other Abenaki persons, including women and children.[35] The two circumstances may have contributed to an order-in-council of 1 July 1839, which has not been located, advising that "legal proceedings be adopted for the purpose of reinvesting the said lands in the Crown."[36]

Noel continued to be drawn into the Durham lands issue in part out of his own and family interests and in part due to the relationship forged with Napier. It may have been in the context of the 1839 order-in-council that Noel, following much research on his part, wrote to Napier in January 1840: "I now send you a general statement how the Indian lands in this township have been disposed of, and by whom the different lots have been taken, whether by lease or not," a document that has not been located. Noel explained he did "not mention the names of the original grantees because you have them," adding that "if I have missed any particulars that may facilitate the intended arrangement about those lands, I can easily make any addition hereafter if required."[37] The absence of any draft letter requesting the information in Napier's letter books suggests the two were, at least in this respect, in personal contact.

Given the uncertainty over the order-in-council's outcome, Durham grantees and their heirs now looked less to leasing their holdings than, despite the restriction on doing so, selling them outright before they were forfeit. In the pattern of his relative Charles Annance, who shared in the immediate family holding, Noel had leased out 300 acres since returning home but in 1840 opted to sell 100 acres for an impressive $162.30. At about the same time, Charles disposed by sale or lease of 200 acres for $150. Over the next dozen years, 1842–53, during which the situation festered, Noel would sell more than 1,000 additional acres of Durham lands in eleven parcels for around $540 in total. Some of it he must have sold on behalf of others, alternatively purchasing or otherwise acquiring others' leases prior to selling the land under his name.[38] Charles similarly dispensed with 350 acres in four parcels for $125.[39] It seems almost certain that it was by this means Noel and the others principally or in part sustained their families.

Even the high-minded Osunkhirhine succumbed. The perennially hard-up preacher anticipated how "I shall be able to pay all I owe when I shall have sold some land I have in a Township called Durham forty miles [or 65 kilometres] up the River St. Francis, as soon as I shall have my share after I and the other heirs shall have made division."

What is clear from his letter of 1836 is that the legalities of doing so did not bother even such a fervent moralist as he was: "A man promised me sometime ago that he will buy what I have as soon as I will bring him in writing from a notary showing that I have got my share … But I found that he changed his mind, he don't like to buy my land unless I obtain a permission from the Governor to sell, because, said he, the Government gave the lands to the Indians and to their heirs not to sell nor lease, but to occupy themselves."[40] Osunkhirhine would have by the summer of 1843 "sold two lots of land that I had in the Township of Durham," as well as leasing out at least one other.[41]

Indicative of how the captivity narratives' legacies continued to operate, among the principal purchasers of Durham land from its sellers was the ambitious Ignace Gill, who although a descendant was not himself an heir.[42] Noel's brother-in-law Ignace Portneuf was not best pleased by how "Ignace Gill has bought several pieces of Indian Land at different times in St. Francis and in the Township of Durham, from different individual Indians, who he has made to believe by his own explanation of Law, that they have a right to sell their lands to him while he well knew that he had no right according to law to make such purchases."[43]

Another consequence of the unsettled situation, Noel reminded Napier in 1840, was that some lessees were still refusing to pay backrent, about which he requested advice.[44] Around this time, Noel and Charles Annance acted on their own volition with unexpected consequences. In 1835 Charles had rented out 100 acres on their behalves to an individual who almost immediately transferred the lease to another person, who then refused to pay the agreed rent of $5.00 per year. The two Annances took the errant lessee to court and on 4 July 1840 won a judgment for him "to pay the said plaintiffs the sum of six pounds and five shillings" plus "twenty shillings & four pence" in costs.[45]

The legal victory counted for naught. Napier informed Noel five days later how "all of the questions you proposed to me some time since in relation to the Legal Rights of Indians, have been answered by the Attorney General in the Negative!!!"[46] When Noel followed up with a more senior official in the Department of Indian Affairs, likely to get the awarded funds from the court case, he was summarily informed that "no lawful ground exists for the interference of the executive government in the matter."[47] That the two Annances had gone beyond the bounds of acceptability for behaviour by Indigenous persons and, at least in the moment, won out had to have grated.

QUEST FOR A MILITARY SERVICE LAND GRANT

While sometimes acting on his own behalf and other times at the behest of other Abenakis over land concerns, not unexpectedly so given his written and oral fluency in English, Noel also employed the relationship he built up with Napier to push his personal agenda. His letter of January 1840 enclosing a list of Durham lands was accompanied by a petition to the governor general for a land grant pursuant on his services in the War of 1812 and in the Quebec Rebellion.[48] The request was consistent with government policy that lands not yet taken up be given to former soldiers.

The 1840 land petition speaks both to Noel Annance's broad base of knowledge and understanding, which had also prompted his earlier request for land in the Pacific Northwest, and to his ingenuity in refashioning his life after his years away. In the petition, he astutely highlighted not only his commendable war service, which was the basis for the request, but also his travel with the respected 1833 expedition. Doing so explained by inference why he had not earlier made the request.

Petition to governor general for a land grant consequent on services in the War of 1812, 20 January 1840

To the most honourable Charles Paulette Thomson Governor General in British North America Capt General and Commander in chief in and over the Provinces of lower and upper Canada &c &c &c and one of Her Majesty's most honorable Privy Council

The memorial of Noel F. Annance, Indian of the Abenaki tribe, Lieut in the Eastern Township loyal volunteers and late Lieut in the Indian Department

Most humbly sheweth

That your Memorialist who served as a lieutenant in the Indian Department in the late war was entitled to a Bounty of land
for his services, but on account of his having been absent from the
province, exploring regions beyond the Rocky Mountains and
more especially his having gone with, and conducted, the Boats of
Capt. Back of the L.A. Expedition in 1833, as far as Great Slave
Lake lost the opportunity of coming forward to put in his claim at
the time his brother officers received theirs.

Thereupon your Memorialist most humbly begs leave to im-
plore your Excellency's goodness that his case may be taken into
consideration to the end that he may obtain something in substi-
tute of what he so undeservedly lost and as in duty bound will
every pray &c &c &c

N.F. Annance

Durham 20 Jany 1840

Source: Petition enclosed in Noel Annance to Napier, 20 January 1840,
Library and Archives Canada, RG10, vol. 99, p. 40951, reel 11470.

Napier took the petition seriously, as Noel ensured he would do by
flattering him: "I enclose also my memorial to the Governor General,
which I beg of you to have kindness to forward, as I think it may have
the desired effect passing thro' your hands."[49]

Noel highlighted a key contact: "If any certificate of my services or
any recommendations as to their merit be required I am happy to think
that Col. Heriot under whom among others, I had the honor to serve,
will be ready and willing to give it."[50] Frederick George Heriot, who
had commanded the Voltigeurs, including Noel, at the Battle of Châteauguay, had charge of administering the land grants given to dis-
banded soldiers in the war's aftermath. Drummondville, which was
located between St Francis and the Durham lands and was where Noel
would teach from time to time, originated under Heriot's oversight and
was where Heriot settled (see map 1). It was Heriot who had on Noel's
return in 1835 arranged an introduction to the governor general so that
Noel could make his lease request for Long Island. In response to the
petition, Heriot was fairly complimentary: "Noel F. Annance served as

Lieutenant in the Eastern Township loyal volunteers, with a party of Indians attached to the Corps during last winter, and he conducted himself to my satisfaction."[51]

Four years later, in 1844, Noel's brother-in-law Ignace Portneuf similarly applied for a land grant, to have his petition summarily rejected by virtue of not having served in "any of the corps entitled to receive land bounty."[52] With Noel, no reason was given. In a letter of the same year uncharacteristically addressed to "Mr. Noel Annance, Late Lieutenant Indian Department," Napier wrote with what almost comes across as a touch of sadness: "I regret to have to inform you that the Indian officers who have claims for services rendered during the later war with the United States of America are not mentioned in the recent circular of the Crown Land's office." The inference left is that land was still being handed out but only to white officers. The claims of "Indian officers," who appear from Napier's words to have been greater in number than simply Noel, had been excluded for what could only have been their indigeneity. To attempt small consolation, Napier added, "in the hope that it may be useful to you, I enclose a certificate of your Services."[53] He also alerted Noel that he would be happy to recommend him for employment on the boundary survey, which job he got.

Apparently left dangling, although intervening correspondence may not have been located or did not survive, Noel in 1849 renewed his application for a land grant consequent on his military service.

Second petition to governor general for a land grant consequent on military service, 2 March 1849

To His excellency the Right hon. the Earl of Elgin and Kincardine, Knight of the most noble order of the Thistle &c &c & Governor General of British N. America &c &c

The petition of Noel Annance, an Indian of the Abenaquais nation of St Francis humbly sheweth:
That your Excellency's petitioner, having served his Sovereign during the last American war, as Lieutenant in the Indian

Department, and having been present at almost every skirmish and battle with the enemy in Lower Canada during that war, as the press of those days can show, was justly entitled to the Bounty of a just and generous sovereign five hundred acres of land of which he has been deprived in consequence of his not having gone thro certain trivial formalities on account of his absence at the time he should have presented his claim; and humbly prays that your Excellency would be pleased to take his petition into favorable consideration that he may obtain a scrip to purchase any ungranted crown land in the townships. And as in duty bound your petitioner will ever pray &c &c

> Noel Annance
> Late lieut. Ind. Dept.
> Durham 2 March 1849

Source: Noel Annance, petition to James Bruce, Earl of Elgin, 2 March 1849, and Napier to Thomas Edmund Campbell, 25 April 1849, Library and Archives Canada, RG10, vol. 606, pp. 50882-3, 50974, reel 11382.

Noel's second petition, which was more explicit than its predecessor, was sent on to the Indian Department to garner a not unexpected response. Napier was again sympathetic, beginning his letter of October 1849, "I regret, that it is not in my power to transmit to you a more favourable answer to your application for a grant of Land, dated 2^d March last."[54] Ever persistent, Noel would subsequently explore with Napier other means of being "compensated" for his military service.[55] Given no further correspondence, it seems unlikely the attempt came to anything.

SEEKING TO RETRIEVE LONG ISLAND

It was not only the Durham situation and a desired concession pursuant on his military service that engaged Noel Annance on the land front. He had not followed up on the Long Island land grant promised him in 1835 by then governor general Lord Aylmer: the "Controller of

Crown land made such a dull work of it, I thought I could do without the grant and still occupy my island." Increasingly regretting his inaction, Noel turned a decade later, as was his wont, to Napier for assistance "to apply for a new lease or grant for my Island where my farm is in the St. Francis River."[56] Napier in turn requested from Noel "the original lease, or a copy of it, or of any other document under which you have occupied the Island in question."[57]

Unable to locate his father's original lease, Noel sent Napier in March 1846 the 1814 document transferring the lease to him, whereupon the Land Department in Montreal, on also being unable to locate the original lease, recommended a simple alternative:[58] "The practice of granting leases has been discontinued but Mr Annance might be permitted to purchase the Island in question at the upset price of 6/per acre which would only amount to £12.0.0 for the whole – whatever back rent that may be due on the lease would have to be paid also."[59] Then came, in Noel's words, unspecified "regulations that interfere with my application."[60]

Noel's concern over his circumstances grew when, at the beginning of 1848, he "was told by a man, versed in the law that I could not will Long Island to my son because the moment I die it becomes the property of the Queen." Noel "told him that idea contained an absurdity, for I never heard that Government made themselves heirs of private property," but he sought assurance from Napier: "In order to confront the sarcastic innuendoes of the man of the law I wish you to be kind enough to inform me as soon as convenient whether that is the case or not."[61]

As well as sending Noel by return post a copy of the preceding year's order-in-council, which so stipulated, Napier submitted a request to the superintendent general of Indian affairs "on behalf of Noel Annance an Indian of the of the Abenequis tribe for reconsideration of the O.C. of 19 March 1847 with a view of securing his family, after his demise, the possession of Long Island in the River St Francis." Napier's request was decidedly respectful of Noel: "On behalf of Noel Annance, a very intelligent and truly loyal Indian, I beg leave to transmit to you the enclosed papers, with a view to ascertain whether the Order in Council of 19th March 1847, could be revised, so as to continue the indulgence therein granted to the family of the applicant after his demise."[62] A response came a month later: "I regret to find, that the indulgence therein granted is confined to your own life."[63] The process of squeezing Indigenous people off the land was ongoing and unrelenting.

BACK TO THE DURHAM LANDS

For all of his concern over Long Island, Noel along with some others kept a watching brief on the Durham lands, about which government interest in resolution had faltered.[64] Noel was, very importantly, not wholly one-sided in his outlook. Concerning a St Francis Abenaki fretting over the amount of rent a tenant paid, Noel reflected, "there is reason in everything, as Horace says, est modus in rebus: sunt certi denique fines quos ultra, citraque nequit consistere rectum [there is a middle ground in all things: and, moreover, certain limits on either side of which right cannot be found]."[65] Noel was similarly honest in reporting to Napier how the Abenaki population at Durham was dwindling, with the result that "there will be only two Indians in Durham perhaps in the course of the summer."[66]

Noel drew on his ongoing relationship with Napier to flag what he considered to be infringements on the common understanding concerning lessees of the Durham lands. Noel was the first to sign a petition of January 1848 by eleven "heirs to the original grantees in the Township of Durham" requesting of the governor general that "Her Majesty's attorney general may be ordered to assist us in compelling ... our tenants on the Indian Reserves in the Township of Durham to pay rent to no one except to the Indians themselves personally."[67]

Likely surprising even the enterprising Noel Annance, the petition garnered action. The governor general, as requested, ordered the attorney general to enquire into the situation, whereupon Napier less than three months later came full circle to Noel for additional information.[68] Noel's lengthy response, citing several examples of infringements respecting the payment of rents, highlights how captivity narratives' legacies operated a century and a half after the event. It was not only outsiders who were taking advantage of Abenakis to their own financial gain but also, and perhaps even more so, Ignace Gill against his kinfolk, including among others Noel's widowed sister, Marie Josephte.

Letter on Durham lands to Department of Indian Affairs, 26 March 1848

Drummondville 26th Mar 1848

To Col. Napier &c
D I Afrs Dear Sir

Your favor of the 17th ultimo enclosing the directions of the Attorney General reached me on the evening of the 18th and in obedience to the instructions thereof I shall take the earliest opportunity to bring everything respecting the matter in question, into some tangible shape, that "effectual proceeding may be adopted" in due time. In our late petition to the Gov. General there was one clause wherein we prayed that our tenants might be notified not to pay rent to any person except to the Indians themselves: because great many seizures have been made on the rents by traders and others on account of some debts and other pretended claims on the property of the Indians. Ignace Gill of St Francis has now nearly all the Indian lands in Durham. He has sued many of the tenants who shewed any doubts of his authority to get the rent on Indian lands. There is a poor woman with two children living in the Indian village quite destitute – her husband left her some ten years ago – he is now living in the U. States. This woman from her condition and helplessness ought to be allowed to receive the rent due on the land of her husband to support the children; but Gill claims the land, and the poor woman never could get the worth of a shilling these ten years. Some means should be taken to put a stop to such proceedings because great wrong and injury are done to the children, and in direct violation of the very Proviso in the Patent Deed intended by the Government to secure the benefits of those lands to the children and heirs of the original Grantees. Gill has sued Robert Millar in the court of Queens Bench because he refused to buy the land he occupies from Gill; the land belongs to my sister widow of the late Pierre Wasaminet. This is the way Gill intends to become Seigneur of Durham
...
I am, Dr Sir,
with profound respect
your
and obedient
Servt
Noel Annance

Note: The remainder of the letter gives a second example and then turns to another topic.
Source: Noel Annance to Napier, 26 March 1848, Library and Archives Canada, RG10, vol. 605, pp. 50279-82, reel 13382.

Noel's and the others' optimism that their concerns over the Durham lands would have a hearing was not borne out.[69] The result of the petition was rather the reverse. Napier may have been duplicitous when on 16 July 1848 he requested that Noel, along with one of the Gills, arrange for "the grantees of the Indian reserve in Durham or their heirs" to meet with him at the end of August in St Francis at the time of the distribution of the annual presents. In the interim, in respect to an enclosed "copy of the list of the said Grantees and Heirs, which appears to have been prepared many years ago and may require to be revised, at the present day – will you be so good as to note thereon the names or their surviving representatives and return it to me as early as may be practicable."[70] Noel must have had every reason to believe something positive was going to result. No information has been located respecting what occurred at the meeting, but six weeks later, rather than launching a court case or otherwise remediating the rent situation, the attorney general recommended, in line with the order-in-council of 1 July 1839, that Durham lands not "occupied for the purpose of settlement by the original grantees or their heirs" be surrendered.[71]

Napier passed the proposal onto Noel with a request he consult as many heirs to the original grantees as possible. Having done so, Noel reported back respecting the inequity of the change in direction: "I found them all averse to the proposed surrender: and all seemed very urgent that the attorney himself should prosecute those fellows who will not pay rent nor give up the land to the Indians according to the express agreement they made with them, before they come to serious blows with them." Noel was very aware of the impetus to the proposed surrender, given that "it appears that those 'certain inhabitants' who petitioned the government last winter are those who refuse to give one third of the crop or give up the land to the Indians according to the agreement made sometimes since" with them. "The leases of the above lots of land expired sometime ago, but the tenants absolutely refused to give one third of the crops or give up the land according to the conditions of the leases."[72]

Rather than the Indian Department attending to Indigenous peoples, as was its function, either on behalf of the attorney general or on behalf of the Indian Department – and it does not matter which since they acted in tandem – it sought to dispossess them. Colin Calloway explains about English-speaking newcomers, whose wishes had priority, that "voicing the argument that had been used to justify dispossession of the Abenakis for generations, they claimed the Abenakis had scarcely made any improvements on their lands and it was a great waste to allow the Indians to hold 'such a large tract in an unsettled, uncultivated state.'"[73] Their perspective echoed the logic being used more generally to dispossess Canada's Indigenous peoples. By virtue of not using the land as whites did, they had no right to it.

Determined to have their way, newcomers became increasingly aggressive. Noel, Osunkhirhine, their relative John Stanislas, who had also attended Moor's Charity School, and one other reported to the superintendent general of Indian affairs in the summer of 1849 respecting "the daily outrages and robberies committed on us by the white people of this place, that they, by continually harassing us, may drive us away from our own lands." They were well aware of how the balance was shifting ever more away from Indigenous people to new arrivals. In 1840 Noel had successfully gone to court, but no more: "We applied to get justice but in vain because they say it requires the oath of six Indians to get a warrant against a white man!!" The quartet implicated Napier: "We have made several applications to Col. Napier for other injuries and outranges committed on us, but all in vain. Therefore, before we are driven the last resource, we beg the interference of our Protector the British government for life is not worthy holding when there is no civil liberty."[74]

Given Napier had charge of Quebec, it was virtually inevitable the 1849 joint letter of protest would be passed on to him for a response. He could not have been more unhelpful: "If justice has been refused you by any magistrate," it was their responsibility to report the case to the secretary of the province and to submit the necessary documentation. Despite having to go through an intermediary or perhaps several of them, very possibly to no avail, Napier contended that "the Law makes no distinction between an Indian and a white man, in regard to civil rights."[75]

The ever persistent Noel would have been even more consternated if he had realized Napier perceived opposition to the government's plan to be masterminded by Noel for his own purposes, as opposed to being widespread. In one sense, it was a backhanded compliment to Noel

that Napier considered he possessed such authority, but it was to no
good purpose. Noel was an easy target with which to deflect responsibility and accountability. In response to a petition from grantees received in the summer of 1849 concerning questionable leases, Napier
reported to the superintendent general of Indian affairs not only that it
was "in the hand of Noel Annance" but also that "I am inclined to
think that he has taken part with the Petitioners in executing the illegal
leases in question."[76]

Even as Napier put the onus on Noel, he continued to use Noel for
his own purposes. In late summer 1849 Napier requested, as he would
also do a year later, that Noel inform "the Indians of Durham, that
their presents will be issued at Saint Francis" in a few days hence.[77]
Given that the two locations were seventy-five kilometres, or forty-five
miles, distant from each other, disseminating the message was no easy
matter. By the fall of 1850, several letters of entreaty later, Noel was, as
he must have considered, at wit's end with nowhere to head.[78]

LOSING LONG ISLAND

It was within this context that two decades of uncertainty over the status of Long Island came to a head. Two very different versions of
events survive. Newcomers' perspective is direct, to the point, and consistent with white self-confidence. According to local notary Joseph-
Charles Saint-Amant, writing four decades after the event, "Thomas
Brady, Esq., J.P." – in other words, the gentleman that Noel might have
been if he were not Indigenous – "claimed to be owner by virtue of
good titles." Saint-Amant having differentiated in the reader's mind between Brady, depicted as a leader in the community and a justice of the
peace, and Annance – "But what mattered the titles of a white man to
an Abenaki chief, a son of the forest?" – he described what ensued:
"One day Mr. Brady went to the island, Annance hidden in a haystack
fired on him. Luckily the murderer missed his target. Mr. Brady left to
very excusably employ force, and Annance soon left the island."[79]

Noel Annance recounted to Napier a more complex series of events,
similarly self-serving and with much the same outcome. The conflict
originated, according to Noel, in neighbour Thomas Brady's seeking in
early 1856 "to hire ten acres of the Island for hay; because his farm

near me is so sandy that on dry seasons no grass can grow on it." On Noel's refusal, Brady offered him "a trifling sum" for the property, which he also turned down.[80] Brady was persistent, and in August 1855 he and four others came to Long Island, cut Noel's grass for hay, and took forceful possession of his house.[81] Napier supported Noel to the extent of appointing an official to enquire into the situation since an Indigenous person had in the eyes of the law no "authority to compel witnesses to come forward," only for Noel to be arrested for a third time on the very day he was to consult with the appointed official. This time it was for "taking some hay out of an apartment in my own house in which I and family were living" in order to share with a neighbour, which Brady represented as theft.[82] Repeatedly imprisoned in faraway Trois-Rivières, Noel would each time eventually be released.

Noel may, or may not, have been the author of his family's fate. In November 1856 Brady sent Napier copies of two leases. The first purported that Noel had three years earlier leased Long Island for ninety-nine years to a third party, and the second was the earlier lease's recent transfer to Brady for £25.[83] Informed, Noel countered in considerable detail as to how the lease was a "trick" given that, as an Indigenous person, he had "no authority to dispose of, or give on a lease, any Island in the river St. Francis."[84]

For Noel, the long harassment campaign seeking to drive him out not only was about what he still considered to be his island but also had practical considerations. Each time, despite being acquitted, "I am dragged away from my family whose daily wants I have to provide for and from a large school under my charge on the main road in Durham near the village."[85] Faced with the imperative of making a living, Noel and his family left Long Island in 1860, if not earlier.[86]

STILL THE DURHAM LANDS

The sequence of events removing Noel Annance and his family from Long Island contrasted sharply with the "Act to Change the Tenure of the Indian Lands in the Township of Durham," passed by the Province of Canada, being Quebec and Ontario, in 1856. Whether or not Noel's many years of advocacy played a role, the act was an about-face. It validated his absolute determination of many years that the lands not be stripped away without recompense: "It is desirable both in the interest of the Indians who do not reside any more on the said lands, and in that of the public of the said locality, that the said transactions should be rendered legal, in order to secure a just compensation to the former, and incontestable titles to the parties now in possession of the said lands." By the act, "all conveyances, sales, promises of sale or emphy-teotic [long-term] leases, shall hereafter be considered as having been made by persons legally qualified to lease, alienate, sell, cede and convey their property, notwithstanding any thing to the contrary contained in the Letters Patent of such lands."[87] Persons who had sold or bought Durham land, among them the captivity narratives' descendants, ranging from Noel Annance and other onetime Moor's students to the venerable Ignace Gill, were validated.

As Noel Annance and the others soon found out, the process set out in the act "to legalize the bargains made with the Indians and the present occupation of these lands" was confusing. It was so much so that in December 1856 Noel, after first offering Superintendent General of Indian Affairs Richard Pennefather a bit of personal background, beseeched him for clarification.[88] Again, Noel by his pen effected change. Per a notation, the letter was "referred to the Hon[ble] The Attorney General East for opinion & report thereon."[89] Noel in the interim bombarded Pennefather respecting specific cases that were unresolvable within the act, which may also have played a role.[90] A clarified act was passed in 1860, of which Noel took advantage to sell off another 260 acres of Durham land in seven parcels between 1860 and 1862, albeit for relatively small amounts, in total somewhat over $200.[91]

Land sales were insufficient, given the loss of Long Island and Noel having only intermittent teaching jobs, to support his family. For the first time in his life, it seems, he asked for help. "Having been afflicted and distressed with various calamities and troubles from various incidents and unforeseen events," Noel petitioned the governor general "for assistance and relief" in December 1861. The petition was, he explained, a direct consequence of the longstanding Durham land disputes, whereby, because he was "a minor" in the eyes of the law, he "could not organize a lawsuit." It was "after much trouble and expense, your Petitioner was compelled to abandon the hopeless struggle and watch for more auspicious days." A note on the request indicated that it was transferred to the Indian Department "for assistance out of Indian Fund," meaning Noel did likely receive some support.[92]

In the interim, Noel persisted as best he could with his pen. In January 1862, citing several acts by their legal definitions, indicating once again his close knowledge of the law, Noel sought a definitive answer as to whether "any contract, bargain, deed or sale of any property, real or personal, made by any Indian ... or any document having reference to such contract or deed made by such Indian be admitted or received into any of H.M's courts in a legal contest between parties." A notation on the letter intended to frame a response was succinct and to the point: "Indians are minors, and can enter into no contract [so] consequently no contract can be referred to."[93] In innumerable letters to government officials, Noel time and again spelled out his full awareness of how the law had become stacked against Indigenous peoples in favour of others, querying "under what circumstances they are considered as minors in the eyes of the law, why an Indian cannot recover his land, or any other property illegally detained by another, by an action in a court of justice."[94]

A year later, in 1863, Noel reminded the governor general of British North America, Viscount Monck, how "the Indians were minors in the eye of the law, not able to obtain redress by a legal process," in consequence of which are "the many expedients, various schemes, artful machinations and roguish intrigues resorted to in order to cheat the poor unprotected Indians."[95] Noel's consternation was shared by others, an 1863 visitor to St Francis being informed how, "if an Indian's rights are threatened or he is otherwise mistreated by the whites he can not seek recourse in the courts on his own but must be represented by his guardian, the government."[96] Noel would repeatedly petition his ultimate guardian in the person of the governor general to no apparent avail.[97]

Noel Annance looked for small openings able to make processes more visible to others and thereby, he hoped, fairer. Respecting the purchase of 150 acres earlier belonging to his father, with the monies being paid to the superintendent general of Indian affairs, Noel sought to know in May 1862, given that he had earlier received a judgment against the purchaser for rent due on the land, why he was not "entitled to the purchase money or at least to the interest thereof."[98] A year later, he painted for Louis-Victor Sicotte, long-time Quebec politician and now attorney general and joint premier of the Province of Canada, a sad picture of events that he as an Indigenous person had been deprived of any capacity to affect: "They will tell the Indian sign this paper and I will pay you and after the poor fellow signed he is told that he has no right to sell and he will get nothing ... The impositions, tricks and frauds practiced upon the Indians defy all description ... There is something very strange in the manner we Indians have been treated these few years past." Speaking to Noel's power of persuasion, or perhaps just to get it out of the way, the letter was sent on to the superintendent general of Indian affairs, which explains its survival.[99] In March 1866 Noel petitioned the governor general as to his inability to act, given that "the Indians are minors in the eyes of the law, not able to obtain redress by a legal process," and he referenced "the many expedients, various schemes, artful machinations and roguish intrigues resorted to, in order to cheat the poor unprotected Indians."[100]

Noel continued to write whomever he considered might be in a position to make a difference in what must have been from his perspective the increasingly vain hope that the individual would seek to do so.[101] What he could not have realized, but survives as notations on his later letters, was that they sometimes caused a bit of a stir. Following Napier's retirement in 1857, Noel's interventions may have given his successors more of a perspective on the ground than they would otherwise have had. His April 1863 letter to Louis-Victor Sicotte was referred to the superintendent general of Indian affairs. Three letters Noel wrote concerning questionable land deals caused their recipient, the deputy superintendent, to pencil on each of them as they were received in respect to the topic at hand, "Let me have this again."[102] Noel's petition of September 1868 to Governor General Lord Monck was "referred to the Deputy Secretary of Indian Affairs for report."[103]

DURHAM LANDS RESOLVED

Noel Annance's persistence made a difference to the resolution of the Durham lands dispute. Not only were somewhat more equitable arrangements concerning them accepted, but Abenaki heirs to the original 1805 grantees also gained a longer breathing space than they would otherwise have done. Noel, Simon Annance, and Peter Paul Osunkhirhine were among those who had thereby taken financial advantage.[104]

Noel continued to press for a full resolution, his last letter located being penned just two weeks before his death in September 1869. Its recipient was Hector-Louis Langevin, who as secretary of state had been responsible for Indian affairs since Canada became a Confederation in 1867.[105] In a "statement and explanation of the present condition of the Indian lands in the Township of Durham," written with a clear hand in persuasive language, Noel pointed out how by now, "with the exception of a few lots, the whole Indian Reserve in the Township of Durham is in the hands of Mr Senécal M.P. who gets all the rent from the occupants of Indian lands."[106] As to why Louis-Adélard Senécal was in this privileged position, the Quebec entrepreneur and politician had acquired the property following Ignace Gill's death in 1865. Indicative of the close ties between these two businessmen whose ambition verged on ruthlessness, four months after the death of Noel Annance, Senécal's daughter Delphine wed Ignace Gill's son Charles, who would a decade and a half later write the Gill family history.[107] He would do so from a wholly white perspective to the extent of excising the Annances from the text as Gill descendants.[108]

Ironically given Noel's earlier unacknowledged translations of one or more New Testament chapters into Abenaki, Charles Gill published about the same time as he did the family history an astute introduction to several recently unearthed, Jesuit-created Abenaki-language manuscripts.[109] For all of the two men's fundamentally different histories and life trajectories, they were not necessarily as far apart in all matters as they would seem to have been.

Noel Annance's letter to Langevin of August 1869 hoped something might be done in the form of an accounting of what had occurred respecting the Durham lands. Noel predicted, "should any enquiry be made very soon many enormous and monstrous irregularities will be found, which will shew what principle and what honesty there is among those squatters on the Indian land."[110] The letter had an effect. Langevin sent it "to WS for action."[111] So nudged, Deputy Superintendent William Spragge initiated precisely such a reckoning. As many documents as possible were collected, although none were requested, at least as far as the report indicates, from Abenaki people, apart from those Noel Annance had submitted on the subject over the years.

The consequence was, all the same, a very detailed and credible report with many attached documents that sought to sort out how events had transpired as they had and to whom parcels now belonged by virtue of the deeds to them. The December 1869 report to the secretary of state gave legitimacy to Noel's three decades of letter writing and to his manoeuvring during these same years in his own and his family's interest: "Noel Francis Annance has sold a great many lots, it appears, however, by deeds of a comparatively old date he purchased from the grantees. It would be a difficult matter, I imagine, to trace these deeds now."[112]

The report laid bare the great differential in access to power and to the law between Abenakis and others determined to have their lands. The report testified to the accuracy of Noel's last letter or possibly took it as a cue to conclude that "most of these lands had been purchased by the late Ignace Gill Esq."[113] Exemplary of the ironies attaching to the long ago captivity narratives was the report's statement, respecting where Noel lived the last five years of his life, as to how "the village of L'Avenir" north of Durham had been built upon 200 acres that Ignace Gill had acquired over time in parcels.[114] Among the properties Gill accumulated was one amounting to 50 acres acquired from Noel in 1862, which could possibly have been on the condition that he continued to live there.[115]

TO SUM UP

By the time of his death in 1869, Noel Annance had come to the end of the road in respect to land. Just as there was no land grant in the offing pursuant to his military service, or in the Pacific Northwest, so his island slipped away, much as did large parts of the St Francis concession, with which Noel was not directly involved. The Durham lands were more complex, with a better outcome. For all that Noel achieved less than he sought, his correspondence tucked away in Library and Archives Canada attests that Indigenous dispossession was contested and that, in some instances, his letters occasioned interested responses. The consequence was, all the same, land no more.

8

To Belong or Not to Belong

The unexpected happened in Noel Annance's later years. He had never been more than at the edge of belonging as the gentleman of his higher education. Returning home to St Francis, he was at the edge of his indigeneity by virtue of his association with the English-speaking, Protestant ethos consequent on the captivity narratives that had formed him. His having dared all his life to be his own person left him with nowhere to head.

Then Noel Annance was given a choice, or so he thought. He had an opportunity to belong. He could become the gentleman of his youth, the gentleman of the War of 1812 and his first optimistic years in the fur trade, the gentleman of his imagination, if at the cost of subordinating his indigeneity. The impetus was an act passed in 1857 making it possible for individual Indigenous persons perceived to have attributes aligning them with the dominant society to be "civilized," and Noel was among the first to apply to be so. For a moment, if not longer, he may have genuinely believed in the government's seeming promise of Indigenous inclusion.

As the years wore on and nothing happened with Noel's application, which suggests that the act was never intended to be taken seriously, as Noel had done, he could not help but be cognizant of his two brothers' and eldest son's searches for belonging. Also educated at Moor's Charity School, they had followed pathways very different from his own. They had each dared but in their own ways and directions.

YOUNGER BROTHER JOSEPH'S PATHWAY

Noel's greatest fraternal separation both in time and in outlook was from his younger brother, Joseph, whose admission to Moor's he had successfully urged in his letter of 1815 and who was subsequently also attracted by the fur trade. If the brothers' paths crossed in the Pacific Northwest, it was prior to Joseph along with a dozen others slipping away in 1825 from a Hudson's Bay Company trapping expedition.

Unlike Noel an ordinary employee rather than officer, the departing twenty-five-year-old had up to then done the job assigned to him. The expedition's journal recorded, shortly before the men's departures, how he along with three others had "left their beaver *en Cache*, stored them in a hiding place which three days later contained 110 Beaver," and how "Annance cast up from ahead with the favourable news of plenty beaver."[1] Joseph and another man "paid their debts" before heading off.[2] His motive for leaving was not to cheat the company but to contest its unwillingness to match American prices for beaver pelts, making it unsurprising that he and the others were given an open invitation to return.[3]

The other departees were Iroquois from Caughnawaga outside of Montreal, highly valued as voyageurs and trappers. Their leader, Ignace Hatchiorauquasha, known as John Gray, was the son of a New England child captive of the Iroquois who had become an interpreter, married an Iroquois woman, and served in both the War of Independence and the War of 1812.[4] According to a common lateral descendant, Annance and Gray stuck together, unsurprising given their literacy and captivity inheritances.[5] Alongside a hundred or so American trappers, the two men shortly after their departure from the Hudson's Bay Company attended a summer rendezvous in central Wyoming. There, companies sold trade goods and staples, and "Mr Annance" exchanged seventeen beaver pelts for sugar, coffee, knives, beads, rings, powder lead, and tobacco to the value of $46.75.[6] The only subsequent certain reference has Joseph among a number of men signing a contract in 1830 at Fort Union, located on the border of Montana and North Dakota, to trap over the next year for an American company.[7]

Joseph Annance was possibly among the dozen families of "Frenchmen and Indians" recorded as having in the summer of 1836 "lately come down from the Rocky Mountains" to settle at the mouth of the Kansas River, the site of present-day Kansas City, Missouri.[8] It was there in 1840 that Joseph's daughter Mary is said to have partnered with John Gray's son Peter, their daughter Louise according to one account being raised by her great-uncle Louis in Maine, which suggests that the brothers kept in correspondence.[9] Not to be found among twenty-six families, including that of John Gray, on a map of the "French Settlement" made in 1840, Joseph had by then, if not earlier, disappeared from view.[10] However his life ended, Joseph Annance lived on his own terms in a part of North America where the distinction between being Indigenous or not was still in flux.

OLDER BROTHER LOUIS'S PATHWAY

Noel's older brother, Louis, similarly followed his own pathway toward belonging. He had early on been drawn back to the New Hampshire of his Moor's schooling. There, he became so well known as a guide that, about the time he left for his family's extended visit to St Francis in 1841, he was sought out for his services by a determined Harvard undergraduate. Future historian Francis Parkman paints a deft portrait of Louis's reputation: "I ... came to Lancaster today to secure the servides of an Indian named Anantz as a guide. He was by far the best hunter in this part of the country, and lived, in part, by guiding parties through the wilderness on the borders of New Hampshire and Canada. He was an educated man, moreover, having passed through Dartmouth College [*sic*], and celebrated through the country for his skill, faithfulness, and courage. But arriving in Lancaster, I found that he was absent."[11] Young Parkman had to content himself with reading through the journal of the head of a geological survey of the year before in which were "preserved a considerable number of Indian legends taken from the lips of Anantz, who is well versed in the traditions of his tribe."[12]

Returning from St Francis in the late 1840s, Louis settled his family just over 300 kilometres, or almost 200 milies, northeast of Lancaster at Moosehead Lake in northern Maine (see map 1). Possibly prospecting where to head, Louis had in the spring of 1846 taken Noel with him to Maine for a visit.[13] The brothers almost certainly remained in contact, as Louis had also done with Joseph.[14] Their common facility with writing had its rewards.

The combination of skills that Louis employed at Moosehead, as he had done earlier at Lancaster, gives every indication of being double-edged. He gave those who hired or otherwise knew him what they wanted to see but with a jolt intended to unsettle their easy assumptions concerning Indigenous people's lack of capacity. According to a man who as a boy knew Louis, "He spoke pure English. He was a great reader and an easy speaker. Although he lived in the solitude of the wilderness, nearly all the time he kept himself well up on current events of the time. He could sit down with an educated person and converse with him on almost any subject."[15] To this "educated Indian of Moosehead lake," as reported by two other locals, "the ways of his White Brothers were acceptable, and he was at all times a respected member of the community."[16]

More so than Noel, but less so than younger brother Joseph, Louis lived on his own terms. By giving those he guided what they wanted to believe, he avoided the vituperation that had befallen Noel for seeking to be accepted for what he sought to become, as opposed to what others wanted him to be. Louis was recalled as a family man who belonged to the Congregational Church but also as a man who had "lived in the old manner," teaching locals "the ways of the woods and lakes, as well as Indian lore," and "having smoked a mixture of tobacco and squaw-bush, half and half."[17] The American popular magazine *Field and Stream*'s flare for the dramatic may somewhat, but certainly not wholly, excuse its rhetoric: "We met near the lake and hurried to camp for breakfast, where the boys [were] entertaining Louis Annance, an old Passamaquoddy Indian. Opening the way to good fellowship by swapping knives ... I enquired the best place to find deer. Pointing to the east, he said, 'right over there, kind o' bog hole. Best place I know' ... He also said 'Moose 'fraid man. Caribou 'fraid like the devil railroad train. Deer, him ain't 'fraid anything."[18] New England writer Henry David Thoreau, who visited the area in 1853 and again in 1857 to hunt moose with Indigenous guides, referred in passing to unnamed "St. Francis Indians" and patronizingly described Abenakis as "the primitive man of America," among other such epitaphs.[19] The question left to the reader of these accounts is who was putting on whom.

ILLUSTRATION 13
Noel Annance's older brother, Louis

The closest to a first-person account of Louis Annance in later life comes from a conversation a year before his death in 1875 in which he described having "wandered into Northern Maine as far as Moosehead lake."[20] The interviewer's lengthy characterization speaks to a dilemma Noel similarly faced, namely that, however fully he engaged literacy's promise, he was still a stereotypical Indigenous person from others' perspectives:

> He was a man of marked natural ability and superior intelligence, and was noted for his kind and generous disposition, his genial and pleasant manners, unimpeachable integrity and strict morality. While possessing all of these traits of a noble and refined manhood, he, at the same time, always retained the natural instincts and peculiarities of his race; for he loved the lone hunting-grounds of his fathers, and devoted many autumns and winters to the adventurous hunt and exciting chase. He was a true child of nature, endowed with faculties that enabled him to fully appreciate her mysteries, wonders, and grandeur.[21]

Respected Maine historian and naturalist Fannie Hardy Eckstorm, born in 1865, caught the contradiction: "Old Louis had been to college; but he hunted and fished and went in the woods like any other Indian."[22]

Louis Annance's ties to the Freemasons, going back to his time in New Hampshire, structured his death, as it likely had his life. Not only did the local lodge conduct his funeral, but a year later it also erected a monument in his honour, described as "simple but dignified."[23] The tribute paid during the funeral encapsulates Louis's and Noel's determination that their lives accord with literacy's promise, as well as the larger society's condescending perspective on their daring to do so: "Although belonging to a race for the most part wanting in the grace and polish of education, he availed himself of some opportunities for mental culture thrown in his way in early life ... Many of the characteristics of his race exhibited themselves in his life, despite the influences of the schools and early associations with the whites."[24]

Just as with Noel in the fur trade, Louis Annance for all of his learning was compartmentalized as Indigenous, if not in his actions, then in his thought process and physical appearance, with all the associated freight. The man who as a boy had known Louis described him as "tall, straight, broad-shouldered," and "copper-colored."[25] In the thinking of his interviewer in old age, Louis had to have been cumbered by the fate of his people: "It seemed to me that the spirit of this aged man was weighted with the errors, oppression, and sorrows of his race, and that the glimpses which education had enabled him to obtain the possibilities of a grander and a higher life, had increased his soul burden ... In his mind were mingled the joys and griefs of a once strong, proud and manly race – weak only because of their inability to grasp the knowledge of a new and strange world."[26]

By virtue of dwelling "in a static and immutable past," Louis Annance seemingly confirmed, Jean O'Brien explains, the comforting stenotype of the day in the emerging dominant society that Indigenous people "could never be modern."[27] They were a relic needing over the short term to be condoned, and written about kindly, until they disappeared altogether into the shadows of the past.

Louis Annance left a large family, with many descendants in Maine and elsewhere into the present day. To the extent that the three brothers and their families kept in touch by post or in person, they must have marvelled at how different their lives had turned out, yet wondered at how similar were perspectives toward them among persons perceiving themselves as white.

SON ARCHIE'S PATHWAY

With Noel's son Archie, it is unclear what motivated him to take the pathway toward belonging, or not so, that he did. Whatever his reasoning, Archie soon decided the enclosed world of St Francis, with an interval at Moor's in the 1840s on the pattern of so many family members, was not for him.

By 1850 Archie Annance had headed out to make life on his own terms across a swath of territory. Respected as a mineralogist, a skill possibly picked up at Moor's, he is remembered as "one of the first prospectors in New Hampshire," with Indian Stream and Annance Gulch both named after him (see map 1).[28] So is Annance River on New Hampshire's border with Maine about 100 kilometres, or 60 miles, east of Sherbrooke, Quebec.[29] Archie described in 1874 how he "had rendered important services to the country in developing the mineral resources of part of the Eastern Townships" and hoped to form a "gold mining company."[30] Consequent on his father's death, Archie unsuccessfuly sought access to the Durham lands granted his paternal grandfather in 1805, and he was as of 1875 living in West Ditton, Quebec, about forty kilometres, or twenty-five miles, west of Lac-Mégantic, possibly awaiting the claim's adjudication, with plans "to move in a northern direction."[31]

Subsequent accounts celebrate Archie's taking chances. By an account of 1886 in *Field and Stream*, no one knew as much about the area's fishing and hunting prospects as did "Annance the Indian who was educated by the State."[32] Living in a small cabin perhaps of his own making, Archie located placer gold, which was likely responsible for his being in 1891 set on and killed in his cabin by whites determined to seize the riches they believed were hidden there.[33]

In the pattern of his uncle Louis, Archie's obituary described him, affectionately for the times, as "our Abenaki Indian" who "was the friend of all the pioneers with whom he lived in harmony."[34] This second *Field and Stream* salute was at one and the same time stereotypical and generous: "The last Indian of the Magalloway River [of northern Maine] is dead. His name was Archie Annance, and he was much beloved by all who had ever the good fortune to fish or trap with him. He disliked civilization, like the most of his race, and naturally took to the woods, though reported to have been educated in his younger days."[35]

Like his uncles Joseph and Louis, Archie assured whites that, yes, Indigenous peoples were, if amusing, surely a thing of the past. Their daring to be their own persons came with a cost, one that, even for the best educated among Indigenous peoples, which they were, could not be overcome.

NOEL'S PATHWAY

Noel wanted more. Unlike his brothers and eldest son, he was all his life unwilling to give newcomers the satisfaction they sought as to Indigenous peoples' inability to compete with them. Although no record survives of his appearance or of how he talked, and despite the fact that he appears never to have been written about or to have had his picture taken, as soon as he put pen to paper he became the gentleman of his higher education. In that moment he belonged. On returning to St Francis, Noel described himself as Abenaki, including at times in his ongoing correspondence with the Department of Indian Affairs, despite the form and content of his letters sending a different message.

Noel's strategy did not equate with comfort with his circumstances, as attested by his response to the Canadian government's 1857 "An Act to Encourage the Gradual Civilization of Indian Tribes," whose goal was "the gradual removal of all legal distinctions between them [Indian tribes] and Her Majesty's Other Canadian Subjects." The act built on the recommendation in the 1844 Bagot Report that Indigenous individuals be able to get a patent for Indigenous land they occupied where "qualified by education, knowledge of the arts and customs of civilized life and habits of industry and prudence, to protect his own interests, and to maintain himself as an independent member of the general community." As to the reasoning, "this proposition is founded upon the conviction, that it is desirable to release the Indians from their present state of tutelage, as soon as they are competent to take care of themselves; that to postpone their emancipation until the whole body is advanced to that stage, would be the most effectual way of retarding that desirable event; and that the example and encouragement held out by the admission of their more enlightened members to all the privileges of a Citizen, will be the highest incentive to exertion."

In making the recommendation, the Bagot commissioners had been particularly aware of how, "in Lower Canada, where Indians are more mixed up with, or closely surrounded by, the white population, there is no evidence of their deriving any harm from the contact; on the contrary, they are reported to be nearly, if not quite, on a par with their Canadian neighbors."[36] The Catholic priest having charge of St Francis may have influenced the Bagot commissioners' perspective by his own view that "I do not know why the Indians are excluded from the enjoyment of the same civil and political rights as all other subjects."[37] It is distressing to speculate that, if not for Indian Department officials defending their turf, the consequence being the Indian Act of 1876, things might have transpired very differently for Indigenous peoples.

The 1857 act perverted the Bagot recommendations. Not satisfied with usurping Indigenous land on various grounds and pretexts, as Noel knew first hand, the Indian Department sought to detach individuals from their ways of life with a faux promise of entering its white counterpart. By the act's provisions, "any such Indian of the male sex, and not under twenty-one years of age, [who] is able to speak, read and write either the english or the french language readily and well, and is sufficiently advanced in the elementary branches of education and is of good moral character and free from debt" could avail himself of the act and would thereupon be examined by the tribe's visiting superintendent, a missionary, and a third appointed person. If meeting the requirements, the individual was to be allotted "a piece of land not exceeding fifty acres out of the land reserved or set apart for the use of his Tribe, and also a sum of money equal to the principal of his share of the annuities and other yearly revenues receivable by or for the use of such Tribe."

A DECEPTIVE ACT

The "gradual civilization" act was deceptive. Although it claimed that "any distinction between the legal rights and liabilities of Indians and those of Her Majesty's other subjects shall cease to apply to any Indian so declared to be enfranchised, who shall no longer be deemed an Indian within the meaning thereof," such persons were multiply dispossessed. The piece of land allotted them was removed from the holdings of the tribe, from which they were now excluded yet perforce living in proximity, almost inevitably creating tensions that could not be remedied. Despite being "liable to taxes and all other obligations and duties under the Municipal and School Laws," enfranchised Indigenous persons possessed "a life estate only therein," meaning that the land could be passed on to "children or lineal descendants" but not to wives and that it was unable to be sold. The consequence was, rather than, in the words of the Bagot Report, the enfranchised person being able to "maintain himself as an independent member of the general community," he was tied legally and geographically to his Indigenous counterparts, from whom by his actions he had almost certainly alienated himself.

BUYING INTO THE ACT

Despite the "gradual civilization" or "emancipation" act's shortcomings, Noel Annance was captured by its broader intent and also, it must be said, by its monetary component, not unexpectedly so given his loss of Long Island and the intermittence of his teaching positions. Initially, Noel considered the enfranchisement process to be straightforward and assumed that, on making the request in 1859, it would be effected almost as a matter of course.[38] In March 1860 he optimistically queried the superintendent general of Indian affairs, Richard T. Pennefather, as to the status of his application, explaining his need for the money due to his financial circumstances.

Letter on enfranchisement to superintendent general of Indian affairs, 2 March 1860

Durham 2ᵈ March 1860

Richard J Pennefather Esq.
        Dear Sir
        Will you be so kind as to inform me if my emancipation has been effected; and if so, I beg that you would be pleased to send me the money, or small part of it; and as soon as I am able I will go down to Quebec to show myself and go thro' the formalities should there be any need for them.
        I have been confined to my bed these several weeks by sickness, and stand in great need of help, having a large family to provide for – .
        In so doing you will confer great favor in your humble servant –
                        Noel Annance

R.T. Pennefather Esq.
Supt Genl I Affrs &c &c
        Quebec

Source: Noel Annance to R.T. Pennefather, 2 March 1860, Library and Archives Canada, RG10, vol. 253, pp. 181270-1, reel 12643.

Noel was soon disabused of his optimism. Not only was the act deceptive, but it also did not much exist in practice. The notation on his letter as to its response, which was posted to Noel on 6 March 1860, reads, "No communication has yet issued for the examination provided by the civilization act. R.T.P."[39] The inference that examinations provided by the act had yet to be organized was misleading at best or a deliberate falsehood at worst, for over a year earlier at least one such event had already transpired in Ontario, which was also under Pennefather's supervision.

On the act's passage in 1857, six Mohawks had applied, whereupon the visiting superintendent in charge of the Six Nations to which they belonged had set up, in accordance with the act's provisions, an examination committee consisting of himself, the local missionary, and a local white businessman. Five of the applicants were rejected, the sixth being examined on 21 March 1859. The official transcript has Elias Hill being asked his baptismal name, his age (twenty-one), the location of his home, his trade (shoemaker), who his employer was, about his indebtedness (none), whether he could "read and write well," and his place of schooling, which was the Mohawk Institution for nine years, where he also learned his trade. He was then asked about his mathematical ability, his knowledge of grammar and geography, the divisions of the globe, and his church membership, as well as to read a chapter of the New Testament and to spell several words.[40] Four witnesses then testified briefly. Elias's employer did so as to his shoemaking skills; a fellow student at the Mohawk Institution, which was an Anglican residential school established in 1828, confirmed Elias's deportment; and two local justices of the peace vouched for his character. Thereupon, the three commissioners deemed Hill "fully entitled to all the privileges of the civilisation act," which were accorded him then or later in the same year.[41] Not only was the process straightforward to the point of simplicity, but it was also firmly in place, contrary to the response given Noel.

PERSISTENCE

Over the next months and years, Noel Annance persisted toward what he termed "the huge project of getting me enfranchised and emancipated from the gentle and protective incubus which incapacitates me to move on the same plane and platform with my other fellow subjects of Her Majesty."[42] His single-minded goal, he explained to the superintendent general of Indian affairs in 1862, was "being converted into a man." He sought "to relieve an educated man from his present condition at once degraded and unworthy of a christian and civilized being; let the Indian sink in the officer, in the teacher of languages, and let all the qualifications which fit a man to be a gentleman be allowed to expiate the crime of being called an Indian."[43] For half a century, Noel had lived between gentility and indigeneity, belonging to neither despite all his daring.

What is clear from Noel Annance's correspondence of the next eight years on the subject of his application, about which over two dozen letters have been located, is that the Department of Indian Affairs was either duplicitous, disinterested, or incapable of administering the act, likely all three. Of potential candidates, he would appear to have exemplified the attributes that were sought. His combination of higher education and military service as an officer twice over was exemplary of what was possible to achieve by, to quote the act's title, "the gradual civilization of Indian tribes." Given that almost all of the letters respecting Noel's application are in a single file, it may well have been that he was being deliberately sidelined. To the extent those in charge considered they had a right to act as they did in response to his application, it may have lain in the act's preamble, which stated that it applied to persons "as shall be found to desire such encouragement and to have deserved it."[44] Noel was not sufficiently docile.

The inference left is not, as historians assert, that no one wanted to be "civilized" but that virtually no one was permitted to be "civilized" and thereby to disrupt a comfortable status quo within the Indian Department and the Department of Indian Affairs more generally.[45] The much cited statement that, "between 1857 and the codification of the Indian Act in 1876, precisely one male, Elias Hill, a Six Nations man who had attended the Mohawk Institute, applied for and received citizenship" is at best misleading.[46] Scattered throughout Indian Affairs files are multiple enquiries from interested persons and from others writing on their behalves.[47]

Noel for his part not only persisted but also recruited others to take advantage of the act. In March 1860, shortly after being informed that the examination process was not yet in place, Noel cheerfully informed the superintendent general of Indian affairs, "I am requested by my son Archibald to inform you that he wishes to avail himself of the emancipation act; he is a single man. You will be good to let me know as soon as convenient, when his emancipation can be effected."[48] In July 1862 Noel reported how "many young people of the village of some education were very much for it, but they have been disappointed" by the lack of a response.[49] The next month, Noel explained the situation to leading Quebec politician George-Étienne Cartier, concluding, "Therefore we, as many as are educated, whether in french or english appeal to you, as the head and first advisor of Her Majesty's Representative to exert your influence with the Executive, that a few of us of the Saint Francis tribe may be enfranchised and be made men capable of dealing with the civilized world with which we have constant intercourse."[50] It was, as these letters attest, not only Noel and his son Archie but also a broad swath of individuals, in St Francis and very possibly across the Canada of the day, who were being sidelined by the Department of Indian Affairs.

TAKING DIRECT ACTION

As the 1860s wore on, Noel despaired that, "after all the instructions and advice I have received in my applications, I find myself in the same untoward predicament in which I was before."[51] Be his approach serious or amusing, nothing ensued. "As for my enfranchisement, I take it to be in abeyance – in dormant state; when it awakens from in its quiet slumber, I may hear some rumors of it."[52]

Noel decided to do something about the situation. In line with his more general strategy of nudging the Department of Indian Affairs into action, he turned to intermediaries with the power, he hoped, to intercede. He took direct action.

In August 1862 Noel "called on" Quebec premier Louis-Victor Sicotte in Quebec City, who arranged on his behalf the appointment of the very respectable Ignace Gill and the long-time St Francis priest Joseph Maurault as his two examiners to attest to his character.[53] Sicotte's intervention secured for Noel Annance the two most prominent individuals associated with St Francis, who by any estimation should have by their recommendations expeditiously permitted him to obtain his goal. Whether or not it was coincidence, that same month Noel sold fifty acres to the acquisitive Ignace Gill in what would be his last recorded sale of Durham land.[54] Whatever the particulars, "I was made to understand that my 'enfranchisement' was to be affected without any further delay."[55]

In response to the naming of examiners, officials requested that Noel get letters from the two men Sicotte had arranged, which he very efficiently did do. Testifying to Noel's qualifications, both were highly positive in respect to the act's requirements. As Ignace Gill wrote to the commissioner of Crown lands, who was also superintendent general of Indian affairs, "The bearer Noel Annance one of [the] Indians of the Abenaki tribe of St. François de Sale wishes to avail himself of the advantages offered by the law 'An Act respecting Civilization and Enfranchisement of Certain Indians' he is a man of good education and sober."[56] Writing in French, Maurault stated, "I the undersigned certify that Noel Annance, the bearer of this message, is a sober man and possessing a good education."[57]

The arrival of the two requisite letters at the Department of Indian Affairs in August 1862 is revealing of its inner workings respecting persons seeking to be enfranchised. The first of three partially legible notes scrawled in pencil on the file containing the two letters commending Noel Annance reads, "Wishes to avail himself of the advantages offered by Law re civilization &c." The second in another hand appears to read, "Que[ry/estion?] Is this the person [who] was the culprit to whom Mr DeLorimier and the Court made appl? To decide as to his legality for enfranchisement." Likely because Noel had at about the same time alerted the Department of Indian Affairs to the sorry state of the St Francis school, the government official sent to investigate, long-time Indian Department interpreter Edward N. DeLorimier, may have sought retaliation against Noel as an interfering busybody. A third notation on the letter in the same hand, which is written sideways and is perhaps a continuation, may read, "Enquire at Secretary's Office re issue of comments of E.N. DeLorimier ... re enfranchising Indians of the Abenakis tribe. L.V.K."[58] The inference left is that not only Noel Annance, but also all Abenakis, were being blackballed for Noel's daring to speak out on their children's behalves.

Unaware of the Department of Indian Affairs' machinations and buoyed by having obtained the two letters of recommendation, Noel persevered. In September 1862 the now seventy-year-old again reminded officials of fellow Abenakis' interest in being enfranchised.[59] With nothing resulting from his application, come December Noel reviewed his situation with incoming Superintendent General William McDougall, reiterating his reasons for seeking to change his status and baldly querying whether "there be any real intention to encourage and promote education and civilization among the Indian Tribes in Canada."

In a mini-autobiography of his life as he perceived it, Noel compared his now "degraded position as an 'Indian'" with his earlier status as a gentleman and an officer. Whether or not it was coincidence, or a genuine response to the respectful tone, the notation reads for the first time on one of Noel's letters, "To be enfranchised."[60]

Letter on enfranchisement to superintendent general of Indian affairs, 1 December 1862

Durham 1st Decem 1862

To:
    the Hon. William McDougall
Sup. Genl. Ind[n] Affairs
    &c &c &c
Honored Sir
    I am very sorry I have given so much trouble to myself and to others in a wild goose chase after that phantom, enfranchisement alias emancipation, that was to liberate me from the thralldom to which I have been subjected by some "untoward accident," and be extricated from that unhallowed and benumbing incubus that paralyzes my civil and political existence. Since 1859 have been petitioning and praying to be enfranchised, pursuant to Act. 20 Vict 26 [Act to Encourage the Gradual Civilization of the Indian Tribes] but I am yet in status quo. Mr. Pennefather told me "if you want to be enfranchised, you must comply with the terms of the act." This I think I have done: Mr

Sicotte at my suggestion consented at his office last August to appoint Ignace Gill Esq and Messr Maurealt our Missionary, commissioners pursuant to Act 20 Vict 26 to examine me as to my fitness to be enfranchised – and both these gentlemen sent down their certificates. Now I am in great anxiety and painful perplexity, expecting to see my name in the official gazette enfranchised – to be converted into a man – a man fit to move in the circle of civil society, to mingle with [the] christian world. I grieve to think of my degraded position as an "Indian." I feel my self ashamed to be among gentleman – tho I have been called a gentleman – an officer – a teacher of languages – but, alas! All this is nothing. To have scanned Homer, Virgil, and Horace, to have traced Euclid through abstruse regions of mathematics has not expiated the crime of being called an "Indian." Therefore I humbly beg that gentlemen in power may feel for my situation and assist me in my humiliation, if there be any real intention to encourage and promote education and civilization among the Indian Tribes in Canada.

I have the honor
to be Sir
with profound respect
Your obd Servant
Noel Annance
Late Lieut Indn Dept

Source: Noel Annance to William McDougall, 1 December 1862, Library and Archives Canada, RG10, vol. 273, pp. 184378-80, reel 12657.

Following up a couple of months later, Noel pushed for closure one way or the other: "I would take it as an act of kindness and charity to be assured whether such a thing is to be realized or not, for I have been praying for it these three years past, and I certainly would be very thankful to be relieved from my intense anxiety." Not only was there once again the notation "To be enfranchised" on the letter, but another notation acknowledged the long history of the application, which was forwarded to yet another official.[61] Three months later, in

May 1863, Noel ended a letter on schooling to Deputy Superintendent William Spragge "with a humble request that I may soon hear about my emancipation."[62]

FUR TRADE INTERLUDE

Even as Noel Annance sought acknowledgment of his gentility through enfranchisement, he was reminded of its pursuit now so long ago in the fur trade. In June 1863, aged seventy-one, three decades after leaving the Hudson's Bay Company (HBC), he was thrust back to a time during which he had at least initially considered he could belong, congruent with his higher education.

The impetus was a request to testify in a Montreal court case about the legal status of offspring of couples who had lived together in the Pacific Northwest without Christian marriage, as Noel himself had done prior to the legal option becoming possible with the arrival of the first Protestant minister in 1834 and the first priests in late 1838. The eldest son of Lachine-born HBC chief factor William Connolly and of a Cree woman named Suzanne had initiated the proceedings against his father's second, white wife to secure a portion of the estate on the grounds that his parents had been wed in accordance with the customs of her people and by their own and others' public assent. Connolly had even taken Suzanne and their six children with him in 1832 when on leave to Lower Canada, where he soon opted to marry his white second cousin Julia Woolrich. Connolly thereafter supported two families, initially both in Montreal. In 1841 he arranged for Suzanne to reside in a Catholic convent at Red River. It was two years after his mother's death in 1862 that John Connolly launched his case, this at a time when his younger sister Amelia was first lady of the two British colonies of Vancouver Island and British Columbia by virtue of her husband James Douglas being governor.[63]

The case was decided for John Connolly, with the decision upheld in the Court of Appeals and then in the Quebec Superior Court, in good part on the basis of witnesses on his behalf, including Noel, who had lived in the Pacific Northwest at the time and could describe the character of such unions.[64] It is because Noel's testimony was repeatedly cited in the published decisions that part of it survives. His words are perforce edited in the sense that he was responding to questions as opposed to making a single coherent speech and in that the sections cited are those supporting the decision. Noel's testimony speaks both to the general character of the fur trade and to his encounter with the family during Connolly's charge of New Caledonia from 1824 to 1831 and with Suzanne at some point after Connolly left her in 1832.

Surviving testimony in *John Connolly v. Julia Woolrich and Thomas R. Johnson etc.*, June 1863

I can see no difference between the marriage contracted in the patriarchal ages and those contracted in the present day, in the North-West, among the Indians: that is buying the girl by giving presents to the father, mothers and brothers of the bride, and sometimes by exchanging presents; that is all the marriage rites that I know in the North-West, among the Indians. The chief or the father will never give his consent to give away his daughter to any man, as a wife, without these marriage rites, because they consider it a disgrace for any girls, without her father or her mother or brother having received this token of marriage, to live with any man. Chiefs of tribes are generally first consulted and any one selected can give away the girl upon those conditions. The ceremony consists of giving away and acceptance. It is not necessary to have anything else. A man cannot legally have more than one wife there, but the Indian chiefs have many wives. A man cannot live quietly with a squaw, in that country, without the performance of the above ceremony, for without it, the brother would even kill his sister and it would be a disgrace for the whole family. The Indians consider me as *Hias Yaye*, because I was the trader, and dealt out goods. There were then no ministers nor priests and no register kept, and the country was ruled by Indian law. The Indian law of marriage, as I have above stated, for the custom of marriage. When the company gives permission to a man or a gentleman to take a wife, the wife is supported by the company, and she will not be supported by the company, unless she is taken with the permission of the company as the man's wife.

The Indian customs do not differ much with regard to marriages. The custom of polygamy prevails universally among the Indians, particularly with the chiefs, in consequence of their ability to support a certain number of wives. I do not say that I have ever known of any persons being murdered in consequence of a regular intercourse between the sexes. I have myself seen them greatly ridiculed, and have heard the women talk especially.

When a man and woman live together, they are called man and wife. I could not say that I ever knew of any distinction being made in the Indian territory or North-West, with regard to any man and woman who live together. The woman is always called the wife of the man with whom she lives, without regard to the manner of marriage. It is always presumed that she has been regularly bought. I am not aware that the Company ever enquire whether a man is legally married before they give supplies to his wife.

When [I] say that a man cannot legally have two wives in the North-West or Hudson's Bay Territory, I do not mean that the Indian law prohibits it, but that the law of the civilized people, that is, the Hudson Bay company's servants, is against it. It is only sometimes that the subject of giving away a girl is mentioned to the chief, and that purely out of deference to him.

The term squaw signifies a woman or wife; a young woman is called a *hunk squaw*. A woman who lives with a man is called that man's squaw, which, in fact, means a wife. If I had a squaw or wife in the Hudson Bay territory, she would be called Annance's squaw – meaning my squaw or wife.

There was a chief at Frazer River, whom I knew well, who had ten squaws or wives. His Indian name was Tascaton [Saseatan in another version of Annance's testimony]. I gave him the name of Joe Pim. He was for a short time a clerk in the North-West Company's office, when I knew him. Here he was a cabinet-maker and fiddler. I do not mean to say that there is any polygamy among white people marrying squaws. I have never known of any instance of a trader or clerk having two wives. I never knew nor heard of a man and women living together in the North-West, without being married.

... I then found at Connolly's post at New Caledonia the family of said William Connolly, consisting of his wife, *as he told me*, and some girls and boys. I remained at New Caledonia, when Mr. and Mrs. Connolly were living there, four or five days, and then returned to my post. They were living there at the time as man and wife. This I know from what I could see, and from what Mr. Connolly told me. He told me several times that she was his wife, and the mother of his children, and that he had been married to her according to the custom of the country; that, at that time, he was seventeen and she was fifteen when they were married.

I boarded at Pion's [with whom Suzanne and her children lived following Connolly's marriage to Julia Woolrich] a week with Mrs. Connolly in Montreal. She was then called Mrs. Connolly.

I never knew or heard of any man and woman living together in the North-West without being married.

Source: Extracted from *Johnstone [sic] et al. v. Connolly* (1869) 17 RJRQ 266, cited in "Johnstone [*sic*] et al. v. Connolly, Court of Appeal, September 7, 1869," *La Revue légale* 1 (1869–70): 282–4, 294, 330, as supplemented by *John Connolly, plaintiff vs. Julia Woolrich, defendant and Thomas R. Johnson, et al., Judgment, July 9, 1867* (Montreal: Montreal Printing and Publishing Company, 1867), 39–40, 45, 49; and by Noel Annance to William Spragge, 5 June 1863, Library and Archives Canada, RG10, vol. 273, pp. 184549-49B, reel 12657, emphasis in original.

Noel's testimony is important not only for its role in establishing an important legal precedent respecting the character of unions formed in the fur trade but also for its validation of his wide-ranging powers of observation and summation. The testimony also speaks to the character of Noel's own family life in the fur trade. In arguing for the validity of unions, he was by inference attesting to the quality of his own union with the unnamed Flathead woman who was the mother of his first three sons, including Archie.

The testimony of Noel Annance, by now in his seventies, underlines his clarity of mind and conceptual capacity. He was in every way mentally and intellectually competent to be enfranchised.

RENEWED VIGOUR

His self-esteem having been boosted by the respect accorded him as a witness in an important legal case, Noel Annance returned to the business at hand with renewed vigour. Not long back home, he reminded the Department of Indian Affairs' deputy superintendent in June 1863 how "Mr Gill and messieur Maurault gave me high recommendation as to fitness to be enfranchised, and it was sent down to the Hon Mr Wm McDougall," then superintendent general of Indian affairs. "I beg leave to say that I am ready now to go down any time to attend the meeting of the Commissioners." However, Noel noted in the letter that other Abenakis were losing patience with a process that was, at best, elusive: "Many of our Indians who can qualify themselves would be willing to be enfranchised if they can get the money and land promised; otherwise they would remain as they are under the protection of the Crown."[65] Writing to Indian Affairs accountant C.D. Walcot on another matter three months later, Noel added an almost plaintive postscript: "P.S. I have had nothing of my enfranchisement for some time past. I hope it will come out soon for I have been waiting for it with great patience. N.A."[66]

It took another year for Noel to lose his patience. Alternatively, letters written in the interim did not survive or have not been located. His March 1864 letter to the deputy superintendent of Indian affairs was curt.

Nothing ensuing, almost as soon as a new commissioner of Crown lands, and hence a new superintendent general of Indian affairs, was appointed in March 1864 in the person of Alexander Campbell, Noel drew his attention to his seemingly endless quest to be enfranchised. Summarizing activity, or rather the lack of it, over the past five years, Noel explained how, from his perspective, Sicotte's removal as premier might have stalled his application, and he especially urged that Campbell give assistance. In making his case, Noel evoked his life course not as his alone but as exemplifying a more general experience among Indigenous peoples, who "consider themselves aggrieved and insulted to be told they are minors, children in the eyes of the law."[67] Such "restrictions should be laid aside," which we know in retrospect would be a long time coming.

Letter on enfranchisement to superintendent general of Indian affairs, 12 March 1864

Durham L'avenir

12th March 1864

William Spragge Esq
S.D.I.Affrs
    Dear Sir
My Enfranchisement
    with profound respect
      I remain
          Your honble servant
          Noel Annance

W. Spragge Esq
D.S.I. Affrs Quebec

Source: Noel Annance to William Spragge, 12 March 1864, Library and Archives Canada, RG10, vol. 273, pp. 184645-6, reel 12657.

Follow-up letter on enfranchisement to incoming superintendent general of Indian affairs, 26 May 1864

L'avenir (Durham) 26th May '64
Hon. Alex Campbell M.P.P.
    Commissioner Lands &c &c &c
        Sir,
          The management of Indian Affairs having been transferred to the Crown Land Depart, I beg leave to draw your honor's attention to a subject which I have submitted to the Indian Depmt. several times since five years past, but I have not yet obtained the object of my petitions.
    Your honorable House passed an Act 20 Vict c 26 [Act to Encourage the Gradual Civilization of the Indian Tribes] by which any Indian with certain qualifications may be converted into a man – and be no more a child. There are many Indians in Canada especially in our Tribe, who are men, well educated, who have

been officers, teachers, clerks and interpreters, who would consider themselves aggrieved and insulted to be told that they are minors, children in the eyes of the law. There may have been a time, when it was necessary to impose some wholesome restrictions on some individuals for their own safety and good for certain reasons but the reasons no longer exist, those restrictions should be laid aside – ratione cessante, lex cessat [reason ceases, the law ceases]. I called on Mr Sicotte in 1862 – August, on the subject of my enfranchisement, and he promised me that it should be effected immediately, but he was removed from his situation before it could be done. Therefore, I humbly beg that our government may take my case into serious and favorable consideration, and deliver me from the disgraceful case of minority. I have given ample proofs that I am fit to be admitted as a member of civil society. If my ancestors were savages, I am not – if they were uncivilized, wild and barbarous I am not: consequently I ought to be treated in a different way; res mutantur et nos mutamur in illis [the times are changing, and we change with them]. A man who has been employed in various situations no matter of what origin, as a gentleman, should not be denied the access to the same privileges as enjoyed by his fellow citizens.

Est modus in rebus; sunt [certi] denique fines quos ultra citraque nequit consistere rectum [there is a middle ground in all things: and, moreover, certain limits on either side of which right cannot be found].

An early answer will much oblige your honor's very humble and obedient

Noel Annance
Late Lieut Ind Dept

Source: Noel Annance to Alexander Campbell, 26 May 1864, Library and Archives Canada, RG10, vol. 273, pp. 184653-5, reel 12657.

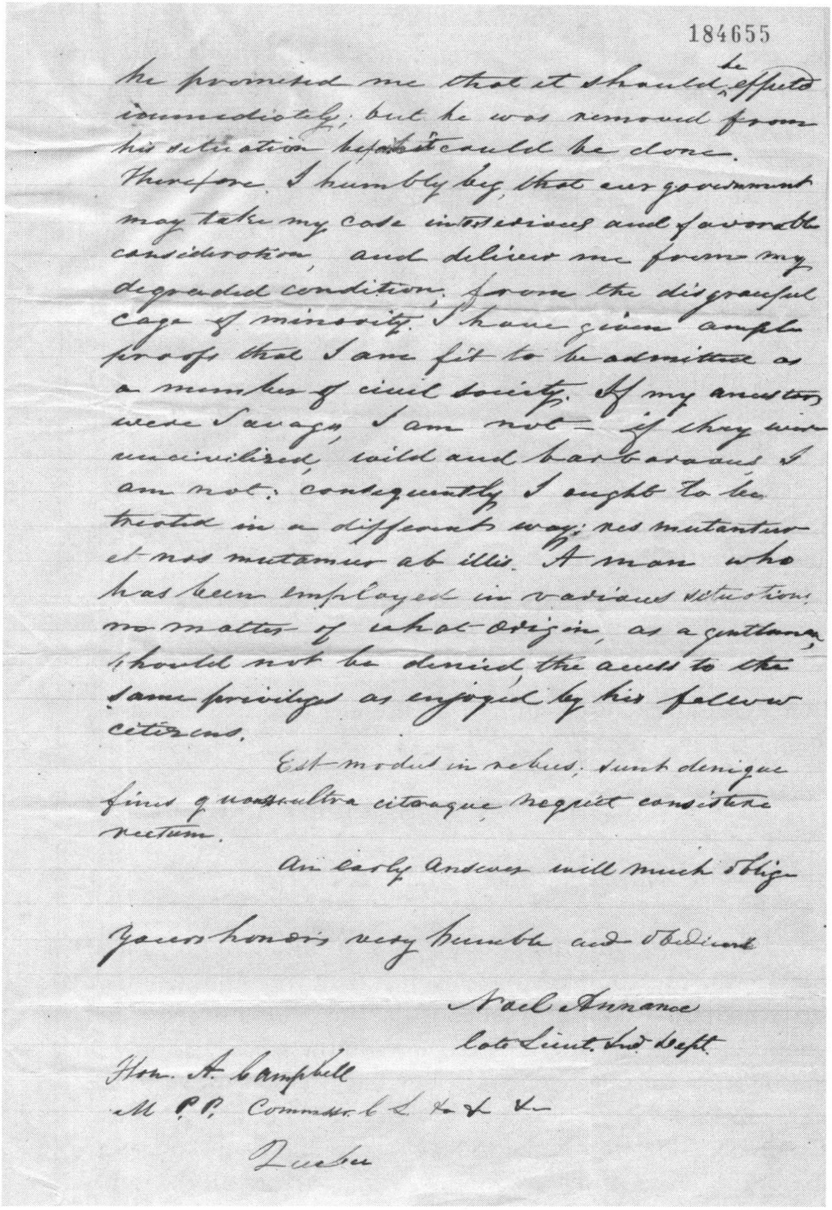

he promised me that it should be effected immediately; but he was removed from his situation before it could be done. Therefore, I humbly beg, that our government may take my case into serious and favorable consideration, and deliver me from my degraded condition, from the disgraceful cage of minority. I have given ample proofs that I am fit to be admitted as a member of civil society. If my ancestors were Savages, I am not — if they were uncivilized, wild and barbarous I am not; consequently I ought to be treated in a different way; *nos mutantur et nos mutamur ab illis.* A man who has been employed in various situations, no matter of what origin, as a gentleman, should not be denied the access to the same privileges as enjoyed by his fellow citizens.

   Est modus in rebus, sunt denique fines quos ultra citraque nequit consistere rectum.

  An early answer will much oblige

Your honor's very humble and obedient

      Noel Annance
      late Lieut. Ind. Dept.

Hon. A. Campbell
M.P.P. Commiss'r I.A. &c &c
   Quebec

ILLUSTRATION 14

Final section of Noel Annance's letter to Superintendent General
of Indian Affairs Alexander Campbell, 26 May 1864

Daring in content, the Campbell letter must have had some effect, as indicated by the notes on its cover, which read, "To be enfranchised" and "Let me have this again," in apparent reference to the larger file of correspondence. Yet nothing happened. It is as though the Department of Indian Affairs was inert in respect to the legislation, or alternatively was determined that Noel should not have his way.

A year later, in February 1865, a frustrated Noel Annance once again tried the political route. His target this time was the premier of the Province of Canada, Étienne Taché. Noel introduced himself in respect to his accomplishments, consistent with the genteel status he sought and also with his writing style, including judicious use of Latin to make the case for his capacity. The letter is also interesting for Noel's slip of the pen as to one of his examiners for enfranchisement, perhaps a reflection of his advancing age, of which, as the letter indicates, he was very aware. He described himself as "an Indian chief," which he had intermittently done since at least 1857, possibly in relation to Noel's being by virtue of his age respected as an elder.[68]

Letter on enfranchisement to joint premier of Canada Étienne Taché, 4 February 1865

Durham L'avenir C.E.
4th Feb. 1865
To the Hon. Sir. Étienne Taché M.P.P. &c &c &c
Honored Sir,
My only excuse and apology for intruding upon your attention on the present occasion must be the grave and urgent necessity which drives me in my present reduced circumstances and unexpected adverse turn of my affairs in the world to apply once more for my enfranchisement which has been promised to me in pursuance to the Act 20 Victoria c 26 [Act to Encourage the Gradual Civilization of the Indian Tribes] and be no longer a minor in the eye of the law, and be admitted into all the rights and privileges enjoyed by all Her Majesty's subjects. Mr Sicotte when in your present position in my interview with him at Quebec fully approved and consented that I should be enfranchised as soon as the Commissioners be named for examining the qualifications

of the Indians who wish to avail themselves of the Act. At my sug-gestion Mr Sicotte got Messrs. Spragge [sic Maurault] and Gill appointed by the Governor, as commissioners to examine me and "others of my description." I have given ample proofs of my fit-ness to be freed from the restriction that binds me down as an uncivilized being, unfit to mix with civil society. I am advanced in years — youthful vigour is leaving my limbs, and activity is fast losing its former elasticity. I see not very far the day coming when I must take my exit, which neither time can impede, nor eternity impair. Therefore before that solemn event arrives, I wish to settle my affairs as a man, as a member of civil society for the dear ob-jects I leave behind. My services during the late American war, the honorable mention made of my name after the battle of Chateau-guay in 1813 as Lieut. in Indian Dept. the medal from the Queen for my exertions in that battle, whereat the invading enemy was repulsed and driven back by a handful of Canadians and Indians, under the late brave Col. [Charles-Michel] de Salaberry ought to entitle me to some consideration in the eyes of our government. I was also commissioned as first Lieutenant in a company of the E.T. loyal volt[igeu]rs in the late troubles in Canada.

Therefore, kind and honored Sir, I humbly beg that you may be kind enough to sympathise in my hard unfortunate condition: it is in your favour to have carried into effect the object of this address.

I shall always say –

Semper honos nomenque tuum laudesque manebunt [Your name and achievements will last forever].

I have the honor
to be with profound
respect
your humble Ser[van]t
Noel Annance
an Indian Chief
late Lt. Indian Dept.

Source: Noel Annance to Étienne Taché," 4 February 1865, Library and Archives Canada, RG10, pp. 184659-62, reel 12657; also Andrée Désilets, "Sir Étienne-Paschal Taché," *Dictionary of Canadian Biography*, online.

Given the letter ended up in the Indian Affairs file, where correspondence respecting Noel Annance's application was grouped together, Taché must have passed it on with purpose. The notation indicates it went in March to the attorney general of Canada East, to be dispatched in April to the Department of Indian Affairs. For good measure, Noel wrote again, a month later in March 1865, to Superintendent General of Indian Affairs Alexander Campbell.[69]

It is virtually certain Noel also wrote during these same years to others possibly able to wield influence who did not pass on their letters to Indian Affairs, and hence they do not survive or have not been located. Noel's virtually annual letters to the governor general of British North America, Viscount Monck, although principally about the Durham lands juggernaut, sometimes contained a percipient sentence, as in 1865: "Your petitioner has only to add that he begs leave to hope that your Excellency be kind enough to accede to his petition – circumstances are low – having been here doing nothing waiting for his enfranchisement for these three years."[70]

TOWARD ENFRANCHISEMENT

The letters, however many there were, did finally have an effect, or perhaps the Department of Indian Affairs acquiesced, if only somewhat so. Very possibly it was at Alexander Campbell's initiative subsequent to Noel's March 1865 letter to him that Deputy Superintendent of Indian Affairs William Spragge informed Noel he would arrive "before the end of May to proceed with my business," only to have nothing happen.[71] Enquiring, Noel was told his enfranchisement had been put on hold but "might occur some time soon."[72] Pressing the matter in the autumn, by which time Noel was in financial difficulty for "not daring to enter into any business which required constant attendance for fear of missing the meeting" at which he would be examined, he was told, as indicated by the notation on the letter, "to be prepared to go to Sorel [eighty kilometres, or fifty miles, distant where the nearest Indian Affairs official was based] whenever notified."[73] Although Noel acquiesced to the request, nothing appears to have ensued.[74]

The correspondence hints that an impediment to fixing a date and a place may have been one of Noel's two witnesses, Joseph Maurault, being unwilling to commit. As Noel had earlier pointed out, "the priest has left the village long ago and yet, he retains his pay, I suppose, as a missionary."[75] Noel's second witness, Ignace Gill, was willing to attend as long as he was given a date "some days in advance," whereas "Revd. Mr. Maurault cannot go to Durham," where Noel was then resident.[76]

Ignace Gill's death on 1 September 1865 made it all the more necessary that Maurault be present, as he was now the only witness. Aware of the situation, Noel groused in September 1865 how, "if I had the means I would go down to Quebec [City] and request his Reverence to go there to perform his duty as a missionary: for he hates to do any thing for the tribe, as he has left the Indian village along ago."[77] The reason for Maurault's reticence may have been his completing a history of the Abenaki people, published in 1866, the same year that he ceased to be in charge. Noel's desire to be enfranchised might not have much mattered, given Maurault's conviction, explained on the book's first page, that "this little tribe" about which he was writing would "soon completely disappear from our country."[78]

A DEBACLE OR NOT?

It took another year and a half, being eight years from the time Noel had so optimistically initiated the enfranchisement process, for a firm date, 23 January 1867, to be set. It was done so hastily and at the last minute to accommodate the elusive priest, Joseph Maurault, then in St Francis. The consequence was a debacle, or so it seems.

The Indian Affairs official in charge reported from Sorel on 3 January how "I am writing to Noel Annance at Durham" to inform him of the upcoming event to be held in St Francis, with no indication of when or whether he actually did so. The letter's destination was in any case erroneous, given that Noel had over the past year and a half corresponded with the Department of Indian Affairs from L'Avenir, sixteen kilometres, or ten miles, distant from Durham and fifty kilometres, or thirty miles, from St Francis. A third factor may have hindered the notification not reaching Noel, if it did so, in time for him to make the long trip. The weather was unstable, as indicated by the official's referring to possibly being "over-taken by a snow storm" on the way to St Francis and to "the state of the roads" delaying letters to Sorel, where he was based, much less to outlying areas.[79]

Whether or not for these reasons, the now seventy-five-year-old Noel Annance did not turn up in St Francis on the appointed day. The official who had attended later informed Deputy Superintendent of Indian Affairs William Spragge of events somewhat defensively: "Having notified Annance in writing him to his address at Durham on the receipt of your first communication to me, I was satisfied that he must have known that he was expected to be present on the 23rd at the Indian village at ten o'clock in the morning, but as owing to the state of the roads he might have been delayed in his journey. I remained the village the afternoon, but Mr Annance did not present himself."[80]

A second, more recent candidate for enfranchisement, the forty-three-year-old namesake son of long-time St Francis chief Ignace Portneuf, who lived locally, did turn up. Based on the official's "personal knowledge," Portneuf was found wanting as to being "sober and industrious" in his "habits and free from debt." To this decision, Portneuf is said to have responded that "he did not see that there was anything which he would gain by being emancipated."[81]

Part of the reason Portneuf reacted as he did may have been his foreknowledge of three St Francis chiefs' determination to hijack the proceedings. By the terms of the legislation, enfranchised persons were to receive land and a monetary sum from their tribe. Clearly aware of the implications, the three signatories, two of whom assented with their marks, were determined to ensure the two candidates would be unsuccessful.

To this end, the Department of Indian Affairs official was on his arrival handed a petition composed in poor French, and so possibly written on their behalf at the last moment. The document asserted in respect to Portneuf and Annance, "we, the undersigned Grand Chiefs of the aforesaid tribe, bound to do justice to all, believe it is our duty to oppose them and to report to you that it is very notorious that the [first] above named often made use of intoxicating drink, and the last above is excessively indebted."[82] The latter, if true respecting Noel, was not surprising given that, as he had informed Department of Indian Affairs officials a year and a half earlier, he dare not take up employment for fear of missing a designated date. The chiefs' response was very similar to that respecting Elias Hill, not expectedly so since the act subverted their authority at a time of diminishing power and resources. Hill was still protesting in 1874, a decade and a half after being emancipated, that he had yet to receive his promised land grant.[83]

It is impossible to know why Noel Annance, who had done due diligence over eight years in the hopes of being enfranchised, did not turn up. Perhaps he was ill, was caught by the weather, or did not receive the letter in time owing to the bad weather or its being misaddressed, or perhaps a combination of factors were to blame. If any of these, then why on finding out did Noel not write officials or others to complain and demand another hearing? It would have been in character for him to follow up, as he continued to do on other topics.[84] If indeed he wrote, the letter or letters have not been located or, possibly, were not retained. The last document in Noel's lengthy enfranchisement file in Indian Affairs records is the official's report on the January 1867 nonmeeting. Or perhaps no letter was sent to him, with the result that he never found out what almost occurred.

Alternatively, it was not a debacle. The other possibility to be considered is that Noel Annance realized at the last moment that he could not do it. He changed his mind. Despite all of his desire for acknowledgment as the gentleman he knew himself to be, he was unwilling to become such at the cost of subordinating his Abenaki self. Given that he continued to write on the Durham lands issue up to his death, it is almost as though he changed his mind and kept the decision private to himself. The Abenaki daring that grounded so much of his life might have again come to the fore.

What matters most in retrospect is not the outcome in respect to the single individual who was Noel Annance but the pathway. For all of the two dozen known letters to a combination of Indian Affairs officials and to persons of some political importance, it took a decade from the law's proclamation for anything to transpire. If Noel experienced the Department of Indian Affairs' general perspective on the 1857 act, the legislation was a sham, and if he was the exception in applying to be enfranchised, unlikely given just the St Francis response as reported by him, then even persons able to interact with the Department of Indian Affairs on its own terms, as Noel had done for a quarter of a century prior to applying for enfranchisement, were not to be permitted their due. Either inference is damning.

DEATH

Noel Annance died two and a half years later. He had rarely been ill prior to his death by unknown causes on 4 September 1869, aged seventy-seven. His health had only infrequently affected his consummate letter writing enough for him to make a note of it, as in January 1848, when he wrote, "The other day I thought I was going to die, the fever took me,"[85] and in July 1862, when he explained, "I have been much afflicted with ophthalmia so much that I can hardly see what I write and beg to be excused for my bad writing."[86] A year and a half after the emancipation debacle, in September 1868, Noel described himself as "now infirm."[87]

Noel Annance's death is revealing of his religiosity, or rather the apparent lack of it. Repeatedly denied a teaching job in St Francis almost certainly for not being sufficiently Catholic, he had not been among the former Moor's students sustaining Osunkhirhine's tiny congregation. All but one of his children located in church records were baptized Catholics, possibly at their mother's initiative. It was also the case that four of them, born between 1846 and 1860, were baptized as Catholics only in 1861 on the death of their unbaptized thirteen-year-old sister. Perhaps at his brother-in-law and cousin Simon Annance's persistence, Noel did transfer his adherence to Protestantism, more specifically to Congregationalism, by the time of his four-year-old son Absalom's baptism in August 1868 a year before Noel's death. Noel was so memorialized and interred not far from his last home in L'Avenir.[88]

TO SUM UP

Noel Annance's quest to become by virtue of enfranchisement the gentleman of his higher education capped his engagement of literacy's promise. The outcome speaks to the fundamental disinterest of the Department of Indian Affairs, and thereby of the Canadian government, in effecting change. Indigenous peoples' exclusion and dispossession were by the time of Noel's death so matter-of-fact that even his highly educated prose, deferent writing style, and ability to importune persons in positions of authority mattered virtually for naught.

For three decades, Noel narrated what he witnessed to the Indian Department, to the Department of Indian Affairs, and to others with the power to effect change. For all that he was, per Duncan Campbell Napier's note of February 1848 to the official in charge, "a very intelligent and truly loyal Indian," his indigeneity trumped his higher education.[89] It is impossible to know whether or not Noel chose to remain so when the much anticipated day for enfranchisement finally came. That he died an enigma is consistent with his life course.

Postscript

The Indian Act of 1876 had been foretold by the time of Noel Annance's death a half-dozen years earlier. Mimicking the Pennefather Report of 1858, the Indian Act confined Indigenous peoples to reserves, with their almost total emphasis on very small-scale agriculture; dispossessed women who had married non-Indigenous men, along with their off-spring across the generations; and separated Indigenous children from their parents into residential schools. The Indian Act gave the Department of Indian Affairs absolute control over the lives of Indigenous peoples. The Pennefather Report had been premised on isolation and separation, exclusion and dispossession, and so it was with the Indian Act, which took inferiority and superiority for granted. The betrayal of Canada's Indigenous peoples would hold for more than a century. In modified form, the Indian Act continues into the present day.

The Indian Act need not have been. An alternative was in view. The Colonial Office, the 1844 Bagot Report, and the majority of missionaries who were queried for the 1858 Pennefather Report looked to Indigenous peoples intermingling on their own terms with the dominant society. The Bagot Report envisaged a future very different from what ensued: "The true and only practicable policy of the Government, with reference to their interests, both of the Indians and the community at large, is to endeavor, gradually, to raise the said Tribes within the British Territory to the level of their white neighbours; to prepare them to undertake the offices and duties of citizens; and, by degrees, to abolish the necessity of its farther interference in their affairs."[1] The Bagot Report was striking in its common sense: "There is nothing in the character of the Indian race which is opposed to such a result. They possess all the higher attributes of the mind ... neither are they wanting in a desire to improve their condition."[2]

The Bagot Report was scathing respecting the inaction of the Indian Department within the Department of Indian Affairs, whose head a dozen years later chaired the Pennefather Commission, established by the Legislative Assembly of the Province of Canada. It is difficult not to conclude that what ensued was tantamount to retribution. Despite requesting missionaries' views, the commission was not unexpectedly "unable to agree with the recommendations of several of these Gentlemen, that the Indians generally should be at one placed on the footing of their white neighbours."[3] The dye was cast. It is intriguing to consider what Canada today would be like if intermingling had been given a chance.

Noel Annance and his similarly educated predecessors and counterparts were one small part of this possible alternative direction. Their writing and their actions testify to what might have been. Indigenous peoples were not inert but dared time and again. They sought entryways to the changes occurring around them without losing sight of who they were as Indigenous peoples. Noel and many others, most of whose stories are yet to be told, searched for belonging consistent with their indigeneity within settings that turned them aside.

Just as the Indian Department could not countenance another policy direction, neither could it condone Indigenous persons daring to speak back on a par with themselves. It was rather the self-serving prejudices of whites, from George Simpson of the Hudson's Bay Company to land-hungry newcomers determined to wrest away the Durham lands, who were condoned by a Canada in the making. What is remarkable in retrospect, and needs an accounting, are the Indigenous and non-Indigenous voices that envisaged another possibility.

Noel Annance lived within this larger setting that stymied his search for belonging. Abenaki daring, captivity narratives, and literacy's promise comprised his inheritance. The circumstances into which Noel was born were exceptional, and he made them more so by engaging literacy's promise with all of the daring he could muster across his life span. As a young man, he was amazingly privileged, educated to a level of very few of his Indigenous or for that matter white contemporaries across North America. His adulthood had two stages: in the first he performed as a gentleman without denying his indigeneity, and in the second he lived as an Indigenous person while using the language of gentility. Both stages were infused with Abenaki daring.

Abenaki daring, like its broader counterpart of Indigenous daring, has taken many forms across time, place, and circumstance. Noel Annance's great-uncle, grandfather, and father had dared in the face of war and its consequences, which had threatened the very existence of their Abenaki homeland of St Francis. Noel's two brothers and his eldest son each dared in his own way, as did their similarly educated predecessors and contemporaries.

Noel's daring reflected his years at Moor's Charity School and more so at Dartmouth College, with their assumption that capacity incurred obligations. That his higher education had transformed him into a gentleman of the day made him no less Abenaki. Determined to be the person he had been educated to become, Noel Annance was as a consequence caught between two ways of being, neither of whose adherents accepted him among their numbers. He did not belong twice over. When he could no longer dare by virtue of his employment, he did so with his pen. He did not crumple.

Noel Annance and his counterparts dared literacy's promise, as had a handful of Indigenous predecessors. Their searches for belonging were their own, be it that of early Harvard student John Wampas, William and Mary counterpart John Nettles, or French-educated Peter Otsiquette. Most fellow students at Moor's, including Samson Occom and and later Noel's second cousin Peter Paul Osunkhirhine, were guided in their searches for belonging by the religious imperative. Noel's two brothers and eldest son, all of whom attended Moor's, devised their own distinctive pathways toward belonging. The few who continued on from Moor's to Dartmouth College had somewhat more options, as with Louis Vincent at Lorette and Noel's father, both of whom founded and sustained local schools.

The young Noel Annance considered it possible through right behaviour to be the gentleman of his higher education even as he was Indigenous, and he crossed a continent with the fur trade in pursuit of inclusion. His determination to make it on an equitable footing, in a setting increasingly unwilling to let him do so, came to naught, whence he returned home to contest Indigenous exclusion with his pen.

With the exception of Duncan Campbell Napier from time to time, officials of the Department of Indian Affairs found Noel a nuisance. They could not countenance that an Indigenous person, in their view inherently inferior to themselves, should not only write in a style and manner equal or superior to their own but also repeatedly point up their failings. Whether or not government officials could have moderated the local priest's stranglehold on schooling, or rather the lack of it, is impossible to know, but they did not try. Noel's persistence in respect to land had consequences. His almost decade of politely and persistently pursuing enfranchisement reads as a reprimand for his daring to do so.

Noel Annance's life in all of its complexity resonates for the present day. To be highly educated and Indigenous may be more practically feasible but still necessitates taking chances. The growing numbers accessing higher education are all too often stymied by a dominant society determined to perceive them, and thereby treat them, as other than themselves. They do not belong. Abenakai daring, more generally Indigenous daring, is no less central to the way ahead than it was for Noel Annance.

Noel Annance's Journal of the Voyage from Fort George to the Fraser River, 18 November to 31 December 1824

George's Fort (Columbia)
Nov/18 – J. 1825

A Journal of a Voyage from Fort George Columbia River to Fraser
River in the winter of 1824 and 1825

Francis N. Annance

Fort George
Nov. 18, 1824

This day we left this place on an expedition to the mouth of Fraser's River which is supposed to empty itself in Puget Sound. Our party headed by James McMillan Esquire, consists of three clerks, an interpreter and thirty six men. Having crossed the Bay, we camped at the west of it, the beginning of the portage [present town of Ilwaco] across the neck of Cape Disappointment.

Nov. 19th

Most tremendous storm of rain and wind last night: this is what we must expect at this season from the nature of the country. We have to contend with boisterous storms and waves, and all the combined powers of the elements and of man. This morning early began the portage, about two thirds of a mile, we found a little lake [Black Lake]: passed thro' this little lake, then came into a swampy prairie [Cranberry Marshes], thro' which a road passes, where the property was carried, and our boats were forced down a small stream [Tarlette Slough] issuing from the little lake and meandering thro' the watery prairie.

Rain again, the whole day. Camped on the portage about two thirds of the way. The soil on the portage was excellent. This is the best spot for a fort: being the centre of all the commercial trade of Indians; and almost the whole of Fort returns pass thro' this place.

Nov. 20th

Again a most fearful storm of thunder, rain and lightning last night! The ground groaned and wept: the trees shrieked with horror, and bowed down with fear; while we awaited with painful anxiety, the probable effects of those dreadful elements that raged over our heads! The night was dark as the middle of darkness, and the surrounding atmosphere appeared a mass of electrified matter. This morning in spite of the rain and cold, we left our encampment and immediately fell into the little river where the tide comes up: here our boats were loaded and going thro' branches and upon and under logs in the little river, we passed thro' a prairie beautifully lined with spruce fur on each side, then fell into the Chinook Bay [Gray's Bay]. The whole length of the portage from one bay to the other being about five miles. Our course on the bay is due north. The Chinooks come to this bay in the fall to catch bon [good] salmon in the little rivers that empty themselves into it. The bay at some places [is] three miles wide. Made about eight miles in the bay and camped on the west side on the point [near the present town of Oysterville]. The country, hilly and mountainous; except on the point to the west, which is low, marshy and well covered with wood and shrub, so that it is almost impossible for man to pass thro'.

Nov. Sunday 21st

Embarked early; hoisted our sails, away we went. Little after P.M. reached the end of the bay, where we are to make a portage; not being able to pass in the open sea with our boats, Make two miles then we camped. The road is upon the sandy beach: most excellent: the sand being hard; some places partially covered with grass and mud.

Nov. 22d

Made about two miles again. The wind has been tremendous. Our boats were brought across the point [Toke Point] from the creek of the bay into the sea this evening. Plenty of geese.

Little out into the woods the country is marshy and encumbered with wood and thickets. It is needless to say, we had rain last night for we have had it every day since we commenced our voyage. In some countries we pray for rain; but in this we receive it in abundance without the intercession of prayers, and enjoy it without gratitude.

Nov. 23

Fine day. The sun shines with all his splendor upon the beautiful and glittering sandy shore. Our boats but one were brought to the end of the portage into a bay called Chehalis Bay or Gray's harbor: this was performed by towing them near the beach inside of the breakers. Continued with the baggage with about half of our men, and made three miles and camped very much fatigued. One of our men finds himself very ill, and unable to walk by a monstrous swelling in one of his feet.

Nov. 24

Fine again. Made two miles this morning then we struck across the point thro' the woods into the bay [near Westport] where our boats are. The road across the point is very bad; full of trees, mud, shrub and every dirty encumbrance. The length is little more than a mile. Our course in the portage has been always north by west: now it is north east across this point. Camped at the bottom of the Bay of Gray's harbor. Rain in the afternoon.

Nov. 25

Rain again this morning. A large canoe full of Indians came to our encampment, going to the way we came. Near twelve o'clock all the canoes came and we set off immediately. Our course is north; then from the point opposite to the sandy point at the entrance of the bay, north east, then almost east, forming something like [a] right angled triangle from our encampment to the entrance of the Chelhalis river to which we must go. Made about seven miles in the last course then encamped, about twelve miles from our last encampment. Bad encampment: every thing is wet. The land is low and the tide comes over it. The mouth of the bay is five or six miles wide. From this bay we see to the north a vast ridge of snowy mountains [Olympic] extending almost in a northwest direction between Puget Sound and the sea.

Nov. 26

Left our encampment early with all possible speed as it rained very hard, made our way to the entrance of the Chehalis river [near Aberdeen]: took breakfast little above the entrance in the midst of rain that left nothing dry about us. The river is about [a] hundred yards wide, and not very deep: very winding near the mouth. About six miles from the entrance, we saw a small village: all the natives fled into the woods at our approach; taking us to be a war party coming upon them. We called them back, stopped a few minutes and went on. The lodges are filthy, full of smoke and stench. This nation is called Chehalis: the first tribe, we met with on our way from the Chinooks of Fort George. There [are] about a hundred men in the whole nation. There is not much beaver in their country; but they have a commercial genius: they go towards the Puget Sound to buy skins, then to Fort George to trade the necessary articles for their commerce. They trade guns, blankets and beads to the other Indians: but the chief medium among themselves, by which they carry on their trade, are little white shells exactly in the shape of our powder horns, somewhat more straight, about one fourth of an Inch in diameter at the big end [dentalium]: these are strung with small cords or sinews and sold by the fathom according to quality. The banks of the river are low thickly encumbered with brushwood for about a mile on each side, then hills and mountains begin to rise. Made four miles, then saw another small village. The same manifestation of fear: some running into the woods, others putting themselves in postures of defense before their doors. These savages know the whites, and expect no harm from them; but they had heard that the Chinooks were coming to make war upon them: this accounts for the agitation in which we found them.

Made five miles from this village and camped opposite to another village. This village was in the same predicament as the others.

Nov. 27

Started early. The water rising fast. Current strong. The country about the same. Passing another village at a fork of our river. This fork is nearly as large as the main river, coming from the north. Rain does not cease. Made about twenty miles then we encamped.

Nov. Sunday 28th

Started as usual. Rain and cold, the river winding, and the current very strong. Came to another fork [Black River] which we must follow to the portage of Puget Sound. This fork is about forty miles from the mouth of the river at the bay. Made eight miles in this fork, then encamped, having found much difficulty on account of lowness of the water. Our departure from the Chehalis Bay to this fork by the general course of the river is, I think, rather to the south: now we go to the north. The point between the two rivers to the country is low, full of bogs, ash, plane and cottonwood. Animals abundant. A fine prairie opposite to the point. A village near our encampment. Our little river is full of salmon half dead [from spawning].

Nov. 29

This morning we saw the sun; but [it] soon disappeared. Made few miles, then came to a prairie on each side of the river. Here we find plenty of water: however we formed un embarras [obstruction] across the river at the beginning.

This morning I went for Pierre Charles, a freeman living with Indians at the principal Haloweema village: he being a good animal hunter, we thought he would be useful to our party. Made about eight miles and encamped on one of the prairies. This is a handsome prairie; full of little knolls or eminences, very convenient for approaching deer. This evening went out, and saw plenty of deer; but the incessant rain prevented us from killing any.

Nov. 30th

Rain again. This morning we sent the sick man off by the Indians and one of our men to take care of him to Fort George.

Pierre Charles came to us and consented to go with us.

Decem 1st

Left our encampment of the prairie des Buttes [meadows of mounds]. I and one of the men went by land to the lake about twelve miles ahead in hopes of finding animals. No elk. Rain, rain! This evening we came to the prairie of the lake and portage where we killed a deer a goose and a salmon. Good supper. We happened to make our fire on a spot where has been an old Indian lodge; in the course of the night, were driven out and nearly devoured by the proprietors of the soil [fleas].

Decem 2d

Went out again but found no elk or rather red deer. Fine day.

Decem 3d

This morning the Boats arrived and began the portage immediately. The road is pretty good; but we are obliged to clear the brush and trees off for the boats to pass. Made nearly two miles then we encamped.

Decem 4

Came to the other end with our baggage; the canoes still behind. The road is muddy, full of trees. Some little rivers to cross. The length, about four miles. Our course here is north west. Pierre Charles killed two red deer [elk].

Decem 5th

This morning went early for the boats and came back at night, having brought the boats near the encampment. Here we found few Indians living upon shells from the salt water, with all the appearance of poverty, impotence and wretchedness.

Decem 6th

The boats were early here and we had the satisfaction to see them put on the water of the famous Puget Sound [at Eld Inlet]. Our course in this bay is north. About ten miles then we came to the principal Bay of the Sound; here we turn[ed] towards east. Saw some Indians, who all fled into the woods, leaving their canoes upon the beach. Sent Pierre Charles who brought them and we spoke with them inquiring for a guide. Made few miles then we turn[ed] almost to the South. Encamped on a point opposite the Nisqually river, the small river emptying itself into the Sound: formerly it was full of beaver; but now much ruined.

Decem 7th

Our course has been winding: now east again across the bay. The fog has been so thick since in the bay we can see but little distance before us. This morning we were nearly lost in crossing the Bay not more [than] six miles wide and many islands on our way. Having attained to the other side we found the village [Steilacoom] where we expect to find guides to take along with us.

Here we engaged the two men and a woman as guides and interpreters and pushed on.

Here our general course is north again. Passed another river called Pouyallup, on the east side also. The Country here on both sides of the Sound has [a] very high reputation for beaver. Made about twenty miles to day then we encamped opposite to a handsome Island [probably Vashon]. The Sound is cut into Bays, points and beautiful islands full of deer.

Decem 8th

Made ten miles then came to a village [Port Madison] of the tribe called Soquams [Suquamish]. We stopped to call upon the chief but he was out fishing. Most of the natives are dispersed about the Islands and creeks fishing.

Here we took breakfast and continued. Here we cross[ed] to the east side of the Sound, being about five miles wide. Here also saw many mountains on both sides. The country seems low for about twenty or thirty miles to the north east, then begins to appear those ridges of mountains that supply all the streams that fall into the Sound, and those that fall into the Columbia between Walla Walla and Okinakan. Passed another river called Sinwams [Skagit River]. All the rivers we have seen are on the north east side: the other side being only a long point between this Sound and a long narrow bay, perhaps part of the Puget Sound; or not, we do not really know. Made about fifteen miles since breakfast then encamped. Rain this evening.

Decem 9th

This morning we passed the bay and river of the nation called Sinahooms [Snohomish]. This is called by [George] Vancouver Possession Bay opposite to two very large islands [Camano and Widbey]. Saw few lodges: the poor natives all fled to the woods. Every thing flies before us. Today one of our guides left us, on account of the news that his Child was sick; but I strongly suspect that he was afraid to venture with us too far.

Saw a large canoe full of Indians who also fled; but we overtook them, and our guides having spoken to them, one of them consented to go with us. Made twenty miles to day then encamped with our Indians and many more came in the evening from the lodges near us and passed the night with us. Fine Indians!

They appear to be mild and well featured and good natured beings: they are very quiet and respectful. The country is beautiful. The Islands are high banked sometimes but thinly covered with fir, intersected with fine little openings or plains full of animals.

Decem 10th

This morning made arrangements with our new guide. Gave him a blanket and he embarked. He is a fine looking fellow; he is said to be the son of the Chief. We also gave [the] other guide and his wife a blanket each. Stopped at the first village as our new guide wished to see his father en passant. There seemed to be much stir in the village: the Indians told us that one of their people was killed last night by a war party of the adjacent tribes; and manifested a desire that we should wait for them, till collected as they were going to the same to avenge the death of their friend. Stopped few minutes: not finding our guide's father, Mr. MacMillan said it was only a hoax to detain us; we pushed off. Made about five miles then four canoes, about fifty or sixty men overtook us, and showed some signs as if they wished to speak with us. We stopped; but they would not speak: asked them what they wanted, they told us to wait for the others, but we told them, we have no time to lose, if they wished to say any thing to us, we are to make a halt at yonder island; and so we went on. We went ashore on the Island [Lummi] with arms; when they saw this, they did not wish to land: our guides spoke to them, and at least with some reluctance they came to us but did not speak. We inquired for the father of our guide and found him in the company: he and two other Chiefs desired to go with us, and embarked then and went off: in fact the whole wanted to go with us; but we took only three. Thus ended the farce of the pretended set out on a war excursion to revenge the cruel death of their poor murdered Brother! The truth of the business was they wanted to collect a respectable band and make a speech to us as long as the Sound itself: for we find Customs house officers in this country as well as on the way from Montreal to Canton; but we were up to their tricks, they did not get many blankets, as they expected. This tribe is called Skatchat [Skagit]: the last nation and place our people from Fort George have seen. The river and country of this nation is said to be full of beaver; and the appearance certainly argues to confirm the report. A small establishment would do well: the natives would hunt if little encouraged. They are fine, stout men.

From the Skatch bay we found a small channel there, a kind of low and grassy isthmus, then fell into a large bay, called by Vancouver Bellingham's Bay. The fog was thick we could not see far; but it seems to be full of Islands large and small. Made about thirty miles then encamped on a very high, long and narrow Island we called Fish Island.

Decem 11th

Strong wind and fair, and we began the day with sails. Here we leave Bellingham's Bay and seemed to follow a large channel stretching into the sea. At the end of our Island the sea appeared to open before us; but we soon discovered very high mountains in the midst of the Ocean, which we take to be the mountains on Vancouver's Island. To the main land, we could not see the high mountains not being sufficiently clear. Made about twenty six miles then encamped on a point, the entrance of a small creek. From this we have a traverse to make straight to our left to Robert's Point about ten miles: while straight forward we can very distinctly see the trees at the end of the Bay, a few yards from which, our guides tell us, passes the famous river we [are] looking for. Here we must wait for a calm day to make the traverse.

Decem Sunday 12th

Strong rain. We remained here. Two red deer killed. Rain, rain and storm!

Decem 13th

Made an attempt to cross; but the wind increasing we veered, meaning to go round the Bay. Before reaching the bottom of the bay, our guides conceived in their heads that they guide us into a small creek, then make a short portage, and fall into Fraser's river at once: we, anxious to feast our eyes with the sight of that far famed stream, went immediately. Our course has been north west: now we got into this little creek it is north east, and sometimes almost east. We find the little river [Nicomekl] very winding and full [of] brush, logs &c. Towards evening we came to the worst place; dragging our boats thro' willows, shrub, briars and beavers' dams till we came to the portage and encamped. The evening we found two Indians, but could get no manner of information. All the natives are very stupid: here you will find no Egyptian to detail to you the history of this country, or converse with you by signs.

Decem 14th

Very weighty rain. Made nearly two miles in the portage. Our boats were partly dragged and partly carried. The portage is handsome prairie [Langley Prairie]. The soil most excellent.

Decem 15th

To day finished the portage and slept at the other end. This morning saw a kind of red deer feeding on the plain, and we killed one.

Decem 16th

Embarked and went down a small river [Salmon]. No language can adequately express the signs and ravages of beaver and red deer, we saw going down this little river. Made about ten miles, then fell into Fraser's river opposite to an Island [McMillan]. Feeling inadequate to give a full description of the river, we can only convey, it is a noble and majestic Stream: and the surrounding country marks thousands of beaver that exist therein and its environs. Made two miles then encamped. Here it is about six or eight hundred yards wide. The ride rises about five feet perpendicular. The course is east. A high mountain [Mount Baker].

Decem 17th

This morning made about two miles [to] another island; opposite to which we found a small village on a small river coming from the north side. The natives are little men; and appear rather shy. In the lodges we saw a sort of loom, with which they manufacture blankets with the hair of dogs and the down of ducks and geese. Proceeding up we saw several Islands. Made about twelve miles then encamped at a point, where our guides told us, there was a large [village] near [the Harrison River]. This evening our guides went to the village to advertise and bring the Indians [Scowlitz] that we may speak with them. To night only one of them came with three Strangers.

Rain all night.

Decem 18th

This morning we were informed that three of our guides had taken a canoe from the village and deserted. The probable cause of this, I think, was, they were going into a far country with them that they would never be able to get back to their homes. Little before twelve the Indians to the number of about fifty came to our camp. We presented a pipe to them to smoke; but they did not know how to make use of it. They all appear very small men; except one big fellow, finely dressed in his way with a clean European blanket and a large Chinook hat ornamented with white shells [dentalium], quite in the style of a Grandee: his is about six feet high and well proportioned. This we took to be a Chief as he appeared to be the leading character. He made us a chart upon the sand, of the river and made more than sixteen to fall into it above. They tell us that the river is covered with ice not far above. After every possible inquiry respecting the country, we gave a letter to be sent by them to the Fort at Kamloops, which they assured us, will reach them in due time: and so we parted better friends than before. The river seems, from this place, to turn due north between high mountains: the same course and appearance I observed above as far as I went down from fort Kamloops last year.

Encamped at our old encampment. Rain without mercy.

Decem 19th

Started early. Passing several Islands and sites of villages, about midday we fell in with the natives again on an island opposite to their village on a little river.

Here we saw the Chief and clothed him and his son.

We also traded some skins from them: and we parted cordially promising and wishing each other better acquaintance. Saw the site of several villages, we came to the beginning of the marshy ground. Here we looked for a place most eligible for a Fort. Having found one, we marked HBC on the trees on the water side and pushed off. The course of the river from the place we turned in is south west; and now near the mouth it runs west. Little below HBC we saw a deserted village nearly a mile long.

Finding no good place below we came back to the village to encamp. This is a terrible large village [possibly Musqueam]! The natives are scattered about in the small rivers catching Salmon. This must contain not less than a thousand men. The houses are very high; the roofs horizontal. There are several channels near the mouth of the river and the ground marshy and full of little ponds and small trees. Near the village there is a beautiful forest of cypress trees.

Decem 20th

Left the village early this morning and made our way to the entrance into the sea. Made a few soundings, found the river four fathoms and some places seven fathoms deep: but as we passed in high tide we cannot be sure as to the depth; but are sure that any vessel can come in to a considerable distance. Our course at present is south west to Point Roberts, whence we are to make the traverse on our way home. To the west we saw Vancouver's Island, about thirty miles. On our way to the point we saw an Indian canoe, but the Indians ran away so could speak to them only at a distance by our guides and went on.

Point Roberts is a fine place for a Fort: well timbered and high: the vessel can anchor at the door and be secure from all winds. At the point on the side of the bay is another village nearly as large as the last. The natives must be very numerous. At the traverse we saw the grandest sight that ever a man wished to behold: in a vast water surrounded with mountains high and low, some covered with everlasting snow, seemed to lose themselves in the heavens! It would require the fire and genius of a Homer to do justice to the scene. So we encamped at the other side of the traverse, having fallen into our old road.

Decem 21st

Started before day, sailed the greatest part of the day. Passed Fish Island and Bellingham's Bay about noon and encamped on the Channel of a grassy isthmus between Bellingham's Bay and Skachat Bay. Made about forty miles.

Decem 22nd

Started early again, passed the Skatchat and the Snahooms or Possession Bay and encamped near our former encampment. About forty miles again.

Decem 23

Dreadful rain all night and very strong wind, so that we cannot stir. Towards evening we made four or five miles then encamped again.

Decem 24

Went off in the night and made the traverse before day: passed the Soquams and Puyalups and came to the village where [we] took our first guides and here we encamped again.

Here we left one of our boats in care of the guide. This near the end of the Sound. From the end of the Sound to Point Roberts at Fraser's River, there are hundred and thirty miles or there abouts. Here we alter our course; we must turn straight to our right thro bays to go to the portage.

Decem 25th

Took leave of our guide before and went off. Breakfasted at the end of the portage and encamped about the middle. Rain again.

Decem 26th

Finished the portage early and went down the fork of the Chehalis river. Made a small portage and encamped little behind our former encampment of the <u>Prairies des buttes</u> on another prairie near the village of Pierre Charles. Here it was determined that we should separate: Mr. McMillan with Mr. Work to go by the Cowlits [River]; and Mr. McKay and myself by Chehalis, our old road.

Late in the afternoon we parted. We found plenty of water in the little river. Encamped at the fork: fine day.

Decem 27th

Fine day again. Passed the Chehalis village encamped on the bay near the portage, made about fifty miles today.

Decem 28th

Arrived early at the portage, made the portage the same day and encamped at the other end.

Decem 29th

Very strong. Moved slower boats round the point and remained here all day on account of the wind.

Decem 30

Left our encampment. The wind still strong. Moved slowly. Encamped on an Island in the bay opposite to our old encampment.

Decem 31st

Fine day. Started very early being determined to get to the Fort today. Made the Cape Disappointment portage and began the Chinook traverse little before sun set and arrived at Fort George sometime after dark.

Thus we finished without any cross accident: performed and seen every thing that was necessary to be done and seen according to the intentions of the Voyage with an expedition and success that were hardly thought of. I may say in the language of Caesar, Veni, vidi, vici: We came, we saw every thing, and overcame every thing.

SOURCES

Noel Annance, "A Journal of a Voyage from Fort George Columbia River to Fraser River in the Winter of 1824 and 1825," Hudson's Bay Company Archives, Archives of Manitoba, B/76/a/1. The journal is reconciled with a transcribed version in Nile Thompson, "Land Untapped and Untrapped," *Cowlitz Historical Quarterly* 22, no. 1 (1991): 6–7.

Notes

PREFACE

1 Among diverse studies from a broad Abenaki perspective are Bourque and Labar, *Uncommon Threads*; Brooks, *Common Pot*; Bruchac, *At the End* and *Bowman's Store*; Masta, *Abenaki Indian Legends*; Wiseman, *Reclaiming the Ancestors* and *Voice of the Dawn*; possibly Ricard, *St.-Francis Abenaki*; and from a children's perspective Gill, *Samuel chez les Abénakis*.

2 Christopher Roy's research on Abenaki sociality illustrates the difficulties of interrogating Abenaki history. Roy's observation that "my informants and I are constantly frustrated by sources which do not anticipate our questions and archives which do not (easily) yield desired data" was borne out in my research. Roy, "Abenaki Sociality," 117.

INTRODUCTION

1 Alexander Rolston Plumley to Asa D. Smith, 4 July 1866, in Plumley, "Reminiscences," 229.

2 Richardson, *History*, 248–50.

3 *Catalogue of the Officers and Members*, 22.

4 The criteria for joining United Fraternity are described in Campion, "Who Was Sylvanus Thayer?" 13.

5 As an example of the ongoing usage of "white," see among many other sources Charland, *Histoire des Abénakis*, 219.

6 King, *Narrative of a Journey*, vol. 1, 119.

7 "Johnstone et al. v. Connolly."

8 King, *Narrative of a Journey*, vol. 1, 50, 66.

9 Noel Annance to William McDougall, 1 December 1862, Library and Archives Canada (LAC), RG10, vol. 273, pp. 184378-80, reel 12657.

10 Noel Annance to Alexander Campbell, 26 May 1864, LAC, RG10, vol. 273, pp. 184653-5, reel 12657.

11 "Report of the Special Commissioners," appendix 21.

12 *Aboriginal Tribes*; *Copies or Extracts.*

13 "Report on the Affairs" and "Report of the Special Commissioners," both unpaginated. The 1858 report's principal attention on Upper Canada was due to Lower Canada's superintendent not providing a detailed report and the commissioners for unexplained reasons not visiting there, as they had Upper Canada. An 1839 unpublished report by J.B. Macaulay on Indigenous peoples' legal status and rights is summarized in Leighton, "Development," 81–5, and described in Harring, *White Man's Law*, 81, as "so shallow and unimaginative that it had little significance."

14 "Indians in the Canadas"; "Indians of British North America"; "Indian Tribes"; "Indians in Canada."

PART ONE

1 William Johnson to the Six Nations Indians, 23 July 1783, and meeting of 24 July 1783, in "Report on the Affairs," vol. 6, appendix T: appendices 47b–47c.

2 Jacques Duchesneau, cited in Havard, "'Protection,'" 124.

3 Havard, "'Protection,'" 117, 122.

4 See, among much writing, Jaenen, "French Sovereignty."

5 Articles of Capitulation, article 40, 8 September 1760, in Shortt and Doughty, *Documents*, 33.

6 "Treaty of Paris," article 4, 10 February 1763, in ibid., 115.

7 "A Proclamation," 7 October 1763, in ibid., 166, 167.

8 That these protocols originating in the Royal Proclamation did not extend to Lower Canada was not, according to Alain Beaulieu, because of "pre-existing policy, but the outcome of a succession of tinkerings." Beaulieu, "Equitable right," 4.

9 Leighton, "Development," 56; also Gwyn, "Sir William Johnson"; Rossie, "Guy Johnson"; and Thomas, "Sir John Johnson."

10 William Johnson to the Six Nations Indians, 23 July 1783, and meeting of 24 July 1783, in "Report on the Affairs," vol. 6, appendix T: appendices 47b–47c.

11 This version of the much disputed origins of the British practice comes from "Indians in Canada [1844]," part 2, 223–23b, 229b–30.

12 "Report on the Affairs," vol. 6, appendix T: appendices 66–9; "Report of the Special Commissioners," appendices 21 and 35.

CHAPTER ONE

1 Axtell, *Natives and Newcomers*, 59–61.

2 Ghere, "Abenaki Factionalism," 9.

3 Dickason, with McNab, *Canada's First Nations*, 94.

4 This summary draws on Day, *Identity*, 1–11; for a detailed account of the movement of peoples during the seventeenth and eighteenth centuries, see 11–65, 110–11.

5 See Duncan Campbell Napier, petition to his superiors, 28 March 1848, Library and Archives Canada (LAC), RG10, vol. 605, p. 50283, reel 13382; and "Copy of the Deeds of Conveyance," 22 August 1700, LAC, RG10, vol. 660, pp. 129–32, reel 13400. St Francis as an entity is reviewed in Day, *Identity*.

6 Earl of Gosford to Lord Glenelg, 13 July 1837, in *Copies or Extracts*, 22, 52. St Francis was only one of a number of such missions the Jesuits began in New France.

7 Ghere, "Abenaki Factionalism," tracks arrivals and departures through the mid-eighteenth century.

8 Day, *Identity*, 6; also 6–65, esp. 63–5, on different hypotheses as to the origins and timing of St Francis arrivals. The larger context is recounted in, among other sources, Nash, "Abiding Frontier"; and Morrison, *Embattled Northeast*.

9 For a comparison, see Beaulieu, Béreau, and Tanguay, *Les Wendats*, 57–82.

10 Day, *Identity*, 41; also for numbers, 42.

11 Little, *Loyalties in Conflict*, 3.

12 Namias, *White Captives*, 5; also 6–7. On slave totals, see Miller and Smith, eds, *Dictionary*, 678; on the taking of Indigenous captives, among other sources, see Newell, "Changing Nature"; and Herndon and Sakatu, "Colonizing."

13 On the diversity of circumstances resulting in capture across time, see the examples in Michno and Michno, *Fate*; VanDerBeets, ed., *Held Captive*; and Steele, *Setting*.

14 Calloway, "Uncertain Destiny," 189.

15 For examples of the power of captivity narratives as retold through time, see Calvert, *Dawn*; and Demos, *Unredeemed Captive*.

16 Calloway and Salisbury, eds, *Reinterpreting*, 14.

17 See, for example, Coleman, *New England Captives*, vol. 1, preface.

18 Baker, *True Stories*; Coleman, *New England Captives*; also Vaughan and Richter, "Crossing."

19 The exact totals were 277, 324, 267, and 536. Vaughan and Richter, "Crossing," 53-4.

20 Ibid., 72.

21 Ibid., 55, 72.

22 The precise totals were 770, 224, and 286. Ibid., 59, 70. In general, less is known about the fate of military than of civilian captives. Ibid., 70.

23 The precise totals are 770, 224, and 286. Ibid., 60.

24 Because more males than females were taken captive, the actual totals were 120 females and 107 males. Ibid., 62-7.

25 Axtell, *Natives and Newcomers*, 189-213. See also Axtell, "White Indians"; Ackerknecht, "'White Indians'"; and Hallowell, "American Indians."

26 Vaughan and Richter, "Crossing," 60-3.

27 Coleman, *New England Captives*, vol. 1, 29.

28 Ibid., vol. 1, 361. Another possibility has Samuel captured on 8 October 1695. Gill, *Notes additionnelles*, 10-13. His birth date was given as 16 or possibly 26 September 1687. Ibid. 8.

29 Hoyt, *Old Families*, vol. 1, 174-5; Gill, *Nouvelles notes*, 7-8.

30 Coleman, *New England Captives*, vol. 1, 79.

31 "Petition of Samuel Gill to Richard Earl of Bollomont, Captain General and Governor in Chief in and over his Maj$^{ty's}$ Province of the Massachusetts Bay in New England, and to the Honorable Council and Representatives of the Province, May 29, 1700," in Gill, *Nouvelles notes*, 7-8. See also Coleman, *New England Captives*, vol. 1, 361. On Gill's background, see Calvert, *Kennebec Wilderness*, 37.

32 "Petition of Samuel Gill to the Lieutenant Governor and His

Majesty's Council of the Province of Massatucicks, May 29, 1701," in Gill, *Nouvelles notes*, 13–16. See also Coleman, *New England Captives*, vol. 1, 362.

33 Gill, *Notes historiques*, 26–31. Although Maurault, *Histoire*, is accurate in respect to the Abenakis and to Gill family genealogy in the second and part of the third generations thanks to the assistance of the Gills' eldest son, the local priest's claims concerning the Gill family's origins were largely "pure imagination" (27) due to Maurault confusing a Gill he had found in an early published history with the senior Samuel Gill (29–30). This information has not, for that reason, been included here.

34 See Gill, *Notes historiques*, 7–8, 17, 19–21. Another version of events doubts Rosalie James's father was a minister. Gill, *Notes additionnelles*, 14–15.

35 Bourne, *History*, 346.

36 Maurault, *Histoire*, 346. See also Charland, "Joseph-Pierre-Anselme Maurault."

37 Among others abducted in 1703 who spent time in St Francis was seven-year-old Esther Wheelwright, who did not leave a precise account of doing so but whose continuing life in New France as a nun is chronicled in lateral descendant Julie Wheelwright's *Esther* and in Kelly, "Esther Wheelwright."

38 Williams, *Redeemed Captive*, 38, reprinted in Vaughan and Clark, eds, *Puritans*, 167–226, and in Haefeli and Sweeney, eds, *Captive Histories*, 92–157, which also describes the circumstances of the publication of Williams's account (89–91). On Maine's being the location where the captures occurred, see Axtell, *Natives and Newcomers*, 209. As evoked in Demos, *Unredeemed Captive*, Williams's daughter Eunice, who was aged seven at the time the family was captured, remained in the Mohawk settlement of Kahnawake, where she wed a local man. A namesake granddaughter a century later married into a St Francis family. See Sadoques, "History and Traditions"; and Bruchac, "Abenaki Connections."

39 Williams, "What Befell"; Haefeli, "Ransoming."

40 Gill, *Notes historiques*, 7; also 8, 17, 22–3, and 31 on how this version of events came down through the family.

41 Ibid., 43, 33.

42 See ibid., 31–3, with its proviso that Samuel Gill might have
    died prior to the autumn of 1754.

43 Ibid., 48; Charland, *Histoire de Saint-François-du-Lac*, 140. See
    also Charland, "Joseph-Louis Gill."

44 Gill, *Notes historiques*, 35, 54; Calvert, *Kennebec Wilderness*,
    33. On the expedition, see Charland, *Histoire des Abénakis*, 145.

45 Gill, *Notes historiques*, 35, and *Notes additionnelles*, 24–5;
    Charland, *Histoire de Saint-François-du-Lac*, 140; Calloway,
    ed., *Dawnland Encounters*, 236.

46 Gill, *Notes historiques*, 58, 63–5.

47 Ibid., 65.

48 Ibid. In 1869 Gabriel Annance's grandson described his grandfa-
    ther in a conversation as Mohawk, but according to ethnohisto-
    rian Gordon Day in *Identity*, 76, "the Abenakis commonly
    equate a person with a foreign tribe if he has one foreign ances-
    tor, so the basis for this tradition of Mohawk ancestry is not
    known" (see also 80).

49 Captivity narratives referencing St Francis are collected together
    in Calloway, *North Country Captives*.

50 Mary Fowler, "Captivity of Mary Fowler, of Hopkinton," in
    Drake, *Indian Captivities*, 140, 142.

51 Entry of 25 June 1855, in King, *Narrative of Titus*, 12.

52 Howe, *Genuine and Correct Account*, 7.

53 Louis Franquet, Report, 27 December 1852, in Franquet,
    Voyages, 174.

54 Howe, *Genuine and Correct Account*, 16.

55 Johnson, *Narrative*, 81. As explained in Ott-Kimmel, "Narra-
    tive," 69, the title page of the second edition published in 1807
    was "corrected and enlarged" from the first edition, which
    unlike the second did not name the Gill family or include the
    self-description of Gill having "an English heart."

56 Johnson, *Narrative*, 64–6.

57 Ibid., 66, 69–70. On the interpreter being Samuel Gill, see Sulte,
    Histoire, 94, which draws on conversations with family histo-
    rian Charles Gill.

58 Maurault, *Histoire*, 348–9, 363; Gill, *Notes historiques*, 54.

59 Johnson, *Narrative*, 67–8.

60 Ibid., 68, 70–3.

61 Ibid., 74.

62 Ibid., 71–2, 74–5, 77.

63 Jeff Amherst to Robert Rogers, 13 September 1759, in Rogers, *Journals*, 140.

64 Robert Rogers to Jeffrey Amherst, 5 November 1759, in ibid., 141–2. See also John Stark, *Reminiscences*, 87n, 160–1.

65 Robert Rogers to Jeffrey Amherst, 5 November 1759, in Rogers, *Journals*, 142. On the conflicting totals, see Day, *Identity*, 43–5.

66 Huden, "White Chief," 200; also 202–3 on the complexities of determining what occurred. Calvert, *Kennebec Wilderness*, 34, contends Xavier survived and "eventually returned home."

67 Day, *Identity*, 61, counts 900 living in St Francis as of 1752, with another 50 to 60 arriving two years later. Charland, *Histoire des Abénakis*, 341, has 342 people living there in 1783 and up to 418 in 1810.

68 Caleb Stark, *Memoir*, 13, 15; also 11–15, 107–8.

69 John Stark, *Reminiscences*, 174.

70 Caleb Stark, *Memoir*, 14.

71 Entry of 27 or 28 June 1855, in King, *Narrative of Titus*, 14.

72 John Stark, *Reminiscences*, 91, 159; Johnson, *Narrative*, 74.

73 Johnson, *Narrative*, 127–8.

74 Maurault, *Histoire*, 562; Gill, *Notes historiques*, 34–5, which states, "There is no basis for saying that Mrs. Johnson's Sabatis was Antoine" (35).

75 Maurault, *Histoire*, 349.

76 St Francis delegation to Superintendent General of Indian Affairs Sir William Johnson, 1768, in Day, *Identity*, 47.

77 Ibid., 60.

78 Calloway, *American Revolution*, 68; also more generally, 65–79. See also, among other sources, Calloway, *Western Abenaki*, 204–23; and Huden, "White Chief."

79 On Annance's activities, see Calloway, *American Revolution*, 73.

80 Elkins, "Reminiscences," 190.

81 The story is told in Charland, *Histoire de Saint-François-du-Lac*, 142–3.

82 George Washington to Congress, 3 November 1779, in Washington, *Writings*, vol. 17, 68–9.

83 *Journals of the Continental Congress*, 12 November 1779 and 7 April 1780.

84 Samuel Huntington to George Washington, 13 April 1780, in Smith et al., eds, *Letters*, vol. 15.

85 See Huden, "White Chief," 340–1.

86 Quoted in Calloway, *American Revolution*, 76; also 82.

87 For detail on the sequence of events centred on St Francis and Joseph-Louis Gill, see Charland, *Histoire de Saint-François-du-Lac*, 144–73. See also Huden, "White Chief," which includes the oath at 350–1; and Calloway, *American Revolution*, 74–84.

88 Calloway, *American Revolution*, 83. See also Charland, "Joseph-Louis Gill."

89 Calloway, *American Revolution*, 92.

90 Grand Council, Deliberations, 1781, in Maurault, *Histoire*, 587–8n2.

91 Francis Annance to Robert Shore Milnes, 25 June 1803, LAC, RG10, vol. 172, pp. 83673-4, reel 2559.

92 Duke of Portland to General Prescott, 4 November 1797, LAC, RG10, vol. 172, pp. 83662-3, reel 2559.

93 For the list of grantees, see "Names of Indians and their families living at St. Francis who lately petitioned His Excellency the Lieut. Governor for a grant of lands," 19 August 1803, LAC, RG10, vol. 172, pp. 83679-82, reel 2559, which includes children's names; also specifying which lots went to which grantees, pp. 83704-05, 83716-17, and for heirs and acreage, pp. 83721-23. See also "Schedule of lands in the Township of Durham granted by Letters Patent dated 26th June 1805 to the Abenaqui Tribe of Indians," LAC, RG10, vol. 304, pp. 204122-4, reel 12276; and Saint-Amant, *L'Avenir*, 55. For the range of original documents generated by the request, see LAC, RG10, vol. 172, pp. 83660-843, reel 2559; and Durham Township Indian Lands Papers, 1816-1873, LAC, RG10, vol. 800, parts 1 and 2, reel 13624.

94 See "Durham Band of Abenaki."

CHAPTER TWO

1 Day, *Identity*, 76.

2 Among general discussions of the meanings attached to literacy, see Lepore, *Name of War*, 26–8.

3 See Szasz, *Indian Education*; and Magnusson, *Education in New France*, 16–63.

4 For a list, see Calloway, *Indian History*, 188–97.

5 Wyss, *English Letters*, 77.

6 Axtell, *Invasion Within*, 351n21. In line with this judgment, Axtell devotes a chapter to the school (179–217). For a sympathetic but measured portrait of Wheelock and the school's beginnings, see Calloway, *Indian History*, 1–14.

7 Wheelock, *Plain and Faithful Narrative*, 21, emphasis in original.

8 Calloway, *Indian History*, 13.

9 John Sauch to Eleazar Wheelock, 10 July 1775, and Joseph Woolley to Eleazar Wheelock, 9 April 1763, in McCallum, *Eleazar Wheelock*, 234, 265.

10 See, among other sources, Love, *Samson Occom*; Johnson, *To Do Good*; Wyss, *English Letters* and *Writing Indians*; Bross and Wyss, eds, *Early Native Literacies*; Peyer, ed., *American Indian Nonfiction*; Peyer, *Tutor'd Mind*; Gale, "Resisting"; Hogsett, "'Tawnee Family'"; Murray, "'Pray Sir'"; and Schneider, "'This Once Savage Heart.'"

11 Wyss, *English Letters*, 37. Captivity narratives give one lens into what occurred in such schools; for other accounts that try to disentangle the phenomenon by drawing on theorists Michel Foucault, James C. Scott, Pierre Bourdieu, and Homi Bhabha, see in particular Schneider, "'This Once Savage Heart'"; and Murray, "'Pray Sir.'"

12 Gale, "Resisting," 137–8.

13 Letter sent by Joseph-Louis, Francis, Joseph-Piche, Robert, Magdélaine, Josephte, and Marie requesting information, 26 February 1768, in Gill, *Notes historiques*, 17; and in Nash, "Abiding Frontier," 256, 363, from original in Archives du Séminaire du Nicolet, Fonds Henry Vassal, F249, A1/3/1.

14 It was the Massachusetts Archives that did so. Gill, *Nouvelles notes*, 5–19.

15 See the appendix in Calloway, *Indian History*, 188–92; also 8, 12, 19–24, 38–40; Paxton, *Joseph Brant*; and Gwyn, "Sir William Johnson."

16 Wheelock, *Continuation* (1775), 19–20. See also McCallum, ed., *Letters*, 293–8, for a list of Indigenous students enrolled from 1754 to 1779.

17 For example, Wyss, *English Letters*, 12, 14, 36, conflates the school's sixteen years in Connecticut with its whole life.

18 McCallum, ed., *Letters*, 19.

19 Dartmouth was not "similarly dedicated to the education of Indians," as had been Moor's, despite the assertions of some scholars, as with Glenn, *American Indian*, 26.

20 Calloway, *Indian History*, 33, 193.

21 Wyss, *English Letters*, 21.

22 Entry of 10 September 1874, in Levi Frisbie, James Dean, and Thomas Kendall, "A Short Account of the Mission," in Wheelock, *Continuation* (1775), 53, emphasis in original.

23 Entries of 11 and 12 September 1874, in Levi Frisbie, James Dean, and Thomas Kendall, "A Short Account of the Mission," in ibid., 53–4, emphasis in original.

24 See student lists in Calloway, *Indian History*, 188–203: McCallum, ed., *Letters*, 293–8; and Kelly, "Dartmouth Indians."

25 "An Authenticated Account of Monies Received and Expended, for the Use of the Indian Charity-School Incorporated with Dartmouth College," in Wheelock, *Continuation* (1771), 36.

26 Ibid., 10, 11, 15, emphasis in original.

27 On girls' training at Moor's, see Richardson, *History*, 37.

28 *Journals of the Continental Congress*, 19 September 1776.

29 William Whipple to Josiah Bartlett, 30 November 1778, in Smith et al., eds, *Letters*, vol. 15.

30 The Rauner Special Collections of the Dartmouth College Library gave generous assistance.

31 Eleazar Wheelock to Francis-Louis Gill, 1 November 1777, in Dartmouth College, Correspondence and Papers, 777601.

32 Calloway, *Indian History*, 194–5, puts the year at 1777, whereas "Report of John Wheelock to Jedidiah Morse at the Request of the Society in Scotland for Propagating Christian

Knowledge, February 25, 1811," in Dartmouth College, Correspondence and Papers, 811175.3, 811419, described the three
Gill grandsons' departure as occurring "a little before" 1780. In
this 1811 report, Wheelock described Anthony Gill, "who has
resided in the same village since he went from the School," as "a
man of regular habits, industrious, attending to the profession of
joinery [woodworking], a good substantial inhabitant, influential and respected by the tribe."

33 Calloway, *Indian History*, 72, 198. See also Kelly, "Dartmouth
Indians," 123.

34 Quoted in Charland, *Histoire des Abénakis*, 158.

35 Francis Annance, petition to Governor General of the Canadas
Sir Robert Shore Milnes, 23 May 1803, Library and Archives
Canada (LAC), RGI-L3L, vol. 32, pp. 16675-6, reel 2505.

36 Lists in Day, *Identity*, 69–70. The latter document was also
signed by Robert and Joseph Gill.

37 Ibid., 71. Among others were Augustin and Thomas Gill.

38 Francis Annance, petition to Governor General of the Canadas
Sir Robert Shore Milnes, 23 May 1803, LAC, RGI-L3L, vol. 32,
pp. 16675-6, reel 2505. See also Day, *Identity*, 70-1, which
enumerates six chiefs in 1808 supporting his request. The 1803
petition referred to an earlier petition, of August 1802, that has
not been located. Long Island was granted on 8 February 1809.
Francis Annance, land document transferring Long Island to
Noel Annance, 24 February 1814, LAC, RG10, vol. 602, pp.
48759-61, reel 13381.

39 H. Van Kamp, 31 December 1805, in Londonderry, *Memoirs*,
vol. 8, 23–5, 33.

40 Chaurette, "Premières écoles autochtones," 27, 40. As of 1799,
the Lorette school enrolled girls alongside boys, having an attendance of 20 and 24 respectively, being the total number of those
aged six to fouerteen in this community of 200 (44).

41 Audet, *Système Scolaire*, vol. 3, 136, 141; also 117–49; and
Curtis, *Ruling by Schooling*, 63. There was a woman teacher
for the girls. John Wheelock to Jedidiah Morse, 12 June 1804,
Dartmouth College, Correspondence and Papers, 804362.1.

42 Doige, *Alphabetical List*, 32; Chaurette, "Premières écoles
autochtones," 40.

43 Tuckerman, *Discourse*, 40–2.

44 Boutevin, "La place"; Chaurette, "Premières écoles autochtones."

45 "T. Annance," in "Canada Sunday School Union," 124. Chaurette determined from attendance records that in 1823 the St Francis school enrolled between eighteen and twenty-five students, except during hunting season, when very few of school age remained in the community. Chaurette, "Premières écoles autochtones," 45.

46 "T. Annance," in "Canada Sunday School Union," 124.

47 Tuckerman, *Discourse*, 41, 43.

48 The name of Noel Annance's mother is taken from marriage record no. 30, 17 August 1836, in *Quebec, Vital and Church Records*.

49 See Richardson, "Dartmouth Indians."

50 On the continued use of the school's name and comparative numbers, see John Wheelock, "Testimonial of Public Examination of Members of Moor's Indian Charity School, August 17, 1810," presented to subscribers of the Honorable Society in Scotland for Propagating Christian Knowledge, 18 August 1810, Dartmouth College, Correspondence and Papers, 810467. Thirty-two boys were scheduled to be examined, of whom two were Indigenous.

51 Calloway, *Indian History*, 70, 195; Graymont, "Thayendanegea [Joseph Brant]."

52 Wheelock, *Continuation* (1775), 25, 28, emphasis in original.

53 John Wheelock to Jedidiah Morse, 19 April 1803, Dartmouth College, Correspondence and Papers, 803269.

54 "Report of John Wheelock to Jedidiah Morse at the Request of the Society in Scotland for Propagating Christian Knowledge, February 25, 1811," in Dartmouth College, Correspondence and Papers, 811175.3, 811419.

55 Francis Annance to John Wheelock, 20 May 1807, Dartmouth College, Correspondence and Papers, 807320.

56 Louis Annance in conversation with John Sprague, 1874, in Sprague, "Louis Annance," 419.

57 John Taubausanda entered three days after Louis Annance, and Paul Joseph Gill did so in October 1803, along with Joseph

Taukerman. "Report of John Wheelock to Jedidiah Morse at the Request of the Society in Scotland for Propagating Christian Knowledge, February 25, 1811," in Dartmouth College, Correspondence and Papers, 811175.3, 811419; Kelly, "Dartmouth Indians," 123.

58 John Wheelock to Jedidiah Morse, 19 April 1803, Dartmouth College, Correspondence and Papers, 803269.

59 Francis Annance to John Wheelock, received 5 October 1803, Dartmouth College, Correspondence and Papers, 803555.

60 John Wheelock to Jedidiah Morse, 12 June 1804, and 15 January 1805, Dartmouth College, Correspondence and Papers, 804362.1, 805115; Charland, *Histoire des Abénakis*, 338.

61 Francis Annance to John Wheelock, 7 August 1805, Dartmouth College, Correspondence and Papers, 805457.

62 M. and Francis Annance to Louis Annance, 14 July 1805, Dartmouth College, Correspondence and Papers, 805414.1.

63 Ibid.

64 John Wheelock to Jedidiah Morse, 1 July 1809, Dartmouth College, Correspondence and Papers, 809401. Some writers have left the impression Louis Annance attended Dartmouth College, but it seems almost certain he did not do so, as he himself explained in a conversation in later life. Sprague, "Louis Annance," 419. Calloway, *Indian History*, 195, does not list Louis Annance among those attending Dartmouth.

65 John Wheelock to Jedidiah Morse, 1 July 1809, Dartmouth College, Correspondence and Papers, 809401; Moor's Indian Charity School Ledger, 6 January 1810, Dartmouth College, Correspondence and Papers, 810106.1, which tabulates his expenses to 5 July 1809. Wheelock's note two years later respecting Louis Annance that he "resides with his father" suggests his awareness Louis's mother had died. "Report of John Wheelock to Jedidiah Morse at the Request of the Society in Scotland for Propagating Christian Knowledge, February 25, 1811," Dartmouth College, Correspondence and Papers, 811175.3, 811419.

66 "Report of John Wheelock to Jedidiah Morse at the Request of the Society in Scotland for Propagating Christian Knowledge, February 25, 1811," Dartmouth College, Correspondence and

Papers, 811175.3, 811419. Louis Annance later claimed he remained at the school until "the war of 1812 was declared and he was summoned home to Canada." Louis Annance in conversation with John Sprague, 1874, in Sprague, "Louis Annance," 419–20.

67 Stanislaus Joseph, whose mother was Francis Annance's sister, arrived in May 1804, followed by William Gill in September 1807. On the former's relationship to Francis Annance, see John Wheelock to Jedidiah Morse, 12 June 1804, Dartmouth College, Correspondence and Papers, 804362.1; on entry dates, see "Report of John Wheelock to Jedidiah Morse at the Request of the Society in Scotland for Propagating Christian Knowledge, February 25, 1811," Dartmouth College, Correspondence and Papers, 811175.3, 811419.

68 Chase, *History*, vol. 1, 635.

69 Kendall, *Travels*, vol. 3, 197.

70 John Wheelock to Jedidiah Morse, 5 September 1808, Dartmouth College, Correspondence and Papers, 808505.

71 John Wheelock to Jedidiah Morse, 1 July 1809, and 28 August 1810, Dartmouth College, Correspondence and Papers, 809401, 810478. The statement of Noel's age as sixteen years in 1808 is consistent with his father's enumeration of his children's ages in his 1803 petition to the governor general.

72 Alexander Rolston Plumley to Asa D. Smith, Dartmouth president, 4 July 1866, in Plumley, "Reminiscences," 229.

73 John Wheelock to Jedidiah Morse, 5 September 1808, Dartmouth College, Correspondence and Papers, 808505. The reference was to Paul Joseph Gill, who was wholly white by descent.

74 John Wheelock to Jedidiah Morse, 1 July 1809, Dartmouth College, Correspondence and Papers, 1 July 1809, 809401.

75 John Wheelock, "Testimonial of Public Examination of Members of Moor's Indian Charity School, August 17, 1810," presented to subscribers of the Honorable Society in Scotland for Propagating Christian Knowledge, 18 August 1810, Dartmouth College, Correspondence and Papers, 810467.

76 Richardson, "Dartmouth Indians"; McCallum, ed., *Letters*, 293–8; Calloway, *Indian History*, 188–203. The students' names

are given on the examination report and also in a separate typed list, both in Dartmouth College, Correspondence and Papers, 810467.

77 John Wheelock, "Testimonial of Public Examination of Members of Moor's Indian Charity School, August 17, 1810," presented to subscribers of the Honorable Society in Scotland for Propagating Christian Knowledge, 18 August 1810, Dartmouth College, Correspondence and Papers, 810467.

78 Alexander Rolston Plumley to Asa D. Smith, Dartmouth president, 4 July 1866, in Plumley, "Reminiscences," 229.

79 See Richardson, *History*, 246.

80 *Catalogue of the Officers and Students.*

81 Richardson, *History*, 277. Noel Annance stood out as a student, as indicated by a Dartmouth visitor two years earlier, when his second cousin Paul Joseph Gill was studying there. Although Robert Gill's son Paul Joseph was wholly white by descent, being at one time the only St Francis student there, he was perceived both as Indigenous and as a geographical outsider. Admitted to Dartmouth in 1806 as the second St Francis student there after Noel's father, Paul Joseph would be dismissed two years later for being "wholly bent on vice." Addendum of Paul Joseph Gill to John Wheelock, 2 March 1810, Dartmouth College, Correspondence and Papers, 809401. In 1812 Paul Joseph Gill was operating a private grammar school in northern New York that promised Latin and Greek along with the basics when he was named to a newly established English-language school in Terrebonne, where he was still teaching two decades later. "Report of John Wheelock to Jedidiah Morse at the Request of the Society in Scotland for Propagating Christian Knowledge, February 25, 1811," Dartmouth College, Correspondence and Papers, 811175.3, 811419; Kendall, *Travels*, vol. 3, 196; Chase, *History*, vol. 1, 635; Audet, *Système Scolaire*, vol. 3, 136, 142, vol. 4, 124, 219, 270–1; Boutevin, "La place," 122–4; Curtis, *Ruling by Schooling*, 70–1; Calloway, *Indian History*, 198; also 71, which mistakenly includes Paul Joseph Gill among "Native Americans at Dartmouth."

82 See Kendall, *Travels*, vol. 3, 195–7.

83 Richardson, *History*, 248–50.

84 *Catalogue of the Officers and Students*; Richardson, *History*, 256–61.

85 "Report of John Wheelock to Jedidiah Morse at the Request of the Society in Scotland for Propagating Christian Knowledge, February 25, 1811," Dartmouth College, Correspondence and Papers, 811175.3, 811419.

86 *Catalogue of the Officers and Members*, 22. The competitor was Social Friends.

87 The other Indigenous United Fraternity member was Peter Hooker Augustine, an Oneida from Green Bay, Wisconsin, where the Oneida had been relocated from New York State following the American War of Independence. He was invited to join in 1828 and, like Noel Annance, did not graduate. See ibid., 35; Calloway, *Indian History*, 198; and Richardson, *History*, 269–70.

88 As examples, see Parish, *Eulogy*, 2, 9; and Webster, *Oration*, 2.

89 See *General Catalogue of Dartmouth*; and *Catalogue of the Members*. Occupations are given for 84 of the 150 who graduated between 1811 and 1814.

90 Francis Annance to John Wheelock, 20 May 1807, Dartmouth College, Correspondence and Papers, 807320.

91 John Wheelock to Jedidiah Morse, 1 July 1809, Dartmouth College, Correspondence and Papers, 809401. For Moor's accounts, see Dartmouth College, Correspondence and Papers, 810106, 811900.2, 812900.3, 813140. On monies allocated for the purpose, see Richardson, "Dartmouth Indians," 525.

92 Moor's accounts, 1810, 1811, 1812, Dartmouth College, Correspondence and Papers, 811900.2, 811103, 812900.3, 8138140. The penultimate text, whose length of two volumes explains the higher cost, was almost certainly Webber, *Mathematics*. The last text, which could not be identified, was listed as "Middlesex col. Music."

93 Moor's accounts, 1812, Dartmouth College, Correspondence and Papers, 812900.3.

94 Richardson, *History*, 275.

95 See, for instance, the writings in Johnson, *To Do Good*.

96 Hill, ed., *College on the Hill*, 206.

97 John Wheelock to Jedediah Morse, 30 December 1813, Dartmouth College, Correspondence and Papers, 813680.2.

PART TWO

1 Frances Slocum, quoted in Ackerknecht, "'White Indians,'" 32; also 18.

2 Milloy, "Era of Civilization," v.

3 Rockwell, *Indian Affairs*, 159.

4 See Garrett, "Dartmouth Alumni."

5 Lord Goderich to Earl Dalhousie, 14 July 1827, and Sir George Murray to Sir J. Kempt, 1 December 1829, in *Aboriginal Tribes*, 5, 60.

6 Earl Dalhousie to William Huskisson, 22 November 1827, in ibid., 6.

7 Major General Charles Henry Darling to Lord Dalhousie, 24 July 1828, enclosed in Dalhousie to Sir George Murray, 27 October 1828, in ibid., 24.

8 For examples, see "Minutes of a Council Held at the Garrison of York," 17 September 1827, in ibid., 14–16.

9 "Minutes of a Speech Made by the Potagunnser Indians," 19 July 1817, in ibid., 17.

10 Indian Department, report, 1829, in ibid., 44. For an 1826 failed attempt to open a nondenominational school, see Milloy, "Era of Civilization," 106–8; and more generally, Chaurette, "Premières écoles autochtones."

11 Major General Charles Henry Darling to Lord Dalhousie, 24 July 1828, enclosed in Dalhousie to Sir George Murray, 27 October 1828, in *Aboriginal Tribes*, 26.

CHAPTER THREE

1 See Calloway, *Indian History*, 198.

2 Sibley, *Biographical Sketches*, vol. 2, 201. For the details, see Bodian, "Long but Thin History."

3 Gookin, *Historical Collection*, 36. See also "Harvard Indian College"; and Sibley, *Biographical Sketches*, vol. 2, 201. The Indian College was located next to where Matthews Hall stands

today, on whose outside wall is a plaque reminding passersby that "Here American Indian and English students lived and worked in accordance with the 1650 Charter calling for the education of the English and Indian youth of this country."

4 Morison, *Founding of Harvard College*, 248.
5 Morison, *Harvard College*, 341–2.
6 Lopenzina, *Red Ink*, 87–126.
7 *Publications of Colonial Society of Massachusetts Collections* 31 (1935): 329, quoted in Szasz, *Indian Education*, 124.
8 See "Digging Veritas."
9 Gookin, *Historical Collection*, 33, 78; Szasz, *Indian Education*, 122–5; Sibley, *Biographical Sketches*, vol. 2, 201–4. On the authorship of a letter attributed to Chesschaumuck, whose surname was variously spelled "Chesh-chaamog," "Cheesh-eteaumuck," and "Cheeshahteaumauck," see Lopenzina, *Red Ink*, 129–33. Respecting the ongoing debate on Indigenous deaths by disease and other means, see Madley, "Reexamining the American Genocide Debate."
10 Gookin, *Historical Collection*, 33, 78; "Digging Veritas"; Bodian, "Long but Thin History"; "Early Native American Resources"; "Remembering Native Sons"; John Leverett, diary, quoted in Sibley, *Biographical Sketches*, vol. 2, 202–3; also Szasz, *Indian Education*, 123–7. Bernd C. Peyer has reprinted surviving writings that, he considers, were very likely "carefully edited – if not entirely rewritten – by members of the faculty." Peyer, *Tutor'd Mind*, 48–51, quotation at 51.
11 "Early Native American Resources"; Baena, "Harvard Indian College." As well, missionary protégé John Sassamon was there for "a few weeks" or possibly a little longer in 1653 but not as a regular student. See Morison, *Harvard College*, 353.
12 Morison, *Harvard College*, 358–9. See also Cogley, *John Eliot's Mission*, 221–2.
13 Quoted in Connole, "Conflict," 66.
14 Morison, *Harvard College*, 356; Wright, "Piety, Politics, and Profit," 87–8.
15 Colonial records in Massachusetts Archives, quoted in Mandell, *Behind the Frontier*, 43.

16 Suffolk County Registry of Deeds, quoted in Connole, "Conflict," 67.

17 This interpretation of Wampas's behaviour and outlook is drawn from Mandell, *Behind the Frontier*, 43–5; and Connole, "Conflict," quotations at 73, 77.

18 Szasz, *Indian Education*, 216–17.

19 *Historical Sketch*, 8; *History of the College*, 42; Axtell, "Williamsburg's Indian School."

20 On the paucity of sources, see Wright, "Piety, Politics, and Profit," 14, 109–25. *Provisional List*, 7, 14, 20, 25, 29–30, 39–40, includes the names of sixteen "Indians" studying at William and Mary, all but one for only a year or two, between 1753 and 1776. On the level of instruction, see Szasz, *Indian Education*, 74; also 67–76. Also useful are Peyer, *Tutor'd Mind*, 33; and *Historical Sketch*, 12.

21 Watson, *Catawba Indian Genealogy*, 73.

22 On David Hutchison, see Fenlon, "Struggle," 14–17, 22.

23 Hutchison, "Catawba Indians," *Palmetto-State Banner* (Columbia, SC), 30 August 1849, quoted in Watson, *Catawba Indian Genealogy*, 73.

24 Ibid., 74.

25 Watson, *History*, 16, 17, emphasis in original.

26 David Hutchison, "Catawba Indians," *Palmetto-State Banner* (Columbia, SC), 30 August 1849, quoted in Watson, *Catawba Indian Genealogy*, 74.

27 Ibid., 73–4.

28 Quoted in Merrill, *Indians' New World*, 242.

29 From John Wyly, "A Copie of the Talk Deliverd by Mr. Drayton to the Catawba Indians, the 8 January 1773, as Nigh as I Can Recolect," quoted in ibid., 242.

30 Gottschalk, *Lafayette*, 102, 141, 284. On the possible circumstances, see Lincklaen, *Travels*, 69n1; Cornelius et al., "Contemporary Oneida Perspectives," 126; Lancaster, "'By the Pens,'" 73.

31 Lafayette to Thomas Jefferson, 18 March 1786, in Chinard, ed., *Letters*, 92.

32 Madame de Lafayette to Thomas Jefferson, end of August 1886, in ibid., 104.

33 *Boston Advertiser*, 6 August 1788, in Morgan, *True Lafayette*, 224n4.

34 Susan Lear, diary, 31 July 1788, in Lancaster, "'By the Pens,'" 72–3; also North, Wedge, and Freeman, *In the Words*, 239.

35 Susan Lear, 1 August 1788, in Lancaster, "'By the Pens,'" 73.

36 Ibid., 74.

37 Hough, ed., *Proceedings*, vol. 1, 178–9, 217, and 246.

38 Watson, *History*, 16.

39 Thomas Morris, memorandum, in Hough, ed., *Proceedings*, vol. 1, 179n1.

40 Entry of 3 September 1791, in Lincklaen, *Travels*, 69.

41 Mary Magdalene Flagg, in North, Wedge, and Freeman, *In the Words*, 239–40.

42 "Chronicle," 214.

43 Thomas Jefferson to Martha Jefferson Randolph, 22 March 1792, in Jefferson, Thomas Jefferson Papers.

44 According to Calloway, *Indian History*, 91, 97, 102, 113, 198–203, thirty Indigenous students attended Dartmouth over the nineteenth century, of whom Seneca Maris Bryant Pierce graduated in 1840, Choctaw Joseph Pitchlynn Folsom in 1854, part-Cherokee DeWitt Duncan in 1861, and Dakota Charles Eastman in 1887. One of the other nineteenth-century college graduates was the social activist Apache Carlos Montezuma, who was raised by whites and received a chemistry degree from the University of Illinois in 1884. See Peyer, ed., *American Indian Nonfiction*, 169, 241–2, and Carney, *Native American Higher Education*, 156–62. Moving into the twentieth century, Winnebago Henry Roe Cloud, who was sustained by a white guardian and similarly committed to Indigenous betterment, graduated from Yale University in 1910, as described in Pfister, *Yale Indian*.

45 Smith, *Mississauga Portraits* and his Peter Jones biography, *Sacred Feathers*. Among other examples, see Perdue, ed., *Cherokee Editor*.

46 Morison, *Harvard College*, 342n1, 360.

47 See Trigger, "Amantacha."

48 Silverman, *Red Brethren*, 56; also 57–8, 70–88; Szasz, "Samson Occom."

49 Samson Occom, "A Short Narrative of My Life," in Peyer, ed., *American Indian Nonfiction*, 47, 48, emphasis in original.

50 Peyer, *Tutor'd Mind*, 54.

51 For founders' names, see Silverman, *Red Brethren*, 59; for cohesiveness over time, including the move to Wisconsin in the 1830s, see Cipolla, *Becoming Brothertown*; and Jarvis, *Brothertown Nation*.

52 Murray, "'Pray Sir,'" 19.

53 Szasz, *Indian Education*, 7.

54 The Department of Indian Affairs files in Library and Archives Canada, which are also at its Héritage website, contain many incoming letters awaiting interrogation that were written in Iroquois or some other Indigenous language.

55 Boutevin, "La place."

56 Warrior, *Tribal Secrets*, 3.

57 For some uses of the Warrior quotation, see Bannet, *Transatlantic Stories*, 159; Lopenzina, *Red Ink*, 198; and Weaver, *That the People Might Live*, 49. Among those following up on Warrior's assessment are Joanna Brooks's edited *Collected Writings of Samson Occom* and the chapters, never mind articles, framed by Occom in books published since the mid-1990s. See, among their number, Bannet, *Transatlantic Stories*, 158–85; Bouwman, "Samson Occom"; Brooks, *Common Pot*, 51–105; Chiles, *Transformable Race*, 31–63; Nelson, "'(I speak like a fool)'"; Peyer, *American Indian Nonfiction*, 43–54, and *Tutuor'd Mind*, 54–116; Roppolo, "Samson Occom"; Round, "Title Pages"; Rubin, *Tears of Repentance*, 114–59; Weyler, *Empowering Words*, 114–44; and Wigginton, "Extending Root."

58 On Joseph Johnson, see his *To Do Good*; Murray, "Joseph Johnson's Diary"; Peyer, *American Indian Nonfiction*, 55–62; and Wyss, *English Letters*, 74–108. Respecting Hendrick Aupaumut, see Chiles, *Transformable Race*, 64–106; Gustafson, "Historical Introduction"; and Peyer, *American Indian Nonfiction*, 63–74. On William Apess, see his *On Our Own Ground*;

and Gura, *Life*; also Brooks, *Common Pot*, 143–218; Dannenberg, "'Where, then'"; Konkle, *Writing Indian Nations*, 97–159; Moore, *That Dream*; Peyer, *American Indian Nonfiction*, 75–84; Peyer, *Tutuor'd Mind*, 117–65; Warrior, *People and the Word*, 1–47; and Weaver, *Red Atlantic* and *That the People Might Live*, 46–85.

59 Brooks, *Common Pot*; Doerfler, Sinclair, and Stark, *Centering Anishinaabeg Studies*; Justice, *Our Fire*; Sinclair and Cariou, eds, *Manitowapow*; Warrior, *People and the Word* and *Tribal Secrets*; Weaver, *That the People Might Live*; Womack, *Red on Red*; Womack, Justice, and Teuton, eds, *Reasoning Together*.

60 Anderson, "Presence," 284.

61 An excellent beginning point for interrogating Osunkhirhine's writing is Boutevin, "La place." On his inheritance and the intricacies of his surname, see Day, *Identity*, 88–90, where "Dartmouth" should read "Moor's."

62 Noel Annance's letters in the files of the Department of Indian Affairs at Library and Archives Canada were compared with those preceding and following them.

63 Louis Annance in conversation with John Sprague, 1874, in Sprague, "Louis Annance," 420.

64 Day, *Identity*, 72; also 62. The Gills are listed as J. Guille, S. Guille, P.J. Guille, G. Gile, and R.W. Guille.

65 Irving, *Officers*, 217; also 215, 218.

66 *Quebec Gazette/Gazette de Québec*, 4 November 1813, in Wood, ed., *Select British Documents*, vol. 2, 398–9. For a detailed account of the battle in its larger context, see Maurault, *Histoire*, 603–13.

67 Wood, ed., *Select British Documents*, vol. 2, 411. The two others commended were fellow lieutenants and interpreters Louis Langlade from Detroit and Bartlet Lyons from Lake of the Two Mountains. Irving, *Officers*, 215, 218.

68 Noel Annance, petition to Charles Stanley, 29 December 1861, Library and Archives Canada (LAC), RG10, vol. 273, pp. 184357-60, reel 12657; "Military Medals."

69 Whatever happened in the interim, Noel Annance's medal came up for auction by Dix Noon Webb Limited in London in Sep-

tember 2006, when it sold over the estimated value of £600-800 for £900. See http://www.dnw.co.uk/auction-archive/catalogue-archive/lot.php?auction_id=94&lot_id=54364.

70 Wood, ed., *Select British Documents*, vol. 3, part 2, 729. The other three companies were Caughnawaga, Lake of the Two Mountains, and St Regis.

71 Wood, ed., *Select British Documents*, vol. 3, part 2, 728.

72 Louis Annance in conversation with John Sprague, 1874, in Sprague, "Louis Annance," 420.

73 Moor's accounts, 1816–18, in Dartmouth College, Correspondence and Papers, 8161901, 819170.

74 Chaurette, "Premières écoles autochtones," 31.

75 Francis Joseph Annance, 1821, cited in Woods, *Cross Cemetery*, 1.

76 The figures come from Ruddel, *Quebec City*, tables 2 and 8, 253, 256.

77 See ibid., 150.

78 Curtis, *Ruling by Schooling*, 133–4, 494, emphasis in original.

79 Francis Annance, petition to Governor General of the Canadas Sir Robert Shore Milnes, 23 May 1803, LAC, RGI-L3L, vol. 32, pp. 16675-6, reel 2505.

80 Louis Annance in conversation with John Sprague, 1874, in Sprague, "Louis Annance," 420.

81 The topic is interrogated in Antaya, "La Traite" and "Chasser." For the earlier time period, see Savoie and Tanguay, "La Noeud"; and for the later, see Gélinas, "La Mauricie"; and LeBel, "Trois facettes."

82 Antaya, "La Traite," 155. The years of employment are not given. The last of the contracts to which Noel Annance agreed was transferred to someone else on his signing up with the North West Company (108n36).

83 Noel Francis Annance, contract signed 8 August 1818, in Voyageurs Database.

84 Ibid.

85 Voyagers Database.

86 Respecting Roman Gill, Michel Gill, and Guillaume Gill, who signed contracts between 1815 and 1816, see Maurault,

Histoire, 363, 365, 368, 376; and for the sundries account of François Guille for 1818–21, see North West Company, Servants' Contracts, 1798–1822.

87 On Ignace Portneuf's service in the War of 1812, see Charland, *Histoire des Abénakis*, 325. In Day, *Identity*, 72, the list of sixty-four St Francis veterans of the War of 1812 with heirs in St Francis in 1844 contains eight Gills and Annances and seven Portneufs. Ignace and Joseph Portneuf's years in the fur trade are tracked in Watson, *Lives Lived*, 789–90.

88 Pierre Charles's years in the fur trade are tracked in Watson, *Lives Lived*, 263–4.

89 Elliott, "Journal of Alexander Ross," 369.

90 Milloy, "Era of Civilization," 3.

91 Noel Francis Annance, contract signed 8 August 1818, in Voyageurs Database. North West Company records are sparse, with nothing otherwise located in respect to Noel Annance.

92 HBC governor and committee to George Simpson, 8 March 1822, in Fleming, ed., *Minutes*, 313; also George Simpson to HBC governor and committee, 16 July 1822, 338, and George Simpson to HBC governor and committee, 5 August 1822, 357–8.

93 Simon Plamondon's years in the fur trade are tracked in Watson, *Lives Lived*, 783–4.

94 Minutes of Council of Northern Department of the Hudson's Bay Company, 2 July 1825, in Fleming, ed., *Minutes*, 115.

95 See Simmons, *Keepers*, 104.

96 Respecting C.W. Bouc and Antoine Hamel, in George Simpson, "Character Book," in Williams, ed., *Hudson's Bay Miscellany*, 202, 215.

97 Respecting John Lee Lewes, John McLeod, James Birnie, John McDougald, Patrick Small, William Sinclair, and Archibald McKinlay, in George Simpson, "Character Book," in ibid., 185, 180, 202, 223, 227, 229; also worded slightly differently respecting John Rowland and James McMillan on 183, Allan McDonnell on 185, John Edward Harriott on 197, Charles Bisbois on 201, John Bell on 202, Nicholas Brown, Thomas Corcoran, and William Cowie on 203, Allan Cameron and George De-

schambeault on 204, Paul Frazer and Henry Fisher on 208, Donald Manson on 221, P.C. Pambrun on 224, J.M. Yale on 230, and "half breeds" generally on 218.

98 Respecting Thomas Frazer, in George Simpson, "Character Book," in ibid., 207; also respecting Frances Grant on 209.

99 Respecting Peter McKenzie, in George Simpson, "Character Book," in ibid., 219.

100 Respecting John Dugald Cameron and John Charles, in George Simpson, "Character Book," in ibid., 173.

101 Respecting William Kittson, in George Simpson, "Character Book," in ibid., 216; also "little Education" respecting Andrew McPherson on 217.

102 Respecting Joseph Beioley, Samuel Black, George Allan, James Douglas, Donald McKenzie, William Nourse, Alexander Robertson, and Richard Rae, in George Simpson, "Character Book," in ibid., 178, 193, 201, 204, 221, 224, 226; also respecting John McLeod and Murdoch McPherson on 220, William G. Rae on 225, and George Ross on 226.

103 Respecting Robert Cowie, Richard Hardisty, John McDonald, and William Swanston, in George Simpson, "Character Book," in ibid., 198, 211, 222, 226; also respecting Nichol Finlayson on 207 and Colin Campbell on 196.

104 Respecting John Bell, in George Simpson, "Character Book," in ibid., 202; also respecting Richard Grant on 211.

105 Respecting Donald Ross, in George Simpson, "Character Book," in ibid., 198.

106 Respecting Peter Skene Ogden, in George Simpson, "Character Book," in ibid., 193; similarly respecting Colin Campbell on 196.

107 Respecting John McLean, in George Simpson, "Character Book," in ibid., 223, with numerous others similarly assessed for reasons that are unclear.

108 Respecting F.N. Annance, John George McTavish, James Keith, John Ballenden, Alexander Hay, Alexander Simpson, and George Barnston, in George Simpson, "Character Book," in ibid., 200, 171, 177, 202, 212, 228, 231. McTavish was so distinguished. In addition, Duncan Finlayson, James Hargrave, and

John McKenzie were described as having a "good Education" on 186, 214, and 223.

109 Respecting John McKenzie, Charles Ross, and Thomas Simpson, in George Simpson, "Character Book," in ibid., 193, 225, 228.

CHAPTER FOUR

1 On the character of the workforce, see Barman, *French Canadians*, 52–75.

2 John McLeod, HBC, Kamloops Report, Spring 1823, in McLeod, Journals and Correspondence.

3 George Simpson to William McIntosh, 15 July 1823, Hudson's Bay Company Archives (HBCA), D.4/2, fo. 52; also partially in Fleming, ed., *Minutes*, 18n1. On Simpson's position, see Galbraith, "George Simpson."

4 Simpson, *Fur Trade*, 113–14.

5 Entry of 21 October 1824, in ibid., 39.

6 Francis Noel Annance, 1825, in HBC, Servants' Characters and Staff Records.

7 John Work, 1825, in ibid.

8 Thomas McKay, 1825, in ibid.

9 Entry of 1 November 1824, in Simpson, Outward Correspondence, D.4/7, fo. 81.

10 George Simpson to John McLeod, 1 November 1824, in Simpson, *Fur Trade*, 247.

11 On Hawaiians in the Pacific Northwest fur trade, see Barman and Watson, *Leaving Paradise*.

12 Thompson, "Land Untapped," 6–7.

13 Annance, "Journal"; Work, "Journal of a Voyage." Although McKay's journal was, along with those of Work and Annance, passed on to Simpson while he was still in the Pacific Northwest, it has not been subsequently cited or located. Simpson, *Fur Trade*, 118.

14 17 December 1824 in Work, "Journal of John Work," 220.

15 Maclachlan, ed., *Fort Langley Journals*, 7.

16 12 December 1824 in Work, "Journal of John Work," 216.

17 Simpson, *Fur Trade*, 114.

18 Running entry of winter 1834–35, in ibid., 118; also "Extracts

from Mr Chief Trader MacMillan's Report of His Voyage and Survey from the Columbia to Frazer's River," 31 December 1824, taken from a copy in the British Archives and thereby likely transmitted to the Foreign Office (248–50).

19 Entry of 4 April 1825, in ibid., 133.

20 George Simpson to John McLoughlin, 10 April 1825, in Simpson, Outward Correspondence, D.4/5, fo. 25d; also fo. 51 and 53.

21 John McLoughlin to HBC chief factors and chief traders, 10 August 1825, in McLoughlin, *Letters, 1825–38*, 304.

22 Douglas, *Journal*, 160.

23 George Simpson to Andrew Colvile, 8 September 1821, in Fleming, ed., *Minutes*, 399. On McDonald, see Cole, *Exile*.

24 See Archibald McDonald to Francis Noel Annance, 12 August 1826, in McDonald, *Blessed Wilderness*, 38–9.

25 See McDonald, *Blessed Wilderness*, 46–56, passim.

26 Archibald McDonald to John Warren Dease, 17 October and 3 December 1826, in ibid., 47, 52.

27 Archibald McDonald to John Warren Dease, 3 December 1826, in ibid., 52.

28 Entry in 2 October 1826, in HBC, Kamloops Post Journal, B97a2, fo. 3.

29 Maclachlan, ed., *Fort Langley Journals*, 254n19; also "Thompson River District Report, 1827," in Simpson, *Part of Dispatch*, 229.

30 HBC, Servants' Characters and Staff Records.

31 George Simpson to HBC governor and committee, 23 February 1826, in Simpson, *Fur Trade*, 267. For the list of names, see Maclachlan, ed., *Fort Langley Journals*, 23.

32 Entry of 28 June 1827, in Maclachlan, ed., *Fort Langley Journals*, 23.

33 Entry of 29 June 1827, in ibid.

34 Entry of 2 July 1827, in ibid., 24.

35 Entry of 5 July 1827, in ibid.

36 Entry of 17 July 1827, in ibid., 26.

37 Akrigg and Akrigg, *1001 British Columbia Place Names*, 18.

38 Entry of 2 July 1827, in Maclachlan, ed., *Fort Langley Journals*, 24.

39 Entry of 27 July 1827, in ibid., 29.

40 Entry of 3 August 1827, in ibid., 30.

41 Entry of 13 August 1827, in ibid.

42 Entries of 10 and 25 January 1828, in ibid., 49, 50.

43 James Macmillan to John McLoughlin, 15 September 1827, in ibid., 243n35.

44 Entry of 26 November 1827, in ibid., 47.

45 Entry of 24 December 1827, in ibid., 48.

46 Entry of 26 December 1827, in ibid.

47 Entry of 11 February 1828, in ibid., 50–1.

48 Allard, "Jason."

49 Entry of 4 April 1828, in Maclachlan, ed., *Fort Langley Journals*, 58.

50 Entry of 5 April 1828, in ibid., 58–9.

51 Entry of 6 April 1828, in ibid., 59.

52 Entry of 11 August 1828, in ibid., 71.

53 HBC, Servants' Characters and Staff Records.

54 "McDonald's Report to the Governor and Council," 25 February 1830, in Maclachlan, ed., *Fort Langley Journals*, 221.

55 Entry of 12 October 1828, in ibid., 81.

56 Ibid., 14, 243n35; Foster, "Indian Trader."

57 Entry of 2 December 1828, in Maclachlan, ed., *Fort Langley Journals*, 88.

58 Entry of 19 December 1828, in ibid., 90.

59 Entry of 21 November 1828, in ibid., 86.

60 Archibald McDonald to HBC governor and Northern Council, 22 March 1829, in McDonald, *Blessed Wilderness*, 65.

61 Entry of 21 March 1829, in Maclachlan, ed., *Fort Langley Journals*, 103; also 100, 102.

62 Entry of 19 April 1829, in ibid., 110.

63 Entry of 3 October 1829, in ibid., 130.

64 Entry of of 23 October 1829, in ibid., 131.

65 Entry of 19 November 1827, in ibid., 46.

66 "McDonald's Report to the Governor and Council," 25 February 1830, in ibid., 222–3.

67 Entry of 14 June 1829, in ibid., 221.

68 Watson, *Lives Lived*, 23.

69 William Cockran to James Hargrave, 9 August 1832, in Brown, *Strangers*, 41.

70 Ibid., 119.

71 Archibald McDonald to John McLoughlin, 14 September 1829, in McDonald, *Blessed Wilderness*, 69–70.

72 Archibald McDonald to John McLoughlin, 14 November 1829, in ibid., 71.

73 Entry of 22 September 1830, in Maclachlan, ed., *Fort Langley Journals*, 160.

74 Archibald McDonald to Francis Ermatinger, 17 July 1826, and Archibald McDonald to George Simpson, 30 July 1826, in McDonald, *Blessed Wilderness*, 36–7.

75 John McLoughlin to Francis Noel Annance, 14 October 1830, in McLoughlin, *Letters, 1829–1832*, 152.

76 John McLoughlin to George Barnston, 30 November 1830 and 4 January 1831, in ibid., 172, 179.

77 John McLoughlin to George Barnston, 4 January 1831, in ibid., 179.

78 Archibald McDonald to John McLoughlin, 20 September 1830 and 10 February 1831, in McDonald, *Blessed Wilderness*, 83, 87.

79 HBC, Servants' Characters and Staff Records; also George Simpson, 1830, in Williams, ed., *Hudson's Bay Miscellany*, 200n3, citing HBCA, A.34/1, fo. 12d.

80 Fuchs, "Native Sons," 9, 64, 65–6; also for the parameters and personnel of Fuchs's study, 9, 236–42.

81 Morag Maclachlan, "Introduction," in Maclachlan, ed., *Fort Langley Journals*, 14; also Maclachlan, "Case for Francis Noel Annance."

82 George Simpson to Andrew Colvile, 20 May 1822, in Simpson, *Fur Trade*, 181.

83 George Simpson to William Smith, 15 March 1827, in Simpson, Outward Correspondence, D.4/15, fo. 18.

84 Ibid. John S. Galbraith parroted Simpson's assertions as though they were common knowledge: "Like the lumbermen and farmers on the St. Lawrence, Abenaki did not depend on furs for their livelihood, but derived their subsistence primarily from the

soil." Galbraith, *Hudson's Bay Company*, 27; also 26, 30–1. See also Gélinas, "La Mauricie."

85 Galbraith, *Hudson's Bay Company*, 27, 30–1.

86 For 1824, see Voyageurs Database. For 1826, see Antaya, "Chasseur," 19fn63; and Antaya, "La Traite," 118–19n67. For 1827, 1828, and 1831, see Antaya, "La Traite," 79, 118, 152–4.

87 Archibald McDonald to Edward Ermatinger, 5 March 1830, in Ermatinger, Inward Correspondence.

88 Among many examples are John Work to Edward Ermatinger, 1 January 1828, and Archibald McDonald to Edward Ermatinger, 20 February 1831, in ibid.; Peter Skene Ogden to John McLeod, 10 March 1831, and Archibald McDonald to John McLeod, 6 September 1831 and 20 February 1833, in McLeod, Journals and Correspondence.

89 Archibald McDonald to Edward Ermatinger, 5 March 1830, in Ermatinger, Inward Correspondence.

90 Fuchs, "Native Sons," 9, 62, passim.

91 Succeeding Scot James McMillan, dispatched west to take charge of Thompson River in 1822, was newly arrived fellow Scot John McLeod, under whom Annance served. Samuel Black was sent west to take charge of Fort Nez Perces not long after Annance left there in 1823, replacing Anglo Canadian John Warren Dease who had similarly been dispatched from east of the Rockies. So were Englishman John Lewes in 1821 to have charge of Spokane House and Irishman Francis Heron in 1829 to have charge of Fort Colvile. In respect to Joseph McGillivray, who arrived in 1826 to take charge of Fort Alexandria in New Caledonia, and his twin brother, Simon, four years later to take over Fort Nez Perces, even though their mother was Cree, their Scots father was a major player in the fur trade whose sons could not be passed over. Others were shunted to the Pacific Northwest because, it appears, they were problems elsewhere, as with the well-educated thirty-five-year-old John Spencer, son of a principal official of the HBC in London, who arrived in 1826 after mismanaging accounts at York Factory and in the English River district. See individual biographies in Watson, *Lives Lived*.

92 Francis Ermatinger to Edward Ermatinger, 18 October 1826, in

Ermatinger, *Fur Trade Letters*, 69; also 64n35; and HBC, Servants' Characters and Staff Records.

93 Minutes of Council of Northern Department, 26 June 1826 and 2 July 1828, in Fleming, ed., *Minutes*, 173, 216; HBC, Servants' Characters and Staff Records.

94 HBC governor and committee to George Simpson, 27 February 1822, in Fleming, ed., *Minutes*, 305.

95 See Raffan, *Emperor*, 139, 145-9, 166, 226-33.

96 John McLoughlin to George Simpson, 16 March 1831, in Simpson, Outward Correspondence, 1830-31, D.4/125, fo. 79, and D.4/18, fo. 68d; also in McLoughlin, *Letters, 1829-1832*, 187-8.

97 George Simpson to John McLoughlin, 1 July 1831, in Simpson, Outward Correspondence, D.4/125, fo. 79, and D.4/18, fo. 68d.

98 John McLoughlin to Francis Heron, 28 June 1831, in McLoughlin, *Letters, 1829-1832*, 199.

99 Entry of 15 November 1831, in HBC, Fort St James Post Journal, B.188/a/16, fo. 56; also Francis Ermatinger to Edward Ermatinger, 24 March 1832, in Ermatinger, *Fur Trade Letters*, 157.

100 The larger context of Simpson's outlook is well described in Galbraith, *Little Emperor*, 109-19.

101 Respecting John Kennedy, in George Simpson, "Character Book," in Williams, ed., *Hudson's Bay Miscellany*, 216.

102 George Simpson, 1830 comment respecting John Kennedy, a surgeon, in George Simpson, "Character Book," in ibid., 216n1.

103 Respecting Roderick McKenzie, in George Simpson, "Character Book," in ibid., 216n1.

104 Ibid., 200, citing HBCA, A.34/1, fo. 12d.

105 Ermatinger, *Fur Trade Letters*, 165n37; also Lahey, *George Simpson*, 131.

106 George Simpson to Thomas Fraser, 12 March 1859, in Simmons, *Keepers*, 108.

107 John Tod to Edward Ermatinger, 18 February 1830, in Ermatinger, Papers.

108 John Tod to Edward Ermatinger, 10 April 1831, in ibid.

109 Belyk, *John Tod*, 83.

110 See Barman, *French Canadians*, 167-92.

111 Entry of 9 July 1833, in Tolmie, *Journals*, 215–16.

112 Both land grants would become fraught as to their legal status, as explained in respect to the Abenakis in chapter 7 and to the Mohawks in, among other sources, Hagopian, "Joseph Brant"; and in Kelsay, *Joseph Brant*, 555–62, and "Tekarinhogen."

113 On Abenakis, see chapter 1; on Brant and the Mohawks, see Paxton, *Joseph Brant*, 49–53. For Brant's and Annance's British counterparts, see Sutherland, Tousignant, and Dionne-Tousignant, "Haldimand"; and Wallot, "Sir Robert Shore Milnes."

114 Buckner, "Matthew Whitworth-Aylmer."

115 Envelope accompanying Francis N. Annance to Lord Aylmer, 20 March 1832, Library and Archives Canada (LAC), Land Petitions of Lower Canada, RG1-L3L, vol. 32, pp. 16698-700, reel 2505.

116 See Wolfenden, "John Tod."

117 Notes on Francis N. Annance to Lord Aylmer, 20 March 1832, LAC, Land Petitions of Lower Canada, RG1-L3L, vol. 32, pp. 16698-700, reel 2505.

118 McDonald, "Short Narrative."

119 Francis Noel Annance to James Murray Yale, 17 October 1832, British Columbia Archives, MS-0182, box 1, file 2, item 17.

120 Ibid.

121 John McLoughlin to P.C. Pambrun, 27 January 1833, HBC, Fort Vancouver Correspondence Books, B.223/b/8, fo. 45d.

122 McDonald, "Short Narrative"; John McLoughlin to George Simpson, 20 March 1833, in Simpson, Inward Correspondence, HBCA, D.5/4, fo. 39d.

CHAPTER FIVE

1 J.E. Harriott to John McLeod, 14 July 1832, in McLeod, Journals and Correspondence.

2 King, *Narrative of a Journey*, vol. 1, 50, 62–3.

3 Ibid., 66.

4 Ibid., 80, 88–9, 91–2.

5 Ibid., 118–19.

6 Ibid., 119; entry of 16 October 1833, in HBC, Fort Simpson (Mackenzie River) Post Journal, B.200/a/15. Entries come from

this version of the journal, unless otherwise noted as being found only in the version E.24/5, which Stuart kept in his possession.

7   James Hargrave to J.G. McTavish, 16 September 1833, in James Hargrave, *Letters*, 255.

8   Entry of 16 October 1833, in HBC, Fort Simpson (NWT) Post Journal.

9   Simpson, *Part of Dispatch*, 25, 39.

10 J.E. Harriott to John McLeod, 24 July 1832, in McLeod, Journals and Correspondence.

11 Smith, "John Stuart."

12 Raffan, *Emperor*, 431.

13 It was on returning in spring 1826 from a trip to England that Simpson lit on Peggy Taylor. The story goes that sometime thereafter, evidencing some uncertainty about the paternity of the child with which she was pregnant, Simpson turned to a confidante: "Pray keep an Eye on the commodity and if she bring forth anything in the proper time & of the right color let them be taken care of but if anything be amiss let the whole be bundled about their business." Quoted in Raffan, *Emperor*, 231. Their son, George, was born at York Factory in February 1827.

14 Van Kirk, *Many Tender Ties*, 276n77, 187; Brown, *Strangers*.

15 A year after Peggy Taylor gave birth to George, named after his father, she and her brother Tom accompanied Simpson on his 1828 trip to the Pacific Northwest, where she again became pregnant. Peggy was left part way back in the spring of 1829 to be with their young son, George, who had been lodged with her sister Mary and John Stuart at the post of which he then had charge about 100 kilometres, or 60 miles, north of Red River. What none of them were told during Simpson's short visit, just before Peggy gave birth, was that he was on his way to England in search of a white wife, an earlier trip having whet his appetite for a lifestyle comparable to that enjoyed by the HBC hierarchy based in London. Kept ignorant of Simpson's intentions, Stuart, as he confided to a friend, subsequently comforted young George as to how he would soon "see his father," at which Peggy "smiled" in anticipation of Simpson's return to his family.

Quoted in Raffan, *Emperor*, 253. Simpson found his white wife in the person of an eighteen-year-old cousin he wed in February 1830, and they settled that summer in the Red River colony. On Simpson's return from England, as he had done with his earlier discards, he married Peggy off to a minor HBC employee, oarsman Amable Hogue, who worked for Simpson and whom she may have known for some time. Five months later, Simpson manoeuvred one of his earlier discards, Mary Keith, to wed his long-time servant, Peggy's brother Tom Taylor. As was usual, the events almost immediately found their way into the gossipy letters exchanged between HBC officers: "The Govrs little tit Bit Peggy Taylor is also Married to Amable Hog what a down fall ... from a Governess to Sow ... Thos Taylor is now attached to this district as Post Master; and as his Beau frair [brother-in-law] is Bourgeois, he will no doubt be raised to clerk in a soon time – he may thank his sisters C--t for that." Lahey, *George Simpson*, 116–17, underlining in original; also Thomas Taylor Sr, HBC, Biographical Sheets; and William Sinclair to Edward Ermatinger, 15 August 1831, in Ermatinger, Papers.

16 Smith, "John Stuart."

17 Respecting John Stuart, in George Simpson, "Character Book," in Williams, ed., *Hudson's Bay Miscellany*, 175.

18 John Stuart to John McLeod, 8 March 1833, in McLeod, Journals and Correspondence.

19 Entry of 20 February 1834, in HBC, Fort Simpson (NWT) Post Journal, E.24/5, as copied by John Stuart. The assertion is inconsistent both with Stuart's initial description of Francis Noel on his arrival and with Stuart writing on 13 December 1833 how "he was sent here as a Gentleman." George Simpson continued to describe Francis Noel to Stuart as a clerk. George Simpson to John Stuart, 4 July 1834, in Simpson, Inward Correspondence, HBCA, D.4/20, fo. 13d–14.

20 Williams, ed., *Hudson's Bay Miscellany*, 174.

21 James Hargrave to John McLeod, 12 June 1827, in James Hargrave, *Letters*, 36.

22 John Stuart to George Simpson, 1 February 1830, quoted in Brown, *Strangers*, 134.

23 John Stuart to John McLeod, 16 March 1833, in McLeod, Journals and Correspondence.

24 John Stuart's observations on the letters are integrated into HBC, Fort Simpson (NWT) Post Journal, E.24/5, as copied by John Stuart. Only this private version of the post journal, kept by Stuart for his own use, contains the letters.

25 Entry of 12 February 1834, in ibid.

26 Entry of 15 February 1834, in ibid.

27 Ibid.

28 Ibid.

29 Respecting John Stuart, in George Simpson, "Character Book," in Williams, ed., *Hudson's Bay Miscellany*, 174.

30 Entry of 13 December 1833, in HBC, Fort Simpson (NWT) Post Journal.

31 Ibid.

32 Entry of 14 December 1833, in ibid.

33 All fifteen notes come from HBC, Fort Simpson (NWT) Post Journal, E.24/5, as copied by John Stuart. Obvious misspellings and grammar errors have been corrected, given that it is unclear whose they were. Stuart's comments accompany the notes in the journal and are not separately cited here.

34 James Hargrave to J.G. McTavish, 5 August 1834, in James Hargrave, *Letters*, 264.

35 HBC, Fort Simpson (NWT) Post Journal, E.24/5, as copied by John Stuart.

36 Entry of 23 March 1834, ibid.

37 John Stuart to John McLeod, 16 March 1833, in McLeod, Journals and Correspondence.

38 Ibid.

39 George Simpson to John Stuart, 4 July 1834, in Simpson, Outward Correspondence, D.4/20, fo. 13d–14.

40 Ibid.

41 James Hargrave to J.G. McTavish, 5 August 1834, in James Hargrave, *Letters*, 264, emphasis in original.

42 Ibid.

43 Ibid., 264–5.

44 Ibid., 265.

45 James Hargrave to J.G. McTavish, 1 December 1834, in James Hargrave, *Letters*, 271.

46 Van Kirk, *Many Tender Ties*, 169–70; also Brown, *Strangers*, 134–6; and Letitia Mactavish to her mother, 9 May 1840, in Letitia Hargrave, *Letters*, 20–1, 20n1, which, giving Stuart's version of events, has Mary Taylor leaving for her health.

47 James Hargrave to Nichol Finlayson, 10 December 1838, in Van Kirk, *Many Tender Ties*, 170.

48 Nicol Finlayson to James Hargrave, 2 June 1842, in James Hargrave, *Hargrave Correspondence*, 400. Mary Taylor's fortunes would later to some extent turn around. Stuart's will, written in 1832, left her £500, but following his death in 1847 a later version turned up that did not mention her and left generous amounts to his two Scots sisters. Although they did not manage totally to disinherit Mary, her legacy was, after legal fees, reduced to a still considerable £350. Van Kirk, *Many Tender Ties*, 276n84; Smith, "John Stuart"; Letitia Hargrave, *Letters*, 20n1, and Letitia Hargrave to her mother, 1 December 1840, on 87.

49 For Annance being at Norway House as of the beginning of August 1834, see James Hargrave to J.G. McTavish, 5 August 1834, in James Hargrave, *Letters*, 265.

50 Thomas Simpson to Donald Ross, 30 July 1834, in Simpson, Outward Correspondence, D.4/20, fo. 24.

51 Donald Ross to Francis Noel Annance, 24 June 1836, in Simpson, Outward Correspondence, D.4/22, fo. 25–25d.

PART THREE

1 The earliest located letter written from St Francis was dated 22 December 1834. See Napier to Noel Annance, 31 January 1835, in Napier, Letterbooks.

2 Lavoie and Vaugeois, eds, *L'Impasse amérindienne*.

3 For the earlier figure, see *Facts*, 14; and on 1844, see "Past and Present Condition of the Indians," in "Report on the Affairs," vol. 4, appendix EEE. Totals are sometimes equated with the number of those who received presents, which was smaller still.

4 "Indians in the Canadas," part 2, 302. Some such observations were made in another hand in the margin, but this one was not.

5 See Leighton, "Duncan Campbell Napier."

6 "Report on the Affairs," vol. 6, appendix T. The report is not paginated. The quotation comes from the report's recommendations in the section entitled "3. Management of the Indian Lands," as opposed to one of the many submissions made to the three commissioners.

7 See Beaulieu, "'Equitable right.'"

8 On duties, see Peter Paul Osunkhirhine to S.L. Pomeroy, 10 September 1857, Osunkhirhine fonds.

9 "Report on the Affairs," vol. 6, appendix T: appendices 53, 88.

10 Ibid., appendix T: appendices 49–50.

11 The monetary value of annuities comes from "Indian Tribes," part 2, 269.

12 According to "Indians in the Canadas," gifts were given out in 1834 to 3,912 individuals in Lower Canada and 12,294 in Upper Canada, of whom, by one estimate, 4,000 of the latter crossed the border from the United States only for that purpose in a tradition going back to Britain's desire to neutralize potential Indigenous adversaries in times of war.

13 House of Commons committee recommendation, in "Indians in the Canadas," part 2, 304. An internal report two years later similarly looked to "immediately reducing & ultimately extinguishing the heavy expenses occasioned to this country by the Indian Department." "Indians of British North America" part 2, 307.

14 "Report on the Affairs," vol. 6, appendix T.

15 Ibid. In line with the report's principal proposal, the Bagot commissioners accepted that all provisions of English and Canadian law equally applied to all persons to the extent of recommending, very controversially from the perspective of chiefs, that reserve land be granted to individual Indigenous persons in fee simple.

16 Ibid.

17 Major General Charles Henry Darling to Lord Dalhousie, 24 July 1828, enclosed in Dalhousie to Sir George Murray, 27 October 1828, in *Aboriginal Tribes*, 30.

18 According to the Bagot Report, in respect to the 17 million acres

of Indigenous land earlier acquired in Upper Canada in exchange for annuities, the Indian Department kept inadequate or no records, administration fees were excessive, and management was "neglectful" due to its "indifference to the interests of the Indians." Per the report, "the system of management hitherto observed, has been throughout defective and injurious to the interests of the Indians." Not only that, but since his appointment in 1837, the Indian Department's chief superintendent, Samuel Jarvis, had not only encouraged Indigenous peoples' bad investments in a self-interested direction but had also pocketed for his own use as much as £30,000, or by other accounts, a lesser amount. "Report on the Affairs," vol. 6, appendix T; "Indians in Canada [1844]," 244; also 237b–254; Leighton, "Development," 71–80, 124, 117–25, 149–51, 156–7; and Leighton and Burns, "Samuel Peter Jarvis."

19 Leighton, "Development," 49, 58, 68–9, 78, 86, 89–90.

20 Harring, *White Man's Law*, 31.

21 Surtees, "Indian Reserve Policy," 91, 94.

22 Harring, *White Man's Law*, 20.

23 "Report of the Special Commissioners." The report is not paginated. The other two members were Froome Talfourd and Thomas Worthington.

24 Missionaries' responses are in "Report of the Special Commissioners," appendix 21. Fourteen of the twenty-three favoured intermingling, seven were ambivalent, and two were opposed.

25 Church of England missionary Frederick A. O'Meara, undated, in "Report of the Special Commissioners," appendix 21.

26 Chippewa missionary S. Waldron, 6 May 1857, in ibid.

27 Six Nations missionaries Abner Nelles and Adam Elliot, undated, in ibid.

28 Caughnawaga missionary T. Eugene Antoine, 27 February 1857, in ibid.

29 St Francis missionary J. Maurault, 20 November 1857, in ibid.

30 T.G. Anderson to Richard T. Pennefather, 19 August 1857, in "Report of the Special Commissioners," appendix 21; also appendix 29.

CHAPTER SIX

1 Noel Annance to Napier, 20 March 1838, Library and Archives Canada (LAC), RG10, vol. 95, pp. 39117-18, reel 11464.

2 By the time Noel returned home, his sisters, Marie Josephte and Marie, were widowed. At some point, along with two of her sons, Marie, who had married a Portneuf cousin, would join her brother Louis on his settling down in northern Maine. Eckstorm, "Old Louis Annance."

3 Marriage, baptismal, and death records in *Quebec, Vital and Church Records* were a principal source of family information. Ignace Portneuf's war wound was sufficiently severe that he received an annual pension from the Indian Department, as in 1844, LAC, RG10, vol. 599, p. 47389, reel 13380, and 1848, LAC, RG10, vol. 174, p. 101029, reel 12505.

4 Listed in the 1825 census of Lower Canada as resident at St Francis, Charles Cadnash Annance was named among those receiving a medal consequent on his service in the War of 1812, including at Châteauguay. "Military Medals." On his briefly being employed at some unknown date, likely during the 1820s, in the fur trade out of St Maurice, see Antaya, "La Traite," 156.

5 Noel Annance to Napier, 9 November 1846, LAC, RG10, vol. 603, pp. 49186-90, reel 13381.

6 Notarized land document transferring Long Island from François Annance to Noel Annance, 24 February 1814, LAC, RG10, vol. 602, pp. 48758-61, reel 13381.

7 Aylmer was pushed out as governor general in August 1835, making the timing feasible, although Annance could also have done so earlier by correspondence. Buckner, "Matthew Whitworth-Aylmer."

8 Noel Annance to Napier, 27 January 1845, LAC, RG10, vol. 600, pp. 47862-4, reel 13380.

9 Noel Annance to Napier, 9 November 1846, LAC, RG10, vol. 603, pp. 49186-90, reel 13381.

10 Marriage record no. 30, 17 August 1836, in *Quebec, Vital and Church Records*.

11 The Indian Department official in charge, James Hughes,

counted "361 souls" living in St Francis as of 15 May 1837. LAC, RG10, vol. 93, pp. 38375-8, reel 11469.

12 Major General Charles Henry Darling to Lord Dalhousie, 24 July 1828, enclosed in Dalhousie to Sir George Murray, 27 October 1828, in *Aboriginal Tribes*, 23.

13 "Indians," in Bouchette, *Topographical Dictionary*, n.p.

14 Council held at St Francis, 30 July 1836, in *Copies or Extracts*, 42–3.

15 Napier to Richard Pennefather, 10 July 1856, LAC, RG10, vol. 226, pp. 134427-8, reel 11538.

16 Chaurette, "Premières écoles autochtones," 109; also on chiefs' illiteracy, 150. This assessment is based on a systematic reading of LAC, RG10, Department of Indian Affairs files respecting Quebec, 1835–69.

17 Maurault, *Histoire*, 377. On spelling variants, see Gill, *Notes historiques*, 42–3.

18 Maurault, *Histoire*, 377.

19 Gill, *Notes historiques*, 62.

20 Roy, "Abenaki Sociality," 21.

21 James Hughes, "Saint Francis," 1837, LAC, RG10, vol. 93, pp. 38375-8, reel 11469.

22 James Armitage to H.L. Langevin, 16 March 1868, LAC, RG10, vol. 303, pp. 203862-76, reel 12676.

23 Gill, *Notes historiques*, 65, 71–2.

24 See Maurault, *Histoire*, 348–76.

25 See, Dubois, *Chant et mission*, vol. 1, 417; also Gill, *Notes historiques*, 73–94. Whether or not he spoke the language, Thomas Gill's grandson Charles was very knowledgeable about written Abenaki. Gill, *Notes sur de vieux manuscrits*.

26 Osunkhirhine to David Greene, 18 August 1838, Osunkhirhine fonds, at which time Osunkhirhine owed Ignace Gill £9/16/9; also Gill, *Notes historiques*, 81–8.

27 Charland, *Histoire de Saint-François-du-Lac*, 247.

28 The calculations are taken from St Francis census records scattered throughout LAC, RG10.

29 James Armitage to H.L. Langevin, 16 March 1868, LAC, RG10, vol. 303, pp. 203862-76, reel 12676; Boutevin, "La place," 303.

In an 1846 letter, Noel Annance referred to "Mr. Gill, postmaster of St. Francis." Noel Annance to Napier, 14 March 1846, LAC, RG10, vol. 602, pp. 48779–80, reel 13381.

30 List in James Armstrong to Joseph Howe, 12 December 1869, LAC, RG10, vol. 304, pp. 204303–4, reel 12677, and in vol. 800, parts 1 and 2, reel 13624.

31 The story is told by Charland in his *Histoire de Saint-François-du-Lac*, 325; and in his "Ignace Gill."

32 The issue was one with which Noel Annance did not engage and is therefore not considered here, despite the tempting wealth of correspondence on efforts to hold on to the St Francis lands in the Indian Department files of LAC, RG10; exemplifying the complexities are Joseph Laurent to William Spragge, 30 April 1867, and James Armitage to H.L. Langevin, 16 March 1868, LAC, RG10, vol. 303, pp. 20596-7, 203862-76, reel 12676.

33 See, for example, the legal trespass case against Edouard Gill described in Napier to Osunkhirhine, 23 and 29 December 1843, 21 February 1844, and 9 April 1844, in Napier, Letterbooks.

34 Napier to Chiefs at St Francis, 14 February 1842, in ibid.

35 Osunkhirhine to Napier, 2 June 1846, LAC, RG10, vol. 603, pp. 49142-5, reel 13381, and 28 February 1844, vol. 599, pp. 42707-10, reel 13379. The culprits included Edward, Alexander, David, and Felix Gill.

36 James Armitage to H.L. Langevin, 16 March 1868, LAC, RG10, vol. 303, pp. 203862-76, reel 12676.

37 Osunkhirhine to David Greene, 22 April 1844, Osunkhirhine fonds.

38 Simon Obomsowine and six other chiefs to Napier, 12 August 1845, LAC, RG10, pp. 48264-5, reel 13380.

39 Ignace Portneuf and three chiefs to Napier, 6 September 1850, LAC, RG10, pp. 51839-42, reel 13383.

40 Ibid.

41 See the list of Indigenous students at Moor's Charity School and Dartmouth College in Calloway, *Indian History*, 188–203.

42 "Rev. P. Béland referring to Abenaquois of St. Francis, dated March 15, 1843," in "Report on the Affairs, vol. 6, appendix T: appendix 8.

43 "Foreign Mission School," 226. For the school's history, see Demos, *Heathen School*; and Cook, *Providential Life*, 86–124.

44 Chaurette, "Premières écoles autochtones," 77, 118.

45 *General Catalogue and a Brief History*, 70.

46 Boutevin, "La place," 124–41, 148–9, 152–5, 176–204, 238–51, 261–6, 272, 277–9, 316–26, 334–5. For Catholic perspectives, see Charland, *Histoire des Abénakis*, 193–217, 231–6; and Maurault, *Histoire*, 617–26. Maurault was the local priest from 1847 to 1866.

47 Osunkhirhine to David Greene, 6 January 1834, Osunkhirhine fonds. Although Osunkhirhine was ordained a Congregational minister, veteran Indian Department official Duncan Campbell Napier considered him a Methodist. Napier, memorandum, n.d. [1834], LAC, RG10, vol. 93, pp. 37794-7, reel 11468.

48 Osunkhirhine to S.B. Treat, 5 June 1851, and Osunkhirhine to David Greene, 6 January 1834, Osunkhirhine fonds; also Chaurette, "Premières écoles autochtones," 31, 40.

49 Maurault, *Histoire*, 619.

50 "Missionary and 30 Indians," petition, 7 July 1832, LAC, RG10, vol. 93, pp. 37798-9, reel 11468.

51 Napier, memorandum, n.d. [1834], LAC, RG10, vol. 93, pp. 37794-7, reel 11468; also Napier to Sueprintendent at Montreal, 28 August 1834, 7 March 1835, and 21 November 1835, in Napier, Letterbooks; and Leighton, "Duncan Campbell Napier."

52 "Native Preachers," *Missionary Herald* 34, no. 1 (1838): 20.

53 James Hughes, "Report of the Superintendent of Indians at Montreal, upon the allegations contained in a Petition from certain Indians of St. Francis dated 3 September 1838," LAC, RG10, vol. 96, p. 39733, reel 11470, underlining in original; Noel Annance and others, petition to Earl of Durham, May 23, 1838, LAC, RG10, vol. 96, pp. 39729-31, reel 11470.

54 Earl of Gosford to Lord Glenelg, 15 February 1837, in *Copies or Extracts*, 20.

55 David Greene to S.B. [*sic*] Annance, 22 September 1836, in Annance, Correspondence, 1.3.2, vol. 1, 190–1.

56 Osunkhirhine to David Greene, 25 October 1836, Osunkhirhine fonds.

57 Petition to Earl of Gosford, Governor General of the Canadas, 19 December 1836, LAC, RG10, vol. 93, pp. 37787-93, reel 11468, and pp. 38166-9, reel 11468.

58 Petition with nineteen signatories and accompanying documents, 27 February and 3 March 1837, LAC, RG10, vol. 93, pp. 38134-45, reel 11468.

59 "Indians of British North America" part 2, 308–308b.

60 Osunkhirhine, James J. Annance, and Joseph John Masta to Napier, 20 June 1837, LAC, RG10, vol. 93, pp. 38140-2, reel 11468.

61 Catholic priest's petition, 6 March 1837, LAC, RG10, vol. 93, pp. 38146-9, reel 11468; complainants' petition signed by Noel Annance, among others, 23 May 1838, LAC, RG10, vol. 96, pp. 39729-31, reel 11470; James Hughes, report, 1 October 1838, and related documents, LAC, RG10, vol. 96, pp. 39726-34, reel 11470; complainants to F.G. Hariot, 22 March 1839, LAC, RG10, vol. 97, pp. 39960-8, reel 11470.

62 Osunkhirhine, James J. Annance, and Joseph John Masta to Napier, 20 June 20, 1837, LAC, RG10, vol. 93, pp. 38140-2, reel 11468.

63 Petition of Noel Annance, Osunkhirhine, and fifteen others to Lord Durham, 3 September 1838, LAC, RG10, vol. 96, pp. 39729-31, reel 11470.

64 Chief Secretary of Lord Durham to Napier, 19 October 1838, LAC, RG10, vol. 96, pp. 39726-8, reel 11470; also Napier to N.F. Annance and P.P. Osunkhirhine, 19 October 1838, in Napier, Letterbooks.

65 James Hughes to Napier, 18 December 1838, LAC, RG10, vol. 96, pp. 39828-9, reel 11470; James Joseph Annance, quoted in Parkman, *Journals*, vol. 1, 332n20.

66 Lord Glenelg to Earl of Gosford, 14 January 1836, in *Copies or Extracts*, 3.

67 Osunkhirhine, James Joseph Annance and Noel Annance to F.G. Heriot, 22 March 1839, LAC, RG10, vol. 97, pp. 39960-8, reel 11470.

68 Osunkhirhine to David Greene, 17 July 1842, Osunkhirhine to S.B. Treat, 5 June 1851, and Osunkhirhine to David Greene, 26 February 1840, Osunkhirhine fonds.

69   Osunkhirhine to David Greene, 6 January 1834, ibid.

70   Osunkhirhine to S.B. Treat, 6 January 1834, ibid.

71   Osunkhirhine to S.L. Pomeroy, December 16, 1856, ibid.

72   Nathan Lord, quoted in Calloway, *Indian History*, 87.

73   Annual registers beginning in 1839 of the Congregational Church, Parish of St Francis, in *Quebec, Vital and Church Records*. According to Calloway, *Indian History*, 84, James Joseph Annance, who died in 1843, spent part of the year guiding hunting parties.

74   Brooks, *Common Pot*, 2, 175, 243, 248-9. Osunkhirhine was known both as Peter Paul Masta after his stepfather and as Peter Paul Wzokhilain or Wzokhiláin.

75   James Thomson to A. Brandram, 1 June 1840, in Thomson, *Letters*.

76   Osunkhirhine to David Greene, 1 November 1841, Osunkhirhine fonds. James Joseph Annance's death on 1 March 1843 is recorded in *Quebec, Vital and Church Records*.

77   Napier to N.F. Annance, 25 April 1842, in Napier, Letterbooks.

78   Napier to N.F. Annance, 9 November 1842, in ibid.

79   Osunkhirhine to David Greene, 27 May 1845, Osunkhirhine fonds.

80   Osunkhirhine to David Greene, 26 October 1846, ibid.

81   Philip Burns to George Simpson, 15 November 1827, in Simpson, Inward Correspondence, Hudson's Bay Company Archives, D.45/2, fo. 349.

82   Louis Annance in conversation with John Sprague, 1874, in Sprague, "Louis Annance," 420.

83   See Porter, *Native American Freemasonry*, 194–8.

84   Osunkhirhine to David Greene, 23 June 1841, Osunkhirhine fonds.

85   Osunkhirhine to David Greene, 4 December 1847, ibid.

86   Ibid.

87   Indian Department memorandum, 14 March 1846, LAC, RG10, vol. 155, pp. 90345-9, reel 11497.

88   Numbers of pupils and the size of the congregation are given in Osunkhirhine's regular reports in letter form to the American Board of Commissioners for Foreign Missions, which are repro-

duced in the Osunkhirhine fonds, the originals being in Osunkhirhine, Correspondence. For St Francis Protestant and Catholic
registers, see *Quebec, Vital and Church Records*; on school enrolment, see Chaurette, "Premières écoles autochtones," 47.

89 Osunkhirhine, "Abenaquis," being extracts from a "Letter of
Osunkhirhine, dated Dec. 15th, 1833," *Missionary Herald* 30,
no. 4 (1834): 141. Subsequent issues of the *Missionary Herald*,
especially 53, no. 1 (1857): 13, contain regular letters from
Osunkhirhine. For two excellent sources on Osunkhirhine's
ongoing and numerous activities, including being for a time St
Francis's government agent, during which he sought to have
St Francis lands sold off to the benefit of individual Abenakis,
including the young men who were his principal supports
against the chiefs, see Osunkhirhine fonds, with the originals
in Osunkhirhine, Correspondence; and his extensive ongoing
correspondence with Indian Department officials scattered
throughout LAC, RG10.

90 "Eastern Township Loyal Volunteers, Pay Lists." "Charles
Annance" is also on the list as a private, but given he signed
with an "x," he was likely not Noel's well-educated cousin.

91 Noel Annance, petition to Charles Stanley, 29 December 1861,
LAC, RG10, vol. 273, pp. 184357-60, reel 12657.

92 Napier to Noel Annance, 24 April 1844, in Napier, Letterbooks.

93 Noel Annance to Napier, 27 January 1845, LAC, RG10, vol. 600,
pp. 47862-4, reel 13380.

94 Napier to F.N. Annance, 4 March 1845, in Napier, Letterbooks.
Noel Annance was based at the time in Bury, Quebec.

95 Noel Annance to Napier, 29 August 1850, LAC, RG10, vol. 607,
p. 51827, reel 13383.

96 "Report on the Affairs," vol. 6, appendix T.

97 "Rev. P. Béland referring to Abenaquois of St. Francis, dated
March 15, 1843," in "Report on the Affairs," vol. 6, appendix
T: appendix 8.

98 Ibid.

99 "An Act to ... Make Provision for Elementary Instruction in
Lower Canada, 9 June 1846," in *Acts for the Promotion of
Public Education*, 7.

100 Napier to F.N. Annance, 1 September 1846, in Napier, Letter-
     books.
101 Noel Annance to Napier, 12 January 1848, LAC, RG10, vol. 605,
     pp. 50151-2, reel 13382.
102 Noel Annance to Napier, 20 January 1848, LAC, RG10, vol. 605,
     pp. 50160-1, reel 13382.
103 "An Act to ... Make Provision for Elementary Instruction in
     Lower Canada, 9 June 1846," in *Acts for the Promotion of Pub-
     lic Education*, 7, 1. On St Francis's inclusion in the act, see note
     in Civil Secretary's Office, Summary of Correspondence, 14
     April 1854, LAC, RG10, vol. 754, no. 7462, unpaginated, reel
     13488.
104 Napier to Noel Annance, 24 January 1848, quoted in Noel
     Annance to Napier, 1 February 1848, LAC, RG10, vol. 600, pp.
     47880-2, reel 13380; Napier, "Respecting the Complaints Pre-
     ferred against the Schoolmaster of St. Francis," n.d., LAC, RG10,
     vol. 93, pp. 37794-7, reel 11468.
105 Noel Annance to Napier, 1 February 1848, LAC, RG10, vol. 600,
     pp. 47880-2, reel 13380.
106 *Seminaire*, 154.
107 Charland, *Histoire des Abénakis*, 200–1, 206–7, 211; Day,
     In Search, 56.
108 Joseph Mauralt to Napier, 27 April 1848, LAC, RG10, vol. 608,
     pp. 50335-8; also Chaurette, "Premières écoles autochtones,"
     31, 34–5, 137–8.
109 Noel Annance to Napier, 26 March 1848, LAC, RG10, vol. 605,
     pp. 50279-83, reel 13382.
110 Chaurette, "Premières écoles autochtones," 31, 34–5, 137–8.
111 Noel Annance to Napier, 22 April 1851, LAC, RG10, vol. 608,
     pp. 52202, reel 13384; Napier to Noel Annance, 29 April 1851,
     in Napier, Letterbooks.
112 Boutevin, "La place," 31.
113 Joseph Maurault to Napier, 6 February 1852, LAC, RG10, vol.
     609, pp. 52727-33, reel 13384.
114 Civil Secretary's Office, Summary of Correspondence, 13 August
     1853, LAC, RG10, vol. 754, no. 6996, unpaginated, reel 13488.
     The petition itself has not been located.

115 Osunkhirhine to S.B. Treat, 22 September 1856, Osunkhirhine fonds.

116 Civil Secretary's Office, Summary of Correspondence, 14 April 1854, LAC, RG10, vol. 754, no. 7462, unpaginated, reel 13488, underlining in original; also 23 February 1854, LAC, RG10, vol. 754, no. 7368, unpaginated, reel 13488; and 11 July 1856, LAC, RG10, vol. 754, no. 7368, unpaginated, reel 13488. The original letters have not been located.

117 Noel Annance to Napier, 8 November 1855, LAC, RG10, vol. 611, pp. 53770-1, reel 13285.

118 Saint-Amant, L'Avenir, 151, 189.

119 See Indian Affairs, Annual Report, 1864, 15, and 1868, 19.

120 "Board of Examiners for the District of Sherbrooke," 14 May 1862, Journal of Education for Lower Canada 6 (1862): 78.

121 Noel Annance to William McDougall, 28 July 1862, LAC, RG10, vol. 273, pp. 184403-10, reel 12657; J.B.E. Dorion to William Sprague respecting identity of Noel Annance, 15 October 1863, LAC, RG 10, vol. 800, reel 13624.

122 On Dorion's activities, see Saint-Amant, L'Avenir, 279–356; and Sylvain, "Jean-Baptiste Éric Dorion."

123 Report of Edward N. De Lorimier to William Spragge, 30 August 1862, LAC, RG10, vol. 283, pp. 191034-9, reel 12663. The quotations are taken from the Indian Department's translation of the report from French into English.

124 See Sylvain, "Jean-Baptiste Éric Dorion."

125 Noel Annance to William McDougall, 1 December 1862, LAC, RG10, vol. 273, pp. 184378-80, reel 12657.

126 Noel Annance to William Spragge, 29 June 1863, LAC, RG10, vol. 273, pp. 184560-1, reel 12657; also Noel Annance to William Spragge, 7 May 1863, LAC, RG10, vol. 273, pp. 184542-5, reel 12657.

127 Indian Affairs, Annual Report, 1868, 32, 1870, 27; on enrolment, see report for 1864 of C.C. Obumsawin to William Spragge, 18 January 1865, LAC, RG10, vol. 611, pp. 53902-3, reel 13385.

CHAPTER SEVEN

1 John Milloy makes this point persuasively in "Era of Civilization."
2 Leighton, "Duncan Campbell Napier."
3 One exception was some very long letters written in Iroquois, the lack of accompanying English translations making it uncertain whether they were read and taken seriously.
4 Charland, "Définition," 282.
5 "Report on the Affairs," vol. 6, appendix T.
6 On the numbers, see Earl of Gosford to Lord Glenelg, 13 July 1837, in *Copies or Extracts*, 50.
7 Ibid.
8 Major General Charles Henry Darling to Lord Dalhousie, 24 July 1828, enclosed in Dalhousie to Sir George Murray, 27 October 1828, in *Aboriginal Tribes*, 23–4.
9 James Hughes, "Saint Francis," 15 May 1837, Library and Archives Canada (LAC), RG10, vol. 93, pp. 38375-8, reel 11469. For the convoluted events implicating whites, the Catholic Church, and also the Abenakis themselves respecting their lands, see Charland, *Histoire des Abénakis*, 219–45; and Jones, "Implementation," 34–43.
10 James Armitage to H.L. Langevin, 16 March 1868, LAC, RG10, vol. 303, pp. 203862-76, reel 12676. That Noel Annance hardly referred to St Francis's agents puts beyond consideration here the contentious power relationship existing between the successive literate agents and almost wholly unschooled chiefs, as described in Department of Indian Affairs files, in LAC, RG10.
11 Earl of Gosford to Lord Glenelg, 13 July 1837, in *Copies or Extracts*, 30, 52.
12 James Armitage to H.L. Langevin, 16 March 1868, LAC, RG10, vol. 303, pp. 203862-76, reel 12676.
13 Osunkhirhine to David Greene, 8 October 1838, Osunkhirhine fonds.
14 Osunkhirhine to David Greene, 4 June 1847, ibid.
15 Osunkhirhine to S.B. Treat, 16 June 1856, ibid.
16 The files in LAC, RG10, are replete with requests and protests respecting the St Francis lands, some of which are described in

Charland, *Histoire des Abénakis*, 219–45, in a chapter appropriately entitled "L'affaire des terres concédées aux blancs."

17 Earl of Gosford to Lord Glenelg, 13 July 1837, in *Copies or Extracts*, 52.

18 See, for example, Barry, "La 'piste Bécancour.'"

19 James Hughes, "Saint Francis," 15 May 1837, LAC, RG10, vol. 93, pp. 38375-8, reel 11469.

20 Duke of Portland to General Prescott, 1 November 1797, LAC, RG10, vol. 172, pp. 83662-3, reel 2559; Francis Annance to Robert Shore Milnes, 25 June 1803, LAC, RG10, vol. 172, pp. 83673-4, reel 2559; "Lease by Francis Joseph Annance Esq.," 20 March 1820, LAC, RG10, vol. 172, pp. 83767-70, reel 2559, with other leases by other grantees following on in time.

21 D.C. Napier to Lt. Col. Cooper, 12 October 1829, in Napier, Letterbooks.

22 Petition signed by thirty-four whites, twenty of them with their "x," to James Kempt, 31 August 1829, LAC, RG10, vol. 172, pp. 83794-5, reel 2559.

23 Duke of Portland to General Prescott, 4 November 1797, LAC, RG10, vol. 172, pp. 83662-3, reel 2559; Francis Annance to Robert Shore Milnes, 25 June 1803, LAC, RG10, vol. 172, pp. 83673-4, reel 2559.

24 "Extract of the Patent," 26 June 1805, and "Extract from a Report of a Committee of the Whole Council Respecting the Waste Lands of the Crown," 23 November 1803, LAC, RG10, vol. 172, pp. 83702-3, 83683-5, reel 2559; also for documents generated by the examination, pp. 83660-878.

25 Napier, report, 28 October 1830, LAC, RG10, vol. 272, pp. 83803-5, reel 2557.

26 Napier to F.N. Annance, 31 January 1835, in Napier, Letterbooks.

27 Napier to F.N. Annance, 2 July 1835, in ibid.

28 The reference to the petition is in Napier to F.N. Annance, 23 February 1838, in ibid.

29 Earl of Gosford to Lord Glenelg, 13 July 1837, enclosure no. 15, in *Copies or Extracts*, 52.

30 Napier to F.N. Annance, 23 February 1838, in Napier, Letter-books.

31 Noel Annance to Napier, 20 March 1838, LAC, RG10, vol. 95, pp. 39116-18, reel 11464.

32 Ibid.

33 Petition signed by thirty-four whites, twenty of them with their "x," to James Kempt, 31 August 1829, LAC, RG10, vol. 172, pp. 83794-5, reel 2559.

34 James Hughes, "Saint Francis," 1837, LAC, RG10, vol. 93, pp. 38375-8, reel 11469.

35 "Statistical Return of the Village of Saint Francis," 21 November 1843, LAC, RG10, vol. 597, pp. 46564-5, reel 13379.

36 See Napier to Thomas Edmund Campbell, 2 August 1849, LAC, RG10, vol. 606, pp. 51130-2, reel 13383.

37 Noel Annance to Napier, 20 January 1840, LAC, RG10, vol. 99, pp. 40947-53, reel 11470.

38 This conclusion was reached in James Armstrong, report to Joseph Howe, 12 December 1869, LAC, RG10, vol. 304, pp. 204287-311, reel 12677.

39 Noel and Charles Annance's leases and sales of Durham lands are calculated from Durham Indian Lands, being an undated list of deeds; from a list, a schedule of documents forwarded with "Report to the Indian Department," and miscellaneous documents, enclosed with James Armstrong to Joseph Howe, Secretary of State for the Provinces, 12 December 1869; and from "Durham Lands – how disposed of," enclosed with James Armstrong to Joseph Howe, Secretary of State for the Provinces, 11 October 1870, all in LAC, RG10, vol. 304, pp. 204114-15, 204122-4, 204138-45, 204288-312, 204313-31, 204665-74, reel 12677; as corroborated by documents later collected together in LAC, RG10, vol. 800, reel 13624, and in Gladue file, in LAC, RG10, vol. 2065, reel 11,148.

40 Osunkhirhine to David Greene, 4 July 1836, Osunkhirhine fonds.

41 Osunkhirhine to David Greene, 17 July 1843, ibid., as corroborated by documents later collected together in LAC, RG 10, vol.

800, reel 13624, and in Gladue file, in LAC, RG10, vol. 2065, reel 11,148.

42 Among the seventeen 1805 grantees were Samuel Gill and Rosalie James's youngest son, Robert, then in his late sixties, and Anthony Gill, who was the eldest son of their eldest son, Robert-Louis Gill, by his second wife. LAC, RG10, vol. 172, pp. 83679-80, reel 2559.

43 Ignace Portneuf and three others to Napier, 23 May 1853, LAC, RG10, vol. 304, pp. 201435, reel 12676.

44 Noel Annance to Napier, 20 January 1840, LAC, RG10, vol. 99, pp. 40947-53, reel 11470.

45 Commissioners Court for the Township of Kinglsey, Noel Annance and Charles Annance vs James Mountain, Judgment, 4 July 1840, LAC, RG10, vol. 304, pp. 204605-6, reel 12677.

46 Napier to F.N. Annance, 9 July 1840, in Napier, Letterbooks.

47 T.W.C. Murdoch to Secretary of Indian Affairs, with copy to Noel Annance, 8 January 1841, LAC, RG10, vol. 101, pp. 41946-8, reel 11741.

48 Noel Annance to Napier, 20 January 1840, LAC, RG10, vol. 99, pp. 40947-53, reel 11470.

49 Noel Annance to Napier, 20 January 1840, LAC, RG10, vol. 99, pp. 40948, reel 11470.

50 Ibid.

51 F.G. Heriot, attached to F.N. Annance to Napier, 20 January 1840, LAC, RG10, vol. 99, pp. 40953, reel 11470; also LaBrèque, "Frederick George Heriot."

52 Ignace Portneuf to Napier, 12 August 1844, and accompanying documents, LAC, RG10, vol. 99, pp. 47471-5, reel 13380; Napier to Portneuf, 20 May 1845, LAC, RG10, vol. 600, pp. 48113-14, reel 13380.

53 Napier to Noel Annance, 24 April 1844, in Napier, Letterbooks.

54 Napier to Noel Annance, 6 October 1849, in ibid.

55 Napier to Noel Annance, 28 March 1851, in ibid.

56 Noel Annance to Napier, 27 January 1845, LAC, RG10, vol. 600, pp. 47862-4, reel 13380. In the letter, Noel shared with Napier his "intention to make a trip to Montreal after the session of

Parliament with a petition concerning my claims for services in the late American war."

57 Napier to F.N. Annance, 16 February 1846, in Napier, Letterbooks.

58 Cover note on Noel Annance to Napier, 14 March 1846, LAC, RG10, vol. 602, pp. 48779-80, reel 13381.

59 T. Bouthellier, statement, 14 August 1846, LAC, RG10, vol. 602, pp. 48940-1, reel 13381; also Napier to Noel Annance, 1 September 1846, in Napier, Letterbooks.

60 Noel Annance to Napier, 9 November 1846, LAC, RG10, vol. 603, pp. 49186-90, reel 13381.

61 Noel Annance to Napier, 12 January 1848, LAC, RG10, vol. 605, pp. 50151-2, reel 13382.

62 Napier to Alexander Campbell, 2 February 1848, LAC, RG10, vol. 605, pp. 50187-9, reel 13382. On Campbell, see Swainson, "Sir Alexander Campbell."

63 Napier to Noel Annance, 17 February 1848, in Napier, Letterbooks.

64 As one example among many in Department of Indian Affairs files, see Louis Degonzague Ottantoson, 18 July and 1 August 1844, LAC, RG10, vol. 599, pp. 47392-9, 47430-1, reel 13380.

65 Noel Annance to Napier, 6 August 1842, LAC, RG10, vol. 597, pp. 46375-8, reel 13379.

66 Noel Annance to Napier, 3 July 1846, LAC, RG10, vol. 603, pp. 49156-7, reel 13381.

67 Petition of Noel Annance and ten others to James Bruce, Earl of Elgin, 7 January 1848, LAC, RG10, vol. 605, pp. 50145-6, reel 13385.

68 Napier to Noel Annance, 17 February 1848, in Napier, Letterbooks.

69 Noel Annance to Napier, 5 July 1848, LAC, RG10, vol. 605, pp. 50452-4, reel 13382.

70 Napier to Noel Annance and Louis Gill, 16 July 1848, in Napier, Letterbooks.

71 Napier to Noel Annance, 16 October 1848, in ibid.

72 Noel Annance to Napier, 21 April 1849, LAC, RG10, vol. 606, pp. 50966-7, reel 13383.

73 Calloway, *Western Abenaki*, 245; also 246–8.
74. Noel Annance and three others to E. Campbell, 20 July 1849, LAC, RG10, vol. 606, p. 51111, reel 13383. Thomas Edmund Campbell was superintendent general of Indian affairs by virtue of being the civil secretary to Governor General James Bruce, Earl of Elgin. Monet, "Thomas Edmund Campbell."
75 Napier to F.N. Annance and three others, 5 September 1849, in Napier, Letterbooks.
76 Napier to Thomas Edmund Campbell, 2 August 1849, LAC, RG10, vol. 606, pp. 51130-2, reel 13383.
77 Napier to Noel Annance, 1 September 1849 and 22 August 1850, in Napier, Letterbooks.
78 Noel Annance to Napier, 23 July 1849, LAC, RG10, vol. 606, p. 51107, reel 13383; Noel Annance to Napier, 21 January 1850, LAC, RG10, vol. 607, p. 51557, reel 13383; Noel Annance to Napier, 5 October 1850, LAC, RG10, vol. 607, p. 51906, reel 13383; Napier to Noel Annance, 19 March and 24 October 1850, in Napier, Letterbooks.
79 Saint-Amant, *L'Avenir*, 56; also on Brady, 103, 215.
80 Noel Annance to Napier, 22 March 1856, LAC, RG10, vol. 611, pp. 53850-3, reel 13385; also La Brèque, "Frederick George Heriot."
81 Civil Secretary's Office, Summary of Correspondence, 15 August 1855, LAC, RG10, vol. 754, unpaginated, reel 13488. The letter has not been located.
82 Noel Annance to Napier, 13 September 1855, LAC, RG10, vol. 611, p. 53752, reel 13385; Noel Annance to Napier, 8 November 1855, LAC, RG10, vol. 611, p. 53770, reel 13385; Noel Annance to Napier, 22 March 1856, LAC, RG10, vol. 611, pp. 53850-3, reel 13385.
83 Thomas Brady to Napier, 17 November 1856, LAC, RG10, vol. 611, p. 53847, reel 13385.
84 Noel Annance to Napier, 22 March 1856, LAC, RG10, vol. 611, pp. 53850-3, reel 13385.
85 Noel Annance to Napier, 8 November 1855, LAC, RG10, vol. 611, p. 53770, reel 13385; Noel Annance to Napier, 14 November 1855, LAC, RG10, vol. 611, p. 53775, reel 13385; N.N.

Bureau's bill of £5 for "defending ... and obtaining the discharge of the said prisoner," 19 June 1856, LAC, RG10, vol. 226, pp. 134223-6, reel 11538; and J.B.E. Dorion to Indian Department, 16 September 1856, LAC, RG10, vol. 228, pp. 135855-8, reel 11539.

86 Noel Annance to William McDougall, 1 December 1862, LAC, RG10, vol. 273, pp. 184378-80, reel 12657.

87 "An Act to Change the Tenure of the Indian Lands in the Township of Durham," 1856; also "An Act Respecting the Indian Lands in the Township of Durham, in the County of Drummond," 1860.

88 Noel Annance to Richard T. Pennefather, 15 December 1856, LAC, RG10, vol. 304, pp. 204579-81, reel 12677. On the complexities from the perspective of a Noel Annance lessee, see Joseph Atkinson to R.J. Pennefather, 3 and 21 June 1858, LAC, RG10, vol. 243, nos 143869, 14413-14, unpaginated, reel 12637.

89 Covering note on Noel Annance to Richard T. Pennefather, 15 December 1856, LAC, RG10, vol. 304, pp. 204579-81, reel 12677.

90 Noel Annance to Richard T. Pennefather, 4 February and 4 April 1858, LAC, RG10, vol. 304, pp. 204583-7, 204592-3, reel 12677; also Noel Annance and Ignace Portneuf to Napier, 23 July 1856, LAC, RG10, vol. 611, pp. 53883-4, reel 13385; Civil Secretary's Office, Summary of Correspondence, 5 March 1856, LAC, RG10, vol. 753, no. 8982, unpaginated, reel 13488; Civil Secretary's Office, Summary of Correspondence, 27 May and 13 October 1857, LAC, RG10, vol. 755, nos 10214 and 10558, unpaginated, reel 13488; and Noel Annance and five others to Pennefather, 4 April 1858, LAC, RG10, vol. 304, pp. 20460-1, reel 12677.

91 "An Act Respecting the Indian Lands in the Township of Durham, in the County of Drummond," 1860; also sale by Noel Annance to William Sutherland, 15 March 1860, enclosed in James Armstrong to Joseph Howe, 12 December 1869, LAC, RG10, vol. 304, nos 204519-23, unpaginated, reel 12677. On an attempted land sale, see Noel Annance to William Spragge, 31

August 1863, LAC, RG10, vol. 273, pp. 184581-8, reel 12657. The documents that were later collected together in LAC, RG10, vol. 800, reel 13624, account for only 125 acres.

92 Noel Annance, petition to Charles Stanley, 29 December 1861, LAC, RG10, vol. 273, pp. 184357-60, reel 12657.

93 Noel Annance to C.T. Walcot, 31 January 1862, LAC, RG10, vol. 273, pp. 184361-4, reel 12657, underlining in original.

94 Noel Annance to E. Parent, 18 September 1862, LAC, RG10, vol. 273, pp. 18448-9, reel 12657.

95 Noel Annance to Viscount Monck, 25 August 1863, LAC, RG10, vol. 303, pp. 203165-9, reel 12676.

96 Schrøder, *Johan Schrøder's Travels*, 75.

97 Noel Annance to Viscount Monck, 25 August 1863, LAC, RG10, vol. 303, pp. 203165-9, reel 12676; Noel Annance to Viscount Monck, 12 June 1865, LAC, RG10, vol. 303, pp. 202958-61, reel 12675; copy of Noel Annance to Viscount Monck, 20 March 1866, LAC, RG10, vol. 303, pp. 203165-8, reel 303; Noel Annance to Viscount Monck, 8 September 1868, LAC, RG10, vol. 304, pp. 203961-5, reel 12676.

98 Noel Annance to Michael Turner, 19 May 1862, LAC, RG10, vol. 273, pp. 184371-73A, reel 12657.

99 Noel Annance to Louis Sicotte, 9 April 1863, LAC, RG10, vol. 273, pp. 184535-8, reel 12657; Désilets, "Louis-Victor Sicotte."

100 Copy of Noel Annance to Lord Viscount Monck, 20 March 1866, LAC, RG10, vol. 303, pp. 203165-8, reel 303.

101 Examples are Noel Annance to C.T. Walcot, 31 March 1862 and 11 September 1863, LAC, RG10, vol. 273, pp. 184364-6, 18400-1, reel 12657; Noel Annance to William Spragge, 5 June, 6 August, and 31 August 1863, LAC, RG10, vol. 273, pp. 184549-49B, 184577-81, 184582-3, reel 12657; Noel Annance to Andrew Russell, 10 April 1866, LAC, RG10, vol. 303, pp. 203176-8, reel 12676; Noel Annance to Governor General Lord Monck, 8 September 1868, LAC, RG10, vol. 304, pp. 203961-5, reel 12676.

102 Noel Annance to William Spragge, 5 June, 15 August, and 25 August 1863, LAC, RG10, vol. 273, pp. 184549-49B, 184577-81, reel 12657, and vol. 303, pp. 203162-63, reel 12676; also

Noel Annance to William Spragge, 31 August 1863, LAC, RG10, vol. 273, pp. 184581-8, reel 12657; and Noel Annance to Viscount Monck, 25 August 1863, LAC, RG10, vol. 303, pp. 203165-9, reel 12676.

103 Cover note on Noel Annance to Governor General Lord Monck, 8 September 1868, LAC, RG10, vol. 304, pp. 203961-5, reel 12676.

104 Indicative of the steps taken toward resolution, see agreement made by Abenaki chiefs, 18 July 1868, in *Indian Treaties*, vol. 2, 269–71.

105 See Désilets, "Sir Hector-Louis Langevin."

106 Noel Annance to Hector L. Langevin, 10 August 1869, LAC, RG10, vol. 304, pp. 204100-11, reel 12677.

107 Gill, *Notes historiques*, 93, 96.

108 See Filteau, Hamelin, and Keyes, "Louis-Adélard Senécal"; Gill, *Notes historiques.*

109 Gill, *Notes sur de vieux manuscrits.*

110 See Désilets, "Sir Hector-Louis Langevin."

111 Noel Annance to Hector L. Langevin, early August 1869, to which are attached notes by Langevin and by William Spragge, 20 August 1869, LAC, RG10, vol. 304, pp. 204100-11, reel 12677.

112 James Armstrong, report to Joseph Howe, 12 December 1869, LAC, RG10, vol. 304, pp. 204287-311, reel 12677; also Durham Township Indian Land Papers, 1816–1873, LAC, RG10, vol. 800, reel 13624.

113 James Armstrong, report to Joseph Howe, 12 December 1869, LAC, RG10, vol. 304, pp. 204287-311, reel 12677.

114 List in ibid.

115 Sale by Noel Annance to Ignace Gill of fifty acres of lot 21, range 2, 16 August 1862, LAC, RG10, vol. 800, reel 13624.

CHAPTER EIGHT

1 Entries of 6, 9, and 15 May 1825, in William Kittson, Snake journal, 1824–25, italics in original, in Ogden, *Peter Skene Ogden's Snake Country Journals*, 231–2.

2 Entry 25 May 1825, in HBC, Snake Country Post Journal, B.202/a/3a, fo. 25.

3 See George Simpson to John McLoughlin, 15 March 1829, in Simpson, *Fur Trade*, 309.

4 Mathias, "Timeline." Mathias's wife was a descendant. The information on John Gray's father is courtesy of the New York State Archives.

5 Salter, website.

6 Morgan, *West*, 123.

7 Joseph Annance, contract signed at Fort Union, 1830, in "Persons Employed," 62.

8 Letter of Van Quickenborne, 4 October 1836, in Barry, "Kansas," 54.

9 "Family Stuff," in Salter, website.

10 Point, *Wilderness Kingdom*, 29; also Garraghan, *Catholic Beginnings*, 110–11. French Settlement's official name was Westport.

11 Francis Parkman, journal, 30 July 1841, in Parkman, *Journals*, vol. 1, 21; also 332–33n20.

12 Francis Parkman, journal, 10 August 1841, in ibid., vol. 1, 36.

13 See Noel Annance to Napier, 3 July 1846, Library and Archives Canada (LAC), RG10, vol. 603, pp. 49156-7, reel 13381. Louis Annance and his family were listed in the 1848 St Francis census. LAC, RG10, vol. 605, pp. 50125-7, reel 13382.

14 Louis Annance explained in 1874, five years after Noel's death, how his brother had collected the dialects of Indigenous peoples. Louis Annance in conversation with John Sprague, 1874, in Sprague, "Louis Annance," 422.

15 Charles D. Shaw, in Eckstorm, "Old Louis Annance," 6.

16 Eckstorm, "Old Louis Annance," 2; Parker, *Native American Families*, 12.

17 Ibid., 7–8; also 5–13, passim.

18 Vreeland, "Game Bag," 422.

19 Thoreau, *Maine Woods*, 126, passim.

20 Louis Annance in conversation with John Sprague, 1874, in Sprague, "Louis Annance," 421. According to local historian

Mary Calvert, Louis arrived in the Greenville area in 1835 and worked principally as a guide. See Calvert, *Kennebec Wilderness*, 37–8.

21 Louis Annance in conversation with John Sprague, 1874, in Sprague, "Louis Annance," 418–19.

22 Eckstorm, "Old Louis Annance," 2.

23 Ibid., 5; also for the text, 7.

24 Summer A. Monson, funeral address on behalf of Freemasons, in Sprague, "Louis Annance," 421–2.

25 Charles D. Shaw, in Eckstorm, "Old Louis Annance," 6.

26 Louis Annance in conversation with John Sprague, 1874, in Sprague, "Louis Annance," 423.

27 O'Brien, *Firsting and Lasting*, 118.

28 Colby, *Colby's Indian History*, 18.

29 See Sandys, "Two Days' Trout Fishing."

30 Archibald Annance to E.A. Meredith, 10 March 1874, and illegible to Archibald Annance, 20 December 1872, LAC, RG10, vol. 1861, file 207, at LAC website.

31 J.W. Hope to Serecetary of the Indian Department, 26 January 1870, LAC, RG10, vol. 800, reel 13624; Archibald Annance to William Spragge, 28 September 1875, LAC, RG10, vol. 1861, file 207, at LAC website.

32 "Letter to the editor."

33 See Charland, "De l'etrange origine."

34 "Notre-Dame des Bois."

35 "New England Waters," 501.

36 "Report on the Affairs," vol. 6, appendix T.

37 "Rev. P. Béland referring to Abenaquois of St. Francis, dated March 15, 1843," in ibid.

38 On the timing of the initial request, see Noel Annance to William McDougall, 1 December 1862, LAC, RG10, vol. 273, pp. 184378–80, reel 12657.

39 Notation on Noel Annance to R.T. Pennefather, 2 March 1860, LAC, RG10, vol. 253, pp. 181270–1, reel 12643.

40 Examination of Elias Hill, 21 March 1859, LAC, RG10, vol. 247, pp. 147492–98, reel 12640; also Six Nations Council Minutes, 1857–59, in Weaver, "Iroquois," 199–200, 211.

41 Examination of Elias Hill, 21 March 1859, LAC, RG10, vol. 247, pp. 147492-8, reel 12640; Indian Branch, Department of the Interior, file notes respecting Elias Hill's petition for an allotment of land and compensation, 1874–76, LAC, RG10, vol. 1930, file 3349, at LAC website. Hill was to be granted thirty acres of land consequent on his enfranchisement, which he had still not received as of 1876.

42 Noel Annance to C.T. Walcott, 8 March 1862, LAC, RG10, vol. 273, pp. 184364-6, reel 12657.

43 Noel Annance to George Sherwood, 10 May 1862, LAC, RG10, vol. 273, pp. 184374-7, reel 12657.

44 "An Act to Encourage the Gradual Civilization of Indian Tribes in this Province, and to Amend the Laws Relating to Indians," no. 58, 1857.

45 See Milloy, "Era of Civilization," 280; also drawing on Milloy, see Francis, *History*, 36; and Miller, *Skyscrapers*, 143.

46 Miller, *Skyscrapers*, 143.

47 One example is J.T. Gilkison to William Spragge, 1 August 1862, LAC, RG10, vol. 286, pp. 102230-1, reel 12665.

48 Noel Annance to Richard T. Pennefather, 13 March 1860, LAC, RG10, vol. 253, pp. 151450-1, reel 12643.

49 Noel Annance to C.T. Walcot, 29 July 1862, LAC, RG10, vol. 273, pp. 184411-12, reel-12657.

50 Noel Annance to George-Étienne Cartier, 27 August 1861, LAC, RG10, vol. 261, pp. 157849-51, reel 12648. On Cartier, see Bonnefant, "George-Étienne Cartier."

51 Noel Annance to C.T. Walcot, 8 March 1862, LAC, RG10, vol. 273, pp. 184364-6, reel 12657; Noel Annance to George Sherwood, 10 March 1862, LAC, RG10, vol. 273, pp. 184374-7, reel 12657.

52 Noel Annance to C.T. Walcot, 29 July 1862, LAC, RG10, vol. 273, pp. 184411-12, reel 12657.

53 Noel Annance to Alexander Campbell, 26 May 1864, LAC, RG10, vol. 273, pp. 184653-5, reel 12657.

54 Sale by Noel Annance to Ignace Gill of fifty acres of lot 21, range 2, 16 August 1862, LAC, RG10, vol. 800, reel 13624.

55 The quotation is taken from Noel Annance to William Mc-

Dougall, 19 February 1863, LAC, RG10, vol. 273, pp. 184511-14, reel 12657.

56 I. Gill to Commissioner of Crown Lands, 4 August 1862, LAC, RG10, vol. 273, pp. 184415, reel 12657.

57 Joseph A. Maurault, 6 August 1862, LAC, RG10, vol. 273, pp. 184416, reel 12657.

58 Untitled file, August 1862, LAC, RG10, vol. 273, pp. 184414, reel 12657. Edward N. DeLorimier had been an Indian Department interpreter at least as far back as 1847. *Canadian Almanac*, 1847, 33.

59 Noel Annance to E. Parent, 18 September 1862, LAC, vol. 273, pp. 1848-49, reel 12567.

60 Noel Annance to William McDougall, 1 December 1862, LAC, RG10, vol. 273, pp. 184378-80, reel 12657.

61 Noel Annance to William McDougall, 19 February 1863, LAC, RG10, vol. 273, pp. 184511-14, reel 12657.

62 Noel Annance to William Spragge, 7 May 1863, LAC, RG10, vol. 273, pp. 184542-5, reel 12657.

63 Peel, "William Connolly" and "Suzanne Connolly."

64 Jennifer S.H. Brown, "Partial Truths," 74–6, and Adele Perry, *Colonial Relations*, 102–7, agree that the decision was more complex in its implications than it appeared on the surface.

65 Noel Annance to William Spragge, 29 June 1863, LAC, RG10, vol. 273, pp. 184560-61, reel 12657.

66 Noel Annance to C.D. Walcot, 11 September 1863, LAC, RG10, vol. 273, pp. 184600-1, reel 12657.

67 Noel Annance to Alexander Campbell, 26 May 1864, LAC, RG10, vol. 273, pp. 184653-5, reel 12657.

68 Noel Annance and three other "Chiefs" to Richard Pennefather, 14 September 1857, LAC, RG10, vol. 236, pp. 140229-32, reel 11542; C.C. Obumsawin to R.T. Pennefather, 18 December 1856, LAC, RG10, vol. 246, pp. 1456247-58, reel 126354; C.C. Obumsawin to R.T. Pennefather, 16 November 1858, LAC, RG10, vol. 245, pp. 145925-7, reel 12634; also Noel Annance, testimonial respecting François Laurent Monlataque, 9 September 1857, LAC, RG10, vol. 248, p. 147688, reel 12640.

69 Noel Annance to Alexander Campbell, 14 March 1865, LAC, RG10, vol. 273, pp. 184781-4, reel 12657.

70 Noel Annance to Viscount Monck, 12 June 1865, LAC, RG10, vol. 303, pp. 202958-61, reel 12675; also reel 12676.

71 Noel Annance to Ignace Gill, 19 June 1865, LAC, RG10, vol. 303, pp. 202968-9, reel 12675.

72 Notation on Noel Annance to William Spragge, 31 August 1865, LAC, RG10, vol. 303, pp. 202982-3, reel 12675.

73 Ibid.

74 The only letter of this time period to have been located, not found in the original, is briefly annotated in Civil Secretary's Office, Summary of Correspondence, 11 October 1866, LAC, RG10, vol. 758, no. 59, unpaginated, reel 13489, as "Enfranchisement."

75 Noel Annance to William Spragge, 7 May 1863, LAC, RG10, vol. 273, pp. 184542-5, reel 12657. On Maurault's activities, see Charland, *Histoire des Abénakis*, 229–31.

76 Ignace Gill to Noel Annance, 26 June 1865, LAC, RG10, vol. 303, pp. 202968-9, reel 12675.

77 Noel Annance to William Spragge, 11 September 1865, LAC, RG10, vol. 303, pp. 202987-90, reel 12675.

78 Maurault, *Histoire*, 1; also on his date of departure, 630.

79 James Armstrong to William Spragge, 3 and 23 January 1867, LAC, RG10, vol. 303, pp. 203227-30, 203249-50, reel 12676.

80 James Armstrong to William Spragge, 25 January 1867, LAC, RG10, vol. 303, pp. 203253-6, reel 12676.

81 Ibid.

82 St Francis priests to William Spragge, 25 January 1867, LAC, RG10, vol. 304, pp. 203881, reel 20676.

83 Petition of Elias Hill to Superintendent General of Indian Affairs, May 1874, and resulting correspondence, 1874–76, LAC, RG10, vol. 1930, file 3349, at LAC website. On the practical difficulties of determining which parcels of Elias Hill's promised land were not already occupied, see J.T. Gilkison to William Spragge, 30 July 1862, LAC, RG10, vol. 286, pp. 192220-28a, reel 12665; also Weaver, "Iroquois," 200.

84 See Noel Annance to Governor General Lord Monck, 8 September 1868, LAC, RG10, vol. 304, pp. 203961-5, reel 12676; and Noel Annance to Hector L. Langevin, 10 August 1869, LAC, RG10, vol. 304, pp. 204100-11, reel 12677.

85 Noel Annance to Napier, 12 January 1848, LAC, RG10, vol. 605, pp. 50151-2, reel 13382.

86 Noel Annance to William McDougall, 28 July 1862, LAC, RG10, vol. 283, pp. 184403-10, reel 12657.

87 Noel Annance to Governor General Lord Monck, 8 September 1868, LAC, RG10, vol. 304, pp. 203961-5, reel 12676.

88 Francis Joseph Annance, 1821, in Woods, *Cross Cemetery*.

89 Napier to Alexander Campbell, 2 February 1848, LAC, RG10, vol. 605, pp. 50187-9, reel 13382.

POSTSCRIPT

1 "Report on the Affairs," vol. 6, appendix T.

2 Ibid.

3 "Report of the Special Commissioners."

Works Cited

Aboriginal Tribes (North America, New South Wales, Van Diemen's Land and British Guiana). London: House of Commons, 1834.

Ackerknecht, Erwin H. "'White Indians': Psychological and Physiological Peculiarities of White Children Abducted and Reared by North American Indians." *Bulletin of the History of Medicine* 15, no. 1 (1944): 15–36.

"An Act Respecting the Indian Lands in the Township of Durham, in the County of Drummond." 1860. http://eco.canadiana.ca/view/oocihm.9_02419/4?r=0&s=1.

"An Act to Change the Tenure of the Indian Lands in the Township of Durham." 1856. http://eco.canadiana.ca/view/oocihm.9_01340/2?r=0&s=1.

"An Act to Encourage the Gradual Civilization of Indian Tribes in this Province, and to Amend the Laws Relating to Indians," no. 58. 1857.

Acts for the Promotion of Public Education in Lower Canada. Toronto: Stewart Derbishire and George Desbarats, 1857.

Akrigg, G.P.V., and Helen Akrigg. *1001 British Columbia Place Names*. Vancouver: Discovery, 1973.

Allard, Jason. "Jason the Fleece Hunter." British Columbia Archives, ms 001, box 16, no. 1.

Anderson, Eric Gary. "The Presence of Early Native Studies: A Response to Stephanie Fitzgerald and Hilary E. Wyss." *American Literary History* 22, no. 2 (2010): 280–8.

Annance, Noel (N.F.). Correspondence. Houghton Library, Harvard University, American Board of Commissioners for Foreign Missions papers.

– (Francis N.). "A Journal of a Voyage from Fort George Columbia River to Fraser River in the Winter of 1824 and 1825." Hudson's Bay Company Archives, Archives of Manitoba, B/76/a/1.

Antaya, François. "Chasser en échange d'un salaire: Les engages améerindiens dans la traite des fourrures du Saint-Maurice, 1798–1831." *Revue d'histoire de l'Améerique française* 63, no. 1 (2009): 5–31.

– "La traite des fourrures dans le basin du Saint-Maurice: Les conditions de travail des engages au début du XIXe siècle (1798–1831)." MA thesis, L'Université du Québec à Trois-Rivères, 2007.

Apess, William. *On Our Own Ground: The Complete Writings of William Apess, a Pequot.* Ed. Barry O'Connell. Amherst: University of Massachusetts Press, 1992.

Audet, Louis-Philippe. *Le Système Scolaire de la Province de Québec.* 6 vols. Quebec City: Les Presses Universitaires Laval, 1952.

Axtell, James. *The Invasion Within: The Contest of Cultures in Colonial North America.* New York: Oxford University Press, 1985.

– *Natives and Newcomers: The Cultural Origins of North America.* New York: Oxford University Press, 2001.

– "The White Indians of Colonial America." *William and Mary Quarterly*, 3rd ser., 32, no. 1 (1975): 55–88.

– "Williamsburg's Indian School." Podcast, 8 November 2010. http://podcast.history.org/2010/11/08/williamsburgs-indian-school.

Baena, Victoria. "The Harvard Indian College." *Harvard Crimson*, 24 March 2011.

Baker, C. Alice. *True Stories of New England Captives Carried to Canada during the Old French and Indian Wars.* Cambridge, MA: E.A. Hall and Company, 1897.

Bannet, Eve Tavor. *Transatlantic Stories and the History of Reading, 1720–1820: Migrant Fictions.* New York: Cambridge University Press, 2011.

Barber, John Warner. *History and Antiquities of New England.* Hartford, CT: H.S. Parsons, 1842.

Barman, Jean. *French Canadians, Furs, and Indigenous Women in the Making of the Pacific Northwest.* Vancouver: UBC Press, 2014.

Barman, Jean, and Bruce McIntyre Watson. *Leaving Paradise: Indigenous Hawaiians in the Pacific Northwest, 1787–1898.* Honolulu: University of Hawaii Press, 2006.

Barry, Gwen. "La 'piste Bécancour': Des campaments abénaquis dans l'arrière-pays." *Recherches amérindiennes au Québec* 33, no. 2 (2003): 93–143.

Barry, Louise. "Kansas before 1854: A Revised Annals." *Kansas Historical Quarterly* 29, no. 1 (1963): 41–81.

Beaulieu, Alain. "'An equitable right to be compensated': The Dispossession of the Aboriginal People of Quebec and the Emergence of a New Legal Rationale (1760–1860)." *Canadian Historical Review* 94, no. 1 (March 2013): 1–27.

Beaulieu, Alain, Stéphanie Béreau, and Jean Tanguay. *Les Wendats du Québec: Territoire, Économie et Identité.* Quebec: Les Édition GID, 2013.

Belyk, Robert C. *John Tod: Rebel in the Ranks.* Victoria, BC: Horsdal and Schubart, 1995.

Bodian, Marian. "The Long but Thin History of Harvard and the Red Man." *Harvard Crimson*, 1 May 1968.

Bonnefant, J.C. "George-Étienne Cartier." *Dictionary of Canadian Biography.* Online.

Bouchette, Joseph. *A Topographical Dictionary of the Province of Lower Canada.* London: Longman, Reed, 1832.

Bourne, Edward Emerson. *The History of Wells and Kennebunk from the Earliest Settlement to the Year 1820.* Portland, ME: Thurston and Company, 1875.

Bourque, Bruce J., and Laureen A. Labar. *Uncommon Threads: Wabanaki Textiles, Clothing, and Costume.* Montreal and Kingston: McGill-Queen's University Press; and Augusta, ME: Maine State Museum, 2009.

Boutevin, Stéphanie. "La place et les usages de l'écriture chez les Hurons et la Abénakis, 1780–1880." PhD diss., Université du Québec à Montréal, 2011.

Bouwman, Heather. "Samson Occom and the Sermonic Tradition." In Kristina Bross and Hilary E. Wyss, eds, *Early Native Literacies in New England: A Documentary and Critical Anthology*, 57–71. Amherst: University of Massachusetts Press, 2008.

British Columbia Archives. Miscellaneous files.

Brooks, Johanna, ed. *The Collected Writings of Samson Occom, Mohegan: Leadership and Literature in Eighteenth-Century Native America.* New York: Oxford University Press, 2006.

Brooks, Lisa. *The Common Pot: The Recovery of Native Space in the Northeast.* Minneapolis: University of Minnesota Press, 2008.

Bross, Kristina, and Hilary E. Wyss, eds. *Early Native Literacies in New England: A Documentary and Critical Anthology*. Amherst: University of Massachusetts Press, 2008.

Brown, Jennifer S.H. "Partial Truths: A Closer Look at Fur Trade Marriage." In Theodore Binnema, Gerhard J. Ens, and R.C. MacLeod, eds, *From Rupert's Land to Canada*, 59–80. Edmonton: University of Alberta Press, 2001.

– *Strangers in Blood: Fur Trade Company Families in Indian Country*. Vancouver: UBC Press, 1980.

Bruchac, Joseph. *At the End of Ridge Road*. Minneapolis: Milkwood, 2005.

– *Bowman's Store: A Journey to Myself*. New York: Dial Books, 1997.

Bruchac, Marge. "Abenaki Connections to 1704: The Sadoques Family and Deerfield, 2004." In Evan Haefli and Kevin Sweeney, eds, *Captive Histories: English, French, and Native Narratives of the 1704 Deerfield Raid*, 262–78. Amherst: University of Massachusetts Press, 2006.

Buckner, Phillip. "Matthew Whitworth-Aylmer, 5th Baron Aylmer." *Dictionary of Canadian Biography*. Online.

Calloway, Colin G. *The American Revolution in Indian Country: Crisis and Diversity in Native American Communities*. Cambridge, UK: Cambridge University Press, 1995.

– *The Indian History of an American Institution: Native Americans and Dartmouth*. Hanover, NH: University Press of New England, 2010.

– *North Country Captives: Selected Narratives of Indian Captivity from Vermont and New Hampshire*. Hanover, NH: University Press of New England, 1992.

– "An Uncertain Destiny: Indian Captivities on the Upper Connecticut River." *Journal of American Studies* 17, no. 2 (1983): 189–210.

– *The Western Abenaki of Vermont, 1600–1800: War, Migration, and the Survival of an Indian People*. Norman: University of Oklahoma Press, 1990.

– ed. *Dawnland Encounters: Indians and Europeans in Northern New England*. Hanover, NH: University Press of New England, 1991.

Calloway, Colin G., and Neil Salisbury, eds. *Reinterpreting New England Indians and the Colonial Experience*. Boston: Colonial Society of Massachusetts, 2003.

Calvert, Mary R. *Dawn over the Kennebec*. Lewiston, ME: Twin City Printery, 1983.

– *The Kennebec Wilderness Awakens*. Lewiston, ME: Twin City Printery, 1986.

Campion, Nardi Reeder. "Who Was Sylvanus Thayer?" *Dartmouth Engineer* 1, no. 1 (2004): 12–16.

"Canada Sunday School Union." *American Sunday School Magazine*, October 1824, 124.

Canadian Almanac and Repository. Toronto: Scobie and Balfour, 1847.

Carney, Cary Michael. *Native American Higher Education in the United States*. New Brunswick, NJ: Transaction, 1999.

Catalogue of the Members of the United Fraternity, Dartmouth College, August, 1818. Hanover, NH: Charles Spear, 1818.

Catalogue of the Officers and Members of the Society of United Fraternity, Dartmouth College, 1840. Concord, NH: Asa McFarland for the Society of United Fraternity, 1840.

Catalogue of the Officers and Students of Dartmouth University, October 1811. Dartmouth College Archives.

Charland, Philippe. "Définition et reconstitution de l'espace territorial du Nord-est Amériquain: La reconstruction de la carte du W8banaki par la toponymie Abénakise au Québec Aln8baïwi kdakina – notre monde à la manière Abénakise." PhD diss., McGill University, 2005.

– "De l'etrange origine toponymique de duex rivières de la region de Mégantic." *Bulletin de la Société de géographique de Québec* 2, no. 1 (2007): 6–10.

Charland, Thomas-M. *Histoire des Abénakis d'Odanak (1675–1937)*. Montreal: Les Éditions du Lévrier, 1964.

– *Histoire de Saint-François-du-Lac*. Ottawa: Collège Dominicain, 1942.

– "Ignace Gill." *Dictionary of Canadian Biography*. Online.

– "Joseph-Louis Gill." *Dictionary of Canadian Biography*. Online.

– "Joseph-Pierre-Anselme Maurault." *Dictionary of Canadian Biography*. Online.

Chase, Frederick. *A History of Dartmouth College and the Town of Hanover New Hampshire*. 2 vols. Cambridge, MA: John Wilson and Son, 1891.

Chaurette, Mathieu. "Les premières écoles autochtones au Québec: Progression, opposition et lutes de pouvoir, 1792–1853." MA thesis, Université du Québec à Montréal, 2011.

Chiles, Katy L. *Transformable Race: Surprising Metamorphoses in the Literature of Early America*. New York: Oxford University Press, 2014.

Chinard, Gilbert, ed. *The Letters of Lafayette and Jefferson*. Baltimore, MD: Johns Hopkins University Press; and Paris: Les Belles Lettres, 1929.

"The Chronicle." *Universal Asylum and Columbian Magazine*, March 1792, 214.

Cipolla, Craig N. *Becoming Brothertown: Native American Ethnogenesis and Endurance in the Modern World*. Tucson: University of Arizona Press, 2013.

Cogley, Richard W. *John Eliot's Mission to the Indians before King Philip's War*. Cambridge, MA: Harvard University Press, 1999.

Colby, Solon B. *Colby's Indian History: Antiquities of the New Hampshire Indians and Their Neighbors*. Exeter, NH: Colby, 1976.

Cole, Jean Murray. *Exile in the Wilderness: The Biography of Chief Factor Archibald McDonald, 1790–1853*. Don Mills, ON: Barnes and MacEachern, 1979,

Coleman, Emma Lewis. *New England Captives Carried to Canada between 1677 and 1760 during the French and Indian Wars*. 2 vols. Portland, ME: Southworth, 1925.

Connole, Daniel A. "Conflict in English and Indian Attitudes Regarding Land Ownership: The Story of John Wampas." *Bulletin of the Massachusetts Archaeological Society* 59, no. 2 (1998): 66–78.

Cook, Christopher L. *The Providential Life and Heritage of Henry Obookiah*. Waimea, Kaua'i, Hawaii: Pa'a Studios, 2015.

Copies or Extracts of Correspondence since 1st April 1835, between the Secretary of State for the Colonies and the Governors of the British North American Provinces Respecting the Indians of Those Provinces. London: House of Commons, 1839.

Cornelius, Amelia, Judy Cornelius, Loretta Metoxen, Eileen Antoine, Liz Obomsawin, and Richard Chrisjohn. "Contemporary Oneida Perspectives on Oneida History." In Laurence M. Hauptman and L. Gordon McLester III, eds, *The Oneida Indian Journey: From New York to Wisconsin, 1784–1860*, 126–42. Madison: University of Wisconsin Press, 1999.

Curtis, Bruce. *Ruling by Schooling Quebec: Conquest to Liberal*

Governmentality – A Historical Sociology. Toronto: University of Toronto Press, 2012.

Dannenberg, Anne Marie. "'Where, then, shall we place the hero of the wilderness?' William Apess's *Eulogy on King Philip* and Other Doctrines of Racial Destiny." In Helen Jaskoski, ed., *Early Native American Writing: New Critical Essays*, 66–82. Cambridge, UK: Cambridge University Press, 1996.

Dartmouth College. Correspondence and Papers. Rauner Special Collections, Dartmouth Library.

Day, Gordon M. *The Identity of the Saint Francis Indians*. Ottawa: National Museums of Canada, 1981.

– *In Search of New England's Native Past: Selected Essays by Gordon M. Day*. Ed. Michael K. Foster and William Cowan. Amherst: University of Massachusetts Press, 1998.

Demos, John. *The Heathen School: A Story of Hope and Betrayal in the Age of the Early Republic*. New York: Alfred A. Knopf, 2014.

– *The Unredeemed Captive: A Family Story from Early America*. New York: Alfred A. Knopf, 1994.

Désilets, Andrée. "Sir Étienne-Paschal Taché." *Dictionary of Canadian Biography*. Online.

– "Sir Hector-Louis Langevin." *Dictionary of Canadian Biography*. Online.

– "Louis-Victor Sicotte." *Dictionary of Canadian Biography*. Online.

Dickason, Olive Patricia, with David T. McNab. *Canada's First Nations: A History of Founding Peoples from Earliest Times*. 4th ed. Don Mills, ON: Oxford University Press, 2009.

"Digging Veritas: The Archaeology and History of the Indian College and Student Life at Colonial Harvard." Peabody Museum of Archaeology and Ethnology, Harvard University. http://www.peabody.harvard.edu/DV-online.

Doerfler, Jill, Niigaanwewidam James Sinclair, and Heidi Kiiwetinepinesiik Stark, eds. *Centering Anishinaabeg Studies: Understanding the World through Stories*. East Lansing: Michigan State University Press; and Winnipeg: University of Manitoba Press, 2013.

Doige, Thomas. *An Alphabetical List of the Merchants, Traders, and Housekeepers, Residing in Montreal*. 2nd ed. Montreal: James Lane, 1820.

Douglas, David. *Journal Kept by David Douglas during His Travels in North America, 1823–1827.* New York: Antiquarian, 1959.

Drake, Samuel G. *Indian Captivities, or Life in the Wigwam.* Auburn, NY: Derby and Miller, 1851.

Dubois, Paul-André. "Chant et mission en Nouvelle-France, Espece de rencontre des cultures." 2 vols. PhD diss., Université Laval, 2004.

"The Durham Band of Abenaki." http://www.nedoba.org/ne-do-ba/menu_dur.html#howto.

"Early Native American Resources in the Harvard University Archives." http://isites.harvard.edu/icb/icb.do?keyword=k18801&tabgroupid=icb.tabgroup23120.

"Eastern Township Loyal Volunteers, Pay Lists, November 1838 to March 1839." *In British Army and Canadian Militia Muster Rolls and Pay Lists, 1795–1850.* Ancestry.ca.

Eckstorm, Fannie Hardy. "Old Louis Annance and His Descendants." Fogler Library, University of Maine, I. Eckstorm papers, box 2, folder 13.

Elkins, Jonathan. "Reminiscences of Jonathan Elkins." In Vermont Historical Society, *Proceedings,* 1919–20, 186–211.

Elliott, T.C. "Journal of Alexander Ross – Snake Country Expedition, 1824." *Oregon Historical Quarterly* 14, no. 4 (1913): 366–85.

Ermatinger, Edward. Inward Correspondence. British Columbia Archives, A/B/40, Er62.4.

– Papers. University of British Columbia Library, Special Collections, H5820.1.E7.A1.

Ermatinger, Francis. *Fur Trade Letters of Francis Ermatinger.* Ed. Lois Halliday McDonald. Glendale, CA: Arthur H. Clark Company, 1980.

Facts Relative to the Canadian Indians Published by Direction of the Aboriginal Committee of the Meeting for Sufferings. London: Harvey and Darton, 1839.

Fenlon, Timothy E. "A Struggle for Survival and Recognition: The Catawba Nation – 1840–1890." MA thesis, Clemson University, 2007.

Filteau, Hélène, Jean Hamelin, and John Keyes, "Louis-Adélard Senécal." *Dictionary of Canadian Biography.* Online.

Fleming, R. Harvey, ed. *Minutes of Council, Northern Department of Rupert Land, 1821–31.* Toronto: Champlain Society, 1940.

"Foreign Mission School." *Christian Herald and Seaman's Magazine,* 3 January 1818, 226.

Foster, John E. "The Indian Trader in the Hudson's Bay Fur Trade Tradition." In Canadian Ethnology Society, *Proceedings of the 2nd Congress,* vol. 2, ed. J. Freeman and J.H. Barkow, 571–85. Ottawa: National Museum of Man, 1976.

Francis, Daniel. *A History of the Native Peoples of Quebec, 1760–1867.* Ottawa: Ministry of Indian Affairs and Northern Development, 1985.

Franquet, Louis. *Voyages et Mémoires sur le Canada par Franquet.* Montreal: Élysée, 1974.

Fuchs, Denise. "Native Sons in Rupert's Land, 1760 to the 1860s." PhD diss., University of Manitoba, 2000.

Galbraith, John S. "George Simpson." *Dictionary of Canadian Biography.* Online.

– *Hudson's Bay Company as an Imperial Factor.* Berkeley: University of California Press, 1957.

– *The Little Emperor: Governor Simpson of the Hudson's Bay Company.* Toronto: Macmillan, 1976.

Gale, Sylvia. "Resisting Functional-Critical Divides: Literacy Education at Moor's Indian Charity School and Tuskegee Institute." PhD diss., University of Texas at Austin, 2008.

Garraghan, Gilbert J. *Catholic Beginnings in Kansas City, Missouri.* Chicago: Loyola University Press, 1920.

Garrett, Kathleen. "Dartmouth Alumni in the Indian Territory." *Chronicles of Oklahoma* 32, no. 2 (1954): 123–41.

Gazette de Québec. Online.

Gazette de Québec: Index from 1764–1824. Online.

Gélinas, Claude. "La Mauricie des Abénaquis au XIXe siècle." *Recherches amérindiennes au Québec* 33, no. 2 (2003): 44–56.

General Catalogue and a Brief History of Kimball Union Academy. Claremont, NH: Claremont Manufacturing Company, 1880.

General Catalogue of Dartmouth College … Graduates. Hanover, NH: Dartmouth College, 1890.

Ghere, David Lyon. "Abenaki Factionalism, Emigration and Social Continuity: Indian Society in Northern New England, 1725 to 1765." PhD diss., University of Maine, 1988.

Gill, Charles. *Notes additionnelles a l'historie de la famille Gill.* Montreal: Eusèbe Senécal et Fils, 1889.

– *Notes historiques sur l'origine de la famille Gill.* Montreal: Eusèbe Senécal et Fils, 1887.

– *Notes sur de vieux manuscrits Abénakis.* Montreal: Eusèbe Senécal et Fils, 1886.

– *Nouvelles notes sur l'histoire de la famille Gill.* Montreal: Eusèbe Senécal et Fils, 1892.

Gill, Pauline. *Samuel chez les Abénakis.* Quebec City: Secundo, 2011.

Glenn, Charles L. *American Indian/First Nations Schooling from the Colonial Period to the Present.* New York: Palgrave Macmillan, 2011.

Gookin, Daniel. *Historical Collection of the Indians in New England.* Boston: Apollo, 1792.

Gottschalk, Louis. *Lafayette between the American and the French Revolution (1783–1789).* Chicago: University of Chicago Press, 1950.

Graymont, Barbara. "Thayendanegea [Joseph Brant]." *Dictionary of Canadian Biography.* Online.

Gura, Philip F. *The Life of William Apess, Pequot.* Chapel Hill: University of North Carolina Press, 2015.

Gustafson, Sandra M. "Historical Introduction to Hendrik Aupaumut's Short Narration" and "Hendrik Aupaumut and the Cultural Middle Ground." In Kristina Bross and Hilary E. Wyss, eds, *Early Native Literacies in New England: A Documentary and Critical Anthology,* 223–50. Amherst: University of Massachusetts Press, 2008.

Gwyn, Julian. "Sir William Johnson." *Dictionary of Canadian Biography.* Online.

Haefeli, Evan. "Ransoming New England Captives in New France." *French Colonial History* 1 (2002): 113–27.

Haefeli, Evan, and Kevin Sweeney, eds. *Captive Histories: English, French, and Native Narratives of the 1704 Deerfield Raid.* Amherst: University of Massachusetts Press, 2006.

Hagopian, John S. "Joseph Brant vs. Peter Russell: A Re-examination

of the Six Nations' Land Transactions in the Grand River Valley."
Social History/Histoire sociale 30, no. 60 (1997): 300–33.

Hallowell, A. Irving. "American Indians, White and Black: The Phenomenon of Transculturalization." *Current Anthropology* 4, no. 5 (1963): 519–31.

Hargrave, James. *The Hargrave Correspondence, 1821–1843.* Toronto: Champlain Society, 1938.

– *Letters from Rupert's Land, 1826–1840: James Hargrave of the Hudson's Bay Company.* Ed. Helen E. Ross. Montreal and Kingston: McGill-Queen's University Press, 2009.

Hargrave, Letitia. *The Letters of Letitia Hargrave.* Ed. Margaret Arnett Macleod. Toronto: Champlain Society, 1947.

Harring, Sidney L. *White Man's Law: Native People in Nineteenth-Century Canadian Jurisprudence.* Toronto: University of Toronto Press, 1998.

"The Harvard Indian College." Peabody Museum of Archaeology and Ethnology, Harvard University. http://www.peabody.harvard.edu/node/477.

Havard, Gilles. "'Protection' and 'Unequal Alliance': The French Conception of Sovereignty." In Robert Engelbert and Guillaume Teasdale, eds, *French and Indians in the Heart of North America, 1630–1815*, 113–37. East Lansing: Michigan State University Press; and Winnipeg: University of Manitoba Press, 2013.

Héritage. http://heritage.canadiana.ca.

Herndon, Ruth Wallis, and Ella Wilcox Sakatu. "Colonizing the Children: Indian Youngsters in Servitude in Early Rhode Island." In Colin G. Calloway and Neil Salisbury, eds, *Reinterpreting New England Indians and the Colonial Experience*, 137–72. Boston: Colonial Society of Massachusetts, 2003.

Hill, Ralph Nading, ed. *The College on the Hill: A Dartmouth Chronicle.* Hanover, NH: Dartmouth Publications, 1964.

Historical Sketch of the College of William and Mary in Virginia. Richmond, VA: Gary and Clemmitt, 1866.

The History of the College of William and Mary. Richmond, VA: J.E. Randolph and English, 1874.

Hogsett, Stacy L.S. "'The Tawnee Family': The Life Course of Indian

Value Adaptation for Eleazar Wheelock's Indian Scholars." PhD diss., University of New Hampshire, 1998.

Hough, Franklin B., ed. *Proceedings of the Commissioners of Indian Affairs … in the State of New York*. 2 vols. Albany, NY: Joel Munsell, 1861.

Howe, Jemima. *A Genuine and Correct Account of the Captivity, Sufferings and Deliverance of Mrs. Jemima Howe*. Boston: Belknap and Young, 1792.

Hoyt, David W. *Old Families of Salisbury and Amesbury, Massachusetts*. Vol. 1. Providence, RI: Snow and Farnham, 1897.

Huden John C. "The White Chief of the St. Francis Abenakis – Some Aspects of Border Warfare: 1690–1790." *Vermont History* 24, no. 3 (1956): 199–210; and 24, no. 4 (1956): 337–54.

Hudson's Bay Company (HBC). Biographical Sheets. Hudson's Bay Company Archives, Archives of Manitoba, online.

– Fort Simpson (Mackenzie River) Post Journal, 1834–35. Hudson's Bay Company Archives, Archives of Manitoba, B.200/a/15.

– Fort Simpson (NWT) Post Journal, 1834–35, as copied by John Stuart. Hudson's Bay Company Archives, Archives of Manitoba, John Stuart papers, E.24/5.

– Fort St James Post Journal, 1830–32. Hudson's Bay Company Archives, Archives of Manitoba, B.188/a/15-21.

– Fort Vancouver Correspondence Books, 1825–33. Hudson's Bay Company Archives, Archives of Manitoba, B.223/b/1-8.

– Kamloops Post Journal. Hudson's Bay Company Archives, Archives of Manitoba, B.97/a/1-3.

– Miscellaneous files. Hudson's Bay Company Archives, Archives of Manitoba.

– Servants' Characters and Staff Records, 1822–30. Hudson's Bay Company Archives, Archives of Manitoba, A.34/1.

– Snake Country Post Journal, 1824–25. Hudson's Bay Company Archives, Archives of Manitoba, B.202/a/3a.

Indian Affairs. *Annual Reports*. 1860s. Online.

"Indians in Canada [1844]." National Archives of the UK, CO47/118, part 2, 220–68 (double pages).

"Indians in the Canadas, 1835." National Archives of the UK, CO47/118, part 2, 282–305 (double pages).

"The Indians of British North America, 1837." National Archives of the UK, CO47/118, part 2, 307–18 (double pages).

Indian Treaties and Surrenders from 1680 to 1890. 2 vols. Ottawa: Brown Chamberlin, 1891.

"Indian Tribes in Canada, 1843." National Archives of the UK, CO47/118, part 2, 269–81 (double pages).

Irving, L. Homfray. *Officers of the British Forces in Canada during the War of 1812–15.* Welland, ON: Welland Tribute Print, 1908.

Jaenen, Cornelius J. "French Sovereignty and Native Nationhood during the French Regime." In J.R. Miller, ed., *Sweet Promises: A Reader on Indian-White Relations in Canada,* 19–42. Toronto: University of Toronto Press, 1991.

Jarvis, Brad D.E. *The Brothertown Nation of Indians: Land Ownership and Nationalism in Early America, 1740–1840.* Lincoln: University of Nebraska Press, 2010.

Jefferson, Thomas. Thomas Jefferson Papers, ser. 1, General Correspondence, 1651–1827. http://memory.loc.gov/cgi-bin/query/P?mtj:17:./temp/~ammem_aaNA.

John Connolly, plaintiff vs. Julia Woolrich, defendant and Thomas R. Johnson, et al., Judgment, July 9, 1867. Montreal: Montreal Printing and Publishing Company, 1867.

Johnson, Joseph. *To Do Good to My Indian Brethren: The Writings of Joseph Johnson, 1751–1776.* Ed. Laura J. Murray. Amherst: University of Massachusetts Press, 1998.

Johnson, Susanna. *A Narrative of the Captivity of Mrs. Johnson.* 2nd ed. Windsor, VT: Alden Spooner, 1807.

"Johnstone [*sic* – Johnson] et al. v. Connolly, Court of Appeal, September 7, 1869." *La Revue légale* 1 (1869–70): 253–400.

Jones, Tristan Rheaume. "The Implementarion of the Abenaki Band Council in Osanak, 1812–1914." MA thesis, Université du Québec à Montréal, 2013.

Journal of Education for Lower Canada.

Journals of the Continental Congress, 1774–1789. Ed. Worthington C. Ford et al. Washington, DC: Library of Congress, 1904–37. https://memory.loc.gov/ammem/amlaw/lwjclink.html.

Justice, Daniel Heath. *Our Fire Survives the Storm: A Cherokee Literary History.* Minneapolis: University of Minnesota Press, 2006.

Kelly, Eric P. "The Dartmouth Indians." *Dartmouth Alumni Magazine*, December 1929, 122–5.

Kelly, Gerald M. "Esther Wheelwright." *Dictionary of Canadian Biography*. Online.

Kelsay, Isabel Thompson. *Joseph Brant, 1743–1807: Man of Two Worlds*. Syracuse, NY: Syracuse University Press, 1984.

– "Tekarinhogen [John Brant]." *Dictionary of Canadian Biography*. Online.

Kendall, Edward Augustus. *Travels through the Northern Parts of the United States in the Years 1807 and 1808*. Vol. 3. New York: I. Riley, 1809.

King, Richard. *Narrative of a Journey to the Shores of the Arctic Ocean in 1833, 1834, and 1835*. 2 vols. London: Richard Bentley, 1836.

King, Titus. *Narrative of Titus King of Northampton, Mass: A Prisoner of the Indians in Canada, 1755–1758*. Hartford: Connecticut Historical Society, 1938.

Konkle, Maureen. *Writing Indian Nations: Native Intellectuals and the Politics of Historiography, 1827–1863*. Chapel Hill: University of North Carolina Press, 2004.

LeBel, Sylvie. "Trois facettes de la coexistence entre les populations autochtones et canadienne en Mauricie (1870–1910)." *Recherches amérindiennes au Québec* 35, no. 1 (2005): 69–80.

LaBrèque, Marie-Paule R. "Frederick George Heriot." *Dictionary of Canadian Biography*. Online.

Lahey, D.T. *George Simpson: Blaze of Glory*. Toronto: Dundurn, 2011.

Lancaster, Jane. "'By the Pens of Females': Girls' Diaries from Rhode Island, 1788–1821." *Rhode Island History* 57, nos 3–4 (1999): 59–113.

Lavoie, Michel, and Denis Vaugeois, eds. *L'Impasse amérindienne: Trois commissions d'enquête à l'origine d'une politique de tutelle et d'assimilation, 1828–1858*. Quebec: Septentrion, 2010.

Leighton, Douglas. "The Development of Federal Indian Policy in Canada, 1840–1890." PhD diss., University of Western Ontario, 1975.

– "Duncan Campbell Napier." *Dictionary of Canadian Biography.* Online.

Leighton, Douglas, and Robert J. Burns. "Samuel Peter Jarvis." *Dictionary of Canadian Biography.* Online.

Lepore, Jill. *The Name of War: King Philip's War and the Origins of American Identity.* New York: Alfred A. Knopf, 1998.

"Letter to the editor." *Field and Stream,* 27 May 1886, 351.

Library and Archives Canada (LAC). Durham Township Indian Lands Papers, 1816–1873. RG10, vol. 800, parts 1–2, reel 13624, with additional materials on reels 13401, 13402, 13625, and elsewhere. http://heritage.canadiana.ca.

– Land Petitions of Lower Canada, 1764–1841. RG1-L3L. http://heritage.canadiana.ca.

– Pre-Confederation Records, Indian Department. RG10. http://heritage.canadiana.ca.

Lincklaen, John. *Travels in the Years 1791 and 1792 in Pennsylvania, New York and Vermont.* New York: G.P. Putnam's Sons, 1897.

Little, J.I. *Loyalties in Conflict: A Canadian Borderland in War and Rebellion, 1812–1840.* Toronto: University of Toronto Press, 2008.

Londonderry, Roert Stewart, Marques of. *Memoirs and Correspondence.* 12 vols. London: H. Colburn, 1850–53.

Lopenzina, Drew. *Red Ink: Native Americans Picking Up the Pen in the Colonial Period.* Albany, NY: SUNY Press, 2012.

Love, W. Deloss. *Samson Occom and the Christian Indians of New England.* Boston: Pilgrim, 1899.

McCallum, James Dow. *Eleazar Wheelock.* New York: Arno Press and New York Times, 1969.

– ed. *Letters of Eleazar Wheelock's Indians.* Hanover, NH: Dartmouth College Publications, 1932.

McDonald, Archibald. *The Blessed Wilderness: Archibald McDonald's Letters from the Columbia, 1822–44.* Ed. Jean Murray Cole. Vancouver: UBC Press, 2001.

– "Short Narrative and a Few Remarks," 1834. British Columbia Archives, A/B/20.

Maclachlan, Morag. "The Case for Francis Noel Annance." *Beaver* 73, no. 2 (1993): 35–9.

– ed. *The Fort Langley Journals, 1827–30*. Vancouver: UBC Press, 1998.

McLeod, John. Journals and Correspondence, 1814–1844. British Columbia Archives, A/B/40, M22k.

McLoughlin, John. *The Letters of John McLoughlin from Fort Vancouver to the Governor and Committee: First Series, 1825–38*. Ed. E.E. Rich. Toronto: Champlain Society, 1941.

– *Letters of Dr. John McLoughlin Written at Fort Vancouver, 1829–1832*. Ed. Burt Brown Barker. Portland, OR: Binford and Morts, 1948.

Madley, Benjamin. "Reexamining the American Genocide Debate: Meanings, Historiography, and New Methods." *American Historical Review* 120, no. 1 (2015): 95–139.

Magnusson, Roger. *Education in New France*. Montreal and Kingston: McGill-Queen's University Press, 1992.

Mandell, Daniel R. *Behind the Frontier: Indians in Eighteenth-Century Eastern Massachusetts*. Lincoln: University of Nebraska Press, 1996.

Masta, Henry Lorne. *Abenaki Indian Legends, Grammar and Place Names*. Victoriaville, QC: La Voix des Bois-Francs, 1932.

Mathias, Bill. "A Timeline of the Life and Times of William L. (Niwentenhroa) Gray and John (Ignace Hatchiorauquasha) Gray." Kansas City Genealogical Society, n.d.

Maurault, Joseph A. *Histoire des Abenakis depuis 1605 jusq'à nos jours*. Sorel, QC: Gazette de Sorel, 1866.

Merrill, James H. *The Indians' New World: Catawbas and Their Neighbors from European Contact through the Era of Removal*. New York: W.W. Norton, 1991.

Michno, Gregory, and Susan Michno. *A Fate Worse Than Death: Indian Captivities in the West, 1830–1885*. Caldwell, ID: Caxton, 2007.

"Military Medals, Awards, and Honours, 1812 to 1867." Library and Archives Canada. http://www.bac-lac.gc.ca/eng/discover/military-heritage/military-medals-1812-1969/pages/military-medals-honours-awards.aspx.

Miller, James R. *Skyscrapers Hide the Heavens: A History of Indian-*

White Relations in Canada. Rev. ed. Toronto: University of Toronto Press, 2000.

Miller, Randall M., and John David Smith, eds. *Dictionary of Afro-American Slavery.* New York: Greenwood, 1988.

Milloy, John Sheridan. "The Era of Civilization: British Policy for the Indians of Canada, 1830–1860." PhD diss., New College, University of Oxford, 1978.

Missionary Herald (Boston).

Monet, Jacques. "Thomas Edmund Campbell." *Dictionary of Canadian Biography.* Online.

Moore, David L. *That Dream Shall Have a Name: Native Americans Rewriting America.* Lincoln: University of Nebraska Press, 2013.

Morgan, Dale L. *The West of William H. Ashley.* Denver, CO: Old West, 1964.

Morgan, George. *The True Lafayette.* Philadelphia: J.B. Lippincott, 1919.

Morison, Samuel Eliot. *The Founding of Harvard College.* Cambridge, MA: Harvard University Press, 1935.

– *Harvard College in the Seventeenth Century.* Cambridge, MA: Harvard University Press, 1936.

Morrison, Kenneth M. *The Embattled Northeast: The Elusive Ideal of Allegiance in Abenaki-Euroamerican Relations.* Berkeley: University of California Press, 1984.

Murray, Laura J. "Joseph Johnson's Diary, Farmington, Connecticut, 18 November 1772 to 1 February 1773." In Kristina Bross and Hilary E. Wyss, eds, *Early Native Literacies in New England: A Documentary and Critical Anthology,* 28–56. Amherst: University of Massachusetts Press, 2008.

– "'Pray Sir, Consider a Little': Rituals of Subordination and Strategies of Resistance in the Letters of Hezakiah Calvin and David Fowler to Eleazar Wheelock." In Helen Jaskoski, ed., *Early Native American Writing: New Critical Essays,* 15–41. Cambridge, UK: Cambridge University Press, 1996.

Namias, June. *White Captives: Gender and Ethnicity on the American Frontier.* Chapel Hill: University of North Carolina Press, 1993.

Napier, Duncan Campbell. Letterbooks, 1826–57. Library and

Archives Canada, RG10, vols 590 (1826–41, 1842–48), 594 (1849–57), reels C-13377-78. http://heritage.canadiana.ca.

Nash, Alice N. "The Abiding Frontier: Family, Gender and Religion in Wabanki History, 1600–1763." PhD diss., Columbia University, 1997.

Nelson, Dana D. "'(I speak like a fool but I am constrained)': Samson Occom's *Short Narrative* and Economies of the Racial Self." In Helen Jaskoski, ed., *Early Native American Writing: New Critical Essays*, 42–65. Cambridge, UK: Cambridge University Press, 1996.

"New England Waters." *Field and Stream*, 9 July 1891, 501.

Newell, Margaret Ellen. "The Changing Nature of Indian Slavery in New England, 1670–1720." In Colin G. Calloway and Neil Salisbury, eds, *Reinterpreting New England Indians and the Colonial Experience*, 106–36. Boston: Colonial Society of Massachusetts, 2003.

North, Louise B., Janet M. Wedge, and Landa M. Freeman. *In the Words of Women: The Revolutionary War and the Birth of the Nation, 1765–1799*. Lanham, MD: Lexington Books, 2011.

North West Company. Servants' Contracts, 1798–1822. Hudson's Bay Company Archives, Archives of Manitoba, F.5/1-3, reel 5M13.

"Notre-Dame des Bois." *Le Pionnier de Sherbrooke*, 10 April 1891.

O'Brien, Jean M. *Firsting and Lasting: Writing Indians out of Existence in New England*. Minneapolis: University of Minnesota Press, 2010.

Occom, Samson. *The Collected Writings of Samson Occom, Mohegan: Leadership and Literature in Eighteenth-Century Native America*. Ed. Johanna Brooks. New York: Oxford University Press, 2006.

Ogden, Peter Skene. *Peter Skene Ogden's Snake Country Journals, 1824–25 and 1825–26*. Ed. E.E. Rich. London: Hudson's Bay Record Society, 1950.

Osunkhirhine, Peter Paul. Correspondence (original letters). Houghton Library, Harvard University, American Board of Commissioners for Foreign Missions papers.

– [as Wzokhilain, Peter Paul]. *Kimzowi Awighigann*. Boston: Crocker and Brewster, 1830.

– Osunkhirhine fonds (microfilm copies of Houghton Library originals). United Church of Canada Archives, CA ON00340/F3387.

Ott-Kimmel, Amy K. "A Narrative of the Captivity of Mrs. Johnson: An Edition." PhD diss., University of Delaware, 2001.

Parish, Elijah. *An Eulogy on John Hubbard*. Hanover, NH: C.W.S. and H. Spear, 1810.

Parker, Everett L. *Native American Families at Moosehead Lake*. Greenville, ME: Moosehead Communications, 2007.

Parkman, Francis. *The Journals of Francis Parkman*. Ed. Mason Wade. 2 vols. New York: Harper and Brothers, 1947.

Paxton, James W. *Joseph Brant and His World: Eighteenth-Century Mohawk Warrior and Statesman*. Toronto: James Lorimer, 2008.

Peel, Bruce. "Suzanne Connolly." *Dictionary of Canadian Biography*. Online.

– "William Connolly." *Dictionary of Canadian Biography*. Online.

Perdue, Theda, ed. *Cherokee Editor: The Writings of Elias Boudinot*. Knoxville: University of Tennessee Press, 1983.

Perry, Adele. *Colonial Relations: The Douglas-Connolly Family and the Nineteenth-Century Imperial World*. Cambridge, UK: Cambridge University Press, 2015.

"Persons Employed for the Upper Missouri Outfit for the Year 1830." Choteau Collection, Missouri Historical Society.

Peyer, Bernd C. *The Tutor'd Mind: Indian Missionary-Writers in Antebellum America*. Amherst: University of Massachusetts Press, 1997.

– ed. *American Indian Nonfiction: An Anthology of Writings, 1760s–1930s*. Norman: University of Oklahoma Press, 2007.

Pfister, Joel. *The Yale Indian: The Education of Henry Roe Cloud*. Durham, NC: Duke University Press, 2009.

Plumley, Alexander Rolston. "Reminiscences of Dartmouth." *New York Observer and Chronicle*, 19 July 1866, 229.

Point, Nicholas. *Wilderness Kingdom: Indian Life in the Rocky Mountains, 1840–1847*. New York: Holt, Rinehart and Winston, 1967.

Porter, Joy. *Native American Freemasonry: Associationalism and Performance in America*. Lincoln: University of Nebraska Press, 2011.

A Provisional List of Alumni, Grammar School Students, Members of the Faculty, and Members of the Board of Visitors of the College of William and Mary in Virginia from 1693 to 1888. Richmond, VA: Division of Purchase and Printing, 1941.

Quebec, Vital and Church Records (Drouin Collection), 1621–1968.
Ancestry.ca.

Raffan, James. *Emperor of the North: Sir George Simpson and the Remarkable Story of the Hudson's Bay Company.* Toronto: Harper-Collins, 2007.

"Remembering Native Sons." *Harvard University Gazette*, 1 May 1997.

"Report of the Special Commissioners Appointed on the 8th of September, 1856, to Investigate Indian Affairs in Canada." *Journal of the Legislative Assembly of the Province of Canada* 16 (1858): unpaginated, 283 pages.

"Report on the Affairs of the Indians in Canada: Sections I and II, January 22, 1844." *Journals of the Legislative Assembly of the Province of Canada* 4 (1844–45): appendix EEE, unpaginated, 44 pages.

"Report on the Affairs of the Indians in Canada: Section III and Appendices." *Journals of the Legislative Assembly of the Province of Canada* 6 (1847): appendix T, unpaginated, 282 pages.

Ricard, Elaine. *The St.-Francis Abenaki Paper Trail, 1790–1900.* 2 vols. Self-published, 2006.

Richardson, Leon Burr. "The Dartmouth Indians." *Dartmouth Alumni Magazine*, June 1930, 524–7.

– *History of Dartmouth College.* Hanover, NH: Dartmouth College Publications, 1932.

Rockwell, Stephen J. *Indian Affairs and the Administrative State in the Nineteenth Century.* New York: Cambridge University Press, 2010.

Rogers, Edward S., and Donald B. Smith, eds. *Aboriginal Ontario: Historical Perspectives on the First Nations.* Toronto: Dundurn, 1994.

Rogers, Robert. *Journals of Major Robert Rogers.* Ed. Franklin B. Hough. Albany, NY: Joel Munsell's Sons, 1883.

Roppolo, Kimberly. "Samson Occom as Writing Instructor: The Search for an Intertribal Rhetoric." In Craig S. Womack, Daniel Heath Justice, and Christopher B. Teuton, eds, *Reasoning Together: The Native Critics Collective*, 303–22. Norman: University of Oklahoma Press, 2008.

Rossie, Jonathan G. "Guy Johnson." *Dictionary of Canadian Biography*. Online.

Round, Phillip H. "Title Pages from Samson Occom's *Sermon Preached at the Execution of Modes Paul*." In Kristina Bross and Hilary E. Wyss, eds, *Early Native Literacies in New England: A Documentary and Critical Anthology*, 72–83. Amherst: University of Massachusetts Press, 2008.

Roy, Christopher A. "Abenaki Sociality and the Work of Family History." PhD diss., Princeton University, 2012.

Rubin, Julius H. *Tears of Repentance: Christian Indian Identity and Community in Colonial Southern New England*. Lincoln: University of Nebraska Press, 2013.

Ruddel, David T. *Quebec City, 1765–1832: The Evolution of a Colonial Town*. Ottawa: Canadian Museum of Civilization, 1987.

Sadoques, Elizabeth M. "The History and Traditions of Eunice Williams and Her Descendants, 1922." In Evan Haefeli and Kevin Sweeney, eds, *Captive Histories: English, French, and Native Narratives of the 1704 Deerfield Raid*, 255–61. Amherst: University of Massachusetts Press, 2006.

Saint-Amant, Joseph-Charles. *L'Avenir: Townships de Durham et de Wickham*. Victoriaville, QC: L'Echo des Bois-francs, 1898. Reprinted as *Un Coin des Cantons de l'Est*. Drummondville, QC: La Parole, 1932.

Salter, John R. Hunter Bear, Jr. Website. http://www.hunterbear.org.

Sandys, Ed. W. "Two Days' Trout Fishing." *Outing: An Illustrated Monthly Magazine of Recreation*, May 1897, 172–6.

Savoie, Sylvie, and Jean Tanguay. "La noeud de l'anciennte amitie: La presence abénaquise sur la rive nord du Saint-Laurent aux XVIIe et XVIIIe siècles." *Recherches amérindiennes au Québec* 33, no. 2 (2003): 29–43.

Schneider, Tammy. "'This Once Savage Heart of Mine': Joseph Johnson, Wheelock's 'Indians,' and the Construction of a Christian/ Indian Identity, 1764–1776." In Colin G. Calloway and Neil Salisbury, eds, *Reinterpreting New England Indians and the Colonial Experience*, 232–63. Boston: Colonial Society of Massachusetts, 2003.

Schrøder, Johan. *Johan Schrøder's Travels in Canada, 1863*. Ed. Orm Øverland. Montreal and Kingston: McGill-Queen's University Press, 1989.

Le Seminaire de Nicolet. Montreal: Imprimerie La Minerve, 1867.

Shortt, Adam, and Arthur G. Doughty, eds. *Documents Relating to the Constitutional History of Canada, 1759–1791*. Ottawa: J. de L. Taché, 1918.

Sibley, John Langdon. *Biographical Sketches of Graduates of Harvard University*. Vol. 2, *1659–1677*. Cambridge, MA: Charles William Sever, 1881.

Silverman, David J. *Red Brethren: The Brothertown and Stockbridge Indians and the Problem of Race in America*. Ithaca, NY: Cornell University Press, 2010.

Simmons, Deirdre. *Keepers of the Record: The History of the Hudson's Bay Company Archives*. Montreal and Kingston: McGill-Queen's University Press, 2007.

Simpson, George. *Fur Trade and Empire: George Simpson's Journal*. Ed. Frederick Merk. Cambridge, MA: Harvard University Press, 1931.

– Inward Correspondence. Hudson's Bay Company Archives, Archives of Manitoba.

– Outward Correspondence. Hudson's Bay Company Archives, Archives of Manitoba.

– *Part of Dispatch from George Simpson*. Ed. E.E. Rich. Toronto: Champlain Society, 1947.

Sinclair, Niigaanwewidam James, and Warren Cariou, eds. *Manitowapow: Aboriginal Writings from the Land of Water*. Winnipeg: Highwater, 2011.

Smith, Donald B. *Mississauga Portraits: Ojibwe Voices from Nineteenth-Century Canada*. Toronto: University of Toronto Press, 2013.

– *Sacred Feathers: The Reverend Peter Jones (Kahkewaquonaby) and the Mississauga Indians*. 2nd ed. Toronto: University of Toronto Press, 2013.

Smith, Paul H., et al., eds. *Letters of Delegates to Congress, 1774–1789*. Vol. 15. Washington, DC: Library of Congress, 1976–2000. Online.

Smith, Shirlee Anne. "John Stuart." *Dictionary of Canadian Biography*. Online.

Sprague, John F. "Louis Annance." *Collections and Proceedings of the Maine Historical Society*, 2nd ser., 3 (1894): 418–23.

Sprague's Journal of Maine History.

Stark, Caleb. *Memoir and Official Correspondence of Gen. John Stark.* Concord, NH: G. Parker Lyon, 1860.

Stark, John. *Reminiscences of the French War.* Concord, NH: Luther Roby, 1831.

Steele, Ian K. *Setting All the Captives Free: Capture, Adjustment, and Recollection in Allegheny Country.* Montreal and Kingston: McGill-Queen's University Press, 2013.

Sulte, Benjamin. *Histoire de Saint-François-du-Lac.* Montreal: Imprimerie de L'Etendard, 1886.

Surtees, Robert J. "Indian Reserve Policy in Upper Canada, 1830–1845." MA thesis, Carleton University, 1966.

Sutherland, Stuart R.J., Pierre Tousignant, and Madeline Dionne-Tousignant. "Sir Frederick Haldimand." *Dictionary of Canadian Biography.* Online.

Swainson, Donald. "Sir Alexander Campbell." *Dictionary of Canadian Biography.* Online.

Sylvain, Philippe. "Jean-Baptiste- ric Dorion." *Dictionary of Canadian Biography.* Online.

Szasz, Margaret Connell. *Indian Education in the American Colonies, 1607–1783.* Albuquerque: University of New Mexico Press, 1988.

– "Samson Occom: Mohegan as Spiritual Intermediary." In Margaret Connell Szasz, ed., *Between Indian and White Worlds: The Cultural Broker*, 61–78. Norman: University of Oklahoma Press, 1994.

Thomas, Earle. "Sir John Johnson." *Dictionary of Canadian Biography.* Online.

Thompson, Nile. "Land Untapped and Untrapped." *Cowlitz Historical Quarterly* 22, no. 1 (1991): 6–7.

Thomson, James Diego. *The Letters of James Diego Thompson.* http://www.jamesdiegothomson.com.

Thoreau, Henry David. *Maine Woods.* Ed. Jeffrey S. Cramer. New Haven, CT: Yale University Press, 2009.

Tolmie, William Fraser. *The Journals of William Fraser Tolmie, Physician and Fur Trader.* Vancouver: Mitchell, 1963.

Trigger, Bruce G. "Amantacha." *Dictionary of Canadian Biography.* Online.

– *Handbook of North American Indians*. Vol. 15, *Northeast*. Washington, DC: Smithsonian Institution, 1978.

Tuckerman, Joseph. *A Discourse Preached before the Society for Propagating the Gospel among the Indians and Others in North America, November 1, 1821*. Cambridge, MA: n.p., 1821.

VanDerBeets, Richard, ed. *Held Captive by Indians: Selected Narratives, 1642–1836*. Knoxville: University of Tennessee Press, 1973.

Van Kirk, Sylvia. *Many Tender Ties: Women in Fur Trade Society, 1670–1870*. Norman: University of Oklahoma Press, 1983.

Vaughan, Alden T., and Edward W. Clark, eds. *Puritans among the Indians: Accounts of Captivity and Redemption, 1676–1724*. Cambridge, MA: Harvard University Press, 1981.

Vaughan, Alden T., and Daniel K. Richter. "Crossing the Cultural Divide: Indians and New Englanders, 1605–1763." In American Antiquarian Society, *Proceedings*, n.s., 90, no. 1 (1980): 23–99.

Voyageurs Database. Compiled by Nicole Fortier, Nicole St-Onge, and Robert Engelbert. At Société historique de Saint-Boniface, http://shsb.mb.ca/en/Voyageurs_database.

Vreeland, Hamilton. "Game Bag and Gun: In Camp on Wilson's Pond." *Field and Stream*, 19 May 1894, 422.

Wallot, Jean-Pierre. "Sir Robert Shore Milnes." *Dictionary of Canadian Biography*. Online.

Warrior, Robert Allen. *The People and the Word: Reading Native Nonfiction*. Minneapolis: University of Minnesota Press, 2005.

– *Tribal Secrets: Recovering American Indian Intellectual Traditions*. Minneapolis: University of Minnesota University Press, 1995.

Washington, George. *The Writings of George Washington*. Ed. John C. Fitzpatrick. 39 vols. Washington, DC: Government Printing Office, 1931–44.

Watson, Bruce McIntyre. *Lives Lived West of the Divide: A Biographical Dictionary of Fur Traders Working West of the Rockies, 1793–1858*. Kelowna, BC: Centre for Social, Spatial, and Economic Justice, University of British Columbia Okanagan, 2010.

Watson, Elkanah. *History of the Rise, Progress, and Existing Condition of the Western Canals*. Albany, NY: D. Steele, 1820.

Watson, Ian. *Catawba Indian Genealogy*. Geneseo, NY: Geneseo Foundation and Department of Anthropology, State University of New York at Geneseo, 1995.

Weaver, Jace. *The Red Atlantic: American Indigenes and the Making of the Modern World, 1000–1927.* Chapel Hill: University of North Carolina Press, 2014.

– *That the People Might Live: Native American Literatures and Native American Community.* New York: Oxford University Press, 1997.

Weaver, Sally M. "The Iroquois: The Consolidation of the Grand River Reserve in the Mid-Nineteenth Century, 1847–1875." In Edward S. Rogers and Donald B. Smith, eds, *Aboriginal Ontario: Historical Perspectives on the First Nations,* 167–212. Toronto: Dundurn, 1994.

Webber, Samuel. *Mathematics Compiled from the Best Authors and Intended to Be the Text-book of the Course of Private Lectures on These Sciences in the University of Cambridge.* Cambridge, UK: Thomas Andrews for University of Cambridge, 1801.

Webster, Stephen P. *An Oration Pronounced before the Society of the Phi Beta Kappa.* Hanover, NH: Moses Davis, 1824.

Weyler, Karen A. *Empowering Words: Outsiders and Authorship in Early America.* Athens: University of Georgia Press, 2013.

Wheelock, Eleazar. *A Continuation of the Narrative of the Indian Charity-School Begun in Lebanon, in Connecticut, and Now Incorporated with Dartmouth-College, in Hanover, in the Province of New Hampshire.* Hartford, NH: Ebenezer Watson, 1775.

– *A Continuation of the Narrative of the Indian Charity School, in Lebanon, in Connecticut, from the Year 1768, to the Incorporation of It with Dartmouth College.* Hartford, NH: Ebenezer Watson, 1771.

– *A Plain and Faithful Narrative of the Original Design, Rise, Progress and Present State of the Indian Charity School at Lebanon, Connecticut.* Boston: Richard and Samuel Draper, 1763.

Wheelwright, Julie Wheelwright. *Esther: The Remarkable True Story of Esther Wheelwright.* Toronto: HarperCollins, 2011.

Wigginton, Caroline. "Extending Root and Branch: Community Regeneration in the Petitions of Samson Occom." In Harold Bloom, ed., *Native American Writers,* new ed., 203–27. New York: Infobase, 2010.

Wilkes, Charles. *Narrative of the United States Exploring Expedition.* 5 vols. Philadelphia: self-published, 1849.

Williams, Glyndwr, ed. *Hudson's Bay Miscellany*. Winnipeg: Hudson's Bay Record Society, 1975.

Williams, John. *The Redeemed Captive*. Ed. Edward W. Clark. 1707. Reprint, Amherst: University of Massachusetts Press, 1976.

Williams, Steven. "What Befell Steven Williams in His Captivity." In Evan Haefeli and Kevin Sweeney, eds, *Captive Histories: English, French, and Native Narratives of the 1704 Deerfield Raid*, 161–70. Amherst: University of Massachusetts Press, 2006.

Wiseman, Frederick Matthew. *Reclaiming the Ancestors: Decolonizing a Taken Prehistory of the Far Northeast*. Hanover, NH: University Press of New England, 2005.

– *The Voice of the Dawn: An Autohistory of the Abenaki Nation*. Hanover, NH: University Press of New England, 2001.

Wolfenden, Madge. "John Tod." *Dictionary of Canadian Biography*. Online.

Womack, Craig S. *Red on Red: Native American Literary Separatism*. Minneapolis: University of Minnesota Press, 1999.

Womack, Craig S., Daniel Heath Justice, and Christopher B. Teuton, eds. *Reasoning Together: The Native Critics Collective*. Norman: University of Oklahoma Press, 2008.

Wood, William, ed. *Select British Documents of the Canadian War of 1812*. 3 vols. Toronto: Champlain Society, 1923.

Woods, R. *Cross Cemetery, Ulverton, Que.* http://www.qfhs-data base.ca/QFHS-virtual-library/Cemeteries/Richmond/QC1069.pdf.

Work, John. "Journal of John Work, November and December, 1824." Ed. T.C. Elliott. *Washington Historical Quarterly* 3, no. 3 (1912): 198–228.

– "Journal of a Voyage from Fort George to the Northward, Winter 1824." British Columbia Archives, A/B/40, W89.2.

Wright, Irvin Lee. "Piety, Politics, and Profit: American Indian Missions in the Colonial Colleges." PhD diss., Montana State University, 1985.

Wyss, Hilary E. *English Letters and Indian Literacies: Reading, Writing, and New England Missionary Schools, 1750–1830*. Philadelphia: University of Pennsylvania Press, 2012.

– *Writing Indians: Literacy, Christianity, and Native Community in Early America*. Amherst: University of Massachusetts Press, 2000.

Wzokhilain or Wzokhiláin [Osunkhirhine], Peter Paul. *Kimzowi Awighigann*. Boston: Crocker and Brewster, 1830.

Index

Names and terms reflect their usage in the text. Notes in parentheses indicate individuals' relationship to Noel Annance, their relationship to the text generally, or in the case of some women, their husband's surname.

Abenaki daring, 3, 5–6, 80, 84, 258–9; as exercised by Abenaki people, 3, 5–6, 11, 18–19, 21, 33–9; as exercised by Noel Annance, 3–8, 66, 84, 87, 95, 100, 114, 122, 124, 143, 148–9, 157, 235, 253, 257–8; as exercised by Noel Annance's family members, 5–6, 7, 34–8, 45, 62–6, 84, 117, 223, 228, 230, 257, 258; as exercised by Noel Annance's peers, 257–8; general manifestation as Indigenous daring, 3, 11, 80, 257, 258; relevance for present day, 11, 80, 257, 259

Abenaki people, 5–6, 18–21, 31–3, 199; migration to St Francis, 19, 21; taking of captives, 18, 21–33; way of life, 26–33, 51–2, 89–90, 112, 153–4, 157, 164–8

Amantacha, Louis (educated in France), 77

An Act to Encourage the Gradual Civilization of Indian Tribes (1857), 231–2; basis in Bagot Report, 231–2, 311n15; deceptive character, 232; administration, 234–6, 244–6, 245–6, 251–3, 253–4; appeal to Noel Annance, 223, 233–40, 244–54; chiefs' opposition, 252–3

Anderson, Eric Gary (scholar), 80

Annacis Island, BC, named after Noel Annance, 104

Annance (Portneuf), Angelique (sister), 50, 161

Annance, Archie (son), 108, 122, 243; adulthood, 161, 185, 229–30, 236, 258; at Moor's, 176, 229; outsider perspectives, 230; search for belonging, 176, 229–30

Annance, Charles (unspecified relationship), 161, 205–6, 313n4

Annance, Francis Joseph (father), 39, 49–51, 53–4, 160, 201; acquisition and use of Long Island, 49–50, 117, 161; acquisition of Durham lands, 37–8, 49, 117; during American War of Independence, 49, 82; at Moor's and Dartmouth, 39, 46–9, 67, 82; outlook, 49–51, 53, 89; respecting Moor's, 52–5, 59, 81; as sachem, 37–8, 49, 53; as schoolmaster, 50–1, 53–4, 86, 168, 286n45

Annance, Gabriel (grandfather), 26–7, 37, 39; accepting of literacy's promise, 46–7; during American War of Independence, 35–8; origins, 26–7, 39, 280n48

Annance, James Joseph (unspecified relationship), 168, 173, 175, 177, 179, 184

Annance, Joseph (brother), 50, 51–2, 84, 160, 223–6, 230, 258; in the fur trade, 90–1, 223–5; at Moor's, 84–6, 90, 223

Annance, Louis (brother), 50, 51–2, 57, 89, 181, 227, 229; as a Freemason, 182, 228; at Moor's, 53–6, 62,